SCOTTISH FANTASY LITERATURE
A Critical Survey

SCOTTISH FANTASY LITERATURE
LITERATURE
A Critical Survey

Colin Manlove

CANONGATE
ACADEMIC

First published in 1994 by Canongate Academic 14 Frederick Street Edinburgh
EH2 2HB

ISBN 1 898410 20 8

British Library Cataloguing-in-Publication Data

A catalogue record for this book
is available on request from the
British Library

The Publishers acknowledge subsidy from the
Scottish Arts Council towards the publication
of this volume

Typeset by Hewer Text Composition Services, Edinburgh
Printed and bound by Bookcraft Ltd, Midsomer Norton

For Scotland
wherever it may be

Acknowledgements

I should like to thank George Mackay Brown, Naomi Mitchison, Alasdair Gray and Margaret Elphinstone, for kindly providing comments and information; George Mackay Brown for permission to quote from *Magnus*, published by Chatto and Windus; Alasdair Gray and Canongate Press for permission to quote from *Lanark*; Margaret Elphinstone and The Women's Press Ltd., London, for permission to quote from *An Apple from a Tree and Other Visions*; Deborah Hunter of the Scottish National Portrait Gallery for her help with the photographs of James Hogg, Thomas Carlyle, George MacDonald, Robert Louis Stevenson, Margaret Oliphant, William Sharp ('Fiona Macleod'), Andrew Lang and J. M. Barrie; and to the Scottish National Portrait Gallery for freely granting me permission to reproduce them; Mrs. Helen Baz for kindly providing the photograph of David Lindsay; Dairmid Gunn for generously allowing me to choose a photograph of Neil Gunn from the Gunn collection at the National Library of Scotland and, together with the Trustees of the National Library of Scotland, for permitting me to reproduce it; Gordon Wright Publishers for permission to reproduce the photograph of George Mackay Brown; Canongate Press for supplying the photograph of Alasdair Gray; and Margaret Elphinstone for providing the photograph of herself. Thanks too to everybody at Canongate for their work on the book; and, as ever, to Sheila Campbell for indefatigably typing it.

Versions of chapters 1, 4 and 6 have previously appeared as articles in the journals *Extrapolation, Swansea Review* and *Studies in Scottish Literature.*

Contents

Plate Section

(between pages 120–121)

1. James Hogg 1770–1835
2. Thomas Carlyle 1795–1881
3. George MacDonald 1824–1905
4. Robert Louis Stevenson 1850–1894
5. Margaret Oliphant 1828–1897
6. William Sharp ('Fiona Macleod') 1855–1905
7. Andrew Lang 1844–1912
8. J. M. Barrie 1860–1937
9. David Lindsay 1876–1945
10. Neil Gunn 1891–1973
11. George Mackay Brown 1921–
12. Alasdair Gray 1934–
13. Margaret Elphinstone 1948–

CHAPTER ONE

Introduction

F ANTASY LITERATURE, THAT is, fiction involving the supernatural, has often been a neglected or undervalued side of national cultures: and this is particularly the case with Scotland. Despite the fact that Scotland is rich in fantasy, no work on the subject yet exists. This is partly because the Scottish literary tradition has always tended to value social realism, partly because many of the main writers of Scottish fantasy have lived outside Scotland. The prejudice of tradition may be readily exposed, though whether it will thereby be dissipated is another matter. The question of its fantasy writers living outside Scotland and often owing much to cultures other than Scottish is more problematic. However, it is not quite so much of a problem as is involved, say, in claiming Joseph Conrad for Poland. Several—Carlyle, George MacDonald, Stevenson, Margaret Oliphant—are already accepted as Scottish writers: and it would not be hard to extend this common perception to Andrew Lang, J. M. Barrie, or David Lindsay, all of whom are frequently seen as 'Scottish'.[1] And it is not as though they were far from their roots, living in England and on occasion returning to Scotland, as many of them did. Nor need the heterogeneity of their works and sources create difficulty: it need not matter that MacDonald wrote semi-Spenserian romance, Stevenson urban Gothic, Barrie 'children's' fiction, or Lindsay transcendentalist science fiction; for if we look at the fantasies written by English authors between about 1850 and 1930 we will find a similar diversity, from the world of marine biology in Kingsley's *The Water-Babies* to the mirror world of inverted logic in Carroll's *Through the Looking Glass* or those of fantastic time-travel in E. Nesbit's *The Story of the Amulet*. 'Fantasy' as a self-aware genre did not really come into being until after 1965 and the 'discovery' of Tolkien by the United States. Nevertheless if the term 'Scottish' is to mean anything beyond ancestry or the early years of many of these writers, it will be necessary to try to find some features common to the fantasies so described, however various they may appear.

The task is not in fact so hard. If we think, it is much easier to speak of Scottish than of English fantasy, in the immediate sense that Scotland has a large and even now still faintly lingering folk- and fairy-tale tradition. *Popular Tales of the West Highlands*, orally collected by J. F. Campbell in four volumes (1860–2), not to mention his posthumous *More West Highland Tales* in two volumes (1940–60) speaks for part of the heritage of one area of Scotland alone. The School of Scottish Studies at Edinburgh University has copious records and recordings of still extant tales from all over Scotland. There are collections of tales from the Borders, Galloway, Fife, Aberdeenshire and from the far north and the islands. To this England can offer E. S. Hartland's *English Fairy and Other Folk Tales* (1890), a one-volume work which takes its tales from chapbooks and published sources, not from a living tradition. England has its classics among these tales, such as 'Jack the Giant-Killer', 'Tom Tit Tot', 'Jack and the Beanstalk' or 'The History of Tom Thumb', but most of them are preservations from a past long gone. Hartland remarks on the lack of folk-tales from England and from lowland Scotland alike, and attributes it to the influence of 'Evangelical Protestantism' and to the spread of education.[2] It is certainly the case in England, at least, that most of the tales collected come from remote western or northern parts of the country. But there may be another reason for this also.

Fairy- and folk-tales appear to flourish, in Northern Europe at least, not only away from religion, education, and indeed large human collectives, but where they are close in origin to the unchanged land. The tales of Grimm come from the fir-covered Hartz mountains; those of Norway from its troll- and undine-haunted fells and fjords; those of Finland from the land's snows and lakes. It is indeed to Germanic and Norse traditions that Scots folk culture looks, rather more than to the slightly more urbane environments that supplied Perrault, Basile, Straparola, or *The Arabian Nights*. The fairies here are gnomes, dwarves, orcs, or trolls, part of the geology, of the rocks: in Germany they are known as *Elementargeister*,[3] and numbers of tales are set in caves or underground or in mines.[4] The tales in such northern traditions are created out of a sense of the inhospitability and the omnipresence of the land. Life is hard, and wresting it from such unwilling ground, generation after generation, leads to a unique bond between men and earth.

Not all the modern Scottish writers we shall speak of have quite this sort of relationship with the environment, but they are all, directly or indirectly, fed by a sense of it. It is hard for many Scots, placed on the thin ribbon of culture of the Forth-Clyde valley, to forget the relatively unpeopled land to the north and south of them: all that geography—that mute but not necessarily insensate mass of moor and mountain, loch and forest—exerts a draw on the spirit. And for those who leave the country, long nesses of their homeland still push after them beneath their feet: they begin to think of their country as a whole as arguably the Englishman less easily does, feel poignantly if often inaccurately its essence in the mountain-born note of the pipes. 'No sentimentalist like a Scots exile,' they say; and Hardy in *The Mayor of Casterbridge* has Christopher Coney ask the émigré and aptly-named Farfrae, ' "What did ye come away from yer own country for, young maister, if ye be so wownded about it?" '[5] Yet there is a sense in which for many Scots their native land comes more clearly into being the further and longer they are away from it. *'We are the land. The elements that created the land live in our bodies,'*[6] writes the novelist Margaret Elphinstone.

This sense of the land is seen in Scots fantasy. Put MacDonald's *Phantastes: A Faerie Romance for Men and Women* (1858) beside his English friend and part-follower Lewis Carroll's *Alice in Wonderland* (1865) and what do we find? MacDonald has a hero called Anodos who wakes up one morning in a strange realm he calls Fairy Land, through which he feels he has to travel. His feet do not sink very heavily into that soil, but we see him walk through forests and plains, voyage on river and ocean, sojourn in cottages and palaces, until in that world he is killed and laid in the earth. In *Alice* there is no journey and little sense of place: Wonderland is a collection of wildly different people and creatures, which Alice meets first severally and then together in the final trial scene, and the narrative is a series of conversations and positions, which go nowhere; and this is curious, since the whole story is set underground.

This posits a case that is perhaps too absolute. There is English fantasy which celebrates the land, such as Kipling's *Puck of Pook's Hill* (1906), or which is rooted in a sense of place, such as T. F. Powys' *Mr Weston's Good Wine* (1927) or Charles Williams's *Descent into Hell* (1937) or J. R. R. Tolkien's *The Lord of the Rings* (1954–5). And there is Scots fantasy which has little to say of land, such as Carlyle's *Sartor Resartus* (1836) or R. L. Stevenson's *Dr Jekyll and Mr Hyde* (1886), which is set in London. It could be argued that Stevenson's London is the urban equivalent of a bleak Scottish moor, or that Hyde himself—goblin-shaped and the expression of the 'underground' side of Jekyll—represents the dark natural self that draws the housed and civilised persona towards it. We could play too with the idea that his childhood experience of the countryside around Entepfuhl is the keystone of the subsequent development of Carlyle's Teufelsdröckh. But really it is a matter of relative emphasis. Hogg, MacDonald, Oliphant, Lang, Fiona Macleod, David Lindsay, Neil Gunn, George Mackay Brown, Alasdair Gray, Margaret Elphinstone—all of them anchor their stories in a landscape recognisably Scottish. With Hogg's *Confessions of a Justified Sinner* (1824) we are in Edinburgh and later in the wilderness of the Southern Uplands—in contrast to Mary Shelley's *Frankenstein* (1818), which starts in Switzerland and has its concluding pursuit in the wastes of the Arctic. MacDonald's Fairy Land has affinities with that of the Scottish folk hero Thomas the Rhymer; and in his *Lilith* (1895) the 'region of the seven dimensions', which coincides with the country about the Scottish home of the protagonist Vane, is a place of moorland, scattered forest, and the odd cottage. Lang, too, takes us to the land of Thomas the Rhymer in his *The Gold of Fairnilee* (1888), which is set in Scotland at the time of Flodden. Most of Fiona Macleod's (pseud. of William Sharp) stories are set on the west coast and the Isles.[7]

Lindsay starts and ends the journey in his *A Voyage to Arcturus* (1920) in Starkness Observatory somewhere on the bleak north-east coast of Scotland. With Gunn, Brown, Gray and Elphinstone we have come to authors who now live in and set their stories in Scottish landscapes, whether urban or pastoral.

In several Scots fantasies we are taken underground—not surprising, given the frequent bareness of the landscape up above. Thus MacDonald's Anodos descends into the earth after his adventures in the Fairy palace, and his *The Princess and the Goblin* (1872) has the miner Curdie defending the palace of the princess Irene from the mining beneath by the goblins. We are in a hellish realm beneath the earth in Margaret Oliphant's 'The Land of Darkness' (1887). The Darling children in Barrie's *Peter Pan* (1904) have a secret hideout beneath the ground of the Never Land. Fairyland in Lang's *The Gold of Fairnilee* is beneath the earth in what can be seen as a land of the dead, 'like a great unending stretch of sand and barren grassy country, beside a grey sea where there was no tide'.[8] Gunn's Old Hector and Young Art in *The Green Isle of the Great Deep* (1944) come to the Gaelic paradise ('Eilan uaine an iomal torra domhain')[9] when they have fallen into the depths of Hazel Pool. And in Alasdair Gray's *Lanark* (1981), the protagonist arrives at his purgatory by letting himself fall through a pair of giant open lips in a graveyard.

There is always the sense of a pull backwards, or even downwards, to one's roots. From wherever he is, the Scots fantasist seems to journey back to his native land. And whatever advances the heroes depicted in such fantasies have made, they seem often to be stripped of them, reduced to bedrock like the landscape itself, as it were. Robert Wringhim in Hogg's *Confessions* is reduced to destitution and death by the evil Gil-Martin; Carlyle's Teufelsdröckh loses his beloved Blumine and comes to see beneath all the appearances and clothes of the world, to the point where he himself disappears from human knowledge. MacDonald's Anodos comes back from Fairy Land having lost his shadow instead of gaining his ideal, and having learned also to yield his lady and to die. The ghosts in Margaret Oliphant's stories are continually drawn back to their localities in this world. The seeker of the light in her 'The Land of Darkness' rejects the dimly-perceived 'whiteness' of possible escape when eventually he finds it:

> It was something from that other sphere—can I tell you what?
> a child perhaps—oh, thought that wrings the heart! for do you
> know what manner of thing a child is? There are none in the
> land of darkness. I turned my back upon the place where that
> whiteness was. On, on, across the waste! On to the cities of
> the night! On, far away from maddening thought, from hope
> that is torment, and from the awful Name![10]

This is reminiscent of Thomson's *The City of Dreadful Night* (1874); but its prose also recalls Morris's 'The Hollow Land' (1856)—and tellingly, for there the gloom and punishment of the dead lands give place to forgiveness and renewal beyond death.

So too in Stevenson's *Dr Jekyll and Mr Hyde*, Jekyll is progressively reduced to Hyde, until he can only die and enter his stunted form permanently. Barrie's children in *Peter Pan* must grow up and lose the form that enabled them to fly with Peter. In *A Voyage to Arcturus*, David Lindsay's hero Maskull is taken to Tormance, a planet filled with luxuriant and enticing people and images which he must reject one after the other, until through his death he finally realises the nature of the true God, Muspel, who is hemmed in by the forces of evil in an isolated tower. 'The truth forced itself on him in all its cold, brutal reality. Muspel was no all-powerful Universe, tolerating from pure indifference the existence side by side with it of another false world, which had no right to be . . . Muspel was fighting for its life . . . against all that is shameful and frightful—against sin masquerading as eternal beauty.'[11] In George Mackay Brown's *Magnus* (1973), the hero loses his lands and yields himself to being slain by his cousin-enemy. Thaw's life in Alasdair Gray's *Lanark* is one of almost unrelieved failure—in art, in relationships, in sex—borne with a stubborn courage to the point where suicide is incontrovertibly proved to be the only act left to him. The characters in Margaret Elphinstone's story-collection *An Apple from a Tree* (1991) often suffer loss: Sarah in 'Green Man' loses the wonder of the alien she met; Helen in 'A Life of Glory' loses her baby and leaves her lover; Peter in 'Islands of Sheep' is stripped of both his reason and his home; Alison in 'An Apple from a Tree' gives up the world of wonder she is offered.

The contrast with English fantasy is striking. There it is true we may often find a stripping process going on, as Kingsley's Tom in *The Water-Babies* leaves his old body behind to become a water-baby; or as C. S. Lewis's Ransom, in *Perelandra* (1943), must go naked and unprepared to Venus to carry out Maleldil's purposes; or as Tolkien's Frodo is worn almost to death to destroy the evil Ring. But the emphasis is not on loss as much as on gain. Ransom and Tom are exposed as they are so that they may develop spiritually. There is usually a happy ending. Middle-earth is saved; so too is the innocence of the Lady of Perelandra; Tom becomes a moral hero and regains Ellie; and in the fantasy of Charles Williams the terrifying irruptions of the Angelicals into the world are reversed, even while those very invasions serve the purpose of showing that the world is in fact a web of immanent supernatural action.

Bareness, too, prevails in the imagery of some of these Scottish fantasies. Even the most colourful, those most bursting with a riot of different pictures, seem to deny images even as they push them forward. MacDonald, it is true, delights in imagery and the imagination, and it is by them that he seeks to work on the minds of his readers. Yet there is a certain refusal, best seen in the way that Anodos in *Phantastes* must continually deny himself the lady he seeks: he is to give up what appears to him 'perfectly lovely', that which is 'more near the face that had been born with me in my soul, than anything I had seen before in nature or art'.[12] It is by no means a *via negativa*, but it is certainly a way of self-denial. In Lindsay's *A Voyage to Arcturus* the clash is at its harshest, in a world full of often searing beauty and vitality, which must be seen and then utterly rejected as the corrupt idiom of Crystalman, the devil. Each hominoid figure that dies, however individual before, reverts in facial expression to the hideous and sickening grin of its creator—for here even creation itself is evil. Even at the end, the character Krag, who is pain, remarks mockingly to Maskull, '"You think you are thoroughly disillusioned, don't you? Well, that may prove to be the last and strongest illusion of all."'[13]

There is something violent, even gleefully savage, in many Scots fantasies. Only someone with a strong sense of sadism and knowledge of what it is to be bullied could have written Hogg's *Confessions*, with its picture of the tormented and delusional Wringhim, or the story of the torture of Lady Wheelhope by the fiend-like Merodach in his 'The Brownie of the Black Haggs'. In Carlyle's *Sartor* there is an explosive quality, not only to the uneven life of Herr Teufelsdröckh, but also in the speed and swing of the style:

> Be of hope! Already streaks of blue peer through our clouds; the thick gloom of Ignorance is rolling asunder, and it will be Day. Mankind will repay with interest their long-accumulated debt: the Anchorite that was scoffed at will be worshipped; the Fraction will become not an Integer only, but a Square and Cube. With astonishment the world will recognise that the Tailor is its Hierophant, and Hierarch, or even its God.[14]

In MacDonald's *Phantastes* there is the absolutism of the self-denial whereby Anodos must totally give up his beloved lady to another; in his *The Princess and Curdie* (1883) the protagonist has to put his hand in a fire to become spiritually aware, and when he sets out to rescue his beleaguered king in a far city, he does so in company with a set of creatures out of nightmare, whose butcherings of the morally louche citizens of Gwyntystorm are lingeringly described; in his *Lilith* (1895) we have a woman 'squelching' into death after being thrown from an upstairs window by Lilith, and Lilith herself has her hand amputated so that she may be pure and sleep her way into bliss. Margaret Oliphant's hopeless world in 'The Land of Darkness' is full of images of exclusion, hatred and violence:

> Then he pulled over me a great movable lens as of a microscope, which concentrated the insupportable light. The wild, hopeless passion that raged within my soul had no

outlet in the immovable apparatus that held me. I was let down among the crowd, and exhibited to them, every secret movement of my being, by some awful process which I have never fathomed. A burning fire was in my brain, flame seemed to run along all my nerves, speechless, horrible, incommunicable fury raged in my soul. But I was like a child—nay, like an image of wood or wax in the pitiless hands that held me. What was the cut of a surgeon's knife to this? And I had thought *that* cruel! And I was powerless, and could do nothing—to blast, to destroy, to burn with this same horrible flame the fiends that surrounded me, as I desired to do.[15]

In Stevenson's *Dr Jekyll and Mr Hyde*, Hyde represents the liberation of energies which are, as we see them, mainly destructive, as in the striking down of a young child or the later clubbing to death of an old man, Sir Danvers Carew: 'next moment, with ape-like fury, he was trampling his victim under foot, and hailing down a storm of blows, under which the bones were audibly shattered and the body jumped upon the roadway'.[16] And this destruction is somehow linked to the very urges of life itself. 'With a transport of glee, I mauled the unresisting body, tasting delight from every blow . . . my lust of evil [was] gratified and stimulated, my love of life screwed to the topmost peg'.[17] Here the emphasis is not far from the carnivorous. Comparison might be found with Wells's *The Invisible Man* (1897), where the hatreds of Griffin are continually checked and baffled. There can be no wish to say that such savagery is central to all Scots fantasy, but it is certainly a recurrent element—the killing of the often amusing pirates in Barrie's *Peter Pan*, the terrible ends of the protagonists in Macleod's 'The Dan-nan-Ron' or 'The Sin-Eater',[18] the continual brutalities and murders that run throughout Lindsay's *A Voyage to Arcturus*, the violent Orcadian past in George Mackay Brown's stories and in *Magnus*, the cruel rejections of Gray's Thaw in the harsh landscape of Glasgow.

The sharpness of Scots fantasy is underscored by its frequent imagery of absolute contrasts, particularly of light and dark. It is, in contrast to English fantasy, full of night scenes. It is at night that Teufelsdröckh in Carlyle's *Sartor Resartus* is overtaken by a carriage containing his beloved Blumine and Herr Towgood, newly-married and en route to their honeymoon; by night that George Colwan in Hogg's *Confessions* is murdered and the later pursuits across country partly occur. So too MacDonald, who translated Novalis's *Hymnen an die Nacht* (1799), has his Anodos move and act mainly by night for a good way into his *Phantastes*, as does Vane in *Lilith*. MacDonald wrote in 1879 a fairy-tale called 'The Day Boy and the Night Girl' (or, 'Photogen and Nycteris'); Stevenson's Jekyll is of day, his Hyde of night. Mrs Oliphant's characters move in realms of darkness and uncertainty (even in the choked daylight of 'A Beleaguered City'), as too do those of Fiona Macleod; *Peter Pan* is full of night scenes, and a good part of the action in the Never Land takes place in darkness. The journey in *A Voyage to Arcturus* begins and ends in the darkness around the tower of the former Starkness Observatory.

So, too, we have the contrasts of the weak Wringhim beside the athletic and sociable George in *The Confessions*; the Everlasting No and the Everlasting Yea in *Sartor*; the white lady beside the Maid of the Alder Tree in *Phantastes*; Jekyll and Hyde; the children and Peter Pan; Crystalman and Muspel in Lindsay; angel and tempter, Magnus and Hakon in Mackay Brown's *Magnus*, Lanark and Thaw in Gray, city and wilderness in Margaret Elphinstone's stories. These opposites are bound to one another, as though the one spawns the other, or each depends on their joint and yet totally oppugnant existence, like seal and man in certain of Fiona Macleod's stories. In English fantasy we more frequently find that any such dualities are overcome in the victory of good. But in Scottish fantasy there is a darker vision, in which doppelgängers and alter egos abound. The affinity here, as in the use of light and dark, is with the Gothic novel, from which at least in part Scots literary fantasy took its inception: we could see similar features in one English fantasy in the Gothic mould—Mervyn Peake's Gormenghast sequence (1946–59). But the word 'affinity' is more appropriate than 'indebtedness': these characteristics are too persistent within Scots fantasies for the latter, and they have an idiom all their own—for instance, their darknesses more frequently occur outside buildings or habitation.

However far the writers of Scots fantasy may be from their roots, they all show something of the influence of Calvinism. Some of them take an almost Manichaean view of the world. In Hogg's *Confessions* and several of his shorter stories it seems largely the devil's territory, a place where too much spiritual care cannot be taken; and yet it is that very Calvinist fastidiousness and consequent pride which proves the ruin of the unfortunate Wringhim. Carlyle's Teufelsdröckh, expelled from university and abandoned by his Blumine, can see the truth of the world only when forced to do without it. We have already seen how both MacDonald's Anodos and Lindsay's Maskull have to dispossess themselves of the world and eventually die out of it. In Mrs Oliphant's stories there are various accommodations with death and with the world beyond it. Stevenson's Jekyll himself is a repressed Calvinist, whose releases of passion take perverted and violent form, in a fog-shrouded London. For Gray's Duncan Thaw the world is a place of bleakness and rejection where the only answer is the self-rejection of death; and in the other world he still finds people whose dragonish or salamandrine forms in part portray the enclosure of repressed passion and refused love. The world is not always so rejected: it has a rare beauty beyond any fantasy in some of Fiona Macleod's tales, in Neil Gunn's *The Green Isle of the Great*

Deep, and in some of George Mackay Brown's stories; and in Margaret Elphinstone's work the land is the prime source of spiritual renewal for mankind. But if we compare English fantasy, we can see that in it there is much more integration with the world, and much more freedom. Tom in Kingsley's *The Water-Babies* breaks out of his old body and swims free in the water, where he meets all sorts of creatures. The world is shown to be a glorious place shot through with continuous divine action in Charles Williams's fantasies. C. S. Lewis's space trilogy transforms an apparently bare and inhospitable universe to a 'celestial commonwealth' teeming with spiritual delight, and shows the previously isolated Earth becoming once more a part of that cosmic society. Part of the effect of Tolkien's *The Lord of the Rings* is to open up the variety of Middle-earth, and show the hobbits becoming citizens of it. In Peake's Gormenghast novels, the castle of the Groans and its inhabitants are given endless delighted description; and this delight coexists with the urge to be free that makes the young Earl Titus quit his home. In general it can be said that there is far more description of places and people in English than in Scottish fantasy. MacDonald and Lindsay are exceptions here, but in each case the image is of less or no value for itself, but only as part of a larger sequence, or else as something to be seen and known and disdained.

The issue of respectability, or of bourgeois complacency, is a frequent one, at least in Victorian Scottish fantasy, inasmuch as it portrays the exposure of rigid values. In Hogg's *Confessions* the priggish Presbyterian Wringhim is shown in his fastidious spiritual pride to be a creature of the devil, so convinced of the rectitude of his ways that he uses any means to try to sustain them; the narrative shows, in his progressive disillusion and flight, the erosion of conscious certainties and entry into a wilderness of self-doubt. Equally, the fanatical tyrant Lady Wheelhope in Hogg's 'The Brownie of the Black Haggs' is degraded to a creature of crazed passion. In Carlyle's *Sartor*, Herr Teufelsdröckh loses all contact with social success and possible marriage, becoming outcast, and therefore more able to see into the heart of life. (It may be remarked that such a critique of respectability is paralleled in earlier German literary fantasy, particularly that of E. T. A. Hoffmann.) MacDonald's Anodos and Vane journey from the conscious external world to a destructured inner one. Stevenson's *Dr Jekyll and Mr Hyde* is an obvious picture of the split between respectability and what it seeks to 'hyde'. In the ape-like form of Hyde we see the further suggestion that all man's civilisation and development constitute a severance from his pre-civilised and primitive self: in short, that evolution is a fiction, and that man is rather regressive than progressive. Barrie's *Peter Pan* shows a flight from the ordered urban family to the wild and adventure-hemmed group of renegade children. In Lindsay's *A Voyage to Arcturus* the proprieties of the high-class séance that opens the novel are shattered by the invasion of the violent Krag;

and all Maskull's 'civilised' susceptibilities are brutally destroyed on Tormance. George Mackay Brown's fantasy frequently shows the savage past behind the apparently pacific present. Margaret Elphinstone plays the primal realities of the land against the civilisation that man all too frequently sets in opposition to it, whether in the antagonism of Peter and Anna in 'Islands of Sheep', or in 'Green Man', where the neat certainties of Sarah's life and art are dissolved by her pastoral alien encounter, or in the opposition between prim urban Alison and wild Nosila in 'An Apple from a Tree'. In English fantasy by contrast we rarely find any concern with respectability or civility.

This undermining of complacent civility goes together with an egalitarian quality in Scottish fantasy. No kings here, no hierarchies: pride is punished, eminence reversed, whether it is in Hogg's Robert Wringhim or his Lady Wheelhope, in MacDonald's Anodos and Vane, or in the apparent gentlemanly station of Dr Jekyll. In English fantasy we have Kings and Queens of Narnia, the Lady or Queen of Perelandra, Earls of Gormenghast, Kings of Rohan and Gondor, and King Arthur: and frequently the protagonist in such works gains a position of eminence from one of relative obscurity. The people in Scottish fantasy on the whole develop no more in importance. This is partly because, as we shall see, their actions often affect no-one but themselves. But there is also a curious modesty or reticence in all this, and one that also has some parallel in their traditional tales or *Märchen*: for, though these deal often with the sort of standard folk narrative that involves a humble nobody in gaining a treasure, a prince or princess, or a kingdom, they nevertheless show a remarkable mixing of high and low, as J. F. Campbell has remarked:

> Kings live in cottages and sit on low stools. When they have coaches, they open the door themselves. The queen saddles the king's horse. The king goes to his own stable when he hears a noise there . . . The fire is on the floor. Supernatural old women are found spinning 'beyond' it, in the warm place of honour, in all primitive dwellings, even in a Lapland tent. The king's mother puts on the fire, and sleeps in the common room, as a peasant does. The cock sleeps on the rafters, the sheep on the floor, the bull behind the door . . . When all Ireland passes in review before the princess, they go in at the front door and out at the back, as they would through a bothy; and even that unexplained personage, the daughter of the king of the skies, has maids who chatter to her as freely as maids do to Highland mistresses. When the prince is at death's door for love of the beautiful lady in the swan's down robe, and the queen mother is in despair, she goes to the kitchen to talk over the matter.[19]

In Scots fantasy the protagonist is most frequently solitary. In Hogg's

Confessions we have the spurned Robert Wringhim looking on at George Colwan and his companions, or alone with the sinister Gil-Martin on Salisbury Crags, or in solitary flight. Carlyle's Teufelsdröckh wanders the world companionless. MacDonald's Anodos is denied all relationships he makes; as, in *Lilith*, is his Vane. In contrast, Kingsley's Tom or Carroll's Alice may be on their own so far as actual companions are concerned, but they are continually entering societies. The central figure of Mrs Oliphant's 'The Land of Darkness' is alone and often persecuted, and the ghosts in others of her stories are often in a solitary limbo between this world and the next. Stevenson's Dr Jekyll becomes increasingly isolated from his friends until he dies locked in his study. Lindsay's Maskull journeys alone across Tormance. Mackay Brown's Magnus is enclosed in his sanctity. Gray's Thaw loses his family and makes no lasting friends in this world. Elphinstone's characters all end alone, whether through accident ('Green Man') or by choice ('An Apple from a Tree'). This is not always the case: in Lang's *The Gold of Fairnilee* young Randal may be forced to sojourn for seven years alone in Fairyland, but he returns to his Borders home and people and to his beloved Jeanie at the end; in *Peter Pan* the children fly together to the Never Land, though both Wendy and Peter end alone; and in Gunn's *The Green Isle of the Great Deep* both Old Hector and Young Art go to the Green Isle, and the relationship of the two of them is one of the central strands of the book. But such a sense of relationship and community is much more common in English fantasy. In one way, for example, *The Lord of the Rings* could be said to be *about* expanding relationships, as the Company of the Ring, itself a little community, is introduced to race after race as it travels through Middle-earth.

In a sense Scots fantasy is inward-looking, concerned to discover something hidden within. It is much more frequently an expression of the psyche of its central figure than is the case in English fantasy. Gil-Martin in Hogg's *Confessions* is a part-projection of Wringhim's mind, Fairy Land and the region of the seven dimensions in MacDonald's *Phantastes* and *Lilith* are the inner spiritual worlds of Anodos and Vane. Stevenson's London, with its mixture of respectability and vice, figures the mind of Jekyll. Barrie's Never Land is what its name signifies, a primarily psychological place. Tormance in *A Voyage to Arcturus* is in part a landscape of Maskull's soul, a picture of an extreme spiritual journey he makes within himself. Most of Elphinstone's landscapes reflect the psyche: the exception, Arizona in 'A Life of Glory', is a source of disorientation. The worlds of English fantasy, however, are often much more clearly 'other'. Tom finds out about the outer world, and the 'miraculous and divine element underlying all physical nature', in *The Water-Babies*; the innocent worlds of Lewis's Malacandra and Perelandra are quite outside the fallen nature of the hero Ransom; the nature of Peake's Gormenghast is that its inhabitants express *it*, not it them; Tolkien's hobbits are literally taken out of themselves in having to journey out of the Shire into the wide and alien realms of Middle-earth.

In Scots fantasy, where a various world is encountered, it often shrinks back into the one thing with which the story began: Anodos is returned to his home from Fairy Land with 'a writhing as of death', becoming 'conscious of a more limited, even a bodily and earthly life';[20] Vane is thrust back into the library of his castle; Jekyll finds he can no longer keep a gap between himself and Hyde; Maskull dies and returns as Nightspore to the observatory tower of Starkness; Elphinstone's 'Green Man', 'An Apple from a Tree' and 'A Life of Glory' put us back with the single characters with whom we began. Much literary fantasy involves a return to where one started from, as Ransom is sent back to Earth or Frodo returns to the Shire—but not with such a sense of reduction. For Frodo and Ransom have gained something new, where Anodos and Maskull have learned, rather, to do without. Scottish fantasy has less of a sense of evolution and progression: more frequently it records stasis or even decline or collapse (Hogg, Oliphant, Stevenson, Gray).

English fantasy more often deals with the quest outwards, where Scots fantasy deals with the inwards search. The former supposes a known objective to be reached—the Other-end-of-Nowhere, the Well at the World's End, the preservation of the innocence of the Lady on Perelandra, the destruction of the One Ring. There are exceptions: in Charles Williams's fantasies the protagonists have to discover the true meaning of the supernatural that has invaded their world; and in T. H. White's *The Once and Future King* Arthur continually searches for an answer to human violence. But it is remarkable how often the element of questioning and of introspective analysis is to be found in Scots fantasy. Hogg's *Confessions* involves a search for the murderer of George Colwan and an inquiry into the nature of Gil-Martin; and by its presentation from different points of view, a search is imposed on the reader into the truth-status of what he or she is told at any point. In Hogg's 'The Brownie of the Black Haggs' we are continuously concerned with the nature of the savage servant Merodach and with why Lady Wheelhope is so fascinated by him. In Carlyle's *Sartor* Herr Teufelsdröckh is searching for a philosophy which will do justice to the vicissitudes of life as he sees and experiences them. *Phantastes* and *Lilith* are, effectively, analyses from superficial to profound levels of the soul: the character of *Lilith* in particular is continuously interrogative. In Mrs Oliphant's 'Earthbound', 'The Library Window', 'The Open Door' or 'A Beleaguered City', the driving impulse is to discover the nature of the apparitions. Both the outside characters and the reader in *Dr Jekyll and Mr Hyde* are trying to find out the true nature of Hyde's connection with Jekyll, being driven ever inwards to the truth in Jekyll's locked chamber. Barrie's *Peter Pan* could be said to constitute a search into the true nature of childhood. Lindsay's Maskull, travelling through the variety of Tormance, is in truth searching for Surtur or Muspel, which is why he was chosen for the journey by Krag. Mackay Brown's Magnus comes to realise the nature of his own life within Christ. Self-examination is of the essence in Gray's *Lanark*; and in Elphinstone's stories there is so much exploration of people's inner worlds that we have in 'Islands of Sheep' a monition against the wrong kind of search into privacy. Whether this idiom of search reflects a Scots uncertainty of identity, or whether it is part of a sense of the hidden nature of truth, buried beneath the flat and uncomplicated surface level (as of the land), cannot be determined: but it may be remarked that Scots fantasy deals more often with the 'vertical' than with the 'horizontal'—with towers, stairs, or, as we saw, realms underground.

There are no journeys in much Scots fantasy: one simply goes further within. This may be why houses so frequently occur in this fantasy, though the house as a place to protect the self is seen as something to be forsaken or invaded; but then it may be, as Mr Raven puts it to Vane in *Lilith*, ' "the more doors you go out of, the farther you get in!" '[21] Much speculation as to the precise house George had been in before his murder fills Hogg's *Confessions*; Carlyle's Teufelsdröckh is obsessed with containers of the self, expressed in his philosophy of clothes ('I . . . have thatched myself over with the dead fleeces of sheep'[22]). MacDonald's Anodos begins his adventures in his bedroom, which, on his waking one morning, he finds transforming itself into Fairy Land; MacDonald's *The Princess and the Goblin* (1872) is largely set within a castle; and in *Lilith* the hero Vane finds the region of the seven dimensions through a mirror in the attic of his house, to which he is frequently returned during his adventures. Lang's *The Gold of Fairnilee* is largely set within and around Randal's Borders home; many of Mrs Oliphant's stories, whether of portraits, windows, or lost wills, take place within houses; Stevenson's Dr Jekyll is increasingly confined to a house; the Darling children in *Peter Pan* are seen as vital parts of a household, from which they fly free and to which, despite Peter's wish to bar the entrance to them, they return; Lindsay's Maskull begins and ends in a tower; the purgatory in Gray's *Lanark* is a huge multi-storey underground building which very few have ever left. The nearest to this in English fantasy is the location of Peake's *Titus Groan* and *Gormenghast* in the huge castle of Gormenghast itself—and that trilogy as we saw is close to Scots fantasy in its Gothic character. Kingsley's Harthover House in *The Water-Babies* is less a house than a meeting place for all sorts of different styles of house, which form a sort of architectural parliament; and it is soon left behind.

In Scottish fantasy the fantastic experience and the world from which it emanates are very close to ours—into which they can come at any time. In the midst of an everyday experience of Edinburgh, Robert

Wringhim in Hogg's *Confessions* moves in a landscape of hell; Carlyle's Teufelsdröckh comes to see the wonder lying all about him; Fairy Land comes into Anodos' house in MacDonald's *Phantastes*, and in his *Lilith* we learn that the region of the seven dimensions coexists bilocally with Vane's home and castle;[23] people from the afterworld inhabit the homes of characters in Mrs Oliphant's stories, while hell in her 'The Land of Darkness' is in part Victorian England; the well beneath which is Fairyland is next to Randal's estate in *The Gold of Fairnilee*; the fantastic existence of Jekyll and Hyde is set in London; Peter Pan comes to London; the Angel of the Loom comes to Earl Magnus in Orkney; Gray's Unthank is only in a sense Glasgow from the other side. But in English fantasy the two worlds are more divided. Tom in *The Water-Babies* has to journey across the world to St Brandan's Fairy Isle, Lewis's Ransom has to go to Mars and Venus, Tolkien's Frodo has to travel across Middle-earth to his goal. Again, there are exceptions: on the one side, there is the fantasy of Charles Williams, where the ordinary world is shown to be supernatural, and on the other Lindsay's *A Voyage to Arcturus*, where the hero must make a journey to and across a far planet.

Corresponding to this mixing of worlds, we find that in Scots fantasy personal identity is often without boundaries, capable of sharing its nature with others. This is obviously the case with Hogg's Robert Wringhim/Gil-Martin, with Stevenson's Jekyll and Hyde, Barrie's Peter and Wendy, or Gray's Thaw and Lanark, who exchange natures with one another. But Carlyle's Teufelsdröckh gradually merges with the world of wonder he discovers, and disappears; Fairy Land in MacDonald's *Phantastes* is in one sense the landscape of the hero Anodos' mind, in which he meets a whole series of forms of himself; the dead who for a short time take over the place of the living in Mrs Oliphant's 'A Beleaquered City' in some way express their natures; and in Margaret Elphinstone's stories characters or places become part of one another, as in 'Green Man' or 'An Apple from a Tree', or one character takes over the mind of another, as in 'Islands of Sheep'.

This inwardness, this self-reflexiveness, in Scots fantasy seems matched in the way that it is quite without the epic dimension of other fantasies, whereby whole worlds or societies may hang on the doings of individuals. Should Charles Williams's protagonists fail to discover the truth of the supernatural invasion their world has suffered locally, the whole world may be overwhelmed, whether it be by the power of the naked principles of life, or the elemental forces contained within the cards of a mystic Tarot pack. If Lewis's Ransom does not succeed in protecting the Lady of Perelandra, the entire planet will fall and God will have to suffer for mortal sin in a new and more terrible guise. If Tolkien's Frodo does not manage to destroy the One Ring, the Dark Lord's power will crush Middle-earth. A whole society takes its life from Arthur's Round Table in T. H. White's *The Once and Future King*. But nothing depends on what Wringhim does, or Teufelsdröckh, or Anodos: they are all outsiders in relation to society anyway—their deeds redound on themselves alone. Even within the epic purview of the whole planet of Tormance in Lindsay's *Voyage to Arcturus*, all of Maskull's adventures serve to develop him further and prepare him for his own death; but the planet itself and its inhabitants are of no concern, are indeed seen as illusions of the corrupt Crystalman. In George Mackay Brown's *Time in a Red Coat* (1984), a strange girl princess travels the world and time, observing human violence in war, hoping, but without apparent success, to tame the 'dragon' that causes it: but the epic dimension the book attempts is *voulu* and over-ambitious, and the reason for that is that Brown's greatest strengths lie in his evocation of the locality he knows—that of the Orkney Islands, in which, significantly, the book ends.

Localism is a part of much Scots fantasy. It is present in the very character of the Scots traditional tale, which occurs in one clan region, where everyone is known to everyone else, and where kings live next door to their subjects. Thus we have Edinburgh and the Borders in Hogg's *Confessions*, Entepfuhl in Carlyle's *Sartor*, the castles in MacDonald's *The Princess and the Goblin* and *Lilith*, the various houses in Mrs Oliphant's stories, the London of Jekyll and Hyde, Lang's Fairnilee, Macleod's Western Isles, Gunn's Caithness, Gray's Glasgow/Unthank, Brown's Orkney, Elphinstone's Galloway. There are exceptions, mainly among those writing from outside Scotland—Barrie, Lindsay. But journeys away from home are much more frequent in English fantasy—Kingsley, Lewis, Tolkien, White. In Scots fantasy there is much more the sense of exploring and transforming the familiar, rather than investigating the strange. Given that the Scots are renowned more as travellers or migrants than the English, this may seem odd.

One feature that may at least be consonant with the absence of the epic or journeying dimension in Scots fantasy is that much of it is short. If we think of the long prose romances of William Morris, the three-volume works of Lewis (the space trilogy), Peake's or Tolkien's works, the seven-book *Chronicles of Narnia* or the four-book *The Once and Future King*, only Gray's *Lanark* comes near them. Where Scots fantasies are of novel-length, two hundred pages or so sees the end of them—Hogg's *Confessions*, Carlyle's *Sartor*, MacDonald's various fantasies, Lindsay's *A Voyage to Arcturus*, Gunn's *The Green Isle of the Great Deep*, George Mackay Brown's *Magnus* or *Time in a Red Coat*, Elphinstone's *The Incomer* or *A Sparrow's Flight* (though here the one takes up from the other). Others are shorter still—Stevenson's *Dr Jekyll and Mr Hyde*, Lang's *The Gold of Fairnilee*, Oliphant's stories of the supernatural, Barrie's *Peter Pan*, the short stories of Macleod or Mackay Brown. The inspiration of Scots fantasy thus operates within a fairly small or compressed compass, both

in terms of its localism and its relative brevity. And we might add that
it is rarely leisurely or expansive in character: description is frequently
terse, characterisation lives by the thumbnail.

Lastly, Scottish fantasy is far less 'fantastic' than its English cousins.
Much of it keeps us within some form of this world, not visiting a magic
realm. Exceptions are MacDonald's Fairy Land, which however in part
is the landscape of the human imagination, Oliphant's 'The Land of
Darkness', which still part-figures the Victorian world, and Lindsay's
Tormance, which again to a considerable extent is a landscape of the
human soul. The point is that Scots fantasy is not frequently concerned
with the supernatural and 'other' for themselves. Its gaze is directed
more in at this world than out at the next. The priggish Arkol in George
Mackay Brown's 'Brig-o-Dread' (*The Sun's Net*, 1976) has to taste after
being slain the bitter truths of the life he has left behind before he may
begin to be acceptable within the realms of death; in Brown's *Magnus* the
saint-to-be is instructed by his angelic visitant to '"weave well upon the
loom of the spirit"',[24] so that his sacrificial death may be a completion
of that spiritual garment. Brown, a Roman Catholic and a writer of
'supernaturalist' fantasy, is in many ways a test case here.

Everyone will have his or her objections to these characterisations, many
of which are already admitted to be only broadly correct and to have
exceptions. What, for instance, of the work of Muriel Spark, whom
some might consider a Scottish writer of fantasy? Her work does not
fit the criteria advanced here: it is international; it does not often hark
back to Scots landscapes but is just as happy in New York or by the
Zambezi; its characters are not generally solitaries; it does not deal in
absolute contrasts; it is not (with the possible exception of *The Driver's
Seat*) particularly violent; and it is not inward-looking. To which we could
reply with arguments as to why it is not to be considered as *Scottish*
fantasy: one might in particular mention that Muriel Spark herself is
such a believer in the value of continually shifting place or country as
to have obliterated her involvement with any one country, including
that of her earliest years.[25] Nevertheless she remains an exception to
our account, and doubtless there may be others. The point has use in
further heightening the fact that the discriminations offered here as to
the nature of Scots fantasy are meant to capture tendencies, dispositions,
broad traits, not to pin everything down in a final and universally valid
definition, even supposing such a thing were possible.

(And there is, one may remark, one fantasy written by an Englishman
which is set in Scotland and exhibits many of the characteristics of
Scottish fantasy—Shakespeare's *Macbeth*. *Macbeth* is 'involved with the
land', there is a steady reduction of the hero, there are absolute contrasts
of light and dark, savagery, a strain of Manichaeism, the theme of desired
respectability, the division of the self, the journey within, and so on. In

this respect perhaps Shakespeare should be made an honorary Scot: certainly he has fully reflected the Scots' psyche as revealed in their fantasy. On the other hand, and in the same way, perhaps the Scot Kenneth Grahame should be made an honorary Englishman, for writing the thoroughly 'Home Counties' *Wind in the Willows*.)

A word on the omission of science fiction here. This is actually a genre quite different in character from fantasy, even if, like fantasy, it does describe imaginary worlds. There has been very little Scottish science fiction—of significant names only Ian Banks or J. T. McIntosh present themselves—and it is almost* all post-war. Further, the continually experimental character of science fiction, and its explorations of alien worlds, make it almost meaningless to speak of any Scottish character it might have. It would belong with Scottish fantasy only to the extent that the subject of interest was the inventiveness of the Scottish imagination. Otherwise it is more usefully to be considered in relation to the development of science fiction as a whole.

For too long now, as we said, primary value has been put by the Scots cultural priesthood, and to some extent by the readership, on 'realism', whether Kailyard or urban; the furthest fantasy could go was with the novels of Sir Walter Scott or John Buchan. Scotland's distinctive literature arguably lies as much in fantasy as in the 'naturalistic' novel, and certainly fantasy is the deepest root behind it. It cannot be without significance that the recent search for a Scottish identity has been accompanied by an upsurge in the writing of fantasy, in George Mackay Brown, in Alasdair Gray, in Margaret Elphinstone. Nor should it escape remark that in these three writers, not to mention Neil Gunn, we see Scots fantasy as at last home-produced. Almost all writers of fantasy before the Second World War write from outside Scotland. Now Scots fantasy, so long looking towards its roots, has at last come back to them. There is something here of value for the future development not only of Scottish culture but for the spiritual wholeness of every individual within it.

Notes

1 As by e.g. Maurice Lindsay, *History of Scottish Literature* (London: Robert Hale, 1977), and Trevor Royle, *The Macmillan Companion to Scottish Literature* (London: Macmillan, 1983).

2 Edwin Sidney Hartland, ed. and introd., *English Fairy and Other Folk Tales* (London: Walter Scott, 1890), pp. xiii–xx. In his foreword to the more recent *Folktales of England*, eds Katharine Briggs and Ruth L. Tongue (London: Routledge and Kegan Paul, 1965), Richard M. Dorson echoes Hartland on the paucity of English fairy tales,

remarking 'how few *Märchen* have come to light in England after a century and a half of scattered searching' (p. vii).

3 See Lutz Röhrich, 'Elementargeister', in *Enzyklopädie des Märchens*, gen. ed. Kurt Ranke (Berlin and New York: Walter de Gruyter, 1977–), vol.3 (1981), 1316–26. Writers of German Romantic fairy-tales or *Kunstmärchen*, such as Novalis and E. T. A. Hoffmann, were particularly stimulated by this tradition, as in turn was George MacDonald in his *The Princess and the Goblin* (1872) and *The Princess and Curdie* (1883).

4 In Britain, the fairies 'most commonly lived underground' (K. M. Briggs, *The Fairies in Tradition and Literature* (London: Routledge and Kegan Paul, 1967), p. 12).

5 Thomas Hardy, *The Mayor of Casterbridge* (London: Macmillan, 1961), p. 56.

6 Margaret Elphinstone, *The Incomer* (London: The Women's Press, 1987), p. 149.

7 These can best be found in the reissues of 1897, *Spiritual Tales, Barbaric Tales*, and *Tragic Romances* by Fiona Macleod (Edinburgh: Patrick Geddes).

8 Andrew Lang, *The Gold of Fairnilee* (Bristol: J. W. Arrowsmith, 1888), p. 65.

9 On this see Campbell, *Popular Tales*, pp. cxviii–ix.

10 Margaret Oliphant, *A Beleaguered City and Other Stories* (Oxford: Oxford University Press, 1988), p. 285.

11 David Lindsay, *A Voyage to Arcturus* (Edinburgh: Canongate, 1992), p. 301.

12 George MacDonald, *Phantastes and Lilith* (London: Gollancz, 1962), pp. 44–5.

13 Lindsay, *A Voyage to Arcturus*, p. 278.

14 Thomas Carlyle, *Sartor Resartus*, eds Kerry McSweeney and Peter Sabor (Oxford: Oxford University Press, 1987), p. 220.

15 Oliphant, *A Beleaguered City*, p. 264.

16 Robert Louis Stevenson, *Strange Case of Dr Jekyll and Mr Hyde* (London: Longmans, Green, 1886), p. 37.

17 Ibid., p. 127.

18 In *Tragic Romances*.

19 Campbell, *Popular Tales*, pp. lxviii–ix.

20 MacDonald, *Phantastes and Lilith*, p. 180.

21 Ibid., p. 194.

22 Carlyle, *Sartor Resartus*, p. 44.

23 *Phantastes and Lilith*, pp. 203–4.

24 George Mackay Brown, *Magnus* (Glasgow: Richard Drew Publishing, 1987), p. 67.

25 She has described herself as 'a constitutional exile' and her early home town Edinburgh as 'a place where I could not hope to be

understood' (Muriel Spark, 'What Images Return' (1962), repr. in Karl Miller, ed., *Memoirs of a Modern Scotland* (London: Faber and Faber, 1970), pp. 151, 152). See also Ruth Whittaker, *The Faith and Fiction of Muriel Spark* (London: Macmillan, 1982), pp. 31–2.

CHAPTER TWO
Beginnings

THE FOLKTALE AND BALLAD

F ANTASY, IN THE shape of the folk- and fairy-tale, is the oldest and first literary genre in Scotland as in any country. For centuries before the first written work, such stories would be told orally, as part of the culture of communities, a means for them of making sense out of lives ringed by mystery and burdened with deprivation. Of those earliest stories we have no record. James Macpherson's celebrated 'Ossian' poems of 1760–3, supposedly a primitive Scottish epic to rival Homer, are in fact largely invention. The stories collected by J. F. Campbell in his *Popular Tales of the West Highlands* (1860–2) are many of them the reworking of narrative motifs traceable to other lands, or else derive from Irish story-cycles and myths: for the folk-tale as we know it is international before it is local. To speak of those that are identifiably Scottish, either wholly or in their mode of telling, one must tread carefully. Further, there are differences between a tale as presented in one part of Scotland or another, or even between one teller and another: the folk-tale is inherently shape-shifting, like many of the characters in it.[1] Nor can we always trust to the written versions that we have, since these sometimes reflect the bias of the transcriber—as with Joseph Jacobs' *Celtic Fairy Tales* (1892), which he adapted to a child readership.

That said, there have been several identifications of particularly Scottish characteristics, and of some peculiarly Scottish tales. We have seen J. F. Campbell's comment on the relative lack of hierarchy, the mingling of the rustic and the royal in such tales, in the last chapter. Campbell also remarks how the giants of Gaelic stories are much nearer men than the supermen of Germany, Scandinavia, Greece or Rome; and points out how not only the giants but the fairies are depicted as having their countries underground, the fairies living in green mounds.[2] In her collection *Scottish Folk Tales* (1976), Ruth Ratcliff remarks, 'All tales in this collection have a particularly Scottish flavour, though similar tales do turn up in the traditions of other countries in slightly different form. What makes these stories special is their setting and their characters, and the characters' way of life.'[3] This however often comes down to minor features, such as the man enchanted to a hoodie crow (in contrast to the frog-prince in Grimm or the supposed monster in the Cupid and Psyche myth) in Campbell's 'The Tale of the Hoodie', or the attempts of two daughters to get rid of their sister by tying her to a peat stack in 'Maol A Chliobain', or the game of shinty played on the lawn of the knight in 'The Rider of Grianaig, and Iain the Soldier's Son';[4] and less specific clan or local traditions, as well as the landscape of hills, glens, lochs, woods and sea-shores, are continuously present. A tale such as 'Conall Cra-Bhuidhe', which has three versions in Campbell, and similar basic narrative to tales from other lands, is yet a uniquely Gaelic story:[5] for example when Conall is sheltering in a bothy from the snow, a group of cats comes in and sings a cronan to him which puts him under an obligation he finally cannot fulfil; whereupon he makes his escape through a turf window, only to be pursued into a nearby pinewood where he shins up a high tree.

Perhaps the most evidently specific of tales are those relating to fairies. In Campbell's collection a good example is 'The Smith and the Fairies',[6] which tells of a smith who finds he has a changeling son and must go to the nearby fairy mound when it opens to recover his natural child. He is told by a sage to go with a bible to protect him, a dirk to stick in the threshold to keep the hill open, and a cock whose crowing will make the fairies disappear. All follows as planned, except that for a year afterwards the rescued boy will not speak.

The best known of Scottish (non-Gaelic) folk- or fairy-tales include 'The Black Bull of Norroway', 'The Well at the World's End', 'Rashie Coat', 'Whuppity Stoorie' and, in ballad form, the Borders stories of 'Tam Lin' and 'Thomas the Rhymer'. Of these only the last two seem unique to Scotland, even if the idea of enforced sojourn in another world is not itself new. 'The Black Bull of Norroway' has analogues going all the way back to the Cupid and Psyche myth, 'The Well at the World's End' can also be seen in Grimms' 'The Three Heads', 'Rashie Coat' in Grimms' 'Ashputtel' (or 'Cinderella'), and 'Whuppity Stoorie' in Grimms' 'Rumpelstiltskin'.[7]

But again, though the bare narrative patterns and characters may be common currency, the individual details put into the story will be much more specific (though they may differ from one Scottish teller to another). This is the ending to the version of 'Whuppity Stoorie' in David Buchan's *Scottish Tradition: A Collection of Scottish Folk Literature*, when the wife names the fairy and escapes her forfeit: 'Gin a fluff o' gunpowder had come out o' the grund, it couldna hae gart the fairy loup heicher nor she did; syne down she came again, dump on her shoe-heels, and whurlin' round, she ran down the brae, scraichin' for rage, like a houlet chased wi' the witches.'[8] The whole tale as told is a vivid account of the self-reliance and learned cunning of a poor Scots peasant woman, abandoned by her husband and tricked by fate; a good touch is how the wife mourned more for her ailing sow than for the loss of her husband.

Baldly told, the tales could often come from anywhere: but their tellers shape them to their own physical and mental landscape. In 'The Cat and the Hard Cheese', two sons go out to see if they can rescue the fortunes of their mother, who is about to be turned out of her house; the first comes on his way to a big castle where a notice on the gate offers work:

> And he rang the bell at the back door; he says, 'Ah see they're advertisin' here fir men.'
>
> He says, 'Oh aye,' he says, 'but,' he says, 'I don't think ye'll ever dae the work.'
>
> 'Well,' he says, 'there nae hairm in tryin.'
>
> He says, 'No, there nae hairm in tryin,' he says, 'but if ye fail,' he says, 'ye see aa they heids stickin on the gate doon there?' he says: 'yours'll be the next.'
>
> 'Ah well,' he says, 'A cannae help it,' he says, 'I'd be as weel deid onyway as goin on like this.'[9]

This whole tale should be read as an example of the way the personality of the teller refashions traditional material: even better would be to hear it on tape, and better still to have heard it from the teller herself, Betsy Whyte, a travelling woman, when she recounted it for several recorders in Montrose and Edinburgh in 1975. The folk-tale, supposedly anonymous, is here made by its teller into an individual work of art.

The fifteenth-century ballads 'Tam Lin' and 'Thomas the Rhymer' are much more specifically products of Scotland, not least because of their debt to native fairy lore. In both a mortal is made thrall to the Queen of Faërie, and forced to live in her country. Both describe men made subject to women: and it must be said that there is a strong 'feminist' element in many Scottish (not Gaelic) fairy tales; England has rather its cunning Dick Whittington or its giant-killing or beanstalk-climbing Jacks. 'Tam Lin' starts with 'fair Janet' who, though warned against Tam Lin as a seducer, still goes to him at Carterhaugh and gives herself to him, and is made pregnant. Rebuked by her family, she returns to Tam to ask him to marry her; but he tells her he is a prisoner of the Fairy Queen, and then instructs her in how to gain him, if she will. She is to stand at Miles Cross on Hallowe'en Night when the fairy folk ride from their mound, and pick him out from the third group that passes her; whereupon the Fairy Queen will turn him into a number of shapes in her arms to try to make her drop him, but if she holds on to him, he will be hers. The whole tale is a picture of feminine resolution—and even of dominance, for Tam is the slave of the Fairy Queen and cannot escape by himself. 'Thomas the Rhymer', which describes how Thomas becomes enthralled to the Fairy Queen for seven years after he kisses her, gives us a still more passive male: for after his initial reckless act, Tam is led about as the queen's helpless captive. Both stories seem to look back to some long-forgotten matriarchy, of which the fairies, now confined to their mounds, seem to be the lost representatives.

Both stories also deal with 'glamour', the enchantment, only part-romantic, that binds both body and spirit. One could argue that Thomas the Rhymer is Tam Lin before Janet met him—though Thomas was to be released after seven years, and Tam was either to be kept or given to the devil. Certainly the two tales could be said to form the halves of a whole: first in the sense that the one shows the beginning of an enchantment, and the other its ending; but also in that 'Thomas the Rhymer' portrays much more a state of being, where 'Tam Lin', which has more action, shows a process of becoming and of continual change.

It is also possible to see the journey of Thomas into Elfland as one into the deepest levels of the unconscious mind, away from sunlit earth to darkness and the unknown, and from the realm of speech to silence (Tam is bid not to utter a word in Elfland).

> O they rade on, and farther on,
>   And they waded through rivers aboon the knee,
> And they saw neither sun nor moon,
>   But they heard the roaring of the sea.

And if 'Thomas the Rhymer' is a journey to the unconscious, 'Tam Lin' is the journey back to the conscious and choosing world, portrayed in the determined activity of a now mortal woman who would have Tam back into the more civil bond of marriage and social and moral acceptability. In this way these ballad fantasies would anticipate an emphasis on the unconscious mind that will be found recurrent in many Scottish fantasies.

Earliest and most pervasive of literary forms though they may be, folk- and fairy-tales had little marked influence on written Scottish literature until the development of a collector's interest in the folk and the vernacular heritage. This could be said to have begun with Allan Ramsay's rather urbane *The Ever Green* (1724), a reworking of poems that first appeared in the Bannatyne Manuscript (1568), and continued ever more strongly through James MacPherson's disingenuous 'Ossian' poems (1760–3), Robert Burns, and in particular Sir Walter Scott's *Minstrelsy of the Scottish Border* (1802–3). Prior to this, the bulk of Scottish literature looks to ancient, classical or English models. And until Burns's 'Tam o' Shanter' (1791), there is not one significant Scottish work which tells a tale of the supernatural. When we speak of 'fantasy' in Scottish literature from the beginnings until Hogg, we must do so in the very limited sense of the use of the fantastical imagination more than of the identifiably supernatural. Many poets write allegories or dream visions in which gods and goddesses appear, but such beings are more the personification of forces both cosmic and earthly than they are to be believed for themselves. Robert Henryson writes a collection of *Moral Fabillis* (c. 1465) founded on Aesop's Fables, but while we have cocks, hens, mice and foxes talking to one another, this supernatural circus is a merely conditional one, the beasts serving as enlivening figures for man and his passions. The truly supernatural, in a believing age, is reserved mainly for Christian contexts.

This said, the story is one well worth telling, not least for the reason that elements of the work of Dunbar, Henryson and others seep through to influence that of some of the writers we shall consider—James Hogg in particular. What might have happened had the Scots imagination not been oriented to foreign literary models, or, after the Reformation, suppressed by doctrinal sobriety, or with the departure of the Scottish court in 1603 left without a cultural and inspirational centre, one can perhaps guess from the force and individuality that breaks the surface of Scotland's best literary works. These are, among others, the visionary poems of the great 'makars'—James I's *The Kingis Quair* (c.1425), Robert Henryson's *The Testament of Cresseid* (c.1460), William Dunbar's 'The Goldyn Targe' and 'The Dance of the sevin deidly Synnis' (c.1495, 1506), Gavin Douglas's 'The Palice of Honour' (1501) and Alexander Montgomerie's *The Cherrie and the Slae* (c.1597). Beyond these until 1760 we have only minor works and imitations. Our assessment of them as fantasies will concern their inventiveness, their recurrent and possibly Scottish features, and where relevant their use of the Christian supernatural.

THE MAKARS (1425–1597)

The Kingis Quair of James I tells of the imprisonment of its author (James was in prison in England from 1406 till 1424) and how one day in spring he sees a lady in the garden beneath his tower and falls in love with her. His pain at imprisonment is now redoubled, and in a dream he makes a plea for help to Venus, to whose celestial sphere he is transported. Venus tells him the remedy lies not in her hands alone, and after promising her support if he behaves as a lover should, sends him, guided by Good Hope, to the palace of Minerva. Minerva in turn then says that she and Venus will put their heads together to determine how to help him, and with further admonitions on good conduct sends him down to the earth again to ask help of Fortune. Fortune stands by a huge turning wheel, on which many of those who climb on fall off to their hurt: but seeing the much-travelled lover trembling at this prospect, she briskly bids him venture all and '"hald thy grippis"' (l.1194);[10] after which he wakes, his fortune brightens, he is released from prison and united with his love.

The poem's originality is not immediately apparent. It owes much to Chaucer and to the work of John Gower and says so (st.197). Chaucer's *The Knight's Tale* is the model for the inamourment from the tower and the springtime setting; his *Book of the Duchess* provides a lover's complaint; his *Parliament of Fowls* gives us a temple of Venus (if the goddess is there treated unfavourably) and his *House of Fame* involves a visit to the Temple of Venus followed by a celestial journey to the Houses of Fame and of Rumour. Gower's *Confessio Amantis* involves a despairing lover who addresses himself to Venus and is then passed on by her to her priest Genius, who instructs him at length in the reconciling of affection with reason and virtue; here the influence on *The Kingis Quair* is both in imagery and in doctrine, and this poem also has a section on Fortune. The influence of Boethius' *De Consolatione Philosophiae*, a seminal text for medieval writers, is also marked, with its stress on acceptance, self-control and cosmic optimism. Beyond this the poem is also influenced strongly by John Lydgate's *Temple of Glas*: indeed it has been said that the aspect of the poem as medley of different forms derives particularly from Lydgate's poem.[11]

This may sound rather damning so far as inspiration is concerned, and it is true that to some extent the novelty of the poem consists in shaking together its various sources with the addition of a bit of local colour—here the actual imprisonment of the supposed author, the fact that James I while in prison fell in love with Lady Joan Beaufort, cousin of Henry V and married her on his release in 1424, and perhaps the complaints at a nearby nightingale who fails to lament in sympathy with the lover's misery. We cannot even assign the tone of abject humility and helplessness on the lover's part to anything singularly idiosyncratic, since we find similar grovelling ineptitude and emotional handlessness on the part of Chaucer's narrator in *The Parliament of Fowls* (though it has been said that this poet goes further in presented naiveté). Novelty—and the poet does set out to write 'sum newe thing' (l. 89)—may be found rather in the way some of the images are presented, and in the unconscious levels at which the poem is fused (here peculiarly justifying its typically medieval use of dream vision).

There may seem nothing original in the supernatural journey:

> Ascending upward ay fro spere to spere
> Through air and water and the hote fyre
> Till that I come unto the circle clere
> Of Signifer, quhare fair, bryght, and schire
> The signis schone,—and in the glade empire
> Of blisfull Venus ane c[a]ryit now
> So sudaynly, almost I wist noght how.
>
> (ll.526–32)

Nothing *original*—except the stress on 'I' and feeling, the sense of wonder in the detail, and the vigour of movement deriving from the run-on lines. These features are seen throughout the poem, and they are distinctive. The lover—let us call him James—comes near to the fantastic impulse in his sense of untutored amazement. From his instruction by Venus, Minerva and Fortune into the ways of the world, one might suppose that he would be more worldly-wise and matter-of-fact by the end: but in fact he concludes with a reply to those who might ask why he has troubled to write this poem, saying that it is a celebration of his astonished gratitude:

> Quho that from hell war croppin onys in hevin
> Wald efter o thank for joy mak six or sevin?
>
> (ll.1271–2)

He then proceeds to pray on behalf of all lovers and to thank the gods, the nightingale that sang to him, even the castle wall from which he first saw his love and the green-clad boughs beneath which she walked. If we were to compare the narrator in Chaucer's *House of Fame*, who is transported through the spheres by a giant eagle, we would find that, typically of Chaucer, he engages in conversation, his fear and amazement being countered by the knowingness of the eagle: what is a journey of discovery in *The Kingis Quair* is in Chaucer rather more a demonstration. The whole of *The Kingis Quair* is interrogative in character, continually questioning experience, down to the least thing:

> 'Quhat lyf is this, that makis birdis dote?
> Quhat may this be, how cummyth it of ought?
> Quhat nedith it to be so dere ybought?'
>
> (ll.248–50)

   The poem is much more personal than its sources: where they consider the nature of love or right behaviour, this one is directed much more at the inner experience of the narrator-lover, who feels himself helpless on the sea of fortune and adrift in the waves of love, and seeks above all from the various deities for stability and a means of finding the control to give him peace. Thus to Venus,

> 'As ye that bene the socour and suete well
> Of remedye, of carefull hertes cure,
> And in the huge weltering wawis fell
> Of lufis rage, blisfull havin and sure,
> O anker and keye of oure gude auenture,
> Ye have your man with his gude will conquest:
> Merci, therefore, and bring his hert to rest.'
>
> (ll.694–700)

As with many others, this stanza shows the drive forward of suspended syntax. The poem is a kind of *Bildungsroman*: James has to reach 'being' by a process of becoming. This may give added meaning to the images of displacement that thread the poem: he is cast adrift on a wild sea of emotional experience, he is cut off from his own country, he is walled off from the world in his prison, he cannot speak to his lady, the goddesses pass him from one to another and from heaven down to earth again. The very use of the interrogative mode throughout suggests displacement from full understanding. The whole poem thus becomes a journey of the spirit. The sea-storm in which James was originally captured represents the lack of control and direction of his youthful emotions; the prison that shuts him from freedom mirrors his fatalistic sense of helplessness; his visits to Venus, Minerva and Fortune signify respectively the growth in him not only of love, but of virtuous and charitable love, then his gaining of reason, and last his readiness to choose the unpredictability of the world out of his own free will. This done, the prison vanishes, and he is united with his lady, because he no longer sees himself as mere helpless victim. Because he has come to terms with his own nature, because he is no longer displaced from what he is, he can meet the world and the object of his love.

The inward-looking aspect of the fantasy in this poem could be said to be its peculiarly Scottish character. There is always something conceptual or even transcendental at the heart of most English visionary poems: but this one puts the sufferings of a particular man in a particular situation first, and the concepts later. The same emphasis on personality and the individual is seen in modern Scottish fantasy, where the action tends to emerge out of particular people, rather than existing on its own, and where the interest is at least as much in idiosyncratic humans as in the supernatural, from Hogg's Robert Wringhim to Stevenson's Jekyll, or Gray's Thaw. (Modern English fantasy is more interested in ideas, adventures and order, whether social, natural or cosmic.)

Henryson's *The Testament of Cresseid* (c. 1460) may seem at first sight removed from the personal, since it is an account of a legendary story from the far past. Yet the poem is actually Henryson's own exploration of Cresseid's 'history' after the action described in Chaucer's *Troilus and Criseyde*, when she has deserted her Trojan lover Troilus for the Grecian Diomede. Chaucer's poem was founded on Boccaccio's *Il Filostrato*, which itself was based on other sources. Henryson says his poem was taken from 'ane uther quhair' (l.61),[12] but that is only a smoke-screen for his own originality: obviously his poem takes its inspiration from Chaucer, but it is still mainly an invention, and as such at once a fantasy, and a more individual poem.

The poem begins with the poet, chilled by a freezing night, seeking warmth by his fire, with a drink in one hand and a book in the other. Reading from the 'uther quhair', he finds that after Diomede had satisfied 'all his appetyte,/And mair' on Cresseid, he rejected her for another. Cresseid eventually returns to her father's house; and one day, in a 'secret Orature', she blames the gods for her rejection by both Troilus and Diomede. She falls into a trance in which she sees the seven planetary gods and goddesses appear before her. They sentence her to lose her beauty and become a leper, for her blasphemy to Venus and Cupid. Cresseid then wakes and finds herself physically ruined, and has to leave her father's house and beg alms in the company of other lepers. One day Troilus passes her band and, half-recognising Cresseid, who is herself part-blind, gives her liberal alms. When Cresseid learns his identity, she is overwhelmed by his nobility and her loss, and dies accepting her guilt.

For us the first concern will be the role of the gods. In themselves they may not be wholly original, deriving from Lydgate's *Assembly of Gods*, but the point is how far they are to be seen only as personifications of natural events—the usual position they occupy in medieval dream narrative—and how far Henryson exploits other possibilities with them. On the first view, it has been pointed out that Henryson, a Christian, would not have believed in pagan gods and goddesses[13]. It has also been argued that, given the conditions of the time, Cresseid could easily have developed leprosy without any supernatural intervention: that the poem is imposing a moral and cosmic pattern on a perfectly natural event.[14] Both these views would give the deities no status in actuality at all: they would only be decorative fictions. Another view, however, would suggest that the deities represent certain universal forces. They are, it is pointed out, introduced as having

> power of all thing generabill
> To reull and steir by thair greit Influence,
> Wedder and wind, and coursis variabill.
>
> (ll. 148–50)

In this light, 'They are the powers against whom Cresseid's conduct has offended, and by whom therefore she is judged and punished. In themselves they are neither friendly nor hostile; they are the indifferent laws of the universe.'[15] Even here, however, the deities are still swallowed in other forces.

These deities are however given marked personalities and a degree of captiousness which makes such explanations of them not wholly satisfactory. Cupid is shown losing his temper at Cresseid's outburst and demanding that she be punished. Saturn is a sort of ghastly version of the aged poet if he had stayed out in the cold:

> His face fronsit, his lyre was lyke the Leid,
> His teith chatterit, and cheverit with the Chin,
> His Ene drowpit, how sonkin in his heid,
> Out of his Nois the Meldrop fast can rin,
> With lippis bla and cheikis leine and thin;
> The Iceschoklis that fra his hair doun hang
> Was wonder greit, and as ane speir als lang.
>
> (ll. 155–61)

This is wonderfully alive, emerging from Henryson's own experience and imagination, and using the power latent in the Scots language to re-animate a standard figure; and he does this with every portrait. The effect is to bring the gods vividly to life, and thus to give them a measure of individual existence. Nor can the judgment they give be called a 'wholly fair' one, since they give it into the hands of two of the deities that are darkly presented—Saturn and Cynthia (the moon): Cynthia indeed has something of the aspect that Cresseid is to be given, being black-spotted, dull and lightless (ll.253–60). The impartial, objective verdict supposed to result from the combination of the highest with the lowest deity seems undermined by the depiction of them as wayward individuals; even allegorising them as Time (Saturn) and Change, their common attributes, will not flatten their rude vitality. But then it almost seems as though Henryson deliberately provokes this reaction, sets up these opposing views of the gods as both real and mere 'devices', as both individuals and concepts, or as impartial and partial, precisely in order to make their natures more fluid.

One of the effects of such fluidity is that it becomes possible to read the gods in psychological terms. As someone well-informed in medical matters, Henryson would certainly have taken into account the effect of planetary forces on Cresseid's body in her catching leprosy: but he would also have believed that the health of the body was dependent on an individual equilibrium or harmony among its several elements and humours. His poem suggests that the gods may not only be powers working on Cresseid from outside, but also symbols of her own inner condition: together she and they can be seen as her spirit at war with itself. The gods, as we have seen represent generation (they have 'power of all thing generabill'); and Cresseid, in deserting Troilus and then in turn being deserted, has rejected true love and generation, and therefore is at war not only with her proper role in creation, but with herself. Her sense of herself, before her vision, is one of being 'clene excludit, as abject odious' (l.133); and her blame of Cupid and Venus at this point measures her refusal to see herself for what she is, as also does her long complaint against Fortune after her sentence has been realised. At the moral level—and the poem is more than moral, it is also tragic—Cresseid has literally to come to terms, so far as she can, with what she is, before she dies: 'Quha findis treuth lat him his Lady ruse:/ Nane but my self as now I will accuse' (ll.573–4). The very diversity and the unfairness of the gods then becomes a picture of her own fragmented spirit; instead of Cupid alone, she gets all the gods in outrage.

To this psychological, or indeed almost psychosomatic, reading of the poem, with the deities as at least partly reflective of Cresseid's inner spiritual state, we might add the context in which she experiences her 'divine' judgments. For she is in 'ane secret Orature' within her father's house, if simply to avoid being seen by people: the context, and the way the gods come down to her while she falls into a dream there, suggest a movement into the most inward places of the mind. The implication is then that Cresseid's spiritual disease translates itself into a physical one. Such a reading cannot, of course, be exclusive: it is part of the poem's force to suggest a variety of interpretations, from the supernatural to the psychosomatic. But it does seem to have strong claim to a place in our understanding of the poem: a poem which is already 'problematic' in the imposition of a moral pattern on a disease which can equally be viewed as having natural causes.

The poem has a very personal tone, like *The Kingis Quair* (which Henryson probably knew). Chaucer is often cited as precedent for this kind of thing, but in fact he is far more reticent and invisible in his work. The whole of *Troilus and Criseyde* arguably has the narrator simply agreeing and sympathising with all that happens until he can stand it no longer; the *Canterbury Tales* are a model of poetic self-effacement. Henryson starts his poem by introducing himself to us in his study, commenting on the weather, saying how it suits his poem's subject and how despite his continued hopes of Venus, he as an old man does not. And then we feel accompanied by him throughout, feel that we learn more about his nature as well as that of Cresseid, through his reactions to his own material: he comes over as a man who has a strong sense of sin and yet an equally strong instinct for compassion, a scholar who wears his learning lightly and with humour, a lawyer with a strong sense of justice who is yet able at least to smile at times in court. We feel him stand ironically apart from the pomp, bluster and ruthless violence of his gods, even while he gives full weight to what they have to say; we sense him not far off, his finger lightly on the spiritual pulse, almost agreeing with Cresseid as he lets her revile the deities as 'Our craibit Goddis' (l.353).

We are back with the imitative mode with Dunbar's 'The Goldyn Targe' (c. 1495), which, for all its poetic vitality, its superb deployment of aureate language without indulgence, is not markedly original or fantastic, save in one respect. The poet finds himself in a luxuriant spring landscape (matched by aureate diction), full of light, leaves and flowers, all described in terms of precious stones reminiscent of the opening of the Middle English poem *Pearl* (c.1450). He then falls asleep in the midst of all this vitality, and dreams that a ship approaches him. There lands from it a group of figures including Nature, Venus, Cupid, several other deities and numbers of allegorical figures such as Beauty, Womanhede, Benigne Luke and Presence. The dreamer is discovered, and we then follow the allegorical tradition of the *Roman de la Rose* as the various personifications begin to assail him; that is, as love tries to conquer him. He is defended however by Reason, who protects him with a golden targe or shield which wards off the various arrows of influence shot at him. Finally he is overwhelmed by Presence, who throws a powder in Reason's eyes: for a while he is favoured by love, but soon all around him is blighted, and the landscape turns from spring to winter. The ship leaves with its company again, and he wakes up. Once more, in the 'real' world, the landscape is joyous and spring-like. The poet then turns to praise other poets, Chaucer, Gower and Lydgate, for transforming the barren cultural landscape of this isle to a new spring through their use of aureate diction: Chaucer is called 'rose of rethoris all,/As in oure tong ane flour imperiall' (ll.253–4),[16] and linked with May and with light. We are left to surmise that the poet has learnt not to identify springtime and joy with love, which is changeable, but now with the continuous spring that is poetry itself[17]—a peculiarly Renaissance emphasis on the value of eloquence. The seasons, like love, change, but the finest poetry is an eternal springtime, and a wellspring flowing and deepening through time: the poet who began with Homer and Cicero (ll.67, 69) ends with Chaucer and his followers and finally with himself, now resolved to hide himself in modesty from their worth. With this, Dunbar seems to end with a sort of priestly devotion to his own craft.

The main original feature of the poem, so far as we are concerned, lies in Dunbar's transformation of a standard trope with a piece of realism. This is the arrival and departure of Venus and company in a ship, where usually in such allegories Venus is simply encountered with her train in a garden. We see the ship approach 'agayn the orient sky' with a blossom-white sail and a mast of bright gold, coming rapidly 'As falcoune swift desyrouse of his pray' till it lands 'Amang the grene rispis and the redis'; and watch a hundred ladies disembark from it and spread over the nearby fields like white lilies (ll.50–66). Nothing at first identifies this as an allegorical scene, and, for the time, we are left to contemplate a vision that seems to belong to fantasy—indeed the poet himself says that it was his 'dremes fantasy' (l.49), which suggests, as with James and with Henryson, a more personal and psychological than a 'given' source for his vision. The departure of the ship is still more dramatic:

> In twynkling of ane eye to schip thai went,
> And swyth up saile unto the top thai stent,
> And with swift course atour the flude thay frak;
> Thay fyrit gunnis wyth powder violent
> Till that the reke raise to the firmament;
> The rochis all resownit wyth the rak,
> For rede it semyt that the raynbow brak;
> Wyth spirit affrayde apon my feet I sprent,
> Amang the clewis so carefull was the crak.
>
> (ll.235–43)

We seem almost to be in the landscape of Mantegna or even Bosch; though Dunbar may owe much to late medieval pageant. A Renaissance ship arrives in an allegory like the locomotive in the pastoral setting of the far future in Michael Moorcock's *The Dancers at the End of Time* (1972–6). It is a wonderful moment, and totally transforms the rigidities of the alle-gorical mode from within, making it much more a genuine 'other world' than a literary convention. Here we have moved to a love of setting which we shall also see in Gavin Douglas and Alexander Montgomerie. But this is true here only of the framing—within the amorous experience in Dunbar's poem the standard literary conventions derived from the *Roman de la Rose* and Prudentius' *Psychomachia* prevail.

Dunbar enlivens allegory and challenges convention in another way in his 'The Dance of the sevin deidly Synnis' (c.1506). Here the novelty consists in setting the seven deadly sins in hell, and having them perform a festive dance for Satan (Mahoun).[18] Because the sins are in their place of origin, dancing at the behest of their supernatural source, they become as real as they are allegorical: here, the poem shows us, is the truth in the representation, and here too is the everlasting consequence for those mortals who give themselves up to any one of them.

> Nixt him [Envy] in dans come Cuvatyce,
> Rute of all evill and grund of vyce,
>   That nevir cowd be content;
> Catyvis, wrechis, and ockeraris,
> Hud pykis, hurdaris, and gadderaris,—
>   All with that warlo went:
> Out of thair throttis thay schot on udder
> Hett moltin gold, me thocht a fudder,
>   As fyreflawcht maist fervent;
> Ay as they tomit thame of schot
> Feyndis fild thame new up to the thrott
>   With gold of allkin prent.
>
>   (ll. 55–66)

In contrast to the flow of 'The Goldyn Targe', this poem utilises vernacular density to give a sense of literally choking, not only here but throughout, in an obstructive medium: the very notion of the dance, which is movement, and the temporal context of the poem, 'Off Februar the fyiftene nycht' (l.1), for that which is everlasting, heightens the sense of eternal entrapment. The dancing sins are free, their victims are bound to wheels, chained at the ankles, locked in infernal bulimia as above, or clamped to each others' genitals. There is comedy throughout the poem, but it is of a grim sort. Lighter is its companion-piece, 'Nixt that a turnament was tryid', which describes a singularly filthy battle instigated by Mahoun in hell between a tailor and a cobbler: this is more a way of cursing two typical swindlers *à l'outrance* than a serious account of hell's nature and our danger of going there; the poem ends quite simply in the poet's mirth. Both of these poems seem prime sources for Burns's 'Tam o' Shanter' (1791), the first particularly with its drunkards and its eldritch hags, the second with its pervasive sense of the common man and its atmosphere of fear.

We return to the 'high' and 'polite' mode of allegory with Gavin Douglas's 'The Palice of Honour' (1501), although the poem utilises the earthy resources of Scots to the full. The poet has a dream in which he sees four successive groups of personages journeying towards the Palace of Honour, led by Minerva, Diana, Venus and the Muses. When he sees Venus' train he hides himself and complains of his love; whereupon he is heard, found and sentenced to die. He is rescued by the Muses, with whose group he now associates himself. This is the same movement from complaint at love to commitment to poetry and eloquence that we saw in 'The Goldyn Targe'; except that here the poet is to become accepted by Venus as her poet in the palace (pp. 65–6).[19]

In this poem we again see the power of Scots allegorists in enlivening the frames of their poems to the point where they take on some of the aspects of fantasy. Here the coming of the vision, the meeting with Venus and the arrival at the palace are all very vivid; elsewhere the encyclopaedic urge behind the poem leads to exhaustive lists of names associated with particular groups (a feature also particularly marked in Sir David Lyndsay's 'The Dreme'). The topography of the journey to the palace consists largely of a list of rivers traversed, but there is a quickening of inspiration as we arrive at a hill with a road of shining marble running upwards around it, and having reached the top, find a lake of fire full of shrieking spirits that has to be traversed (they are quickly labelled as people who fell victim to lust).

The palace itself is tantalisingly less one place than a changing assemblage of architectural possibilities; we are later to find that Honour itself is a virtue of no easy or worldly definition.

> Pinnakillis, fyellis, turnpekkis mony one,
> Gilt birneist torris, quhilk like to Phebus schone,
> Skarsment, reprise, corbell, and battelingis,
> Fulȝery, bordouris of mony precious stone,
> Subtile muldrie wrocht mony day agone,
> On buttereis, jalme, pillaris and plesand springis,
> Quick imagerie with mony lustie singis,
> Thair micht be sene, and mony worthie wichtis,
> Befoir the ȝet arrayit all at richtis.
>
> (p. 55)

Honour too is now a virtue that partakes in Christ (p. 79), now the highest mode of secular behaviour where no reward is sought save that of doing good (pp. 74–5). The palace is 'heuinlie' and covered with '*sancta sanctorum*' (p. 55), yet it contains Venus and, as examples of Honour, such standard reprobates as Semiramis and Medea. The virtue that is the way to Honour cannot easily be described, 'The world can not considder quhat it is' (p. 75). It is the unnamed god that, abruptly and briefly happened upon within four lines, strikes the poet down with its brightness and is withdrawn from our view (p. 72).

The shifting rooms and swirling personages of the castle portray a far less certain reality than the earlier part of the poem, with its desert landscape:

> This laithlie flude rumland as thonder routit,
> In quhome the fisch ȝelland as eluis schoutit,
> Thair ȝelpis wilde my heiring all fordeifit
> Thay grym monstures my spreits abhorrit and doutit.
> Not throw the soyl bot muskane treis sproutit,
> Combust, barrant, vnblomit and vnleifit,
> Auld rottin runtis quhairin na sap was leifit,
> Moch, all waist, widderit with granit moutit,
> A ganand den, quhair murtherars men reifit.
>
>   (p. 8)

This landscape in part expresses the poet's misery in love: the poem began in the May season, but changed to this after he gave anguished complaint of his wretchedness in love in the prologue (though it later changes back to May while he is still wretched (st. 26)). The consistent emphasis of the poem on the poet's feelings about everything that happens to him serves to heighten this. We may suppose that the journey to the Palace of Honour is a journey inwards to the deepest levels of the mind and spirit: this is furthered by the idea of four different companies travelling there as to a focus, and the change of context from nature to the interior of a building. The poem thus not only expresses in its details the mind of the poet, but also expresses a movement to a progressively more unstructured, unconscious area of that mind. In short it ends as a dream in which alone can true reality be found. In this aspect the poem might be said to anticipate some of the later characteristics of Scottish fantasy.

Sir David Lyndsay's early poem 'The Dreme' (1528), a rather dull tour of hell, heaven, paradise and then, as climax, Scotland, is occasionally able to see things afresh. The poet's vision comes to him when, wakeful on a January night, he dresses and walks down on the seashore till he comes upon a little cave high up in a crag; there he resolves to sit and write poetry, but falls asleep and has his vision instead. He copies Dunbar by having himself woken up afterwards by a ship firing its guns (ll.1016–29). He has the poetic impulse to make his journey wondrous (ll.368–71) but generally fails to rise to it, preferring to stick to an inert slavery to Dante and to his own compendiously instructive purposes. One moment juts out, however: it is when he visits Purgatory,

Quhare mony babbis war, makand drery mone,
  Because they wantit the fruitioun
  Of God, quhilk was ane gret punytioun:
  Of Baptisme, thay wantit the ansenze:
Upwart we went, and left that myrtheles menze.
(ll. 353–7)[20]

One can feel that Lyndsay himself knew all too well that dread sound.

Lyndsay's magnificent *Ane Pleasant Satyre of the Thrie Estaitis* (originally 1540) is a morality play in the tradition of the medieval *Everyman* (c.1500). It is not properly a fantasy, describing in allegorical terms the unmasking and removal of corruption from the king's court, and from the spiritual and temporal estates of the realm. Though its backdrop is belief in heaven and hell, particularly the latter, there is nothing very supernatural in it, save perhaps for the agent of Divine Correction, who is however seen in no different light from that of the mundane figures. The vigour of the play comes from the way Lyndsay has seen reality through the spectacles of allegory: one feels very often that there are identifiable historical figures behind the personifications, and we know that the play was written out of a sense of the menace of national corruption. Here then allegory comes into reality, rather than the other way round: this world rather than a visionary one is being given a strange new life.

Alexander Montgomerie's very popular *The Cherrie and the Slae* (c.1597), the last of the great Scottish visionary poems, looks back to the allegorical 'King Hart', possibly by Gavin Douglas, describing a man's life in a personified sequence representing his changing years and spiritual condition. By now we have reached a point where there can be an interest in the movements of the mind and spirit for themselves. In *The Cherrie and the Slae* the poet is in a spring landscape by a river, and is met by Cupid, who offers him a turn with his wings and bow and arrows; recklessly the poet agrees, but wounds himself with an arrow, whereupon Cupid recovers his gear and flies off, leaving the poet wretched. The poet now sees a cherry tree growing on the top of a steep rock on the other side of the river, and a sloe-bush growing by a pit into which the river falls. He is drawn to the cherries, but fear of the risk involved deters him: an allegorical battle between his various faculties and inclinations for and against—such as Dread, Danger, Courage, Reason, Experience—occupies the bulk of the poem until a resolution is reached to make the attempt. Having crossed the river and climbed the rock, the poet finds that the tree drops its berries from on high into his hands. He ends giving thanks to God.[21]

Its discursive character may make this poem seem the least 'fantastic' of those considered, but certain features belie this. It has often been asked what the experience with Cupid has to do with the long argument about a cherry. C. S. Lewis implicitly equates the cherry with the amorous centre of the *Roman de la Rose*, seeing Montgomerie's poem as the last gasp of a geriatric tradition.[22] The poet however has not fallen in love when he meets Cupid: he simply wants to play god. It has well been pointed out that Cupid is also called 'Cupido', meaning Cupidity here, and that the poet's flight is likened to that of Icarus.[23] He is irresponsibly ambitious: his ascent with Cupid's wings is fraudulent, as his eventual ascent of the rock will not be. His cupidity here is aimless: he will strike with his arrows whoever he likes, whereas his quest for the cherries is both specific and a desire for a literally higher object. It is possible then to see the poem moving from secular to sacred having. The fruit hangs 'betwixt me and the sky,/ Halfe gate almost to Heaven' (ll.338–9); reference is later made to Adam and Eve and the Fall of Man (ll.1124–6), reminding us of another fruit whose miserable issue the gaining of the cherries may reverse (the bitter sloes here may be the fruits available to us in our fallen state). The rock and the pit may be the rock and hard place; the associations of pits need no comment, and the rock may be from St Peter (*petrus*, a rock) who holds the keys to heaven. To get to the cherries, the poet must cross the river (be baptised?); the cherries fall into his hand like grace itself, given, not simply gained; and, at the end, the poet grounds his cure and his success on God alone.

> Yea, blessed bee his holy Name,
> Who did from death to life recleame
> Mee, who was so unkinde.

Here then the poem would have a clear supernatural and fantastic dimension.

But what is the need for the long allegorical debate? In part what is being portrayed, as in other poems we have considered, is an inward moral and spiritual journey. Mere ignorant emotion for and against at first sways the poet, but gradually more sophisticated faculties such as Wit, Skill, Experience and Reason are called into play, and eventually they achieve a reconciliation and relative harmony among all the warring elements (something that does not happen in 'King Hart') in the purpose of gaining the cherries. Spiritual riot becomes order, and the poet is able to make the choice of virtue which alone is the path to unearned, freely-given grace.

Yet we can go further than this. The pit in the river can suggest the unconscious, just as the height may hint at its obverse, the super-conscious, the transcendent. The allegorical process is one of analysis to a deeper and still deeper level of understanding. The journey to the cherry tree is part of that process, because it can only be successfully made when the spiritual movement is complete. The poet's distance from the tree, on its rock on the other side of the river, measures his distance from his true self. The journey itself is scarcely described (ll.

1572–5): it is effectively performed in the allegorical resolution. That resolution may seem a very intellectual and conscious thing, and so it is: but it is also the poet journeying within to his truest nature. Only a literal reading would see grace dropping out of the heavens on to the wide earth like manna here: grace springs in the soul, and what has happened is that the poet has cleared away all his mental obstructiveness and made himself uniquely open to it. In its subtle use of allegory to figure a deepening process of inner education, Montgomerie's poem parallels Spenser's contemporary *The Faerie Queene* (1589–96).

INTERMISSION (1597–1760)

'Qha douttis dremis is bot phantasye?'[24] After Montgomerie, there is something of a great gap in Scottish fantasy until the late eighteenth century. The allegorical tradition of the 'makars' had died out, and the severities, first of the post-Reformation aesthetic landscape, then of rationalism, empiricism and finally of Enlightenment common sense, denied the use of the supernatural in literature and frowned on all but the most modest flights of the creative imagination. In England that did not prevent figures such as Milton or Pope, but Scotland, with a far scantier population and no court, had no such figures to offer and no centre for them if it had; and in addition the Kirk ruled and controlled where the King did not.[25] (Our best books of the Covenanting period are those written long after it, such as Scott's *Old Mortality* (1816) or John Buchan's *Witch Wood* (1927).) Into this long gap we might throw some of the wilder parts of Sir Thomas Urquhart's translation of Rabelais (1653, 1693), but even so there the fantasy comes from Rabelais himself and the additions are mainly of a rhetorical nature;[26] or perhaps the reworking of Ariosto, Tasso and Spenser in Patrick Gordon's *The First booke of the famous Historye of Penardo and Laissa* (Dort, 1615).

ROMANTIC FANTASY (1760–1830)

Fantasy begins once more with James Macpherson's 'Ossian' poems (1760–3). By this pre-Romantic point, the imagination, so long a spurned mental faculty, was coming into favour as a source and subject for literature. The 'Ossian' poems are heroic stories of battles between Irish and invading armies of the semi-mythological time of the Gaelic invasions, stories supposedly told by the son of the warrior-king Fingal, Ossian, in the third century. In these poems we see the first deliberate use of the supernatural for its own sake, to add a *frisson* of awe; previous works we have considered assume that it exists, but this one is the first to be surprised that it may. Even so, the supernatural is as yet only incidentally deployed, and usually in the guise of dreams.

The main fantastic element of these poems is in their strong use of the imagination, creating not only a picture of departed heroic worth, full of fierce gloom, but of a unique kinship between such heroic acts and the land on which they take place. Not a human deed but it is shot through with meteorology and geography:

> Lubar is bright before me in the windings of its vale. On either side, on their hills, rise the tall forms of the kings. Their people are poured around them, bending forward to their words: as if their fathers spoke descending from the winds. But they themselves are like two rocks in the midst; each with its dark head of pines, when they are seen in the desert, above low-sailing mist. High on their faces are streams, which spread their foam on blasts of wind![27]

The land itself has almost given birth to these human forms, which as readily flow back into it with a melancholy that matches its own dark aspect:

> 'Ossian, carry me to my hills! Raise the stones of my renown. Place the horn of a deer: place my sword by my side. The torrent hereafter may raise the earth: the hunter may find the steel and say, "This has been Oscar's sword, the pride of other years!"'[28]

Battles are like weather or water, swirling about the intermittently rock-like heroes. All is in movement, whirl and tumult about shifting foci, like colliding galaxies.

> 'Thou hast seen the sun retire, red and slow behind his cloud: night gathering round on the mountain, while the unfrequent blast roared in the narrow vales. At length the rain beats hard: thunder rolls in peals. Lightning glances on the rocks! Spirits ride on beams of fire! The strength of the mountain-streams comes roaring down the hills. Such was the noise of battle . . .!'[29]

The language itself now has all the craggy abruptness of the land, now the flow of the streams and storms that dash over it. When an actual struggle through waves to a sea-shore is described, it is hard to distinguish it from metaphor.[30]

This is quite different from earlier fantasy. Here the emphasis is on wild and indefinite feeling, rather than on spiritual instruction and discipline. Nature and landscape begin to play a much more active part. In Macpherson's poetry mind and setting are made coterminous: the inner world is expressed not by cultural and allegorical figures, but by wild nature. The movement is now not so much towards the establishment of a self (even Henryson's Cresseid comes to see and accept what she is), but towards the dissolution of personal identity. What was seen as stable in earlier fantasy now begins to lose shape.

Effectively 'Ossian' mythologises Scotland, gives it a speaking identity. If the heroes Ossian described have gone, the land expressed in them has not. (There are those who see in these poems the poetic victory of the Highlands over the Lowlands.[31]) This proximity to the land, together with their unstructured narratives, puts these works close to the particular character of Scottish fantasy. The nationalist urge behind *Fingal* and *Temora* is also inescapable. Macpherson's first production of Ossianic verse in 1760 had excited the *literati* of Edinburgh to the belief that Scotland might have an indigenous epic to match those of Homer or Virgil: and Macpherson answered their wildest hopes by returning with *Fingal*. What was not known at first was that Macpherson was not transcribing an epic from any poet called Ossian, but was adapting some Gaelic legendary material to his own purposes, binding it to unified narratives and infusing it with poetry, metaphor and feeling that were all his own. In that sense Macpherson was a fraud: he gave Scotland a primitive epic it never had. But that did not stop his work strongly exciting the imaginations of his age, from those of Thomas Gray or Horace Walpole to those of such German Romantic writers of fantasy as Novalis or Tieck. And it did not inhibit the mythologising of Scotland, at least for those who lived outside it. One of the most influential proponents of 'Ossian' was Napoleon; and Macpherson's body of poems could be said to have been singly responsible for the late eighteenth- and nineteenth-century fascination with Scotland's wildness.[32] In Macpherson we see a prime symptom and source of that Romantic enthusiasm for the imagination that was to give renewed life to fantasy, in Scotland itself no less than elsewhere.

The nationalist fervour that set scholars all over Europe hunting out the primitive literature of their native lands had less self-conscious expression in the more vernacular work of Robert Burns's 'Tam o' Shanter' (1791), the tale of a drunken farmer's supposed encounter with witches, warlocks and the devil while riding home at night from the inn past Alloway kirkyard. The poem is based on a Galloway folk-tale,[33] and exploits popular lore concerning the dealings of witches and the devil. Burns's treatment of the supernatural is as much comical as serious: he is still the eighteenth-century man of common sense as much as the pre-Romantic of the excited imagination. As well as shuddering at the items on the altar before the devil,

> A murderer's banes in gibbet airns;
> Twa span-lang, wee, unchristen'd bairns;
> A thief, new cuttit frae a rape—
> Wi' his last gasp his gab did gape . . .
> (ll. 131–4)

we are also bid to shudder in a different way at the aged witches who strip off their clothes as the dancing gets hot:

> wither'd beldams, auld an' droll,
> Rigwoodie hags, wad spean a foal,
> Lowping an' flinging on a crummock,
> I wonder didna turn thy stomach.
>
> (ll. 159–62)

The possibility is also present that what Tam sees is a product of his drunken wits; Burns will not allow the supernatural to pass unchallenged. Comical too is the way Tam alerts the coven to his presence by calling out in excitement when one of the near-naked witches turns out to be a beauty.

What Burns does is exploit a range of feelings in this poem: he plays with our emotions as with different strings, and out of them all makes a strangely harmonious medley. The poem moves us from bar-room jollity to far different mirth and festivity in the storm-filled outside world of the kirkyard, from mock-moralising about good wifely counsel, through elegy at the frailty of happiness ('But pleasures are like poppies spread,/ You seize the flow'r, its bloom is shed!' (ll. 59–60)) to the mixture of serious and comic threat in the witches' pursuit. In a sense Burns gives us a democratic reality that mixes all forms of experience, one without frontiers. English and broad Scots language, Augustan, Gothic and folk-tale modes mix together. Tam's wife's prophecy of his eventual drunken fate easily blends natural with supernatural, foretelling that he

> wad be found, deep drown'd in Doon!
> Or catch'd wi' warlocks in the mirk
> By Alloway's auld, haunted kirk.
>
> (ll. 30–32)

It is the one that we would take as less likely that comes true. The poem is irrepressibly plural:

> When chapman billies leave the street
> And drouthy neebors neebors meet;
> As market-days are wearin late,
> An' folk begin to tak the gate;
> While we sit sousing at the nappy,
> An' gettin' fou and unco happy,
> We think na on the lang Scots miles,
> The mosses, waters, slaps, and styles.
>
> (ll. 1–8)

Many an adjective, noun or comparison is put two or three ways—'A bletherin', blusterin', drunken blellum', 'favours secret, sweet and precious', 'hornpipes, jigs, strathspeys an' reels'; Tam's disturbance of the witches is likened to awakening a swarm of bees, stimulating hounds in pursuit of a hare or chasing a thief. Tam is so much the life and soul that he creates company, of whatever sort, wherever he goes. The poem shows a love of crowds and conviviality: a greater threat than the witches is perhaps the solitary menace of the wife left at home, 'Gathering her brows like gathering storm,/ Nursing her wrath to keep it warm' (ll.11–12). The supernatural threat Tam may elude: her he cannot escape. The expansive imagination that dilates outwards to the witches shrinks back to cold domestic reality. Here, as much as in the comic tone, we see Burns's countering of fantasy with fact.

A somewhat more serious, if still reserved, treatment of the supernatural is to be found in one or two tales by Sir Walter Scott, especially 'Wandering Willie's Tale' (in *Redgauntlet* (1824), Letter XI) and 'The Tapestried Chamber' (1828). Scott is even better known for his collection of ballads, *Minstrelsy of the Scottish Border* (1802–3), which gives to Scottish literature the ballads of the supernatural 'Tam Lin' and 'Thomas the Rhymer'. The whole of Scott's work can in a sense be seen as fantastic, in that through his various historical novels and poems he gives to many almost blank periods of Scottish culture a literature they never had and a life they never recorded. Some of the novels are themselves part-fantasies, such as *The Bride of Lammermoor* (1819) and *The Monastery* (1820). These and the short stories of the supernatural introduce an element of contemporary Gothic horror into Scots literature, something also being done in the writings of Scott's friend and near-neighbour James Hogg; aside from those and 'Ossian', Scotland is remarkable in having little or nothing to offer of the Gothic novels that flooded in such a stream from English presses from the 1760s through to the 1820s.[34]

Scott is less interested in the supernatural for itself than in its effects on people. His essay of 1827, 'On the Supernatural in Fictitious Composition; and particularly on the Works of Ernest Theodore William Hoffmann', deserves attention here as the first of its kind. Scott objects to Hoffmann that he let into his stories too much of the magical and the fantastic and did not sufficiently control his imagination with 'sober reason'.[35] There is a vein of eighteenth-century conservatism running under Scott's attitude to the use of the marvellous: he holds the view that in an 'enlightened' age 'the belief in prodigies and supernatural events has gradually declined in proportion to the advancement of human knowledge'; and that therefore 'the supernatural in fictitious composition requires to be managed with considerable delicacy, as criticism begins to be more on the alert.' For Scott therefore such 'supernatural appearances in fictitious narrative ought to be rare, brief, indistinct, and such as may become a being to us so incomprehensible.'[36] In his own stories we find that the supernatural appearance or event is single and more or less open to a natural

explanation in terms of prior knowledge ('My Aunt Margaret's Mirror'), coincidence ('The Two Drovers'), or the witness dreaming ('The
Tapestried Chamber') or being drunk ('Wandering Willie's Tale');
further, the emphasis of the stories is on what is revealed about human
beings rather than about the supernatural—in 'The Two Drovers' and
'The Highland Widow' the concern with human relationships, the one
between two friends who fall out, and the other between a mother
and her son, is so dominant as virtually to drive out the interest in
the magical.

In both the stories we shall consider, the interest centres, as in all
modern Scottish fantasy, on the instability of the self. In Macpherson's
'Ossian', the lineaments of the heroes grow indistinct as they become
parts of the landscape and weather in which they move. The threat to
Tam o' Shanter is of being caught and torn apart, symbolised in the tail
ripped from Tam's horse. In Hogg's *The Confessions of a Justified Sinner*
we shall find a character who struggles against the knowledge that the
devil is within him. Scott's tales explore the relative capacity of the self
to remain assured in the face of the supernatural.

'The Tapestried Chamber' is set in England, and describes a general
who, returning from the American War of Independence, happens to
pass through a town near which he comes upon the castle of an old
friend, now Lord Woodville, who welcomes him and bids him stay.
General Browne passes the night in an old tapestried room, and the next
day is found in some agitation, wishing to leave at once. He eventually
tells Woodville that he encountered a terrifying female apparition in
his room, and on being led to the family portrait gallery, is able to
identify it with a picture of an old lady in a dress fashionable at the
end of the seventeenth century. Woodville tells him, in the mannered
style typical of this story, '"If that be the case . . . there can remain
no longer any doubt of the horrible reality of your apparition. This is
the picture of a wretched ancestress of mine, of whose crimes a black
and fearful catalogue is recorded in the family history."'[37] He goes on to
mention that these crimes included incest and unnatural murder. It then
turns out however that Woodville has used his friend Browne, whose
courage is evident, to test the room, which had a sinister reputation
that had persuaded him, till Browne's opportune arrival, to keep it
closed up: in short, that he has used his friend as a supernatural
surveyor.

The story is more subtle than first appears. No account is given of
the General's actual experience, which is reported to Woodville the
next day: having got him to the room Scott simply remarks, 'Here,
contrary to the custom of this species of tale, we leave the General.'
The report however does not lack for vivacity. The General describes
how when he went to bed he suddenly saw an old woman pass by the
bed with her back to him, and, thinking she might be someone living at

the castle who had lost her way, he coughed to alert her to his presence: whereupon,

> 'She turned slowly round, but, gracious Heaven! my lord, what a countenance did she display to me! There was no longer any question what she was, or any thought of her being a living being. Upon a face which wore the fixed features of a corpse were imprinted the traces of the vilest and most hideous passions which had animated her while she lived. The body of some atrocious criminal seemed to have been given up from the grave, and the soul restored from the penal fire, in order to form, for a space, a union with the ancient accomplice of its guilt. I started up in bed, and sat upright, supporting myself on my palms, as I gazed on this horrible spectre. The hag made, as it seemed, a single and swift stride to the bed where I lay, and squatted herself down upon it, in precisely the same attitude which I had assumed in the extremity of horror, advancing her diabolical countenance within half a yard of mine, with a grin which seemed to intimate the malice and the derision of an incarnate fiend.[38]

This totally unmans the General, and he faints. The terror of the scene lies in the way what is seen at a remove then becomes active and close, leaping on the bed and staring back at the beholder face to face. Moreover there is something hideously intimate in this meeting on the bed, and in the way the hag precisely mimics the bodily posture of the General. There are many suggestions in this story of dark things beneath the surface of the mind. Woodville is effectively a deceiver: he seems the perfect host and friend, but actually he is sizing the General up to test a room of which he well knows the history, and merely for the purpose of making available another room for guests in the castle. And whatever Woodville may say about the lady, she is his ancestress, and he participates in her blood. As for the General, he is reduced from an urbane man of courage to a nervous and disarrayed wreck who cannot present himself in human company. Appearances thus deceive: the mannered and rational surface conceals unimagined depths; the hag mirrors the General in her attitude. The castle, as often in Gothic novels, is suggestive of mind, with the inner and sealed chamber that of the dark id, which reason would rather deny and repress. And the whole story at first encourages us in the sunlit and optimistic view of human nature that flatters our wishes, only to take away all our assumptions until there is no basis of trust left. But we can go wider than this, to suggest that what Scott is effectively portraying in this story is the weakness and fraudulence of the eighteenth-century habit of mind which gave primacy to reason and to social appearance, and ignored and suppressed the imagination—which, so suppressed, took on the lineaments of the pit. Of that the hag herself is an emblem, her corrupt heyday having been in that period when an emphasis on politeness in high society was particularly matched by sexual licence—the Restoration. In that sense Scott's story is a plea for the very fantasy-making faculty that goes into its creation—the imagination.

Good manners and rational surfaces are hardly the issue with Scott's Redgauntlet in 'Wandering Willie's Tale'. Redgauntlet is a coarse and violent laird of the manor who goes to hell after his death. The story concerns his servant the piper Steenie, who acts as Redgauntlet's financial steward and collects the rents from his tenants: his improvident management of the estate puts him two terms behind with the rent owing, and he has to borrow from a money lender. But just after he pays Redgauntlet the rent and the latter has to sign the receipt, Redgauntlet dies, and his heir demands evidence of payment from Steenie which he cannot supply. However, he is enabled through the interested help of the devil to visit hell and secure a receipt from Redgauntlet, provided he resists the many temptations put in his way. He does, and takes the receipt and the information that the money itself is to be found in 'the Cat's Cradle' back to the new lord, who rejects the receipt as of infernal provenance, but knowing the Cat's Cradle to be the top of a ruined turret goes there and finds the money and much more besides.

Effectively the story is the triumph of the canny Scot over the uncanny: with care and a steady devotion to his own interests, Steenie makes a profit out of hell itself. The story is also a picture of 'following': Redgauntlet follows the ways of the devil, his servant Dougal follows him to hell, Sir John Redgauntlet follows his father as laird, and throughout the story there pops up the old Redgauntlet's ape. But Steenie keeps himself apart: he is with but not of Redgauntlet's party; he succeeds in frustrating even hell's attempts to make him one of its company; he is a survivor, who keeps his counsel. The whole story describes how he escapes from obligation, in the matter of the rent money he owes and which Redgauntlet and his son successively demand of him.

And yet in a sense not even he may be quite his own man in the story: for there is a way in which the events seem determined by some larger power. Redgauntlet has an uncommon liking for him; he frets himself into a fit of the gout because Steenie has left the castle and has not come by noon with the rent—neither of which issues was mentioned in the narrative before. When Steenie comes with the money he finds only the Laird, Dougal and the pet ape, 'a thing that hadna chanced to him before'.[39] Redgauntlet then strangely bids Dougal take Steenie downstairs for a brandy. But just as they are leaving, the Laird screams that his feet and throat are burning ('hell, hell, hell, and its flames, was aye the word in his mouth'), and dies before the receipt can be written. All this apparently motiveless coincidence puts Steenie in his predicament with Sir John: it is as though events are arranged to try him. Too dry and cynical a view of human nature is present in his story for us to see Steenie as a character reformed by his affliction: but his actions are not unsuited to those that might be seen as satirically fitted to the Covenanting Kirk of which he ends as a member—a careful regard for one's own spiritual welfare and an amassing of spiritual benefit for the rainy day of death. And the emphasis on hell in the story is one peculiarly present in Calvinism. In Steenie we might then have a mocking picture of one of the elect, tried by supernatural affliction to manifest his acceptability to a higher Lord than Sir John, and able by a matchless fastidiousness to which he has no real title to pass through the power of hell. None of this of course is in the lugubrious moral of subsequent family decline that Wandering Willie draws from it.

To the list of writers of Scottish fantasy we might—just—add Byron's name. Byron's mother was Scots and he lived between the years of four and ten in Aberdeenshire; he wrote an imitation of 'Ossian', 'The Death of Calmar and Orla', and several youthful poems regretting his departure from the Highlands, 'Lachin y Gair', 'I would I were a careless child' and 'When I roved a young Highlander' (though the last is already regretting rather more the loss of a girl who 'endear'd the rude scene'). All these were published in his *Hours of Idleness* in 1807, when he was just nineteen. Those who would claim Byron for Scotland point to his later *Don Juan*, Canto X, stanza 17, where he declares, 'I am half a Scot by birth, and bred/ A whole one'[40]—though this ignores the somewhat sentimental context and the admission that 'it may seem a schoolboy's whine', together with the clichéd and literary view of Scotland it presents (stanzas 18, 19). We should not make too much of Byron's Scottish links: the traditions and interests that fed his poetry are primarily English and international. However, his fantastic works, which include the satanic *Vision of Judgment* (1822) and the darker, more Gothic *Manfred* (1817), *Cain* (1821) and *Heaven and Earth* (1822), all show an ambition for the ultimate (heaven, hell and beyond) and an enthusiasm for rebels and outcasts (Satan, Cain, Manfred, the angels who coupled with mortals) which, though of Romantic provenance, could also be said to be in the Scottish character. James Hogg admired Byron for his 'native energy'.

By now, via 'Ossian', Burns and Scott, we have arrived at the sort of Romantic emphasis on the imagination and on feeling which is fertile ground for the writing of fantasy, and for the appearance of a writer prepared to make fantasy a central part of his literary output. That first writer is James Hogg, the Ettrick Shepherd.

Notes

1 See e.g. Stith Thompson, *The Folktale* (New York: Holt, Rinehart and Winston, 1946). Scotland, so geographically various as it is, has a range of folk regions, from Galloway to the North East, and from the Borders to the Western Highlands and Islands.

2 J. F. Campbell, ed., *Popular Tales of the West Highlands*, 4 vols (Edinburgh: Edmonston and Douglas, 1860–2), I, c–ci.

3 Ruth Ratcliff (reteller), *Scottish Folk Tales* (London: Frederick Muller, 1976), pp. 7–8.

4 Campbell, *Popular Tales*, I, 63, 251–2; III, 1–2.

5 Campbell, I, 103ff.

6 Campbell, II, 47–50.

7 The tales were first collected by Robert Chambers, *Popular Rhymes of Scotland* (Edinburgh, 1826); and are repr. in David Buchan, ed., *Scottish Tradition: A Collection of Scottish Folk Literature* (London: Routledge, 1984). For the ballads, and their several versions, see F. J. Child, *The English and Scottish Ballads*, 5 vols (New York: Folklore Press, 1957), I, nos 37, 39 (pp. 325–6 and 353–6 are Scott's texts).

8 Buchan, *Scottish Tradition*, p. 29.

9 Ibid., p. 34.

10 References are to James I of Scotland, *The Kingis Quair*, ed. John Norton-Smith (Oxford: Clarendon Press, 1971).

11 Norton-Smith, pp. xii–xiii.

12 References are to *The Poems and Fables of Robert Henryson*, ed. H. Harvey Wood (Edinburgh: Oliver and Boyd, 1958).

13 Thomas W. Craik, 'The Substance and Structure of *The Testament of Cresseid*', in Adam J. Aitken, Matthew P. McDiarmid and Derick S. Thomson, eds, *Bards and Makars* (Glasgow: Glasgow University Press, 1977), p. 25.

14 Matthew P. McDiarmid, 'Robert Henryson in his Poems', in *Bards and Makars*, p. 37.

15 John MacQueen, *Robert Henryson: A Study of the Major Narrative Poems* (Oxford: Clarendon Press, 1967), p. 70.

16 References are to William Dunbar, *Poems*, ed. James Kinsley (Oxford: Clarendon Press, 1958).

17 See also Priscilla Bawcutt, *Dunbar the Makar* (Oxford: Clarendon Press, 1992), p. 311.

18 Bawcutt, p. 287.

19 References for 'The Palice of Honour' are to *The Poetical Works of Gavin Douglas*, ed. John Small, 4 vols (Edinburgh: William Patterson, 1874), I, 1–81.

20 References for 'The Dreme' are to *The Works of Sir David Lyndsay of the Mount*, ed. David Laing, 3 vols (Edinburgh: William Patterson, 1879), I, 1–39.

21 References are to the Wreittoun version (1646) of *The Cherrie and the Slae*, in *Poems of Alexander Montgomerie, and other pieces from Laing MS No.447*, Supplementary Volume, Scottish Text Society 59, ed. George Stevenson (Edinburgh: Blackwood, 1910), pp. 72–108.

22 C. S. Lewis, *The Allegory of Love: A Study in Medieval Tradition* (New York: Oxford University Press, 1958), pp. 258–9.

23 R. D. S. Jack, *Alexander Montgomerie* (Edinburgh: Scottish Academic Press, 1985), pp. 111–12.

24 First line of poem on dreams by 'Lichtoun monicus' from *The Bannatyne Manuscript*, 1568, 4 vols (Glasgow: Hunterian Club, 1896), II, 289.

25 David Reid, 'Prose after Knox', in R. D. S. Jack, ed., *The History of Scottish Literature, Volume 1, Origins to 1660* (Aberdeen: Aberdeen University Press, 1988), p. 184. For a more cheerful view of the period in its poetry, see Michael Spiller, 'Poetry after the Union, 1603–1660', in the same volume, pp. 141–62.

26 For an example (it is an exuberant expansion of a list), see Rabelais, *Gargantua and Pantagruel*, trans. Sir Thomas Urquhart and Peter Le Motteux, 2 vols (London: David Nutt, 1900), II, 73–4 (from Rabelais, Book 3, ch.13).

27 *The Poems of Ossian*, trans. James Macpherson, ed. William Sharp (Edinburgh: Patrick Geddes, 1896), p. 281 (*Temora*, Book V).

28 Ibid., pp. 230–1 (*Temora*, Book I).

29 Ibid., p. 82 (*Fingal*, Book IV).

30 Ibid., pp. 64–5 (*Fingal*, Book III).

31 Andrew Hook, 'Scotland and Romanticism: the International Scene', in *The History of Scottish Literature, Volume 2, 1660–1800*, ed. Andrew Hook (Aberdeen: Aberdeen University Press, 1987), p. 316.

32 Ibid.

33 Namely 'Adam Forrester and Lucky Hair', repr. in Alan Temperley, ed., *Tales of Galloway* (London: Skilton and Shaw, 1979), pp. 74–7.

34 At least so a survey of Montague Summers, *A Gothic Bibliography* (London: Fortune Press, 1941; repr. 1964) suggests. There are occasional English writers using Scotland as a scene, such as Mrs Isaacs, *Glenmore Abbey, or, The Lady of the Rock* (1805), or Hannah Maria Jones (later Mrs Lowndes), *The Scottish Chieftains, or, The Perils of Love and War* (1831).

35 Scott, op. cit., repr. in Sir Walter Scott, *On Novelists and Fiction*, ed. Ioan Williams (London: Routledge, 1968), p. 335; see also pp. 348, 352, 353.

36 Ibid., pp. 313, 314, 316.

37 *The Supernatural Short Stories of Sir Walter Scott*, ed. Michael Hayes (London: John Calder, 1977), p. 30.

38 Ibid., pp. 25–6.

39 Ibid., p. 80.

40 Cited in Edwin Morgan, 'Scottish Poetry in the Nineteenth Century',
    in *The History of Scottish Literature, Volume 3, The Nineteenth Century*,
    ed. Douglas Gifford (Aberdeen: Aberdeen University Press, 1988),
    p. 339. Morgan gives a full account of Byron's claim to Scottishness
    (pp. 339–40).

CHAPTER THREE

James Hogg

Hogg is the first significant Scots writer of fantasy, and that is peculiarly appropriate, since of all the writers we shall look at in this book he is the one most directly steeped in the folk-tale and ballad tradition of Scotland, the one who most catches up the past and passes it on to the future. Hogg was the son of an Ettrick shepherd, and spent much of his life as a shepherd or farmer, apart from ten years from 1810–20 pursuing a literary life in Edinburgh. Visitors to his early Borders home might find themselves passing the time in a cave-like bothy where he lived while tending his sheep: but whether there or at his later cottage at Altrive, they were sure of good company, whisky and Hogg's amazing ability on the fiddle, to which he sang his songs. The land and the tales and songs of its people were part of Hogg's being. His brother William records how 'He was remarkably fond of hearing stories, and our mother to keep us boys quiet would often tell us tales of kings, giants, knights, fairies, kelpies, brownies etc. etc.'[1] But it was not only from his mother, and in his childhood, that Hogg was to hear such stories: they were part of the oral tradition of the community to which he belonged. The titles of some of his own stories express this—'The Cameronian Preacher's Tale', 'Tibby Hyslop's Dream', 'The Wife of Lochmaben', 'The Hunt of Eildon'. Hogg is literally closer to Scotland than almost any other writer we shall consider. This makes him a unique focus of the past: not only Scottish folk-tradition, but for example the voices of Dunbar and of Henryson as tuned by that tradition are to be heard in his poetry.

Yet we do Hogg wrong to see him simply in his pastoral and 'folk' mode, or to accept at face value his assertions that he avoided books to preserve his originality.[2] He also had an ambition to succeed among the *literati*, an ambition well satisfied during some of his years in Edinburgh, when his work was reaching a wide and educated public through *Blackwood's Magazine*; and again in 1832 when he was lionised during a stay in London. His sources for some of his works were as readily the eighteenth-century novelists, the Gothic novelists, Burns, Scott, Wordsworth or Milton, as they were oral or traditional for others. It has even been suggested that his *The Private Memoirs and Confessions of a Justified Sinner* may have been influenced by E. T. A. Hoffmann's *Die Elixiere des Teufels* (*The Devil's Elixirs*) published at the same time in June 1824, through his friendship since 1813 with the translator R. P. Gillies.[3] *The Confessions*, Hogg's best known work, is an intellectuals' book, with an intellectual as its protagonist—even if it does effectively condemn the intellect in its portrayal of the downfall of a religious bigot whose conviction of his personal salvation blinds him to the discordant reality all about him. If we delight in the popular mode of Hogg's ballad 'Kilmeny' (1813) about a girl's visit to heaven, then we also acknowledge his other treatment of the subject with much more learned, aureate and mixed style, *The Pilgrims of the Sun* (1815). Hogg's rural background is certainly the strongest influence in his life, but variability is also one of his most marked characteristics.

Variety certainly marks his fantasy. There is 'Kilmeny' in comparison to *The Pilgrims of the Sun*, and both in contrast to *The Confessions*. Even within *The Confessions* variability is seen in the way that the story is told first by an Editor and then from inside by the 'justified sinner' Robert Wringhim himself. From grave to gay, from high religious vision to supernatural *frisson*, from literary to oral, Hogg's supernatural stories span a considerable range. So too Hogg gives us varying pictures of the reality of the supernatural. In *The Confessions* we are left uncertain as to whether the mysterious figure Gil-Martin is the devil or a projection of the unfortunate Wringhim's mind; the fearsome being in *The Brownie of Bodsbeck* (1818) turns out to be a wounded and deformed Cameronian called John Brown; the monkey-like Merodach of 'The Brownie of the Black Haggs' (1828) who torments to death the evil Lady Wheelhope, is all too satanically real. In one direction the impulse is to persuade us of the existence of a just and loving God ('The Wife of Lochmaben' (1820), 'The Cameronian Preacher's Tale' (1829)); in another we are rather to be convinced of the power of the devil ('Tibby Hyslop's Dream' (1827), 'George Dobson's Expedition to Hell' (1827)). And if in 'The Prodigal Son' (1829) Calvinism is seen in a favourable light beside worldly behaviour, in *The Confessions* the reverse is the case. There is difference, too, in the way the supernatural appears in Hogg's poetry as compared to his prose. The prose is more sombre: it is rooted to the earth, often pervaded by darkness, in a world troubled by the inroads of devils, witches, goblins and spirits; this is a world too of temptation, of moral uncertainty and even of perceptual uncertainty, as in *The Confessions*; and murder is one of the recurrent themes. But in the poetry, the earth and even fire ('George Dobson's Expedition to Hell') of the prose are changed to the elements of air and water: fairies and mermaids are more often the supernatural beings met, and flights through the air or upward to heaven are described.

Any account of Hogg's fantasy, therefore, should give place to this variety. Here we shall be considering four very different works: 'Kilmeny' (with *The Pilgrims of the Sun*), the ballad 'The Witch of Fife', 'The Brownie of the Black Haggs' and *The Confessions*. These are perhaps the best and best-known: but there are many others we could have chosen. In particular the reader is referred to that amazing compendium of fantasy, earthy comedy and martial quest that makes up Hogg's *The Three Perils of Man* (1822).[4] Although this is more incidentally magical than a consistent story of the fantastic, it shows Hogg's invention at its most various and exuberant.

To start with 'Kilmeny'. This has sometimes been viewed as one of the most beautiful and mysterious of poems in the Scots or any language. It forms one of the seventeen poems of *The Queen's Wake* (1813), in which Hogg imagines a gathering of bards set by Mary Queen of Scots at her homecoming from overseas to compete for the prize of a harp. These poems include ballads of love, battle, war and magic, as well as the comic 'The Witch of Fife' and 'The Abbot M'Kinnon' which describes how the spirit of St Columba returns to cleanse the isle of Iona of sin. Each bard is given his own character, and comes from a different part of Scotland, so that characterisation is as much by surroundings as by person, and we are made to feel that in some sense all Scotland is pouring its treasures at Queen Mary's feet.[5] The bard who sings the thirteenth song, of Kilmeny, comes from the forest of Glen-Ample and the moors of Ern (Earn) in Perthshire, and is named Drummond; he lives alone, in loving communion with God, contemplation of His ways and wonder at His heavenly plan,

> Till his rapt soul would leave her home
> In visionary worlds to roam.

Drummond prefers primitive to modern poetic modes, and the lays of his 'rude forefathers' to the 'florid films of modern rhyme'; but this belies the poetic subtlety of his poem. Of the seventeen poems in *The Queen's Wake* only this one and 'The Witch of Fife' are told in Scots dialect, and while this may portray the fierce primitivism of the poet, it serves also, as in 'The Witch', to establish a unique relation between the poet and his subject.

'Kilmeny' is the story of a pure maid who goes walking and disappears, returning only after a long time to tell of how she was taken to a place on the borders of heaven and granted a vision of the future of Scotland and mankind. But this plain account belies the manner in which the poem is told. Typically Hogg uses a traditional or known form (here the ballad and the folk-tale of abduction by fairies) to produce a quite different effect—not the dark fatalism of ballad, nor the sense of supernatural power over mortals in the tales of 'Tam Lin' or 'Thomas the Rhymer'; but the awakening of feelings associated with both before transcending them. This is the first stanza:

> Bonny Kilmeny gaed up the glen;
> But it wasna to meet Duneira's men,
> Nor the rosy monk of the isle to see,
> For Kilmeny was pure as pure could be.

It was only to hear the yorlin sing,
And pu' the cress-flower round the spring;
The scarlet hypp and the hindberrye,
And the nut that hang frae the hazel tree;
For Kilmeny was pure as pure could be.
But lang may her minny look o'er the wa',
And lang may she seek i' the green-wood shaw;
Lang the laird of Duneira blame,
And lang, lang greet or Kilmeny come hame![6]

The ballad form sets up expectations in us. We begin to think that either
she has come to grief, in the way of many ballads with their heavy
ironies on 'lang, lang'; or else she may like Thomas the Rhymer have
lost herself in faërie. In this way the poem tests our own mortal way of
seeing, like that of Kilmeny's mother, who blames Duneira. But of course
its primary function is to set up a mystery—if not Duneira or any monk,
then what?—and being mystified is one step towards eventual mystic
unknowing. It is a peculiarity of Hogg's fantasy to enjoy the pleasures
of multiple possibility.

The stanza is full too of images of mortality—the privileged and
colloquial familiarity of the poet with his subject, the possible all-too-
human motives that might have led Kilmeny forth, the recriminations
of the mother. But beyond these there is also a mortality that is pure,
like Kilmeny herself or the innocent motive of joy that leads her,
or nature itself: the lines describing the yellowhammer, the flower,
the fruit and the nut fall in clear drops of syntax, each item closely
bound to the nature of Kilmeny, as she takes pleasure to hear or to
gather. Such a sense of spiritual contour bands, from the lowest and
weakest levels of our human nature to the highest and beyond, is to
run through the poem.

The next stanza brings Kilmeny back.

When many a day had come and fled,
When grief grew calm, and hope was dead,
When mess for Kilmeny's soul had been sung,
When the bedes-man had prayed, and the dead-bell rung,
Late, late in a gloamin, when all was still,
When the fringe was red on the westlin hill,
The wood was sere, the moon i' the wane,
The reek o' the cot hung over the plain,
Like a little wee cloud in the world its lane;
When the ingle lowed with an eiry leme,
Late, late in the gloaming Kilmeny came hame!

Here, as in the last stanza, Hogg is a master of detail: we see the cot
clearly on the plain, and yet at the same time it is almost a sym-

bol of isolated human life. Indeed, one of the distinctive features of Hogg's fantasy is its grip on common reality, its mixing of the supernatural and the everyday: we feel he has been there, he has seen these things. For all her supernatural life Kilmeny returns to her home. The stanza starts with time and grief passing in typical way, using generalised diction, viewed from an almost Olympian standpoint; then it literally homes in and stops with one particular evening. Kilmeny comes back when all is still—still in the spiritual sense, here mirrored in the worn quietude of nature, with the sere wood and the waning moon. The long suspended sentence ending in Kilmeny's return is an obvious way of increasing suspense. But the way it surrounds the rest of the stanza suggests both her detachment from the world, like a larger ironic ring about its needless gestures and small concerns, and at the same time her love for it, circling it with care and returning to it. And all the time the air of waiting is giving to every natural thing a kind of electrostatic charge: we read not only of the red fringe, the wood, the cot or the ingle, but also feel moving inwards through these things the tread of that which is coming.

And of course, to consider the poem in strict order, we do not till the end of the stanza know who or what is coming, and when we do, we still do not know where from. The poem gradually prepares us for the 'fantasy', and that fantasy is to be far beyond conceiving. When Kilmeny comes home we may still see it as the return of a ghost at the no-time of twilight, but the poem is to take us out of ourselves and our assumptions, just as Kilmeny was taken out of her world. On her return she is wearing a lily-coloured skirt and a birch-green ribbon, and carrying roses; and with those who meet her we wonder where she got them and where she has been: for the lily suggests death, the birch return from death (or heaven) and the roses life and passion.[7] So far we could think that she is one of the dead brought back to life, or else a ghost, or possibly one who is returning from some strange land of faërie; and certainly Hogg's footnote to the poem, in which he describes attested accounts of returns by people who once inexplicably disappeared, farther persuades us to this more 'secular' level of reading.[8]

We come a little closer to understanding in the next stanza: but we are warned that Kilmeny herself could not say where she had been nor describe it. Indeed at first she could seem almost cataleptic in her stillness of demeanour, were it not for the way her stillness is compared to nature, which plays a recurrent part in the poem, always suggesting innocence, calm, or peace: 'still was her look, and as still was her ee, / As the stillness that lay on the emerant lea, / Or the mist that sleeps on a waveless sea.' When she speaks, we feel a sense of divine ventriloquism, but again this is transfigured by the imagery of nature and super-nature:

> Kilmeny had been where the cock never crew,
> Where the rain never fell, and the wind never blew.
> But it seemed as the harp of the sky had rung,
> And the airs of heaven played round her tongue,
> When she spake of the lovely forms she had seen,
> And a land where sin had never been;
> A land of love, and a land of light,
> Withouten sun, or moon, or night:
> Where the river swa'd a living stream,
> And the light a pure celestial beam:
> The land of vision it would seem,
> A still, an everlasting dream.

A land of vision it might indeed seem, but we are nearer to guessing what it may be. There is a curious sense of paradox set up by the first two lines, where the syntax is very blunt and assertive and yet is talking of what did not happen. The negatives of this place, rainless, windless, timeless, sinless, match Kilmeny's own inability to say what it was like; yet they also invite us beyond to a transcendental understanding of a river that is a living stream and light a celestial beam. The lack of verbs in the last six lines helps convey a sense of stillness, and yet at the same time each line seems an attempt to say what cannot be said, until the last two rather fall away in a mortal attempt at summary. (George MacDonald, who used this stanza in his *At the Back of the North Wind* to try to convey the strange region his boy-hero Diamond visited, also felt this.[9])

So far the poem has been a deepening mystery, a gradual undermining of assumption after assumption until only the furthest things may remain—in fact it has taken us on something like a journey beyond ourselves and our mortal ways of understanding. Thereafter, however it becomes more explicit: the symbolic and mysterious mode gives way to direct statement. Spirits of the long-dead and angels surround Kilmeny, telling her that she has been chosen for this vision of heaven because she alone in centuries has had sufficient purity, and through her 'Now shall the land of spirits see,/ Now it shall ken what a woman may be!' They lead Kilmeny in 'the light of a sunless day' through 'emerald fields . . . of dazzling glow', and bathe her deep in the stream of life; they bear her on over 'Unnumbered groves' and 'The lowermost vales of the storied heaven', until they can see 'heaven's blue gates with sapphires glow'. They seat her on a 'purple sward' (rather feeble phrase this) to view heaven, but after a few lines describing how she did not see a sun but 'a crystal dome of a thousand dies'; nor land, but 'an endless whirl of glory and light' amid which angels came and went, we are told that 'She hid her een frae the dazzling view;/ She looked again and the scene was new.' The definiteness of location is for that very reason undefined: it is alien to Hogg's genius to be fixed.

The new scene becomes a prophetic vision (rather like Gray's 'The Bard') of future history beyond Queen Mary up to and past the French Revolution. The gaze is turned from heaven back to earth. Such continued concern with earthly affairs was also present in Dante's *Paradiso*, but there it was a part of heaven; here it seems rather that heaven has been too much for Kilmeny and the poet, and prophecy has taken the place of mystery.[10] Certainly the next movement of the poem after this granted vision of future history is for Kilmeny to return home herself to her own Perthshire locality, and to pass the month left to her amidst the beasts and birds of the mortal nature she knows. The poem ends with what must seem something of an anti-climax and also a pathetic fallacy, after the vision of heaven and the insight into the violence of future human history: we find nature twining Edenically and without much poetic vitality about Kilmeny as she gives herself in solitude to its ministry—

> wherever her peaceful form appeared,
> The wild beasts of the hill were cheered;
> The wolf played blythly round the field,
> The lordly byson lowed and kneeled;
> The dun deer wooed with manner bland,
> And cowered aneath her lilly hand.

This descends to a zoological catalogue of animal admirers, flatly listed. The life has rather gone from the poem.

Hogg was never again to hit the beauty of the vision that he grasped at the outset of 'Kilmeny'. All his surest poetic instincts, all his own natural speech, all his deepest longings there come together in some of the subtlest poetry he wrote. Perhaps it is because Hogg is not fully a contemplative that his poem cannot rest in the vision of heaven, but must keep moving into other contexts. 'Be mine to sing of visions that have been,/ And cherish hope of visions yet to be,' he wrote in his poem 'Superstition' (1815); and certainly Kilmeny is in continual motion throughout the poem.[11] It was Hogg's purpose to show how the best things of earth were linked to heaven, but while he finds the journey outward from earth a natural one, the return trip is less comfortable or easy.

The Pilgrims of the Sun (1815) in a sense tells the story of 'Kilmeny' over again.[12] Mary Lee of Carelha' is taken out of her body on a guided tour of the heavens by an angel called Cela. Like the poem itself, she is much more consciously a Christian than Kilmeny, having long read and thought 'Of the ways of Heaven and Nature's plan' (p. 32); and to that extent she is more in tune with the vision, less a particular individual. She is conveyed near to the throne of God, then taken back via the different spheres dependant on the heavens to earth once more. The earth here is seen as '"yon cloudy spot"' (p. 43). There is a definite strain in this poem, as in 'Kilmeny', of world-rejection. In heaven Mary is instructed in the divine scheme and the evolutionary progress of souls inwards from sphere to sphere. The poem has been praised for the use by Hogg of ballad form in the first part, Miltonic style in the second (which describes heaven), Augustan satiric mode in the third and the idiom of ghost story in the fourth (where Mary returns), as a *tour de force* of poetic variety,[13] but it is arguable that these shifts of style mirror an uneasiness with the subject, and Hogg's poetry here has hardly any of the life or detail of 'Kilmeny'. There are frequent exclamations of inability to describe what is seen, but while this of course has to be true, it does beg the question; and we are often to feel that where in 'Kilmeny' we were driven towards heaven by the poem's reticence and mystery, here we are driven away by a poem which tries to be too definite. Where Kilmeny is shown her vision by angelic spirits, Mary Lee and Cela actively search out theirs, as they fly about the central core of heaven trying to see further in. Hogg was clearly fascinated by the topic of heaven, but here he seems to have chosen the wrong method by which to describe it. He is not so much in sympathy with the intellectual Mary Lee, and her motives for beholding heaven seem as much those of curiosity as of devotion.

In the second part of the poem we do find an at least idiosyncratic description of the core of heaven as a great triangular vale narrowing in from the outer margins of heaven, lined on either side of which in increasing size are the palaces of seraphs and archangels until 'closing the lengthened files,/ Stood the pavilion of the eternal God!' But the style that in 'Kilmeny' was so precise in its ignorance, is here inexact in knowledge:

> Far far away, thro' regions of delight
> They journeyed on—not like the earthly pilgrim,
> Fainting with hunger, thirst, and burning feet,
> But, leaning forward on the liquid air,
> Like twin-born eagles, skimmed the fields of light,
> Circling the pales of heaven. In joyous mood,
> Sometimes thro' groves of shady depth they strayed,
> Arm linked in arm, as lovers walk the earth;
> Or rested in the bowers where roses hung,
> And flow'rets holding everlasting sweetness.
> And they would light upon celestial hills
> Of beauteous softened green, and converse hold
> With beings like themselves in form and mind;
> Then, rising lightly from the velvet breast
> Of the green mountain, down upon the vales

They swooped amain by lawns and streams of life;
Then over mighty hills an arch they threw
Formed like the rainbow.—Never since the time
That God outspread the glowing fields of heaven
Were two such travellers seen!

(pp. 44–5)

Lacking in ability to make this heaven wonderful, Hogg falls back on the travellers themselves. No-one wishes to linger on a poet's difficulties, but these are instructive: with his sympathies not fully engaged, Hogg makes the rather irrelevant contrast with earthly pilgrims, or feebly likens the pair to 'twin-born eagles' or earthly lovers; we find them variously and abruptly flying, walking, lying or sitting through a range of celestial clichés from 'groves of shady depth' or 'bowers where roses hung' to 'celestial hills/ Of beauteous softened green' or 'lawns and streams of life'. It is not surprising that we become a little alienated from the travellers, who come over as a mixture of peering tourists and low-flying aircraft. And as we are hurried from vaguely-felt place to place, we begin to be distanced from this heaven: and this is not because of the Miltonic and high style, for Milton was capable of detail, precision and mystery far beyond this. But if the poem does not very well succeed, it shows the enormous energy of Hogg's imagination, which so persists in its quest of the ultimate.

That energy is also seen in variety, in Hogg's almost Chaucerian readiness to write in a whole range of genres. One could almost disbelieve that the same man who wrote 'Kilmeny' also composed the uproarious 'Witch of Fife' (1813), where magical powers create pleasure and misrule. In this poem a witch-wife returns to her home and husband in Fife to tell him of her many wild pleasures as a witch, not excluding a midnight orgy with warlocks in Lapland. Her husband is unmoved by any of her adventures, until she describes how she and her friends drank the Bishop of Carlisle's well-guarded wine. He follows her to Carlisle, but becomes so drunk that he is captured: in the original version he is then burnt; but, at the outraged behest of Sir Walter Scott, Hogg gladly had him rescued by his wife at the last moment.[14] Hogg was quite as ready to have the poem end with a moral blaming women, as with one telling each man 'nevir [to] curse his puir auld wife,/ Rychte wicked altho scho be.'

Variety is almost a distinguishing feature of this poem. The wife is a Fife carlin, a truant witch, and by magical transformation a damsel to delight a warlock. The husband is now a sturdy moraliser telling the wife, '"Ye had better sleipe in yer bed at hame,/ Wi yer deire littil bairnis and me"'; and now a witch and a reveller himself, pursuing his wife to Carlisle and the Bishop's wine. The wife describes three quite different places she visits on her nocturnal excursions: first, Ben

Lomond, in the country not far from their home; then across the sea
to Norway and by flight overland to the great magical 'rave' party in
Lapland; and then to the urban pleasures of Carlisle. The first trip is by
magic horse, the second by enchanted cockle-shell, and the third is by
unaided flight. One could even see a continual change of element, from
the earth of Ben Lomond, across the water to Norway, through the air
to Carlisle and there, so far as the old man is concerned, in and out of
the fire.

Here too Hogg delights in the interplay of the domestic and the
supernatural, as in a different way we saw him do in 'Kilmeny'. Being a
witch and getting up into the wide air has literally given the wife ideas a
bit above her station: she clearly delights in being part of the supernatural
fast set. Her husband, meanwhile, feels out of his element, suspicious of
all this magical new-fangledness. But, like Kilmeny, the wife has come
home, and the poem interplays domestic and supernatural impulses;
again, at the end, she comes back to rescue him. So too the pleasures of
the wife as a witch are partly illicit, involving copulation with warlocks,
and partly innocent, being pleasure at the natural beauties of Lomond
or the ocean or simply in flying. At the pipe of the 'wee wee man' who
appears on Ben Lomond,

> 'The corby craw cam gledgin near,
>   The ern gede veeryng bye;
> And the troutis laup out of the Leven Louch,
>   Charmit with the melodye.'

Magic is expressed and enjoyed in the ordinary things of nature.

In the midst of the description of supernatural adventures, much of
the pleasure of the poem also arises out of the relation of the old man
and his wife. By an unusual reverse, it is not the husband in this poem
who is being scolded for straying, but the wife: yet he, who seems so
staunch a pillar of the domestic virtues of home and hearth, soon reveals
his true colours when she mentions the Bishop of Carlisle's wine. About
the relationship of the two we cannot speculate far, but we may consider
that the husband seems to value the wife for her domestic duties rather
than for herself, and is ready to put her below wine for his pleasures.
Yet she has come back to him, and does tell him what she has been
doing, and in the revised ending does come to save him at the last:
there is the hint that they matter more to one another than they know.
On this level of reading we may take the wife's witchery as an escape
from the confines of marital life. Indeed both of them in the end opt
for a measure of free and amoral truancy, even if the husband pays for
it; both of them leave the cottage by the chimney, symbol of home and
hearth, for the wide air.

The supernatural in this poem is literally super-natural (even to the
extent of flying above the ground or defying the sea). The whole point

here is the things one can do by magic that are barred to one in everyday repetitive existence; the three very different journeys by the wife are here symbolic. The poem is full of images of bounds broken; and the fantasy is to some extent the gratification of the wildest wishes of the imagination, which may be why more censure of witchcraft is blunted here.[15] There is increasing liberation in the sense that the journeys go further afield, and in that by the time they fly to Carlisle they no longer depend on material aids. The music and dancing on Ben Lomond are wild with freedom, waking the white sea-mew on Loch Leven, making the trout leap out of the water and the weasels start from their holes. On the journey to Norway the power of the sea is defied by a cockle-shell boat. A stanza portraying the sea's power in hurling the witches upwards before sinking them in the depths of a trough is followed by one describing how when they could not climb the waves they simply pierced through them:

> 'As fast as the hail, as fast as the gale,
>   As fast as the midnycht leme,
> We borit the breiste of the burstyng swale,
>   Or fluffit i' the flotyng faem.'

In Lapland the witches escape their eldritch forms and are transformed to beauties. The journey to Carlisle is made possible by a word that can also '"lokkis and baris undo"': so that they enter '"free as ayr"' into the vault of the Bishop of Carlisle. This magic word is not only a means to supernatural flight, but is also symbolic of all that wars with restraint in human life: the witch-wife says that if it were generally known, '"It wald turn this warld all upside down,/ And make it warse than hell"':

> 'For all the lasses in the land
>   Wald munt the wynd and fly;
> And the men wald doff their doublets syde,
>   And after them wald ply.'

The last image of release in the poem, if we except the wine 'liberated' from the Bishop of Carlisle's vaults, is in the revised ending where the witch-wife arrives to save her little old man from the fire, uttering a word that causes his manacles to fall off and him to fly up into the air back to Fife.

Nevertheless in this poem, in contrast to 'Kilmeny', the fantasy does not go beyond the world: everything happens within it, and if there is an exotic journey to Norway, it is flanked on either side by trips to Ben Lomond and Carlisle; and much of the tale is narrated in a Fife cottage. The journeys, dances and revels of the witches take place in the midst of a nature of 'muntaine muir and dale' or wild ocean; there is constant mention of beasts and birds, and in Lapland with spirits of the earth, fairies, genii and mermaids. The escape portrayed here is not to a wider realm of the spirit above, but to a fuller expression of the passional nature below: this magic is of this world, and the world in turn partakes in it. The strength of the poem lies in its peculiar fusion of an instinct for wild, free beauty with the simpler pleasures of tricking the Bishop of Carlisle or getting drunk; and in the setting of all this in the context of lowly home and hearth.

However, in its fusion of the colloquial and the supernatural 'The Witch of Fife' is as we said not wholly unlike 'Kilmeny'. And the two poems share one further feature which distinguishes them from the prose tales we shall now consider, and indeed from much of Hogg's 'supernaturalist' prose fiction. In them the whole direction is out from the world or from confines to freedom: the supernatural is reached or enjoyed via an outward journey. But in the prose we shall find that the characteristic movement is rather that, as in Scottish fantasy generally, the supernatural comes inwards, that the mortal world is gradually penetrated, eroded or even destroyed by it. Every assurance of the hero in 'George Dobson's Expedition to Hell' is stripped away until he realises that he has journeyed to an inescapable hell; every beauty who approaches Jock Allanson in 'Mary Burnet' (1828) is an apparition sent to draw him to his eventual death; John Macmillan in 'The Cameronian Preacher's Tale', who slew his rival Walter Johnstone, is brought to his own death by supernatural means; the ghost of the murdered wife in 'The Barber of Duncow' (1831) enters her aunt's cottage to tell where her body may be found and to demand justice.[16]

To this process of the supernatural coming in rather than the mortal going out, the tale, 'The Brownie of the Black Haggs' (1828) is no exception. Here a laird's wife, Lady Sprot of Wheelhope, who has long tyrannised her servants and been a frequent agent in the murder of Covenanters, is herself tormented and finally slain by a new servant of particularly sinister nature. This servant has a simian aspect, has a senile face on a young body, and is forever mocking the lady to her distraction: his name in Merodach, which was the name of the city-god of Babylon in the Bible (Exodus 7), while 'Evil-Merodach' was the son and successor of Nebuchadnezzar, King of Babylon. Lady Wheelhope detests him, but when she finally succeeds in having him removed, is so obsessed by him that she follows him everywhere, to her eventual ruin and death.

As we said, if 'Kilmeny' and 'The Witch of Fife' portray an expansion, an increase of freedom, this story, as with much of the prose, portrays increasing confinement and helplessness. The obvious moral level of 'The Brownie of the Black Haggs' is that of the biter bit: she who tormented and tortured others has the same done to herself; in some sense Merodach may be seen as an indirect agent of divine retribution. But in addition the move is one whereby Lady Wheelhope is reduced from unrestrained tyranny to total impotence, her life wholly dependent upon a detested other. There is no better image of her helplessness than her attempts to strike Merodach:

> At one time she guided her blow towards him, and he at the same instant avoided it with such dexterity, that she knocked down the chief hind, or foresman; and then Merodach giggled so heartily, that, lifting the kitchen poker, she threw it at him with a full design of knocking out his brains; but the missle only broke every plate and ashet on the kitchen dresser.[17]

The contrast is additionally heightened by the fact that Lady Wheelhope is a large woman, where Merodach is a little skipping thing.

Then again we have a strange relationship between the two, in that her very hatred and loathing of Merodach comes to bind Lady Wheelhope closer to him almost than a husband (somewhat reminiscent of the attraction-repulsion of Beatrice-Joanna and the ugly De Flores in Thomas Middleton's play *The Changeling* (1653)). At first she asks the laird her husband to send Merodach away, knowing the threat he is to her; but then in time she comes to expend all her hatred and lust for vengeance on Merodach, to such an extent that

> She could not stay from the creature's presence, for in the intervals when absent from him, she spent her breath in curses and execrations, and then not able to rest, she ran again to seek him, her eyes gleaming with the anticipated delights of vengeance.
>
> (p. 98)

This sounds like a love-relationship founded on hate: and indeed one of the effects of the tale is to show the nature and power of hatred, first in Lady Wheelhope, then reflected back at her in the features of the leering Merodach. Doubtless something sado-masochistic is woven into the tale: it is fair to say that the rain of blows from Merodach to which Lady Wheelhope subjects herself by the end is the obverse of sexual congress; we may suppose that she who once delighted in inflicting pain is as ready by the end to receive it. The strangeness of her relationship with Merodach is caught in the way that her attempt to murder him in his bed is described as 'the lady had been seeking Merodach's bed by night, on some horrible intent' (p. 100); and later, when Merodach has finally been expelled from the house after the murder of Lady Wheelhope's son, and when Lady Wheelhope has just said that he must not go because she wants the pleasure of dismembering him, she immediately 'eloped after him' (p. 102). They are referred to as 'this unaccountable couple' and as 'the fascinated pair' (p. 100). So far as the servant Wattie Blythe then sees it, the two are but lovers, and their apparent antagonism nothing to the point: '"nipping an' scarting are Scots folk's wooing"' (p. 103). Merodach's role as 'familiar' seems to have more sense than one.

Despite being badly beaten by Merodach, who returns her saying '"I have scourged, I have spurned and kicked her, afflicting her night and day, and yet from my side she will not depart"' (p. 105), Lady Wheelhope continues to follow him until eventually she disappears, and her buried body is later found 'mangled and wounded in a most shocking manner, the fiendish creature having manifestly tormented her to death' (p. 106).

The story refuses to conclude about Merodach's nature, but like much of Hogg's work, leaves open as many possibilities as it can. Merodach may be a supernatural agent, and if so may be simply a brownie, or an angel or a devil in disguise, engineering retribution. Equally he could just be an externalisation of some conscience in Lady Wheelhope which, like the worm, finally turns. Or again, as we have seen, he could be the perfect foil to her violence, the key to a sado-masochistic relationship she has long blindly been seeking. So far as her relations with her husband the laird are concerned—a stupid 'stump', 'A big, dun-faced, pluffy body, that cared neither for good nor evil, and did not well know the one from the other' (p. 94)—her violent behaviour can in part be seen as a reaction to the emptiness there, a violence that literally finds its match in Merodach.

But then again there may be a more metaphysical way of looking at Lady Wheelhope's relation with Merodach. For she exhibits the sort of 'mystery of iniquity' that is attributed to the evil Claggart in Melville's 'Billy Budd' (1891):

> When the Sprots were lairds of Wheelhope, which is now a long time ago, there was one of the ladies who was very badly spoken of in the country. People did not just openly assert that Lady Wheelhope was a witch, but every one had an aversion even at hearing her named; and when by chance she happened to be mentioned, old men would shake their heads and say, 'Ah, let us alane o' her! The less ye meddle wi' her the better.' Auld wives would give over spinning, and, as a pretence for hearing what might be said about her, poke in the fire with the tongs, cocking up their ears all the while; and then, after some meaning coughs, hems, and haws, would haply say, 'Hech-wow, sirs! An a' be true that's said!' or something equally wise and decisive as that.
>
> In short, Lady Wheelhope was accounted a very bad woman.
>
> (p. 94)

In short, rather more than a bad woman: it is clear that she seems to have some deep and unspeakable iniquity about her, which verges on the mysterious. And if we take Merodach as the ultimate image or the last analysis of her evil, then here he has unmistakably satanic qualities that reflect on her. With Lady Wheelhope we have someone for whose murderous behaviour no cause is assigned: it simply emerges spontaneously. Moreover its most particular object is Christians: 'Whenever she found out any of the servant men of the laird's establishment for religious characters, she soon gave them up to the military, and got them shot; and several girls that were regular in their devotions, she was supposed to have popped off with poison' (p. 94).

We have also seen, in 'Kilmeny' and 'The Witch of Fife', how Hogg mixes the domestic and the supernatural life in a cottage with mystic visions of heaven or magical journeys to Lapland. In this story his penchant for multiple effects is shown also in the vein of humour that runs through the most savage moments. The sudden flippancy of the last phrase quoted, 'popped off with poison', is typical of the tone of the piece, which has a derisive, Merodach-like edge to its serious intent, and where we find murdering servants or Covenanters is on a par with shattering the dinner service. The slightly digressive portrait towards the end of the tale of the lengthy debate between the laird's old shepherd and his wife about what has become of Lady Wheelhope—morally a mixture of self-righteous religiosity, stupidity, greed, superstition and complacent satisfaction at the downfall of their betters, but humanly a superb comedy of the interplay of a married pair's frailties—is a classic instance of this.

Multiplicity of truth, reality and tone in the tale is reinforced by the use of different perspectives throughout. We open with the reticences of old men and women on the subject of Lady Wheelhope; we have the hopeless inadequacy of the laird's response to her evil, '"I wish she maunna hae gotten something she has been the waur of"' (p. 95); and we have Bessie and Wattie Blythe whose marital battle of the sexes determines their different attitudes to Lady Wheelhope's behaviour, and whose joint desire for the reward offered for the lady's return unites them. At the end we are told that the story was long ago told to the narrator 'by an old man, named Adam Halliday, whose great grandfather, Thomas Halliday, was one of those that found the body and buried it' (p. 106), so that we are left uncertain as to how far the tale we have been given was as narrated by Thomas Halliday, retold by Adam Halliday or recalled by the narrator himself. As for the narrator within the story, he is highly idiosyncratic, referring human peculiarities to parallels he has witnessed in collie dogs or hounds and foxes, and certainly filling the tale with a bluff colloquialism. Further, he takes no certain standpoint, declaring at one point of the speculations concerning Merodach's nature, 'What he was I do not know, and therefore will not pretend to say' (p. 102), and at another speaking of 'the hellish looks of the Brownie' (p. 105), and ending a story to whose events he has given unquestioning credit with 'But, upon the whole, I scarcely believe the tale can be true.'

The use of multiple narration, not to mention the exploration of the ambiguities of evil, is more amply deployed in *The Confessions of a Justified Sinner*, with its sources in the literature of the double and of the shadow.[18] The story is told from two viewpoints: first, that of an 'Editor', and secondly, that of one of the characters in the story, one Robert Wringhim, a fanatical believer in his own divine election; and at the end we have first 'Hogg' himself, describing how this story of the period 1687–1712 came to light in 1823, and then the Editor again, correcting Hogg's version of events. The bare bones of the story itself concern the enmity of one religiously inclined brother for another, more worldly one, and the eventual murder of the latter; the Editor's narrative then deals with the process by which the guilt of the first brother Robert Wringhim is determined, while that of this 'justified sinner' himself describes how he was brought to the murder for the best of motives by a companion called Gil-Martin, from whom and from justice he variously struggled to escape until he met a wretched end. So far as the Fieldingesque Editor is concerned, the issue is a mainly straightforward though exceptional one of hatred of one sort of brother for another, rather reminiscent of that of Blifil for Tom Jones in Fielding's *Tom Jones*. But on the other side, Robert Wringhim tells how when he was finally convinced of his being marked out from other men by divine election, he met the person he came to call Gil-Martin, who encouraged him to acts of violence against the Lord's supposed enemies, or those in peril of their souls—prominent among whom was to be his own brother George—in order to testify to his own election and bear witness to God's judgments. In short we have two versions of the same event, neither of them conclusive.

At the same time, events which are left amazing in the Editor's narrative—a man known not to be present and yet who was seen to call on George on the night of his murder, the dead George appearing in apparent full health and vigour—are given explanation in terms of the shape-shifting Gil-Martin in Robert's narrative. But there we also have the problem of Gil-Martin himself: is he actually a devil, or (as in 'The Brownie of the Black Haggs') may he not equally be seen as a projection of Robert's own nature in absolutely evil terms, rather like the gigantic reflection of him his brother George sees on Arthur's Seat?[19] Nor can we give easy credence to Robert's story, when he admits that he is a constitutional liar;[20] and as for the Editor who tells the first part, his bias in favour of the one brother is plain enough. Throughout, we may note, the story is concerned with perception and identity: what was the nature of the apparent apparition of his brother that George saw on Arthur's Seat, how could Robert Wringhim be in so many places at once, who came for George on the night of his death, what shape did Wringhim take that allowed his miraculous escape from the law?

The uncertainties and mysteries here doubtless express Hogg's delight in such *frissons*. But in this particular story they also in part arise out of a recurrent motif of 'separation from reality'. Because certain people variously cut themselves off from the rest of mankind, the world they inhabit becomes shot through with doubt. This is an exceptional theme for Hogg here, but he is dealing with people possessed of pride, and with intellectuals whose theories about themselves exist in total dismissal of the common empirical facts about them. In almost all of Hogg's other supernatural tales the extraordinary events spring from, are rooted in or return to the ordinariness of domestic life—even those concerning the psychopathic Lady Wheelhope of 'The Brownie of the Black Haggs', where the lady's behaviour occurs within her house and is largely immersed in and commented on by the lives of all about her, including her domestic servants. But Robert Wringhim is to have no companion at all apart from the enigmatic Gil-Martin, and is to be driven out of house after house till he dies on an uninhabited moor. We start with Robert's mother, who early separated herself from her husband, out of a sexual horror and a Calvinist contempt for his easy ways. Then Robert drops his father's name of Colwan and takes the surname of his mother's religious adviser, the Rev. Mr Wringhim; this helps to cast doubt on his parentage.

But the most singular severance from reality is that arising out of the doctrine of election. Once Robert believes himself chosen, every other action and person in the world thereafter serves only to illuminate this divine choice. Such a belief is founded not on empirical proof, but on the inner conviction of the heart, and here too on pride: and thus it is that in this book external reality in the shape(s) of Gil-Martin may play as many tricks as it wishes with the likes of Robert Wringhim, but will in no way shake their assurance of salvation. So it is that we see an ostensibly redeemed Christian finding theoretic sanction for the removal by murder of all he deems sinners:

> From that moment, I conceived it decreed, not that I should be a minister of the gospel, but a champion of it, to cut off the enemies of the Lord from the face of the earth; and I rejoiced in the commission, finding it more congenial to my nature to be cutting sinners off with the sword, than to be haranguing them from the pulpit, striving to produce an effect, which God, by his act of absolute predestination, had for ever rendered impracticable . . . Seeing that God had from all eternity decided the fate of every individual that was to be born of woman, how vain was it in man to endeavour to save those whom their Maker had, by an unchangeable decree, doomed to destruction . . .
>
> (pp. 122–3)

Convinced as he is of his salvation, possessed too of enormous pride, he is easy prey for the figure he calls Gil-Martin to cut him off from all saving intercourse with the external world. He is incapable, too, of recognising Gil-Martin's true nature, first through his pride, which would not let him believe that any but God's agents would be able to converse with him, and later by his fear, which refuses to allow that the entire edifice on which he has built his life may have been undermined by the devil. It is true that Hogg captures a truth concerning the nature of extreme puritanism here, the belief that the world shapes itself into purpose about the redeemed: but it is not Calvinism itself that is here being attacked so much as the self-deception that, fuelled by pride, it can admit. We may surmise that such self-delusion at the core of the book will propagate itself into general uncertainty of the kind that we have seen and experienced.

But even this does not quite catch everything that is in the story. The Editor at the end declares, 'What can this work be? Sure, you will say, it must be an allegory; or (as the writer calls it) a religious PARABLE, showing the dreadful danger of self-righteousness? I cannot tell' (p. 240). It seems fair to say that in some sense the story also shows the limits of all human perception. Two narrators to give different versions of the same happenings, one of them a biased commentator living more than a century after Wringhim's death, the other a constitutional liar; continual visual uncertainty, darkness, mist, legal proceedings to determine this or that 'fact'; a creature of disguise that can assume the form of anyone it pleases; and most of all someone whose passions are presented as so distorted that he cannot recognise the devil even when he flaunts his horns before him—'Lord, thou knowest all that I have done for thy cause on earth! Why then art thou laying thy hands so sore upon me? Why hast thou set me as a butt of thy malice? But thy will must be done! Thou wilt repay me in a better world' (p. 239). One irony of the story is that those supernatural beings identified with ultimate reality, God and the devil, are here the most shifting and equivocal of all.

One is tempted to ask why Hogg should have been so interested in the theme of perception in this story. Perhaps it was his answer to the eighteenth-century empiricists who were so sure of the independent existence of external phenomena, extending even to a transcendent supernatural realm. But it would be better to centre the story in Hogg's curiosity concerning the supernatural in any manifestation—heavenly, fiendish, faërian or mind-made, and his delight in its mystery: the particular theme or message of the story is for this book only, and is not really found extensively elsewhere in his work; so far as patterns of meaning are concerned, these always seem to emerge from Hogg trying his hand, as though he was in a workshop, continually surprising himself at the varying shapes that were coming off his lathe. But for the core we look to the varying delights Hogg chronicles in his poem 'Superstition' (1815) and in his tale 'Mary Burnet' (1828):

I must . . . relate scenes so far out of the way of usual events, that the sophisticated gloss and polish thrown over the modern philosophic mind, may feel tainted by such antiquated breathings of superstition. Nevertheless, be it mine to cherish the visions that have been, as well as the hope of visions yet in reserve, far in the ocean of eternity, beyond the stars and the sun. For, after all, what is the soul of man without these? What but a cold phlegmatic influence, so inclosed within the walls of modern scepticism, as scarcely to be envied by the spirits of the beasts that perish?[21]

In that anti-rational thrust, in that reach for a world beyond or beneath the confines of human consciousness, Hogg strikes a note that we will hear throughout our account of Scottish fantasy.

Notes

1 William Hogg (brother) in Mrs (Mary Gray Hogg) Garden, *Memorials of James Hogg, the Ettrick Shepherd*, 3rd edn (Paisley: Alexander Gardner, 1903), p. 13. On Hogg's life see James Hogg, *Memoir of the Author's Life and Familiar Anecdotes of Sir Walter Scott* (first published 1832), ed. Douglas S. Mack (Edinburgh: Scottish Academic Press, 1972); and Allen Lang Strout, *The Life and Letters of James Hogg, the Ettrick Shepherd, Vol. I, 1770–1825* (Lubbock, Texas: Texas Tech Press, 1946)—the typescript of Vol.II is in the National Library of Scotland.

2 John Carey mentions this assertion in his edition of James Hogg, *The Private Memoirs and Confessions of a Justified Sinner* (London: Oxford University Press, 1969), p. xiii; he is perhaps referring to Hogg's *Memoir*, p. 19.

3 Carey, ed. cit., p. xxi.

4 Recently reissued with an introduction and notes by Douglas Gifford (Edinburgh: Scottish Academic Press, 1989).

5 Thomas Crawford, 'James Hogg: The Play of Region and Nation', in Douglas Gifford, ed., *The History of Scottish Literature, Volume 3, The Nineteenth Century* (Aberdeen: Aberdeen University Press, 1988), p. 91, observes, 'Region and nation inform both the structure and texture of *The Queen's Wake*: it is a deliberate attempt to write not just about Ettrick, but about at least the majority of the regions that comprise the nation.'

6 References for *The Queen's Wake* generally are to *The Works of the Ettrick Shepherd*, edited by the Rev. Thomas Thomson, 2 vols (London: Blackie, 1876). This is the fullest edition available of all Hogg's poetry and prose tales. References for 'Kilmeny', *The Pilgrims of the Sun* and

'The Witch of Fife' are taken from the more accessible James Hogg, *Selected Poems and Songs*, ed. David Groves (Edinburgh: Scottish Academic Press, 1986).

7 The return here is reminiscent of that of the three sons in the ballad 'The Wife of Usher's Well', whose hats were 'o' the birk'.

8 It is remarkable how many early commentators looked no further than faërie for the land Kilmeny visited: see Douglas S. Mack in his edition of James Hogg, *Selected Poems* (Oxford: Clarendon Press, 1970), pp. xxii–iii, finally dispelling this view and identifying the land as heaven.

9 MacDonald, *At the Back of the North Wind* (1871) (London: Dent, 1956), p. 95, 'The last two lines are the shepherd's [Hogg's] own remark, and a matter of opinion.'

10 This is also the view of Mack, ed., *Selected Poems*, pp. xxv–vi; contrast, however, Nelson C. Smith, *James Hogg* (Boston: Twayne, 1980), pp. 132–3.

11 Groves, ed., *Selected Poems and Songs*, pp. xiv–xxiii, sees the journey as a basic pattern in Hogg's work: 'the mind discovers itself through motion, transition, and process, rather than through any static or idealised image of itself' (this point is actually made in relation to Hogg's analogous mode of composition).

12 Douglas Gifford, *James Hogg* (Edinburgh: Ramsay Head Press, 1976), pp. 55–6, finds the impulse behind 'Kilmeny' in several of Hogg's works, including the poems 'Elen of Reigh' (1829) and 'A Greek Pastoral' (1830), the prose tales 'The Hunt of Eildon' (1818) and 'Mary Burnet' (1828) and the dramatic tale 'The Haunted Glen' (1817). However it should be said that while those stories portray disappearances, they none of them depict the strange lands the mortals are taken to.

13 Smith, pp. 133–7, and Groves, pp. xxiv–v; less so Mack, ed. *Selected Poems*, p. 93, and Gifford, p. 62.

14 Hogg, '*Memoir*', pp. 123–4. Groves prints both endings.

15 As it is not so much in Hogg's tale 'The Witches of Traquair' (1828).

16 All these are reprinted in James Hogg, *Selected Stories and Sketches*, ed. Douglas S. Mack (Edinburgh: Scottish Academic Press, 1982).

17 Ibid., p. 96. References are to this edition.

18 Gifford, pp. 141–2, suggests sources in the Gothic novel. Douglas Mack emphasises Scott's *Old Mortality* (1817) and in particular John Galt's *Ringan Gilhaize* (1823), in his '"The Rage of Fanaticism in Former Days": James Hogg's *Confession* [sic] *of a Justified Sinner* and the Controversy over *Old Mortality*', in Ian Campbell, ed., *Nineteenth-Century Scottish Fiction: Critical Essays* (Manchester: Carcanet, 1979), pp. 38–50. The most recent and suggestive shadow-and-devil story is Adelbert von Chamisso's *Peter Schlemihl* (1814; tr. 1824).

19 Hogg however offers scientific explanation for such a phenomenon in his 'Nature's Magic Lantern' (1837), repr. in *Works, Volume I: Tales and Sketches*, pp. 459–62.
20 Hogg, *Confessions*, ed. Carey, p. 108. References are to this text.
21 Hogg, 'Mary Burnet', *Selected Stories and Sketches*, p. 71.

CHAPTER FOUR

Carlyle, *Sartor Resartus* (1836)

ARLYLE MET JAMES HOGG only once, just after he had written
Sartor Resartus and while he was on his first visit to London
from Scotland, early in 1832. His impression of Hogg then
suggests only moderate sympathy, through he was intrigued enough
to give Hogg three times the space in his Notebook he afforded Galt
or Lockhart: 'speaks Scotch, and mostly narrative absurdity (or even
obscenity) therewith. Appears in the mingled character of zany and
raree show . . . His poetic talent is authentic, yet his intellect seems
of the weakest . . . The man is a very curious *specimen.*'[1] One wonders
what Hogg made of the then escapee from Craigenputtock. Yet *Sartor
Resartus* has considerable similarities with Hogg's *Confessions of a Justified
Sinner*, particularly in the use of a (more or less confused) Editor and of
a double narrative; and there has been an argument that Carlyle as well
as Hogg wrote within a common contemporary Scottish interest in the
psychic double.[2]

However there are very real differences between Carlyle and Hogg as
writers. All his literary life Carlyle had a vision of the divine reality in
the universe which he wished to promulgate; Hogg had no such fixed
world-view or axe to grind—he delighted rather in different attitudes
from work to work. Hogg is much more both for the fictive, and for
the local: general truths do not excite him; thus he creates stories about
individuals, where Carlyle (in *The French Revolution* and *Frederick the Great*)
uncovers the divine meaning of history, or (in *Sartor Resartus*) reveals the
supernatural basis of all creation. And where Hogg looks to Scotland for
all his stories and situations, Carlyle never does: his ambitious spirit
includes a disdain for what he sees as the parochial, and his gaze is international and ultimately eternal, looking beyond all time and space.

Sartor Resartus ('the tailor retailored') is Carlyle's only fantasy, in the
sense that it sets out to give us a supernatural and wondrous vision of
life. It is also his first large-scale work, written in 1831 while he was
still in Scotland, living in isolation with his wife Jane at the farmhouse
of Craigenputtock in Dumfriesshire. It is in part a metaphor (or clothing)
for Carlyle's own spiritual development. Brought up in a sternly Calvinist
family in the farming town of Ecclefechan in Dumfriesshire, Carlyle
was sent to Edinburgh University, where he studied mathematics and
where, in the atmosphere of late-Enlightenment scepticism, he lost his
faith. Years of directionless misery followed until gradually, through his

knowledge of German idealist writers such as Kant, Goethe, Schiller and Fichte, he refashioned for himself a faith which found a present God in every meanest thing and behind every historical event in the universe.[3] This renewed trust in divine immanence owed nothing to Christian orthodoxy or to the Bible, but had much in common with the strong Calvinist sense of God: for Carlyle the old forms and stories of Christianity, so challenged by the new mechanism of his age, and so overthrown in his own personal experience, were reborn out of the old husks. God, the divine tailor or *sartor*, was reclothed.[4] It was to proclaim this that *Sartor Resartus* was written. It was intended, in its way, as a new bible, without dogma, to show to his age that beyond the obscurations of our life ' "this fair Universe, were it in the meanest province thereof, is in very deed the star-domed City of God; that through every star, through every grass-blade, and most through every Living Soul, the glory of a present God still beams" '.[5]

Yet anything less like a bible could hardly be imagined. What we are given is a philosophy of clothes, as expounded by an obscure German 'Professor of Things in General' from a university of Weissnichtwo ('know-not-where'); this professor labours under the extraordinary name of Diogenes Teufelsdröckh ('Devil's dung'). His philosophy is relayed to us in fragmentary form by an often baffled English Editor; it maintains that all activities and phenomena in life may be considered under the dual aspect of clothes, either as emblematic of a deeper reality or as obstructive to the vision of naked truth. The whole book comes in three sections. In the first, some account is given of the aspect and character of the professor, together with chapters expounding the bases of his clothes philosophy: this material is derived partly from first-hand acquaintance, partly from report and partly through the professor's 'just-published' book, *Die Kleider ihr Werden und Wirken* ('Clothes, their Origin and Influence'). Then, in the second section, we have a biography of the professor, describing how he developed his philosophy through his experience of life's vicissitudes (primarily in terms of an amorous reverse): this material has to be ordered by the Editor out of six paper bags of highly miscellaneous and often irrelevant material sent to him rather late from Germany. We are to suppose that in the Editor's terms the whole first section of the book has been an unnecessary marking of time and disclosure of material which would have better followed the life of its proponent. In the last section of the book we return to exposition of the clothes philosophy. Add to this the fact that the book tells no story, does not give even the life without interruptions, and is presented as a series of fragmentary observations or else biographical tableaux, and one is left with still less of a clear, or graspable, new theology.

The work also refuses us any intellectual certainties. We do not know how seriously to take Herr Diogenes Teufelsdröckh or his philosophy; we are bewildered by the presence of the (often confused) Editor; we do not know if, given the chaotic material with which he has been presented, the Editor has given us an accurate picture of Teufelsdröckh's life and views; he himself wonders, as we may of Carlyle, whether the whole thing may be a hoax (pp. 152–3). We are battered by continual irrelevancies, shifts of tone from grave to gay, and by a philosophy which is not so much a philosophy as a series of intuitions. We do not even know how to take the crucial heart of the book, the account of how Teufelsdröckh lost his beloved Blumine to another, and thereupon entered a dark night of the soul, described as the 'Everlasting No'. Teufelsdröckh's enamourment with this lady—and we have his wild and ungainly figure before us too—is described as a potentially violent firework, ignited at a bland social gathering for 'Aesthetic Tea'; he loses Blumine to someone with more money, an Englishman, who prospers under the name of Herr Towgood ('Tough-gut'); even in the midst of his pains his tone 'has more of riancy, even of levity, than we could have expected' (p. 142); the very shrillness with which his despair is uttered, seeing the Heavens and the Earth as the 'boundless Jaws of a devouring Monster, wherein I, palpitating, waited to be devoured' (p. 128), suggests a disproportion with its amorous cause. An account which in part founds itself on Goethe's *Sorrows of Werther* is everywhere subverted by the mocking laughter of Jean Paul Richter. The effect on us is quite simply to leave us in uncertainty, at once presented with a clear scheme of spiritual development and denied it—unable even to have the assurance of being ignorant.[6]

Yet Carlyle may be seen as having chosen this mode as the one most consonant with the nature of his vision, and as the one most able to succeed in its propagation. That vision essentially involves an unravelling, a destructuring of those cloth-webs of mind, sight and reality that blind us to wonder:

> 'But deepest of all illusory Appearances, for hiding Wonder, as for many other ends, are your two grand fundamental world-enveloping Appearances, SPACE and TIME. These, as spun and woven for us from before Birth itself, to clothe our celestial ME for dwelling here, and yet to blind it,—lie all-embracing, as the universal canvass, or warp and woof, whereby all minor Illusions, in this Phantasm Existence, weave and paint themselves. In vain, while here on Earth, shall you endeavour to strip them off; you can, at best, but rend them asunder for moments, and look through.'
>
> (p. 197)

It is such a looking-through that *Sartor Resartus* attempts: and one way to do so is to break down all structures and certainties, including those of art itself. Carlyle's sources are many of them writers with similar or near-similar intent, such as Laurence Sterne (of *Tristram Shandy*) or the German writers E. T. A. Hoffmann, Novalis and Richter (of *Titan*).

Thus we find Carlyle in 'On History' (1830) rejecting narrative because it separates a little world of sense off from the rest of the universe: 'Alas for our "chains," or chainlets, of "causes and effects," which we so assiduously track through certain handbreadths of years and square miles, when the whole is a broad, deep Immensity, and each atom is "chained" and complected with all!'[7]

But more to our purpose here: if our existence is founded on unfathomable mystery, if every meanest thing is based on wonder and the unknown infinite, then it would be appropriate for the book that tells us so to try to show that by itself being a mystery which we struggle and fail to grasp. Admittedly, there is a great difference between mere confusion or bafflement, and true mystery: but the one, which knocks away the certainties of the mind that thinks to grasp and thereby to know life, may be a way to approach the other. '"This Dreaming,"' says Teufelsdröckh, '"this Somnambulism is what we on Earth call Life; wherein the most indeed undoubtingly wander, as if they knew right hand from left; yet they only are wise who know that they know nothing"' (p. 43). Or as Carlyle put it in his contemporary 'Characteristics' (1831):

> Boundless as is the domain of man, it is but a small fractional proportion of it that he rules with Consciousness and by Forethought: what he can contrive, nay, what he can altogether know and comprehend, is essentially the mechanical, small; the great is ever, in one sense or other, the vital; it is essentially the mysterious, and only the surface of it can be understood.[8]

If that is so, then the dismantling of intellectual and other certainties is an essential preliminary to grasping the true wonder of reality. And in this sense every device that subserves this purpose is an agent in the creation of fantasy.[9] In this emphasis on the unstructured and the unconscious, Carlyle is peculiarly a writer of Scottish fantasy.

One of the means by which this dismantling is done is through the frequent 'contradictions' in the book. What, for example, *are* clothes? Is Herr Teufelsdröckh's clothes philosophy founded on fetishism; or is he a would-be tailor? For much of his account of clothes, particularly of their history and development, seems to show a fascination with them for themselves, irrespective of any meaning they may be made to have. Thus on the German fashionable dress of the fifteenth century he shows a clear love of the bizarre garments in their own right:

> 'Rich men, I find, have *Teusinke*' (a perhaps untranslateable article); 'also a silver girdle, whereat hang little bells; so that when a man walks it is with continual jingling. Some few, of musical turn, have a whole chime of bells (*Glockenspiel*) fastened there; which especially, in sudden whirls, and the other accidents of walking, has a grateful effect. Observe too

> how fond they are of peaks, and Gothic-arch intersections.
> The male world wears peaked caps, an ell-long, which hang
> bobbing over the side (*schief*): their shoes are peaked in front,
> also to the length of an ell (and laced on the side with tags);
> even the wooden shoes have their ell-long noses: some also
> clap bells on the peak.'
>
> (p. 38)

Throughout the early presentation of the clothes philosophy we are
shifted continually between 'clothes-as-metaphors' to actual accounts
of fashion 'so learned, precise, graphical', that at one point the Editor
is led to ask whether Teufelsdröckh's 'philosophy' would not do as well
as a companion piece to 'Mr Merrick's valuable Work *On Ancient Armour?'*
(p. 37). Yet elsewhere the metaphoric radiates in all directions: clothes are
like bodies, screens of the eternal behind life, societies are knit together
as clothes, Time and Space are as clothes that hide us from wonder,
words and style as the garment of thought may act as concealments (as
at pp. 57–8), Teufelsdröckh's enigmatic nature is as clothing, and last
but not least, the very form of this book, which elaborately hoaxes us
with the existence of a German professor who is in part a disguise of
Carlyle himself, is one more such illusive vestment.

Nor is this all the contradictoriness there is on clothes, for Teufelsdröckh
also continually veers between seeing clothes as mere obscuring rags
to be flung aside for true vision, and viewing them as the outward
manifestations of the divine. Thus on the one hand we learn that
'"The beginning of all Wisdom is to look fixedly on Clothes . . . till
they become *transparent*"' (p. 52); and on the other that clothes are '"a
mystic grove-encircled shrine for the Holy in man"' (p. 32). It is typical
of this book so to balance the 'No' and the 'Yes', to give us one chapter
entitled 'The World in Clothes' and another 'The World Out of Clothes';
and then even openly to acknowledge the fact:

> Nothing that he [Teufelsdröckh] sees but has more than a
> common meaning, but has two meanings; thus, if in the
> highest Imperial Sceptre and Charlemagne-Mantle, as well
> as in the poorest Ox-goad and Gypsy-Blanket, he finds Prose,
> Decay, Contemptibility; there is in each sort Poetry also, and
> a reverend Worth.
>
> (p. 52)

Thus too Teufelsdröckh can condemn tailors in one place and laud them
in another (pp. 44–5, 218–20); can speak of kings as distinguished from
carmen by no more than their clothes, and elsewhere see them as
'Heaven-chosen' (pp. 50, 188); can praise the worship of symbols by
mankind and pass on without pause to depict '"five hundred living
soldiers sabred into crows' meat, for a piece of glazed cotton, which

they called their Flag; which, had you sold it at any market-cross, would not have brought above three groschen"' (p. 168).[10]

So much by way of throwing the reader's mind into a state of relative uncertainty, where it may more readily be susceptible to the wonder beneath life. Such wonder is not the common medium of the book, but rises intermittently, in great fountains of (in)comprehension. The book becomes a mirror of the world, a mélange of different impulses and intermittent revelations: it is like a medium of different density, when we shift from the 'superficial' to the 'profound' and back again without warning.

> In the way of replenishing thy purse, or otherwise aiding thy digestive faculty, O British Reader . . . [this philosophy] leads to nothing, and there is no use in it; but rather the reverse, for it costs thee somewhat. Nevertheless, if through this unpromising Horngate, Teufelsdröckh, and we by means of him, have led thee into the true Land of Dreams; and through the Clothes-Screen, as through a magical *Pierre-Pertuis*, thou lookest, even for moments, into the region of the Wonderful, and seest and feelest that thy daily life is girt with Wonder, and based on Wonder, and thy very blankets and breeches are Miracles,—then art thou profited beyond money's worth; and hast a thankfulness towards our Professor; nay, perhaps in many a literary Tea-circle, wilt open thy kind lips, and audibly express that same.
>
> (pp. 204–5)

There are as many banal moments in the book as wondrous ones, as many ridiculous as sublime, as many assaults on that which is antagonistic to fantasy as realisations of the fantastic itself.

How then is the fantastic realised? One vessel of it is the peculiar Diogenes Teufelsdröckh himself, wholly an invention of Carlyle's and certainly a creature from beyond nature so far as his nominal parents are concerned, since he is given to them as a baby by a mysterious stranger as in a fairy-tale, and comes to them complete with a birth certificate attesting his extraordinary name. There is then, the freakish throughout the story, a medium with which we would certainly feel uncomfortable and would tend to reject, were it not that we are forced to accommodate ourselves to it from the start:

> Considering our present advanced state of culture, and how the Torch of Science has now been brandished and borne about, with more or less effect, for five thousand years and upwards; how, in these times especially, not only the Torch still burns, and perhaps more fiercely than ever, but immunerable Rush-lights, and Sulphur-matches, kindled thereat, are also glancing in every direction, so

that not the smallest cranny or doghole in Nature or Art
can remain unilluminated,—it might strike the reflective
mind with some surprise that hitherto little or nothing of
a fundamental character, whether in the way of Philosophy
or History, has been written on the subject of Clothes.

(p. 3)

Not at all surprising, one might suppose: what on earth or anywhere else
has a philosophy of clothes got to do with the advancement of science?
Nevertheless science itself has taken a beating in that first sentence, even
as it is apparently praised as the foundation of progress: the imagery
of fire and light suggests both its incendiary danger and its intrusive
vulgarity. But we are to be shown that this so seemingly absurd clothes
philosophy is not simply what it appears, but the key to life and eternity.
What we thought might be a mere discourse on fashion or the wardrobe
is to be a means of apprehending not only the truth about society but
of God Himself. Before we know what is happening our knowledge of
clothes is metamorphosing: within a page we are being asked to think
of our clothes as concealments for our souls and selves; within a few
chapters we are to consider the military and the police of a country as
a protective apron, society itself as a tissue of clothing woven together,
and Time and Space themselves as the clothing mediums of our lives,
whereby we cannot see further than them to the eternal. This capacity
to show the hidden significances and depths of an apparently trivial
thing is an act of fantasy-making: and that is precisely the removal of
the clothes of our familiar vision till we see the wonder that is hid. Indeed
most people are seen as a different sort of fantasists themselves, happier
to cling to their habituated delusions concerning reality than to pierce to
the truth. Here the world is rightly seen upside-down: the apparently
alien, idiosyncratic and absurd Teufelsdröckh and his philosophy of
clothes are closer to what centrally matters to us almost than our very
souls; what seemed mere detritus or disturbing anarchy, Teufelsdröckh,
'devil's dung', is in truth God-given (*vom Himmel gesandt*).

Part of the technique is to show how all seemingly so isolated or
insignificant things may, rightly viewed, be linked to a greater whole, as
separate threads to one universal garment. In the sphere of *Sartor Resartus*
itself this is seen in the way the seemingly absurd clothes philosophy is
made sole key to the universe and to the understanding of God; and also
in the way that the apparently separate, fragmented chapters or even
attitudes all gradually come together in a deeper unity. It is precisely
the fragmentation of thought and society caused by materialism that
Sartor opposes, and does so by working in the opposite direction, taking
the seemingly divided and discordant and showing them to be part of
a larger harmony:

'Wondrous truly are the bonds that unite us one and all;

whether by the soft binding of Love, or the iron chaining of Necessity, as we like to choose it. More than once, have I said to myself, of some perhaps whimsically strutting Figure, such as provokes whimsical thoughts: "Wert thou, my little Brotherkin, suddenly covered up with even the largest imaginable Glass-bell,—what a thing it were, not for thyself only, but for the world! Post Letters, more or fewer, from all the four winds, impinge against thy Glass walls, but must drop unread: neither from within comes there question or response into any Postbag: thy Thoughts fall into no friendly ear or heart, thy Manufacture into no purchasing hand; thou art no longer a circulating venous-arterial Heart, that, taking and giving, circulatest through all Space and all Time: there has a Hole fallen out in the immeasurable, universal World-tissue, which must be darned up again!"'

(pp. 185–6)

The fantasy serves the purpose of bringing the idea before us with particular vividness: and here its very absurdity demonstrates how it cannot be true, how this figure that takes such pride in its self can no more divide itself from its necessary links with its fellow man than it could survive under a glass bell. The very technique here denies isolation, as the image itself and incoming letters sliding off the glass fades into a more generalised picture of disconnection from the world. To the soul that, less vain, but still lonely, feels that there is no longer a religion, a church or a God, Teufelsdröckh likewise bids us look to hidden connections far more real than outward forms:

'Be of comfort! Thou are not alone, if thou have Faith. Spake we not of a Communion of Saints, unseen, yet not unreal, accompanying and brother-like embracing thee, so thou be worthy? . . . Neither say that thou hast now no symbol of the Godlike. Is not God's Universe a Symbol of the Godlike; is not Immensity a Temple; is not Man's History, and Men's History, a perpetual Evangile? Listen, and for organ-music thou wilt ever, as of old, hear the Morning Stars sing together.'

(p. 192)

Carlyle's book also sets out to remove the staleness of our vision of the world, that custom and habit based, or even institutionalised, mode of perception that leads us, after we have seen a thing five times, utterly to lose the vivid reality it had when we saw it first. We speak of miracles, says Teufelsdröckh, but we forget that every operation of nature is miracle: '"Am I to view the Stupendous with stupid indifference, because I have seen it twice, or two hundred, or two million times?"' (p. 196). (Numerous Victorians were later to use this argument to sustain their faith in an immanent God.) We think that ghosts are miraculous; and Dr Johnson longed to see one: but '"The good Doctor was a Ghost, as actual and authentic as heart could wish; well nigh a million of Ghosts were travelling the streets by his side"', for '"Are we not Spirits, shaped into a body, into an Appearance; and that fade away again into air, and Invisibility?"' (p. 200). In this aim of restoring wonder, *Sartor* is very close to J. R. R. Tolkien's view of one of the central functions of fantasy, 'Recovery', the regaining of a clear view of things that habitual perception has blurred:[11] though Carlyle's aim is more immediately religious, to show the foundation of such wonder in God. In this context we find Teufelsdröckh attacking names, which in his view '"are but one kind of such Custom-woven, wonder-hiding garments"' (p. 196).[12] In a sense then this book must be a war against words, or at least against that vocabulary that classifies—a sort of deconstruction, parallel to that carried out on our habitual and blinkered ways of thinking (as at pp. 43, 194–5). The name 'Teufelsdröckh', for example, flaunts its translation 'Devil's dung' before us, only as seen to suggest that its owner is in fact the reverse of devilish: yet no sooner may we be comfortable with that than we find Teufelsdröckh revealing to us that each human soul has within it '"an authentic Demon-Empire"' which is the source of vision (p. 197). One of the central impulses beneath all this is antipathy to the static (also seen in Hogg), a sense that the universe exists in ever-changing movement: '"Thinkest thou there is aught motionless; without Force, and utterly dead?"' (p. 55); '"all . . . works together with all; is borne forward on the bottomless, shoreless flood of Action, and lives through perpetual metamorphoses"' (p. 56).[13] The so solid world we live on is but an '"air image"', a '"habitable flowery Earth-rind"', floating on a fiery nether abyss (p. 197).

To turn things inside out, to make them seem new, to thrust them together with items with which they seem to have no connection, is part of Teufelsdröckh's metaphoric-fantastic style. Man is compared in his clothing of himself to horses, to his disadvantage: for the horse is '"his own sempster and weaver and spinner: nay his own bootmaker, jeweller, and man-milliner"' (p. 44). Napoleon was unknowingly God's missionary, teaching through the mouths of his cannon '"that great doctrine, *La carrière ouverte aux talens* (The Tools to him that can handle them), which is our ultimate Political Evangile, wherein alone can Liberty lie"' (p. 136). Since clothes may be considered to be the expressions of the indwelling soul, then discarded clothes may be the more worshipped because no longer obscured by the passions of their erstwhile wearers: and thus we have the picture of Teufelsdröckh passing with awe and reverence among the old clothes of Monmouth Street Market (pp. 183–4). Elsewhere, '"The Journalists are now the true Kings and Clergy"', or they are the preaching friars of a new Church to be founded in literature (pp. 35, 191). Man is distinguished by the fact that he is a tool-making animal, and one of the products of this is clothes: this has been brought to such a state of refinement that now,

> He digs up certain black stones from the bosom of the Earth, and says to them, *Transport me, and this luggage, at the rate of five-and-thirty miles an hour*; and they do it [the Liverpool Steam-carriage]: he collects, apparently by lot, six hundred and fifty-eight miscellaneous individuals, and says to them, *Make this nation toil for us, bleed for us, hunger, and sorrow, and sin for us*; and they do it [The British House of Commons]."'
>
> (p. 33)

Not only do we have the bizarre collocation of a steam-carriage with a parliament, but both are in turn related as tools to clothes. It is typical of *Sartor* that elsewhere almost every one of these items or notions is derided or denied: man is far better made than any horse (pp. 174–5), war is a horrific absurdity (pp. 133–4), clothes are mere rotten concealments from the truth (pp. 44–5, 52), newspapers are of negligible significance beside clothes (p. 166), man is not at all the only tool-making animal (p. 150), steam-engines and scientific advance are a blight (p. 127). But everywhere we find this technique of throwing things into lights in which we never saw them before, because we never saw them truly:

> 'In vain thou deniest it,' says the Professor [speaking to mankind]; 'thou *art* my Brother. Thy very Hatred, thy very Envy, those foolish lies thou tellest of me in thy splenetic humour: what is all this but an inverted Sympathy? Were I a Steam-engine, wouldst thou take the trouble to tell Lies of me? Not thou! I should grind all unheeded, whether badly or well.'
>
> (p. 185)

It may be a questionable argument, but it serves for the moment to dislocate our certainties, make us see through to a wonder that our passions would normally never admit. Or there is the classic image of inversion whereby war is portrayed as the deadly collision of two groups of men, born and bred in often widely separated parts of the world and having no quarrel with one another, brought together by no other impulse than to act as proxies for the mutual hostility of their two 'governors'. Thus, thirty supposed 'Natural Enemies of the French' are chosen from their home town of Dumdrudge, which can ill afford the skills it has nurtured them to exercise, and dispatched to some remote place: meanwhile come '"to that same spot"'

> 'thirty similar French artisans, from a French Dumdrudge, in like manner wending: till at length, after infinite effort, the two parties come into actual juxta-position; and Thirty stands

fronting Thirty, each with a gun in his hand. Straightway the word "Fire!" is given; and they blow the souls out of one another; and in place of sixty brisk useful craftsmen, the world has sixty dead carcasses, which it must bury, and anew shed tears for.

(p. 134).

Last here, we can speak of Teufelsdröckh's actual language. This may be called fantastical in its use of conceits, its piling of synonyms and plurals, its inversions, shifts of mood and direction, and frequent parentheses—fantastical, that is, in the way that it so constantly refuses a settled mode or grammar that we continually have to attend to it as an almost living thing, like a shadow that throws itself in all directions:

'Reader, the heaven-inspired melodious Singer; loftiest Serene Highness; nay thy own amber-locked, snow-and-rose-bloom Maiden, worthy to glide sylphlike almost on air, whom thou lovest, worshippest as a divine Presence, which indeed, symbolically taken, she is,—has descended, like thyself, from that same hair-mantled, flint-hurling Aboriginal Anthropophagus! Out of the eater cometh forth meat; out of the strong cometh forth sweetness. What changes are wrought not by Time, yet in Time! For not Mankind only, but all that Mankind does or beholds, is in continual growth, re-genesis and self-perfecting vitality. Cast forth thy Act, thy Word, into the ever-living, ever-working Universe: it is a seed-grain that cannot die; unnoticed to-day (says one) it will be found flourishing as a Banyan-grove (perhaps, alas, as a Hemlock-forest!) after a thousand years.

(p. 31)

The switches between personal address and general statement, indicative, exclamatory and imperative moods; the confusion as to what is being described in the first sentence, whether the reader, or three ways of talking about the maiden, or three separate beings; the multiple verbs, adjectives, nouns—'lovest, worshippest', 'hair-mantled, flint-hurling Aboriginal', 'growth, re-genesis, and self-perfecting vitality'; the shift from apparent adoration at the opening to satire (beauty founded in the Aboriginal), to perfectibility again—these and other features give to the passage not only a prodigious energy, but make it assume the aspect of some tentacular creature.[14] It is a style which can be said, in its constant disruptions and alterations of thrust, to break through to Teufelsdröckh's picture of the fantastic universe itself: 'So spiritual (*geistig*) is our whole daily Life: all that we do springs out of Mystery, Spirit, invisible Force; only like a little Cloud-image, or Armida's Palace, air-built, does the Actual body itself forth from the great mystic Deep"' (pp. 131–2). So too with the cloud-images of words, the 'garment of style', which are one with bodies, societies, religions, Time and Space themselves, in the aspect of clothes.

And just as words are not separate from other forms of existence, and indeed the idea of separation itself is anathema in Teufelsdröckh's philosophy, so words are to be one with what they describe, as in the magic of primitive language where myth or 'metaphor' and reality were undivided. '"Be not the slave of Words,"' Teufelsdröckh enjoins, '"is not the Distant, the Dead, while I love it, and long for it, and mourn for it, Here, in the genuine sense, as truly as the floor I stand on?"' (p. 43). To one for whom nothing is '"Detached, separated"' (p. 56), and Time and Space chimeras, this very book is not the sole production of Diogenes Teufelsdröckh and his publisher '"but [of] Cadmus of Thebes, Faust of Mentz, and innumerable others whom thou knowest not"' (p. 186). Words and symbols must be in continual movement to bring to us '"new Fire from Heaven"' (p. 170). That style where words and things are finally at one Teufelsdröckh finds in the universe, whose author is God: '"a Volume written in celestial hieroglyphics, in the true Sacred-writing"', with '"its Words, Sentences, and grand descriptive Pages, poetical and philosophical, spread out through Solar Systems, and Thousands of Years"' (p. 195).

Notes

1 Carlyle, 'Extracts from a Note Book', in J. A. Froude, *Thomas Carlyle: A History of the First Forty Years of his Life, 1795–1835*, 2 vols (London: Longmans, 1882), II, p. 234.

2 Thomas C. Richardson, 'Carlyle and the Scottish Tradition of the Double', in Horst W. Drescher, ed., *Thomas Carlyle 1981*: Papers Given at the International Thomas Carlyle Centenary Symposium (Frankfurt am Main: Peter Lang, 1983), pp. 351–64.

3 For accounts of Carlyle's life, see Froude, op.cit. and his *Thomas Carlyle: A History of his Life in London, 1834–1881*, 2 vols (London: Longmans, 1884). A useful short account is A. L. Le Quesne, *Carlyle* (Oxford: Oxford University Press, 1982).

4 On the sources and development of Carlyle's religious outlook, see John D. Rosenberg, *Carlyle and the Burden of History* (Oxford: Clarendon Press, 1985); and Ruth ap Roberts, *The Ancient Dialect: Thomas Carlyle and Comparative Religion* (Berkeley: University of California Press, 1988), pp. 1–44.

5 Carlyle, *Sartor Resartus*, eds Kerry McSweeney and Peter Sabor (Oxford: Oxford University Press, 1987), p. 200. Page references are to this edition.

6 On the fragmentary, multiple and often contradictory nature of *Sartor*, see G. B. Tennyson, *Sartor Called Resartus: The Genesis, Structure, and Style of Thomas Carlyle's First Major Work* (Princeton: Princeton University Press, 1965); Albert LaValley, *Carlyle and the Idea of the Modern* (New Haven: Yale University Press, 1968), pp. 56–118; G. H. Brookes, *The Rhetorical Form of Carlyle's Sartor Resartus* (Berkeley: University of California Press, 1972). There is frequently a tendency however to extract definite meaning, and to see Carlyle's humour as simply subserving a serious and moral purpose, without allowing that his vision contains the everlasting interaction of both sides, of the 'no' and the 'yea'. On this see my '"Perpetual Metamorphoses": The Refusal of Certainty in Carlyle's *Sartor Resartus*', *Swansea Review*, 2 (Nov., 1986), pp. 19–36.

7 Carlyle, *Critical and Miscellaneous Essays*, 5 vols (London: Chapman and Hall, 1899), II, p. 89.

8 *Critical and Miscellaneous Essays*, III, p. 3.

9 Ibid, p. 40: 'Metaphysical Speculation, if a necessary evil, is the forerunner of much good . . . The principle of life, which now struggles painfully, in the outer, thin and barren domain of the Conscious or Mechanical, may then withdraw into its inner sanctuaries, its abysses of mystery and miracle; withdraw deeper than ever into that domain of the Unconscious, by nature infinite and inexhaustible; and creatively work there.'

10 Carlyle's own thought, it should be noted, is marked by contradiction: see David Daiches, *Carlyle: The Paradox Reconsidered*, Thomas Green Lectures no. 6 (Edinburgh: The Carlyle Society, 1981).

11 J. R. R. Tolkien, 'On Fairy-Stories', *Tree and Leaf* (London: Allen and Unwin, 1964), pp. 50–3.

12 Though typically he elsewhere praises them, at pp. 67–8.

13 On change see also 'Characteristics', *Critical and Miscellaneous Essays*, III, pp. 37–9.

14 Carlyle's style everywhere manifests some of these tendencies, but never to such a degree as in *Sartor*.

CHAPTER FIVE

George MacDonald

I N GEORGE MACDONALD we have the writer who could fairly be said to be the founder of much modern fantasy. In the strange new worlds he created, his extraordinary range of symbolism and his emphasis on the imagination, he demonstrated the reach and power of fantasy, and released a spring for many subsequent writers. The key to his achievement was the unique place he gave in his work to the powers of the unconscious mind—the forces he saw as latent in the dark and unknown portion of our being. In this he is peculiarly a writer of Scottish fantasy.

Such an interest in the unconscious we have just seen in Carlyle's work. MacDonald owed a considerable debt to Carlyle: his recent biographer William Raeper writes, 'For Carlyle, the great enemy was mechanism, and MacDonald, who read deeply in Carlyle and absorbed many of the same German influences, wrote under his shadow, espousing many of the same theories.'[1] However, we should also bear in mind that an interest in the inner life is, as we saw in the introduction, characteristic of much Scottish fantasy. Further, Carlyle's interest in the unconscious is not so much in the mind itself as in the world, and the sea of divine imagination in which it swims. Nevertheless MacDonald does clearly 'follow' Carlyle: and it will provide a way into his work to show how far this is the case.

MacDonald, brought up in Huntly, Aberdeenshire, experienced similar early Calvinist influences to those of Carlyle. Like Carlyle he studied a science at university—in his case Chemistry and Natural Philosophy (Physics) at Aberdeen University from 1841-5. Like Carlyle too he then felt in himself a deeper religious calling, though in his case it became a specifically Christian one. However, his first ministry, at Trinity Congregational Church at Arundel, came to an early end in 1853 when his parishioners disapproved of numbers of his 'heterodox' opinions, particularly that the heathen might be given a second chance and that animals might be saved. Thereafter, despite a move to the more liberal theological territory of Manchester, MacDonald was unable to secure another living; and for the fifty remaining years of his life had to support himself and his growing family mainly by writing, supplemented by lecturing; and to minister outside the church and in his *Unspoken Sermons*. Thus like Carlyle he had his life to reconstruct for himself, and had to survive by his pen.[2]

With Carlyle MacDonald shared a debt to the German idealists and writers of *Kunstmärchen;*[3] and like Carlyle he believed with them in the supreme creative power of the unconscious imagination. It was probably through reading Carlyle's work, particularly *Sartor Resartus,* that MacDonald developed his own view of the world as a symbolic fabric, a vesture of the eternal, in and beneath which is an immanent, ever-working God. And from Carlyle, as much as from his own experience, he drew his view of a Christianity that existed outside Church and even creed or Bible, found often more at work in the meanest city street than in the finest cathedral. Yet the differences between the two writers are also striking. Carlyle's idealism is all directed towards understanding this world aright, and towards living and working within it: but MacDonald's gaze all his life is more towards the world that lies beyond this one. *Sartor Resartus* is an attempt to make us see this world in a new way; but almost all MacDonald's fantasies describe journeys to worlds that are in some sense fundamentally other than this one. And Carlyle's gaze is directed towards the spiritual improvement of mankind and society, where MacDonald's concern is much more with the development of single individuals—almost all his protagonists are alone. While MacDonald wrote twenty-five novels of 'real life' besides his fantasy, none of them like Carlyle's works displays any commitment to this world or desire to solve its ills by any means but reliance on individual charity and faith in God.

MacDonald's fantasies are few beside his novels, but they embody his deepest literary and spiritual ideals. There are only two substantial adult ones, *Phantastes* (1858) and *Lilith* (1895), written in a fragmentary mode not wholly unlike that of Carlyle's *Sartor,* and for similar 'deconstructionist', 'pro-unconscious' reasons. *Phantastes* was not a literary success and MacDonald turned to writing novels, in part because as his publisher insisted, they 'paid'.[4] (Mrs Oliphant we shall see had to follow a not dissimilar course in her literary career.) But in the interim MacDonald wrote numbers of fantasies for children, including *At the Back of the North Wind* (1871), *The Princess and the Goblin* (1872) and *The Princess and Curdie* (1883), all of which were popular; and several shorter fairy stories, owing debts variously to folk tales, Novalis and his friend Lewis Carroll's work, under the title *Dealings with the Fairies,* in 1867. These children's stories, unlike *Phantastes* and *Lilith,* have clear plots, characters and narrative directions, even if their ultimate vision is often the same. We might explain this by saying that the style of *Phantastes* and *Lilith* is used to break down the rigidities of adult consciousness, while children may be said already to inhabit the unconscious naturally; but we might equally allow that MacDonald saw that writing clearly would ensure broad appeal. But, so far as MacDonald himself was concerned, 'I do not write for children, but for the childlike, whether of five, or fifty, or seventy-five.'[5]

'Unconsciousness' in all its forms, including those of sleep and death, is central to MacDonald's vision in his fantasy. Many of his ideas on the imagination and on the fairy-tale he found in the German Romantic writer Novalis. For Novalis the dream was the true form of reality, and fairy-tales, since they were similarly unstructured, were the highest of literary modes (by 'fairy-tale' Novalis meant its Romantic form, as expressed in the *Märchen* of Goethe or his own fantasy novel *Heinrich von Ofterdingen*, 1802). 'A fairy-tale is like a dream-picture without coherence, a collection of wonderful things and occurrences'; 'Everything is a fairy-tale'; 'Our life is no dream, but it should and will perhaps become one.'[6] The part of the mind which mirrors this is the unconscious imagination. But MacDonald differs from Novalis vitally, in that for him this vision is not wonderful in itself, but because it is immediately shot through with the divine. Beautiful and stimulating though the products of the unconscious imagination may be, they are nothing without God. And God, for MacDonald, lives in that unconscious.[7] Where Carlyle saw the imagination as the route to once more seeing the outside universe to be founded in God, MacDonald brings divine immanence still closer by saying that the workings of the imagination are directly those of God inside man:

> God sits in that chamber of our being in which the candle of our consciousness goes out in darkness, and sends forth from thence wonderful gifts into the light of that understanding which is His candle.[8]

Thus, 'If we . . . consider the so-called creative faculty in man, we shall find that in no *primary* sense is this faculty creative. Indeed a man is rather *being thought* than thinking, when a new thought arises in his mind.'[9] In this way the expressions of the imagination, which MacDonald calls fairy-tales, have God as their true author, though His words may be blurred through the filtering of the human being who does the writing. The only way to understand a fairy-tale will be 'unconsciously' like a child, who lets it work freely on him.[10] The 'best' fairy tale will encourage this state of unconsciousness.

The effect in *Phantastes* is marked. The work presents itself in the aspect of a dream. The central figure, Anodos (Greek for 'having no way' or 'wandering'), awakes one morning to find that the furniture of his bedroom has turned into the natural landscape of Fairy Land, and thereafter journeys through this strange country, happening on even stranger, and, at the narrative level, largely unconnected, beings and adventures, from a carnivorous Ash-tree, an elusive white maiden, an errant knight in rusty armour, a sinister shadow, or a fairy palace, to a trio of giants or a forest church with a wolf as its hidden god. We have no idea of what is coming next: Anodos after a short while says he can 'only act and wander',[11] and that 'it is no use trying to account for things in Fairy Land; and one who travels there soon forgets the very idea of doing so, and takes everything as it comes; like a child, who, being in a chronic condition of wonder, is surprised at nothing' (p. 33). Fairy Land has changing faces, from the wooded aspect of Keats's *Lamia* to marbled interiors suggesting Poe, or giants out of Spenser or folk-tale to a mystic sea-cottage owing something to Novalis. Nor even is Fairy Land the constant context: in the fairy palace, Anodos comes upon a library in which he reads a story of a strange planet with a dead sea, and another tale of magically-blighted love out of the German *Kunstmärchen* tradition; and in each case he does not merely read, but participates in the story, so that it is as real as his own, 'Mine was the whole story' (p. 81).

Part of the impulse here is to erode our categorisations of things, our desire to grasp and know reality: but the point is also to show that 'No shining belt or gleaming moon, no red and green glory in a self-encircling twin-star, but has a relation with the hidden things of a man's soul, and, it may be, with the secret history of his body as well' (p. 83). The violation of the 'fictional microcosm' with interpolated stories thus serves to dissolve away our certainties, to show reality far larger, more mysterious, and more of a piece than we could ever have known. Anodos' shadow, which he acquires in part as a result of his own previous possessiveness within Fairy Land, is partly a symbol of the appropriating tendency of our minds: its effect is to *reduce* phenomena. It kills or blights the living things on which it falls, and it denies wonder. A child with a magical device which embodies the poetic powers of both simile and metaphor, becomes under its gaze 'a commonplace boy, with a rough broad-brimmed straw hat . . . The toys he carried were a multiplying glass and a kaleidoscope' (p. 66). It becomes Anodos' abiding aim to rid himself of this wonder-killing shadow. The style of *Phantastes* seems significant here, for no being or place in it is ever given a name, except for the uncertain name of the hero; and the language continually shifts from the vague or mysterious to the forensic and precise, as though nothing can quite be brought into focus: in this way the fixing power of the shadow is countered. This is Anodos when he sees the form of a reposing woman in a block of alabaster he finds in a cave:

> I could not see the expression of the whole. What I did see appeared to me perfectly lovely; more near the face that had been born with me in my soul, than anything I had seen before in nature or art. The actual outlines of the rest of the form were so indistinct, that the more than semi-opacity of the alabaster seemed insufficient to account for the fact; and I conjectured that a light robe added its obscurity.
>
> (pp. 44–5)

The emotional response of the second sentence is countered by the tone of clinical analysis in the next.

It is possible for us to detect certain patterns in *Phantastes*. For instance, the white lady that Anodos eventually releases from the marble through song seems related to a statue of a woman he also finds in the fairy palace and again sings into life; and this woman is met again through the narrative. The shadow Anodos acquires is responsible for several of his acts of possessiveness and pride through the story. And possessiveness is his fault with the white lady: every time he releases her he tries to seize her and is rebuffed. Actually she was herself previously 'seized' in the sense of being a statue. We begin to see that possessiveness itself is a 'theme' in the story: and there are other features of it related to this. Anodos early on meets two evil creatures, a predatory Ash-tree and a seducing Alder-tree which seek to possess and then to devour him; two interpolated stories describe people who are selfish in love, and one, the story of a strange planet where lovers live apart and 'die of their desire' (p. 87), seems to question the reverse behaviour also. Later Anodos feels misplaced pride at his part in the slaying of three giants that menaced a kingdom, and ends up shut in a tower of his own self-admiring egoism. The end of the story, after Anodos gives away his lady for another, and gives his life to save other people, makes the theme explicit: 'I knew now, that it is by loving, and not by being loved, that one can come nearest the soul of another; yea, that where two love, it is the loving of each other, and not the being beloved by each other, that originates and perfects and assures their blessedness' (p. 179). Perhaps this last is an instance of MacDonald putting his human interpretations on to the material welling up from the unconscious—seeking as it were to possess his own material. He once asked of his readership, 'A fairytale, a sonata, a gathering storm, a limitless night, seizes you and sweeps you away: do you begin at once to wrestle with it and ask whence its power over you, whither it is carrying you?'[12] Perhaps on occasion, as a creator of a mystifying fantasy of the unconscious, one is tempted to help oneself and one's readers to understand it a little.

Nevertheless there remains quite enough mystery at the heart of the book to resist even this kind of possessiveness. Indeed it may be that the mixture of ascertainable significance and lack of it is a larger mirror of the mixture of precision and vagueness in the style; and that each undercuts the other, so that we can rest on neither clarity nor the lack of it. The book is full of symbols and events that resist patterning while speaking powerfully. Why is an Ash-tree the predator of the woods? What is the significance of the fairy palace with its strange pool, its mystic library, its many halls of dancers? Who is the old woman who lives in a submersible cottage in the midst of the sea? As these images pass before us, each one as strange as the last, each floating up from some secret depth in the narrative, with no obvious interconnection, displacing any assumptions we might make, dissolving our ability to make interpretations, we enter a kind of subconscious mode of comprehension, begin to feel too that what we are experiencing is a series of pictures emerging from the depths of a mind. Another way of putting this is to say that *Phantastes*, as its name suggests, is a picture of the imagination, the creative unconscious, which here is that of Anodos, who in entering Fairy Land may be seen as having gone into his own mental darkness. Because of the way the style works on us, we may not feel we are merely reading a book, but that we are responding to an immediately active sequence. In the potent fairy books Anodos found in the library of the palace, he felt himself not a reader but a participant in the adventures, and one book 'glowed and flashed the thoughts upon the soul, with such a power that the medium disappeared from the consciousness, and it was occupied only with the things themselves' (p. 89).

Only by such means will we be able to feel that the dreaming mind that is *Phantastes* is not solely the mind of Anodos himself, lit by the riot of merely neurotic phantoms, but that it is part of a larger Dreamer. Part of the paradox here is that the work so readily lends itself to Freudian or Jungian analysis in terms of mother symbols.[13] MacDonald's picture of the unconscious here is no facile one: he gives full scope to it in its aspect of a jungle of secret urges, and as a picture of the innermost and most naked forms of the best and worst desires that govern our lives;[14] but he lets that jungle shimmer before us, now and then piercing through to a further apprehension of a deeper reality of which our lives are but a distortion. Of this Anodos' elusive white lady, who threads Fairy Land, and the wholly untaught songs that well from Anodos to wake her, are perhaps symbols. And of this perhaps the mystic bath in the fairy palace, the benign moon, the cottage in the sea or the sudden visions of the purity of Fairy Land may be a more direct experience. 'A man may well himself discover truth in what he wrote; for he was dealing all the time with things that came from thoughts beyond his own.'[15]

Yet there is a sense of elegy about *Phantastes*, the feeling that somehow the full experience of Fairy Land's potential has eluded Anodos. However heroic it is in him, he still has to give up the white lady to her knight, still has to die out of Fairy Land through an act of sacrifice, and even has to leave the rich life he enjoys beyond death, 'dying' back into the old life as a mortal man, 'Sinking from such a state of ideal bliss, into the world of shadows which again closed around and infolded me' (p. 180). Back home, he feels the loss of the promise of his journey: 'Thus I, who set out to find my Ideal, came back rejoicing that I had lost my Shadow.' Earlier he had remarked, 'Alas! I brought nothing with me out of Fairy Land, but memories—memories' (p. 40). At the end, he is left doubting whether he will be able to translate his experience of Fairy Land into his everyday life or will have to live it over again. All he seems to have left is the intuition that his friend the Beech tree of Fairy Land speaks to him distantly through the leaves of a tree in his own world, telling him that '"A great good is coming—is coming—is coming to thee, Anodos"': an assertion to which he resolutely commits his trust as he ends:

> Yet I know that good is coming to me—that good is always coming; though few have at all times the simplicity and the courage to believe it. What we call evil, is the only and best shape, which, for the person and his condition at the time, could be assumed by the best good. And so, *Farewell*.

For all its originality and power—indeed because of them—*Phantastes* did not make MacDonald much money, and the reviews were at best mixed, some finding it confusing, others a singular experiment. (*Lilith* was to have a still less happy reception from the reviewers.) It was not till this century, and particularly through C. S. Lewis, that its importance and power came to be realised.[16] After its publication, MacDonald wrote little for five years apart from a Celtic tale of second sight, *The Portent* (1864); but then he embarked on a career of (Christian) novel writing, from which he was to derive both pleasure and the makings of a living. His children's fantasies fitted more readily than *Phantastes* into a ready-made market for such works, even while in themselves they constituted a revolution in Victorian juvenile fantasy. It was not till the end of his literary life that MacDonald felt prepared to return to the radical literary mode of *Phantastes*, in his other adult fantasy, *Lilith* (1895).

Lilith, written in the same destructured idiom, forms a companion piece with *Phantastes*. Both involve a young man just come of age who enters and explores a strange realm before being returned to this world. The central figure Vane finds himself in the 'region of the seven dimensions' when he follows a bent old man up to the attic of his house and through a huge mirror. In this new world Vane, like Anodos, becomes enamoured of a woman (Lilith) he brings to life, here by saving her from a giant leech that comes to suck her blood by night: but she is as evil as the Maid of the Alder in *Phantastes*. During the early stages of his (several) visits to this strange bare land, Vane is invited by the figure he followed there (who turns out to be a form of Adam) to visit his cottage. There he meets Eve also, and is shown a huge dormitory full of sleeping dead below the ground: she and Adam invite him to lie down on an empty bed prepared for him and sleep to await the cock-crow of eternity, but he refuses and flees. After this his adventures are haphazard, involving encounters with dancing skeletons, a group of children called the Little Ones, the evil woman Lilith with whom he falls in love, the people of a city called Bulika, and a mass of hideous monsters in a place called the Bad Burrow; until in the end he returns with many of those he has met to Adam's house to sleep. Though there is much more interconnection of the adventures than in *Phantastes*, and though unlike Anodos Vane stays in the same area of the fantastic land, *Lilith* still has quite enough of fragmentation, from the sheer diversity and tenuous links of its characters, events and symbols, to approach the dream-like quality of *Phantastes*. In both books the final chapter quotes Novalis, 'Our life is no dream, but it should and will perhaps become one.' Vane is reassured that his dream was not of his own making, but given to him by God.

But the two works are also very different. In *Phantastes* the strange world entered is in part symbol of this mortal and fallen life; but in *Lilith* the region of the seven dimensions is the world beyond death, with hell, purgatory and heaven. God as the basis of the dream is more remote or hidden in *Phantastes*, where in *Lilith* the Christian element is much more evident, with Adam, Eve, Lilith, the Great Shadow (Satan), Jesus, the Last Days, God Himself; the last being reached, through a narrative that has amounted to a process of deepening spiritual awareness, at the end, when Vane finally approaches the clouded throne of the Ancient of Days. We feel in *Phantastes* that everything for the time revolves about Anodos, whose story this is, and whose inner mind is the landscape; but in *Lilith* 'other people' matter as much as Vane, who will be only one of the sleepers in the multitudinous house of the dead. In *Lilith* Vane may be dreaming; but he may as readily be being dreamt by someone else. Where in *Phantastes* we dealt with the unconscious in an individual, here we deal much more with that of the race, the collective human unconscious in God—which may in part be why we have reference to traditional personages, symbols and narratives from the Bible. We have moved in a sense closer to God in this book, stripping away the obscuring individuality and mortality of *Phantastes*. The landscape of *Phantastes* was largely wooded and confusing, and there was little connection between Anodos' adventures; in *Lilith* the country is much barer, and events as we saw cohere much more. It would not be impossible to see *Lilith* as a deepening analysis of *Phantastes*—to put the two works together as a journey through the changing strata of the imagination towards God. MacDonald indeed saw *Lilith* as a mandate sent to him direct by God.[17]

Phantastes and *Lilith* may also be seen as joined together, through their very differences, into one huge Christian fantasy.[18] For it is possible to see *Phantastes* as dealing with the first part of Christian history, where *Lilith* evidently describes the last. For one thing, *Phantastes* is very much concerned with the idea of making and creating, has a protagonist who is a poet, and is scattered with songs, stories and poems and reflections on their nature: the hint that Fairy Land itself is a larger version of one of Anodos' songs, or a story like the interpolated one about life on the strange planet, is continually present. Fairy Land too often suggests a paradise, but one now so frequently obscured by the monsters of fallen passion or diseased imagination, that only from time to time does its original purity gleam through the murk (for example, pp. 61, 78). And when through disobedience Anodos acquires a shadow that blights all he sees, we feel that there has been something in the nature of a fall in Fairy Land.

At the end of the narrative we find Anodos turned to a sacrificing Christ figure as he lays down his life to rescue ignorant forest worshippers from their delusion. *Lilith*, on the other hand, is clearly concerned with death and resurrection at the end of time. If we were to see *Phantastes* and *Lilith* as portraying First and Last Things in this way, then it would be reasonable to ask whether the fairy-tales published by MacDonald between them fill in some of the middle stages of this Christian history.

The books can be seen as linked, at a less specifically Christian level, by the way they balance or invert one another.[19] In *Phantastes* Anodos meets a number of maternal figures, and gradually has to learn how to live his life independent of them; but in *Lilith* Vane must learn to be passive, to give himself up and lie down and sleep. Anodos enters Fairy Land when he is asleep, and throughout the story must come increasingly awake and aware—one sign of which is the way he becomes more purposive as the story goes on. Vane, on the contrary, enters the region of the seven dimensions in full wakefulness, continually asking, or being asked questions by the strange Mr Raven; he comes to leave his conscious mind behind, and enter the unconscious tide of the universe. In *Phantastes* Anodos is frequently being asked *not* to do things, but Vane is invited to do and to give way. *Phantastes* in contrast to *Lilith* is full of people being woken up—the white lady, the enchanted lady in the story of Cosmo von Wehrstahl, the ignorant worshippers at the end. *Phantastes* too has a linear plot: Anodos goes 'on, and . . . through' Fairy Land (p. 61), moving always eastward, never re-crossing any land. *Lilith* has Vane in one place, indeed in a sense he never leaves his house: his adventures in the 'region of the seven dimensions' continually circle about the cottage of Adam and Eve, until at last he enters it. Anodos goes forward spiritually, but Vane's development is rather towards an understanding and acceptance of his identity—or, in Mr Raven's words, '"No one can say he is himself, until first he knows that he *is*, and then what *himself* is"' (p. 196). Thus *Phantastes* is concerned more with spiritual becoming (what is it to be?), and *Lilith* with spiritual being (what is being?); the one is more involved with ethics, the other with ontology. In *Phantastes* the hero is prepared for a life in the mortal world; in *Lilith* Vane has to ready himself for eternity.

While *Lilith* and *Phantastes* go together, *Lilith* still has its own individuality and way of working on us. MacDonald's art here, if we can call it that, may be in part that of the grotesque. In *Phantastes* Anodos inhabits a semi-medieval landscape into which most of the various jarring elements are merged: but in *Lilith* there is much more of a sense of the opposition of the various elements and of their extreme peculiarities. (Certainly the very story describes constant warfare, between Lilith and all other mortals, or the Little Ones and the Giants, or the fighting dead, or Mara and Lilith, where *Phantastes* has no such conflict.) Here we have a silent librarian who turns into a loquacious raven talking metaphysics, and this bird into Adam himself; a pair of married skeletons engaged in a violent dispute; and two 'women', one good, one evil, who both assume the forms of leopardesses by night. Each element of the story is bizarre in itself and still more so together with the others. The effect is like that violent yoking-together of heterogeneous ideas (as Dr Johnson put it) that we see in metaphysical poetry. There is also a sense of strain that comes from the way many elements of the story have been pitched to the point of becoming repulsive: this ranges from the sugary sentimentality of the Little Ones in their nests, for example referring to Christ as the '"beautifullest man"' saying to them, '"'Ou's all mine's, 'ickle ones: come along!"' (p. 416), to the account of the 'heavy squelch' as Lilith throws a woman, now reduced to 'a pulpy mass', from a window in Bulika (p. 299), or the amputation of Lilith's evil hand by Adam with his sword to make her repent (pp. 389–90). In a sense the highest spiritual matters are linked to the lowest or most repugnant emotional or physical ones: if we are talking of likeness to metaphysical poetry, it is Richard Crashaw who comes first to mind here.

In one way the style of uniting extreme opposites could suggest the compositional power of God: thus hyacinths in the region of the seven dimensions grow through a piano in Vane's house in his own world (pp. 203–4), the raven in the faërian cemetery turns the worms of the earth to beautiful flying things (p. 201), or a pigeon is transformed to a prayer (p. 206). This is also suggested in the way faërian truth exists by inversion of our normal modes of understanding, as when Mr Raven tells Vane, '"the more doors you go out of, the farther you get in!"' (p. 194), or '"Nothing but truth can appear; and whatever is must seem"' (p. 272)—indeed also by the very marriage of the juggling intellect to deep spiritual realities. But the violence of this union is matched by the tension of potential discord. The world Vane finds is one of dis-joining: Lilith has been banished by Adam, on whose kind she preys, the Little Ones and the Giants are polarised opposites, the landscape is one of severed communities—Bulika here, the Little Ones there, somewhere else the warring dead, the Bad Burrow, Mara's cottage. Even the faculties of the mind seem scattered, if we consider the intellect as residing with Adam, sentiment with the Little Ones, passion with Lilith, soul with Mara. The idea of *Lilith* is that all come together, as Lilith is brought to Adam's cottage to be healed and to sleep, and as the Little Ones also lie down there; the motif that concludes the book is one of atonement ('at-one-ment'), '"Death shall be the atonemaker; you shall sleep together"' (p. 386). But still there remains the sense to us that this yoking-together is as much forced as real, because of the very extremity of the opposites involved: certainly the way Lilith is forced to repent, to cease to be her self, is instructive here. At this level, the book might rather be said to be mirroring the broken condition of reality as we know it, as much as the uniting force of God. And at this level too the style of the book begins to confess itself inadequate, the language of man rather than of God:

> . . . it involves a constant struggle to say what cannot be said with even an approach to precision, the things recorded being, in their nature and in that of the creatures concerned in them, so inexpressibly different from any possible events of this economy, that I can present them only by giving, in the forms and language of life in this world, the modes in which they affected me—not the things themselves, but the feelings they woke in me.
>
> (p. 227)

The divine truths that are taught by such startling means in *Lilith* are conveyed more gently and indirectly in MacDonald's fairy-tales for children.[20] *At the Back of the North Wind* (1871) never goes quite the overtly Christian distance of *Lilith*: there may be some who will feel that because of that it gets further. The North Wind blows on Diamond through chinks in his bedroom at night, and calls him out to meet her. She is a grand lady, who says she has to carry out her work, some of it terrible to human life, but because of a far-off song, which is coming nearer, she knows all will be well in the end. She takes Diamond on several aerial journeys, and shows him her work. Once, she takes him to the North Pole and he goes through her to the country at her back: it is a place of wonder that almost breaks his heart, but he can remember no more than fragments of it, and those to whom he speaks of it think he has been dreaming, or else has '"a tile loose"'.[21] In between these journeys we follow Diamond's life as a cab-man's son in London. The narrative is thus a mixture of seemingly mundane city life, exciting supernatural journeys through the wider world, and mystic significances in what is the ultimate journey, to North Wind's back.

This mixture gives a peculiarly Christian effect in that it suggests the marriage of God and man, magic and mortality, even as God's sub-vicar North Wind comes down to Diamond. Stranger suggestions are present in the names of some of the characters and places—Mr Raymond (ray of the world), Joseph and Martha (Diamond's parents), Paradise Row, Dulcimer (Diamond's baby sister), The Wilderness, Mr Dyves; and names relating to crystals, Mr Coleman, old Sal, Ruby, Diamond.[22] These names have some of them allegorical, some of them symbolic and biblical meaning: but the fact that they occur together with more ordinary ones such as Nanny, Mr Evans, London, Mrs Crump, Hoxton, once again suggests the interpenetration of the ordinary and the divine. The very structure of the book, continually slipping between world and world, conveys this interpenetration: in *Phantastes* and *Lilith* there was much more sense of leaving this world behind, as Anodos and Vane went into other realms.

A central idea behind the book is that there may be much more to a person or thing than we think. Diamond is a London child, but he is also a child for whom Christ came down; and in his ordinary acts of driving a cab for his father or singing to his baby brother, he is living within the idiom of Christ: 'The little boy was just as much one of God's messengers as if he had been an angel with a flaming sword, going out to fight the devil' (p. 148). North Wind is 'only' the wind, but she is also pain, suffering and death; and beyond that, as part of the song of the universe, she is a sub-vicar of God, imbued with something of His dreadful love and power. Even the horse, Ruby, may turn out to be an angel in disguise. Diamond may have seen North Wind in his dreams, but those dreams are real pictures of the world and of the precincts of Heaven. Where in *Phantastes* and *Lilith* the dream takes us further into the mind, in *At the Back of the North Wind* we move outwards to the whole world and beyond. Here dreams, like illnesses, or even death, are not the true forms of reality: they are the cloaks under which the divine makes itself known to mortal life.

All of MacDonald's fantasies that we have looked at so far take us from one world to another, the real to the fantastic one. But in the 'Curdie' books, *The Princess and the Goblin* (1872) and *The Princess and Curdie* (1883), we are in the same world all the time. That world is one out of Grimm and the German Romantic fairy-tale writers, the realm of the *Märchen*, with a castle, mines, and a walled city across a barren wilderness; and the characters are a humble hero, who has a princess to rescue or a kingdom to save, a helpful old woman, and a group of wicked fairies. This world bears analogous or mythic rather than direct relationship to ours. It is what Tolkien would have called a 'sub-created' or secondary world (rather like his own Middle-earth, or Mervyn Peake's Gormenghast),[23] a 'new' nature or country with its own rules and operations without reference to ours; and it is one of the first significant ones in modern fantasy. Here we look not directly at the imagination itself, or at its operation, but rather at one of its finished products. This world is one which 'could still be going on' when we have shut the book. Its solidity seems almost reinforced by the rocky medium in which both stories are set.

The Princess and the Goblin has two centres. One involves the 'story': the young Princess Irene has been left under care in his country castle by her 'King-papa'; the goblins who live in mines beneath plot to seize her and the kingdom by marrying her to their Prince Harelip; but Curdie, the son of one of the miners in the human part of the mine, saves Irene, helped unknown to him by a strange old lady Irene has got to know in the attics of her home. This lady is the other centre of the book. She has little to do with what goes on below stairs, except in helping Irene to rescue Curdie at one point. At first, she seems an old woman with a spinning wheel, with the quaint belief that she is Irene's 'great-great-grandmother': but later she appears as a grand and beautiful woman surrounded by mystic doves, a moon-like light and a fire of burning roses. Once, after Irene has got dirty helping Curdie in the mines, she puts her in a silver bath that seems to have no bottom, 'but the stars shining miles away, as it seemed, in a great blue gulf', while from somewhere the lady sings a song that gives her deep joy.[24] Much of Irene's time with her is spent in conversation and in being shown these magic things. This mystic lady seems almost more concerned with being than with doing, with that side of life concerned with contemplation rather than action. The two centres of the book contrast in these terms. To the aspect of contemplation one can add the way Irene sees or rather is allowed to see more of the lady's nature every time she meets her, so that the quaint old fairy-tale lady out of Grimm or Andersen in her first meeting gradually becomes a mystic woman of almost seraphic power. When Irene is placed in the bottomless bath, her 'contemplation' of the lady's nature has also reached its own full depth. And we may remark, this happens just as Curdie in the mines has finally plumbed the goblins' mining intentions, and sees that they are digging towards the king's house. Thus the 'action' side and the 'contemplation' side of the story interweave with one another, suggesting, like 'Irene', peace or divine stillness at the heart of life—like the deep soul or God in man, like the lady in relation to this book.

This is also seen in the symbolism of the book's setting. We have the goblins who live in the mines beneath, the humans who live on the surface and the mystic lady living at the top of the castle. These can be paralleled to the three levels of the mind—the sub-conscious, the conscious and the super-conscious, or, in Freudian terms, the id, the ego and the superego.[25] The stairs that lead to the old lady are the stairs up to the 'wider vision' (MacDonald was always fascinated by stairs):[26] we notice how each time Irene climbs them the lady seems to expand further beyond the walls of her room, whether in passing through it into the night, or in revealing the bottomless bath; the process goes still further in *The Princess and Curdie* where the walls disappear altogether to leave 'the great sky, and the stars, and beneath . . . nothing—only darkness!' (p. 215). The goblins, by contrast, are enclosed in their caverns, and finally choked in them by the flood released by Curdie. The symbolic shape suggested is not simply a vertical, but a funnel spreading out into the heavens. And yet, such symbolism is for MacDonald only one way of putting it. Elsewhere as we have seen he can speak of God as working in the depths of our unconscious imaginations, sending up wonderful gifts and images to the surface. And in *The Princess and Curdie* we are to find that the old lady has now also become a habituée of the mines, known to the local miners as Old Mother Wotherwop. In *The Princess and the goblin* MacDonald has polarised the two aspects of the same faculty, the imagination *in* the one full of corrupt and monstrous images in goblin shape, the other pregnant with divine symbols, but both chaotic and dreamlike—because in this book he is peculiarly intent on opening our gaze upwards and outwards. Every mystic object or action of the lady's, up there in the attic between earth and heaven points us further: if she is the soul, she is also suggestive of an angel operative within the universe.

But we should not over-emphasise the transcendent aspect of the book. It is also very human, domestic and even comical. If contemplation is one of the centres, action is the other. If the old lady (and the feminine) is at the heart of one side of the book, Curdie is the main figure in the other. And Irene 'relates to' this mortal youth Curdie as much as to the lady: her relations are pre-sexual or simply those of boy and girl with him, if they are strange or mystical with the lady. And there is also the element of class, with Curdie as the poor miner's son and Irene as the princess—even if Curdie is too bold and Irene too naturally friendly to mention it. Page after page of the book is full of Curdie's comments on the habits of goblins or his sometimes comic dealings with them (stamping on their over-sensitive feet); or of Irene's conversations with her slightly careless and ignorant nurse Lootie; or of the extremely natural interactions of Irene as a slightly nervous young girl with her great-great-grandmother—now having her dress cleaned, now being bathed, now being given a ball of thread, even if all these things are also magical at the same time. Indeed Irene's relations with the mystic lady herself are a striking blend of the domestic and the supernatural.

> 'It is so silly of people—I don't mean you, for you are such a tiny, and couldn't know better—but it *is* so silly of people to fancy that old age means crookedness and witheredness and feebleness and sticks and spectacles and rheumatism and forgetfulness! It is so silly! Old age has nothing whatever to do with all that. The right old age means strength and beauty and mirth and courage and clear eyes and strong painless limbs. I am older than you are able to think, and— '
>
> 'And look at you, grandmother!' cried Irene, jumping up and flinging her arms about her neck.
>
> (p. 86)

Even in *At the Back of the North Wind* there was not this sort of relationship between Diamond and North Wind; and there will not be between the old lady and Curdie in *The Princess and Curdie*.

In *The Princess and Curdie* we are much more continuously involved in the world. The king, who at the end of *The Princess and the Goblin* took Irene away with him, is now old and sick, and at the mercy of a powerful faction of his subjects, who seek to end his life and seize power by slowly poisoning him with false medicines. Curdie, trained by the mystic old lady, and with a band of extraordinary beast-helpers, sets out for the city of Gwyntystorm to effect a rescue. He is able to save the king, and at a subsequent battle, in which the doves of the old lady take part as winged javelins, the evil forces are overthrown and the old king restored; Irene and Curdie marry, and later rule the kingdom. But victory is short-lived, for we learn that, after their deaths without issue, the people return to their evil ways, and Gwyntystorm is destroyed. The view seems that restoration of the world is insecure, and only transformation of the spirit may remain, and perhaps find for itself a more lasting habitation outside mortality.

This is a darker book than *The Princess and the Goblin*: but necessarily. Irene and Curdie are here young adults confronting a threat to their world rather than a semi-comical plot against Irene herself. (Though it is true that in almost all MacDonald's work comedy is confined to childhood.) The concern is man's materialism. Curdie at the outset has sunk from the scepticism that prevented him from seeing the old lady in *The Princess and the Goblin* to the beginnings of mere selfish materialism; but he is rescued from this by the lady. The 'citizens' of Gwyntystorm live only for profit, and a cabal of them are at work to kill the king and seize the kingdom. The book begins and ends with direct images of materiality in the form of the ores that miners take from the ground—permissible where used for social good, but self-destructive when seized with greed.

In this book there is a divorce between matter and spirit, not a marriage, as in the previous books. North Wind said that people saw her in a good or evil shape depending on the nature of their vision, but here no such link is finally present: the old lady may tell Curdie and his father in the mine that the way people see her depends on the sort of people they are, but she actually states the position as a dualism, '"Shapes are only dresses, Curdie, and dresses are only names. That which is inside is the same all the time"' (p. 209). Evil is thus much harder to detect here. Curdie can only tell the inner spiritual nature of any creature after his hands have been specially (and agonisingly) treated in the lady's strange rose-fire. Otherwise we have in Gwyntystorm a whole range of greedy or hypocritical people whose true bestial selves are hidden. So too the crazy animal forms of the creatures that accompany Curdie are no longer an index to their natures. This is the shape of the 'dog' Lina that Curdie meets in the lady's room:

She had a very short body, and very long legs made like an
elephant's, so that in lying down she kneeled with both pairs.
Her tail, which dragged on the floor behind her, was twice as
long and quite as thick as her body. Her head was something
between that of a polar bear and a snake. Her eyes were dark
green, with a yellow light in them. Her under teeth came up
like a fringe of icicles, only very white, outside of her upper
lip. Her throat looked as if the hair had been plucked off. It
showed a skin white and smooth.

(pp. 222–3)

Yet inside this grotesque and terrifying body Curdie feels, when asked
to hold Lina's paw, the hand of a child.

This book has certain affinities with *Lilith*. In some ways it stands to *The
Princess and the Goblin* as *Lilith* does to *Phantastes*. Here imagery of division
and oppugnancy rather than of reconciliation prevails. Here we are with
societies rather than with the individual. And here we look with more
hope to death than to life. There is a strong sense of death, 'good' death,
in *The Princess and Curdie*. Images of sacrifice, of purgatorial punishment,
of the dissolution of the body, recur in it; and there is a feeling of some
further world beyond this through the sacramental imagery in the book
(particularly of the 'old lady', who here seems more clearly an angel). This
is reinforced by the sense of great spiritual pressure, and of an author
who speaks often directly from some further region of understanding:
'There is this difference between the growth of some human beings and
that of others: in the one case it is a continuous dying, in the other a
continuous resurrection' (p. 180). At the heart of the book, in the midst
of the darkness and the spiritual bolts of lightning cast against the sinful,
we feel a hint of the world poised on the edge of transformation, about to
pass away beyond the old husk to a new and more glorious form. This
is part of the song that Curdie hears the lady sing as she spins:

> The stars are spinning their threads
> And the clouds are the dust that flies,
> And the suns are weaving them up
> For the time when the sleepers shall rise.
>
> The ocean in music rolls,
> And gems are turning to eyes,
> And the trees are gathering souls,
> For the day when the sleepers shall rise.
> (p. 217)[27]

Apart from his longer children's fantasies, MacDonald also wrote a
number of shorter fairy-tales, many of them published as *Dealings with
the Fairies* (1867). These are extremely various, ranging from the comic
'The Light Princess', in which the heroine is cursed with a lack of gravity

in both senses of the word, to 'The Carasoyn', in which fairies who have stolen human children are made to return them, or 'The Giant's Heart', in which children who have escaped from a wicked giant find his heart where he has put it 'out to nurse' and try to reform him under threat. Nearly all the stories deal with an outwitting of the supernatural, with which no relationship is established as in MacDonald's other fantasy. These tales are often *jeux d'esprit*, less closely linked to MacDonald's deepest impulses.

One exception here is 'The Golden Key', owing more to Novalis and the German Romantic fairy-tale than to the traditional tale: this describes two children journeying through a strange symbolic landscape to reach a country above them, 'whence the shadows fall'. This story is like *Phantastes* in that it is a journey both through the world as seen by the divine imagination, and through the unconscious itself; but unlike *Phantastes* the divine is here much clearer, and the images, rather than expressing the hero's confusions and mortality, all point forward to deeper and higher levels of awareness, united in the girl Tangle's journey downwards into the depths of the earth and the boy Mossy's pilgrimage upwards to a mountain.[28]

If we now put together all the fantasies by MacDonald we have looked at, we can see how they share certain characteristics. An interest in dreams is seen in many of them: *Phantastes*, 'The Golden Key' and *Lilith* have dream-structures, North Wind in *At the Back of the North Wind* visits Diamond only when he is asleep, and Irene in *The Princess and the Goblin* is the only one to see her 'grandmother'. Their landscapes or settings are often suggestive of the unconscious mind (even down to the mountain described at the beginning of *The Princess and Curdie*, thrown up from the molten fire in the earth's darkness beneath). Death too is a recurrent motif: Anodos has to die out of his old self, Vane has to lie down in death with the sleepers in Adam's house, Diamond's acquaintance with North Wind ends in his death, Mossy and Tangle leave this world. Death and sleep are closely intertwined, and so too dreaming: to dream aright one must let go of the conscious self, and the true condition of life both before and after death is that of a dream. Again, a vein of otherworldliness runs through these works: though Anodos and Vane are forced back into this world at the end of their stories, they long for the divine realms they have glimpsed; Mossy and Tangle reach the land 'whence the shadows fall'; Diamond arrives at the back of the North Wind; the mortal world that Irene and Curdie save soon fails again and they must look to be better hope of another.

There is also something of a pattern of development among these works. In *Phantastes* and *Lilith* reality is frail: one's bedroom may turn to a faërian glade, the attic of one's house may open on the 'region of the seven dimensions'; and faërie itself may collapse under one, as Anodos and Vane are removed from it at the ends of their stories. Neither of these books has a clear ending, or closure. *At the Back of the North Wind* also shifts from one kind of reality to another, but now as much to show the true nature of this world as to move us to another realm. The Curdie books keep us wholly within one world, if *The Princess and Curdie* bids us look beyond its travails. It could be said that reality is less secure in *Phantastes* and *Lilith* because the first deals with (poetic) creation, the inception of things, and the second with their ending: so that in either case the world is unstable, either not fully formed or losing form. This of course is not the case with the 'middle' books: and we might assign them to the middle stages of (Christian) history, where the other two deal with the First and the Last Things. Thus the issues in those middle books are much more moral conduct in this world, faith in the unseen in the midst of an obscuring medium, and the overcoming of greed and materialism. Taken together, the whole journey, if we may call it that, of MacDonald in his fantasy is like that of Anodos in *Phantastes* going into, through and out of Fairy Land.

But for MacDonald development does not mean only the linear, and certainly not any wholesale superseding of the past. We do not simply 'go on, and . . . through', but like Anodos or Vane return to the houses we started from. And the best of the past must remain continually present, if we are to develop at all: 'He who will be a man, and will not be a child, must—he cannot help himself—become a little man, that is, a dwarf.'[29] So *Phantastes* and *Lilith* form a circle of development, and we begin and end with the mining of a mountain in the 'Princess' books, and Anodos and Vane are returned to the world having for the time lost Fairy Land or bliss, but with new knowledge of their own natures and of that of the creation about them.

> For the movements of man's life are in spirals: we go back whence we came, ever returning on our former traces, only upon a higher level, on the next upward coil of the spiral, so that it is a going back and a going forward ever and both at once.[30]

Notes

1　William Raeper, *George MacDonald* (Tring, Herts.: Lion Publishing, 1987), p. 183.
2　On MacDonald's life, see Raeper, and Greville MacDonald, *George MacDonald and His Wife* (London: Allen and Unwin, 1924).
3　On MacDonald's German sources, see R. L. Wolff, *The Golden Key: A Study of the Fiction of George MacDonald* (New Haven: Yale University Press, 1961).

4 *George MacDonald and His Wife*, p. 318.
5 MacDonald 'The Fantastic Imagination', *A Dish of Orts: Chiefly Papers on the Imagination, and on Shakspere* (London: Sampson Low, 1893), p. 317.
6 Translated from Novalis, *Fragmente* (1798–9), in *Schriften*, eds Paul Kluckhohn and Richard Samuel, 3 vols (Stuttgart: Kohlhammer, 1960–8), III, p. 454, no. 986; p. 377, no. 620; and p. 281, no. 237.
7 See also my *Modern Fantasy: Five Studies* (Cambridge: Cambridge University Press, 1975), ch. 3.
8 MacDonald, 'The Imagination', *A Dish of Orts*, p. 25.
9 Ibid., p. 4.
10 'The Fantastic Imagination', pp. 321–2.
11 MacDonald, *Phantastes and Lilith* (London: Gollancz, 1962), p. 40. References for both *Phantastes* and *Lilith* are to this edition.
12 'The Fantastic Imagination', p. 319. MacDonald protests a shade too much in this essay that he will not assign a definite meaning to his fairy-tales—see pp. 316–21.
13 See e.g. Wolff, op.cit.; David Holbrook, Introduction to *Phantastes* (London: Dent, 1983); and C. N. Manlove, 'Circularity in Fantasy: George MacDonald', *The Impulse of Fantasy Literature* (London: Macmillan, 1983), esp. pp. 82–3, 164–5.
14 See e.g. 'The Imagination', p. 25: 'If the dark portion of our own being were the origin of our imaginations, we might well fear the apparition of such monsters as would be generated in the sickness of a decay which could never feel—only declare—a slow return towards primeval chaos. But the Maker is our Light.'
15 'The Fantastic Imagination', p. 321.
16 Lewis records his first momentous encounter with *Phantastes* (in 1916) in his *Surprised by Joy: The Shape of my Early Life* (London: Bles, 1955), pp. 168–71. See also his assessment of *Phantastes* and others of MacDonald's fantasies in his *George MacDonald: An Anthology* (London: Bles, 1946), pp. 14–18, repr. in *Phantastes and Lilith*, pp. 8–11.
17 *George MacDonald and His Wife*, p. 548. This did not prevent him from trying to clarify God's message through six manuscript revisions.
18 Manlove, 'The Circle of the Imagination', pp. 74–92.
19 Ibid.
20 On the children's fantasies, see also my *Christian Fantasy: from 1200 to the Present* (London: Macmillan, 1992), pp. 164–82 *passim*.
21 MacDonald, *At the Back of the North Wind* (London: Dent, 1956), p. 251. References are to this edition.
22 These observations have been made by Lesley Smith (née Willis), in an unpublished book, 'George MacDonald's Fantasy for Children: "Light Out of Darkness" in *At the Back of the North Wind*, *The Princess and the Goblin* and *The Princess and Curdie*', chs 1, 2; she provides a

fascinating biblical and Jungian interpretation of *At the Back of the North Wind*.

23 Tolkien, 'On Fairy-Stories', *Tree and Leaf* (London: Allen and Unwin, 1964), pp. 43–50 (section on 'fantasy').

24 MacDonald, *The Princess and the Goblin and The Princess and Curdie*, ed. Roderick McGillis (Oxford: Oxford University Press, 1990), p. 124. References to both works are to this edition.

25 See e.g. Tony Tanner, 'Mountains and Depths—An Approach to Nineteenth-Century Dualism', *Review of English Literature*, 3, 4 (Oct., 1962), pp. 52–4. Compare also MacDonald, *Malcolm* (London: Henry S. King, 1875), II, p. 157, where we are told, 'The cellars are the metaphysics, the garrets the poetry of the house'; and the garrets are 'in harmony with the highest spiritual instincts'.

26 *George MacDonald and His Wife*, pp. 347–9, 481–2, 530.

27 For a fuller consideration of this song, see Manlove, *Christian Fantasy*, pp. 174–6.

28 See also *Christian Fantasy*, pp. 168–9, on the symbolism of the story.

29 'The Fantastic Imagination', p. 322.

30 MacDonald, *England's Antiphon* (London: Macmillan, 1874), p. 256.

CHAPTER SIX

Stevenson, *Dr Jekyll and Mr Hyde* (1886)

S TEVENSON'S *Dr Jekyll and Mr Hyde* is probably the best known of Scottish fantasies, because more than any other it is a mythic analysis of the nature of modern man. Carlyle's attack on the dangers of mechanism, and his espousal of the divine unconscious in *Sartor* make him a unique prophet for his time more than for the less religious twentieth century, but Stevenson's picture of man's nature at war with itself has somehow had perennial force, because of the peculiar modern divorce of the public from the private self, particularly in the institutionalised job. Stevenson's story addresses not only our urge for respectability, but our lust for perfect lives, the bourgeois belief, now sustained by advertising, that one can live a standardised life without pain, or loss, or corruption, or ugliness. In his own life Stevenson lived these things in the tension he saw between his father's and his own public pronouncements and secret deeds: but more than this, in the continual 'war in the members' of a lifelong battle with sickness.

And yet Stevenson almost missed the point when he first wrote the story in three days, after it came to him in a dream. It was his wife who saw how he had gone wrong in making Jekyll 'bad all through' and Hyde only a disguise; he had missed the 'allegory' within the story.[1] Three further days, and Stevenson had the final version written, a version which on publication was to be an instant and lasting success. Now he gave place to Hyde as half of Jekyll's nature, and thus not so simply outcast or reprehensible. It was in effect Stevenson's acknowledgment of what he was to call the creative 'Brownies' within himself. In his 'A Chapter on Dreams' (1888), he speaks of his best and most macabre stories being sent up from his subconscious by forces outside his control, forces which he can only arrange into intelligible stories. He, Stevenson, is but a conscious self, a respectable public persona with some aptitudes in the craft of writing: but the true producer of his fiction, who creates through his dreams, is 'some Brownie, some Familiar, some unseen collaborator, whom I keep locked in a back garret, while I get all the praise'.[2] He then portrays his *Dr Jekyll and Mr Hyde* as being born out of three scenes given to him in a dream. Thus, by making Hyde half of Jekyll's nature, Stevenson acknowledged his own nature, and gave the Brownies their due. More than this, he admitted that half of his story was the creation of figures with the amoral force of Hyde.

The story had sources other than the Brownies, however. It has become a truism that it represents in part Stevenson's own reaction to his Scottish Calvinist upbringing and his sense of the gap between respectable Edinburgh family and public life and the low life elsewhere pursued by the men, including himself, who were pillars of society. As a symbol of that doubleness he had long been fascinated by the story of Deacon Brodie, Edinburgh cabinet maker by day and grave robber by night. And he was drawn to the literature of the double also, and in particular no doubt to Hogg's *Confessions*, then recently reprinted (1865, 1876) in Thomson's edition of Hogg's *Works*. The *Confessions* gives us, in Gil-Martin, a Hyde figure in relation to Robert Wringhim's Jekyll—even if Wringhim is much more evidently puffed up by pride, convinced as he is of his divine respectability rather than a merely social one. The literature of the double goes far beyond Hogg, of course, into the German Romantic fairy-tale or the Gothic novel. Its importance is that it is in effect a psychological analysis: that which would in earlier literature have been simply seen as the 'other', an outsider (as, say, Lovelace still is to the heroine of Richardson's *Clarissa*) now had to be admitted to be half of the self, the *alter ego*. It is fair to say that this reflects how from a previous 'identity' modern man has become a multiple and uncertain self. An instance of this is Adelbert von Chamisso's *Peter Schlemihl* (1814) in which a man sells his shadow to the devil in return for pleasure, only to find life unendurable without it: his shadow is his dark self, his id or unconscious, which he has sought to remove so that his conscious self or ego may have absolute power. A further seminal text here is Mary Shelley's *Frankenstein* (1818), in which, by seeking to emulate the creative power of God, Frankenstein releases what is to him the demonic in the shape of the monster—which is, looked at one way, his own id, with which he in his respectable pride will admit no kinship or ties of obligation, and which therefore becomes renegade. *Frankenstein* is of course the only such story before *Jekyll and Hyde* to use scientific methods to bring the situation into being.

George MacDonald's work also frequently deals with doubles, but Stevenson does not mention it. Both writers deal with the unconscious, and 'warn' of the dangers of its repression, but MacDonald's objective is a Christian one. Stevenson is fascinated by the unconscious as subversive of moral and social norms: MacDonald sees it as the only home of spiritual health, the resort of God in man. They really belong to two opposed classes of fantasy: the one directed to transcendent and sacred ends, the other to subversive and secular ones. As if in keeping with this there seems no evidence that they ever met. Nevertheless it remains the case that the interest shown in the unconscious by Stevenson's fantasy is one that has been shared by all the Scottish fantasies we have looked at so far. From Hogg's Gil-Martin or Merodach, the unconscious world of Carlyle's Teufelsdröckh, or the dreams of MacDonald's fantasies to this, there is a straight, if variegated line. This urge to come to terms with the dark and forested side of the self seems a peculiarly Scottish trait in its constancy: in geographical terms it might be construed as the attempt of the civilised and educated Lowlands to accommodate themselves to the nameless tracts of the Highlands; in personal terms it may represent Scotland's only dialogue with its more barbaric and dark emotions. For it is the frequent absence of such a dialogue elsewhere in Scotland's culture that is its acute limitation. This interest at any rate will be found to provide a continuing thread through many of the fantasies considered in this book.

Dr Jekyll and Mr Hyde might be termed 'urban Gothic'. The Gothic novel usually employs as its setting some remote land, castle, tarn or wilderness: but here the hideous events take place in the midst of the relatively peopled streets of London. In part this is because it is the purpose of this novel to show the dark side of man's respectable and citified self. Indeed the other side of the city, its fog-shrouded nature, its slums, inhabited by Hyde, its labyrinthine streets, threaded by Hyde, may symbolise the repressed unconscious itself. But the exposure goes beyond Jekyll alone: it relates also to those more apparently respectable friends and acquaintances with whom he is surrounded, and who inhabit the same city. In this context the story most recalls *Oliver Twist*, where Fagin and his gang are the rejected side of the story and yet represent, beneath all the moralising, the products of the respectable and the bourgeois who remove themselves from them. And *Dr Jekyll and Mr Hyde* is like *Oliver Twist* in being told from multiple narrative centres (unusual for Stevenson): this reinforces the sense of a society and its involvement. Stevenson's story would lack force if Jekyll were an exception: the object is to implicate all society, and even the reader, in what Jekyll is and does. This is a story in which Hyde finally comes together with Jekyll: it is also a narrative in which many other apparently quite separate items are shown to be strangely implicated with one another. The other fantasies we have looked at have often moved towards some deeper understanding of the world or the mind: but this book, more so even than Hogg's *Confessions*, where Robert Wringhin resists the truth to the last, is implosive, involving not the enrichment but the destruction of being. It is fantasy's other, and darker, face.

The impulse to separate areas of life is a particularly Victorian one. The public world is radically divorced from the private one, 'civilised' life from its dark undergrowth and urges, the conscious from the repressed unconscious, 'high' from 'low', industrial advance from its social consequences, Christian faith from scientific knowledge, criticism of national ills from any revolutionary impulse, charity from any notion of worker's rights. Only by compartmentalising reality, by keeping antagonistic forces separate from one another, could an increasingly precarious personal, political and social assurance be maintained. It is not surprising that so many material objects fill Victorian homes, and so many different offices are fulfilled by people: the society is inherently atomistic. It is partly this impulse that Carlyle inveighed against in his attack on the 'Detached, separate', and his attempt to show nature as a divine organism in which all items are interrelated. Stevenson's book follows this example, but goes further and to revolutionary lengths in that it not only suggests that all things are interrelated, but that they should be voluntarily brought into intimate unity, lest they collide as explosively as here. The very polarities with which his book is filled—good and evil, light and dark, respectable and violent, rich houses and slums, all initially brought into contiguity in one city—measure the pressure to break down such dualities. This short and claustrophobic work, in which every word tells, and every move pushes in on Jekyll, is one under enormous spiritual pressure, like a star at the point of collapsing inwards. It is such a collapse that the story describes.

The narrative, in brief, is that Dr Henry Jekyll, living a respectable life in London, has discovered a chemical means of releasing his amoral energies in another and brutish form of himself called Mr Hyde. Thus separated, he satisfies numbers of his darker urges and carries out at least one murder, before he finds he can no longer readily sustain the form of Jekyll and avoid discovery, and, as the now trapped Hyde, kills himself. We know none of this till late, however, for the narrative is first told through friends of Jekyll's, who gradually become alarmed at his behaviour and resolve to discover its cause, finally breaking in on him at the point of his death as Hyde.

Throughout the story, seemingly unrelated people or incidents are brought together. Jekyll and Hyde, at first so disparate, are shown to be increasingly involved with one another to the point where they merge. First we have a connection via a cheque, signed by Jekyll, with which Hyde buys off the father of a girl he attacks; then there is the strange fact that the worthy Jekyll has made his will in favour of the repulsive Hyde; then Jekyll asks the lawyer Utterson to look after Hyde's interests should he, Jekyll, disappear; then Hyde is given a key and free access to Jekyll's house; then Jekyll's appearance and health begin to degenerate, there is a recognition of a similarity between the handwriting of Hyde and of Jekyll, and so on. This is strikingly seen also in the way that a certain 'blind' house identified early on as the resort of Hyde is not till later revealed to back on to the house of Jekyll, of which it in fact forms the laboratory (pp. 8–10, 17–18, 19–20); previously we had no reason to believe other than that Jekyll's house was elsewhere in London; and indeed one character specified that Jekyll did not live there but '"in some square or other"' (p. 11).

The narrative itself, as outlined in the chapter titles on the contents page, might be mistaken for a collection of separate short stories rather than a sequence of events: 'Story of the Door'; 'Search for Mr Hyde'; 'Dr Jekyll Was Quite at Ease'; 'The Carew Murder Case'; 'Incident of the

Letter'; 'Remarkable Incident of Dr Lanyon'; 'Incident at the Window'; 'The Last Night'; 'Dr Lanyon's Narrative'; 'Henry Jekyll's Full Statement of the Case'. Indeed the last title reads like a lawyer's summing up, and the whole could be seen as a legal presentation of a case (the full title of the story is *Strange Case of Dr Jekyll and Mr Hyde*), with apparently separate pieces of evidence brought together to argue a position which only becomes fully apparent at the last: and to this we might add the fact that the early part of the story is told through the lawyer Utterson, and that his concern for most of the time is with investigation into particular deeds of Hyde's and their possible relation to Jekyll. Yet it is not as static as that sounds, for the evidence is not all available to Utterson at the outset, but comes piecemeal: and he himself is not directed to one particular objective from the first, but moves from casual interest to vital concern as the narrative proceeds; nor does he ever unearth the full truth for himself, but is told it in Jekyll's last letter. Here again the seemingly random or disconnected come together to make a coherent sequence; the neglected house, accidentally encountered by Utterson and his companion Enfield on one of their Sunday rambles, leads to a story connected with its door, and this to Hyde and an eventual link with Jekyll.

There are two sides to the narrative: the seen and the unseen. On the one hand there are the investigations of Utterson; and on the other is the story of Jekyll's relations with Hyde. The two sides compare almost as conscious and unconscious. In a sense they never meet until the last: Jekyll develops on his own, and his development and no other person determines his fate, while the other characters try by indirections to find directions out, and operate more or less in isolation from Jekyll. The narrative seen through Utterson, Enfield, Lanyon and the objective narrator himself is effectively the public world, of society and London itself, where that seen through Jekyll is essentially private. Little is said within Jekyll's narrative of the actual deeds of Hyde when abroad in London, for these are recounted by the public figures: what is at issue is the effect of these deeds on Jekyll. The irony of Jekyll's situation is that his normal public self is seen as shut away—as the chapter 'Incident at the Window' conveys—while for all his name, and his fundamentally anti-social self, Hyde inhabits the streets and acts and speaks. The two narratives are related in another way. The narrowing investigations of Utterson and others can be seen as the outside world working in; they end by symbolically breaking down the door to the inner sanctum of Jekyll's house: but in the Jekyll-Hyde narrative the case is rather one of the inside working out, of Hyde, whom Jekyll constantly images as something violent locked within him, breaking out to the point where he engulfs Jekyll. The story thus has a network of oppositions informing and playing through it, which suggests a far tighter bonding between the various aspects of the tale than might at first sight appear.

This is illustrated in the early description of a bustling London by-street with one strange building:

> The street was small and what is called quiet, but it drove
> a thriving trade on the week-days. The inhabitants were all
> doing well, it seemed, and all emulously hoping to do better
> still, and laying out the surplus of their gains in coquetry;
> so that the shop fronts stood along that thoroughfare with
> an air of invitation, like rows of smiling saleswomen. Even
> on Sunday, when it veiled its more florid charms and lay
> comparatively empty of passage, the street shone out in
> contrast to its dingy neighbourhood, like a fire in a forest;
> and with its freshly painted shutters, well-polished brasses
> and general cleanliness and gaiety of note, instantly caught
> and pleased the eye of the passenger.
>
> Two doors from one corner, on the left hand going east, the
> line was broken by the entry of a court; and just at that point,
> a certain sinister block of building thrust forward its gable
> on the street. It was two storeys high; showed no window,
> nothing but a door on the lower storey and a blind forehead of
> discoloured wall on the upper; and bore in every feature, the
> marks of prolonged and sordid negligence. The door, which
> was equipped with neither bell nor knocker, was blistered
> and distained. Tramps slouched into the recess and struck
> matches on the panels; children kept shop upon the steps;
> the schoolboy had tried his knife on the mouldings; and for
> close on a generation, no-one had appeared to drive away
> these random visitors or to repair their ravages.
>
> (pp. 8–9)

The street of shops looks outward to a public; it is concerned with putting on a fine front and drawing people in. The building that juts forward has only an unopened door, no windows, and neither bell nor knocker on the door: its preoccupation is with exclusion, its ruinous appearance an indication that it would invite no-one. Yet it is part of the street, even if it is not integrated with it but thrusts its way forward. Both the street and the house are personified: the street drives a thriving trade, the shop fronts invite 'like rows of smiling saleswomen', and veil their more florid charms on Sundays; while the 'sinister block of building' (which 'sinister' may be the left hand to the street's right, and certainly is 'on the left hand going east'), 'thrust[s] forth its gable on the street', has 'a blind forehead of discoloured wall' and bears 'the marks of . . . negligence' in every feature. It is not too much of a leap to see the shops as suggestive of the respectable, ambitious, civil area of mind—in short, all that Jekyll is to seem to be, if on a higher class level—and this bare block of building (with its 'blind forehead') in its midst as the intrusive and unfathomable unconscious area of that same mind.[3] Enfield later says of this building that whether anyone lives there is obscure, '"for the buildings are so packed together about that court, that it's hard to say where one ends and another begins"' (p. 12). The street and the building together seem almost to form a composite whole, the one, by the extremity of its cheer and vitality, seeming almost to beget the other—variety producing uniformity, care neglect, light darkness.

And that last duality reminds us of the two recorded instances of Hyde's evil. Each involves his meeting by night, alone, with an innocent—in the first instance, a child, which he tramples on as if it is not there, and in the second, at the opposite end of life, and yet also child-like, a good old man, Sir Danvers Carew, M.P., member of the establishment, whom he also tramples. The fact that each act involves a meeting is in itself significant: it is as though Hyde conjoins momentarily with the other half of the larger whole from which he comes. But for the story the most significant aspect of these meetings, particularly the second, is the way that the innocence is described in such a way as to suggest that somehow evil is generated out of its very existence:

> A maid servant living alone in a house not far from the river, had gone upstairs to bed about eleven. Although a fog rolled over the city in the small hours, the early part of the night was cloudless, and the lane, which the maid's window overlooked, was brilliantly lit by the full moon. It seems she was romantically given, for she sat down upon her box, which stood immediately under the window, and fell into a dream of musing. Never (she used to say, with streaming tears, when she narrated that experience) never had she felt more at peace with all men or thought more kindly of the world. And as she so sat she became aware of an aged and beautiful gentleman with white hair, drawing near along the lane; and advancing to meet him, another and very small gentleman, to whom at first she paid less attention. When they had come within speech (which was just under the maid's eyes) the older man bowed and accosted the other with a very pretty manner of politeness. It did not seem as if the subject of his address were of great importance; indeed, from his pointing, it sometimes appeared as if he were only inquiring his way; but the moon shone on his face as he spoke, and the girl was pleased to watch it, it seemed to breathe such an innocent and old-world kindness of disposition, yet with something high too, as of a well-founded self-content. Presently her eye wandered to the other, and she was surprised to recognise in him a certain Mr Hyde, who had once visited her master and for whom she had conceived a dislike. He had in his hand a heavy cane, with

which he was trifling; but he answered never a word, and seemed to listen with an ill-contained impatience. And then all of a sudden he broke out in a great flame of anger, stamping with his foot, brandishing the cane, and carrying on (as the maid described it) like a madman. The old gentleman took a step back, with the air of one very much surprised and a trifle hurt; and at that Mr Hyde broke out of all bounds and clubbed him to the earth. And next moment, with ape-like fury, he was trampling his victim under foot, and hailing down a storm of blows, under which the bones were audibly shattered and the body jumped upon the roadway. At the horror of these sights and sounds, the maid fainted.

(pp. 25–6)

The girl had never felt more at peace that evening, never felt more kindly of the world: as she so thinks, the good old man appears, and simultaneously the smaller man, to whom she pays less attention. Stevenson liked melodrama, true: how better to produce this than by the contrast of the pleasant thoughts with the horrors that ensue, the physical destruction of the old man by the other? Yet the insistence on the observation of the scene by a mind, and by a mind in a state of near-holiness, followed at once by the appearance of the old gentleman and the other, suggests a causal relation. Projections of mind are the basis of the whole story, in the sense that Hyde is a portion of the soul given concrete existence. At the same time the very existence of the good old man seems to generate the other, its opposite; and certainly, at a more evident level, provokes Hyde's extremest evil. It might conceivably be said that the whole scene is a projection of the maid's mind; but the main point here is that innocence, whether in the form of her thoughts or in the appearance of the old man, begets its opposite.

And this of course has a bearing on the whole story. If innocence and corruption go so together, who is free? (It is a question also asked by Hawthorne, Melville, James and Conrad.) Jekyll poses the question in his discovery 'that man is not truly one, but truly two' (p. 61). In him 'with even a deeper trench than in the majority of men, [were] severed . . . those provinces of good and ill which divide and compound man's dual nature' (p. 60). Seen this way, Jekyll is simply an extrapolation of the nature of all men. And he locates the origin of his Hyde personality in an excessive love of life (pp. 62–3, 70, 74): extreme vitality begets a creature of death. Utterson the lawyer, like Banquo in Shakespeare's *Macbeth*, is aware of 'the cursed thoughts that nature/ Gives way to in repose', and of his own potential for wrong:[4] he broods 'awhile on his own past, groping in all the corners of memory, lest by chance some Jack-in-the-Box of an old iniquity should leap to light there. His past was fairly blameless; few men could read the rolls of their life with less apprehension; yet he was humbled to the dust by the many ill things he had done' (pp. 20–1). Utterson's imagination is 'enslaved' by Hyde: he dreams repeatedly of the image of Hyde treading down the little girl like a Juggernaut, and becomes obsessed by the desire to behold the as yet unknown features of Hyde; 'by all lights and at all hours of solitude or concourse' he posts himself by the haunt of Hyde to satisfy this wish, saying, ' "If he be Mr Hyde . . . I shall be Mr Seek" ' (p. 17). His knowledge of Hyde's legal connection with Jekyll is given an air of strangeness by the manner of presentation: he is walking with Enfield before we have heard anything of Jekyll or of Hyde, and Enfield describes Hyde's violence to the girl; then Utterson reveals that he knows something of Hyde already, more indeed than Enfield himself. It is Utterson's stick which in the hands of Hyde strikes down Sir Danvers Carew. It is Utterson who in the end is made the beneficiary of Jekyll's will in place of Hyde.

If these facts raise questions, there are other, and related, issues. Why is it that people have difficulty in recollecting Hyde's appearance? Why is it that all people who meet Hyde are peculiarly repelled by him? When Enfield beholds Hyde after the incident with the child,

> 'there was one curious circumstance. I had taken a loathing to my gentleman at first sight. So had the child's family, which was only natural. But the doctor's case was what struck me. He was the usual cut and dry apothecary, of no particular age and colour, with a strong Edinburgh accent, and about as emotional as a bagpipe. Well, sir, he was like the rest of us; every time he looked at my prisoner, I saw that Sawbones turn sick and white with the desire to kill him. I knew what was in his mind, just as he knew what was in mine . . .
>
> (pp. 9–10)

Again, when Utterson has seen Hyde, he is left 'the picture of disquietude', feeling 'hitherto unknown disgust, loathing and fear', from which he comes finally to the moral conclusion that Hyde has 'Satan's signature' on him (p. 19). As for Dr Lanyon, he registers a more physical reaction to 'the odd, subjective disturbance caused by his [Hyde's] neighbourhood': 'At the time, I set it down to some idiosyncratic, personal distaste, and merely wondered at the acuteness of the symptoms; but I have since had reason to believe the cause to lie much deeper in the nature of man, and to turn on some nobler hinge than the principle of hatred' (p. 56). But suppose what all these different individuals are violently responding to and refusing is the Hyde in themselves?[5] Jekyll suggests as much when he says that the 'visible misgiving of the flesh' that he observes in people when confronted with Hyde occurs 'because all human beings, as we meet them, are commingled out of good and evil: and Edward Hyde, alone in the ranks of mankind, was pure evil' (p. 64). And indeed Jekyll himself is an instructive case on the subject:

for in Hyde he sees all the energy and lust for life in man that is tied down by restraint and the respectability of the normal social self (p. 63); yet he comes to try to disown Hyde as though he were an alien, an evil being wholly disconnected from himself (pp. 74–5).

There is thus a tendency in the story to suggest the interrelation of the various characters with Hyde, through the very discontinuities sought by the characters and apparently practised by the narrative. The insistence on disconnection and alienness makes us, particularly in a story about man's two selves, look also for links and nearnesses. We start with one quaint pair, the respectable lawyer Utterson with his friend Enfield: we end with an extreme version of their division in Jekyll and Hyde. The whole landscape of the story, with its city streets, darkness and fog, can be seen as images of a journey into the interior: certainly the narrative moves progressively inwards from the streets into buildings—the trampling of the child is seen by Enfield while out walking, the killing of the old man is witnessed from a house, Doctors Lanyon and Jekyll die in their houses. What we have here could be said to be something like the journey in Conrad's *Heart of Darkness*. The procedure of the story suggests that Hyde can lie at the end of a journey into the respectable self—the self not just of Jekyll but of Utterson or of Lanyon. Jekyll's is an extreme case: it is what we can come to in the last analysis; and this seems to be why we only come to a full statement of that case as the last item in this narrative.

What are we to make of the concluding 'full statement' by Jekyll? One problem is the relative importance of Jekyll's scientific knowledge and his discovery of the identity-changing drug. Jekyll begins his statement with no mention of this drug or of any researches. First, he tells us that the two selves, the Jekyll and the Hyde, were already considerably divided in himself before his scientific experiments cast any 'side light' on his condition.[6] It is a curious rehearsal:

> I was born in the year 18– to a large fortune, endowed besides with excellent parts, inclined by nature to industry, fond of the respect of the wise and good among my fellow-men, and thus, as might have been supposed, with every guarantee of an honourable and distinguished future. And indeed the worst of my faults was a certain impatient gaiety of disposition, such as has made the happiness of many, but such as I found it hard to reconcile with my imperious desire to carry my head high, and wear a more than commonly grave countenance before the public.
>
> (p. 60)

From this one would suppose a merely inconvenient ebullience of temperament such as might be imagined fairly common in men who wish to be respectable. Yet even here things have shifted. In the first sentence, he was endowed with many excellencies and was fond of the respect of the wise and the good: so far there seems nothing amiss in this. But by the second sentence this has become more dubious, 'my imperious desire to carry my head high, and wear a more than commonly grave countenance before the public': now he is more of a mask, greedy of respect while not necessarily deserving of it. And simultaneously, the other side of him is to shift throughout the whole long paragraph which the above passage opens, from 'a profound duplicity of life', to 'irregularities', 'faults', 'plunged in shame' (p. 60). In a sense, what we witness here is an enactment of the widening gulf in Jekyll himself: as he speaks, what were peccadilloes turn to sins and what was the respectable display of one's talents becomes a craving for praise. But in part this is exactly the case in his life itself. He has allowed his wilder spirit some outlet, but having done so is the more coldly determined to be respectable: he has split himself, because the more he gives his energies vent the more strongly they tug against his impulse towards public acceptance and renown, and therefore the stronger *that* impulse becomes until he digs a trench in himself and has to live two lives, each of which fights for dominance in him.

The drug Jekyll discovers is thus only an alleviation of a situation which he himself has created through numbers of voluntary acts: it allows him to put into concrete form the duality he has begotten in himself, and in so doing to remove the pain. By so separating the two he is able to let the darker side go its own way, convinced that its deeds will not affect him. And thus further separated, the dark side does become darker. Put in the order that we have here, with Jekyll first furthering the split in himself, the drug is a mere catalyst permitting him to carry the process to the limit: it is, almost, reducible to a mere mechanism for allowing the full expression of his nature. To this extent the drug itself is quite unimportant: and this is seen again at the end of the story, when Jekyll finds it increasingly difficult to escape from the form of Hyde. He blames the chemicals he scours London for, convinced that it was an undiscoverable impurity in the original salts that facilitated his transformations, and dies feeling sure that the mere exhaustion of a chemical has finally fixed him to the being of Hyde. But in the same way that throughout the story Jekyll's acceptable ambition turns to a mask of worthiness, so his belief that Hyde is the sole repository of his evil gradually becomes mistaken. When he begins to find himself transformed involuntarily as it seems, into Hyde, we realise that it is not the habitual use of the chemicals but the habitual decision to use them which has led to this. In other words, Jekyll becomes more and more of a sham until he *is* Hyde. The man who began by letting Hyde out ends by having to let him in. The drug's part in the whole business might be put in the same way that Mephistophilis in Marlowe's *Dr Faustus* puts it: Mephistophilis dismisses the doctor's magical powers in calling him up, 'That was the cause, but yet *per accidens*'; Faustus is told that it was his apostasy, not his skill, that called the devil forth. 'Je-kyll', 'I kill', self-killer, thus seems an apt description of the protagonist here.[7] (And of course Hyde kills *himself* in the end.)

A second issue that arises with Jekyll's 'full statement' is precisely who is talking, and whether we should credit him. As he writes, he is on the verge of losing the last shred of his Jekyll-ness and becoming Hyde wholly and irrevocably, a Hyde that Jekyll himself has created. He wanted to be free of the war in his nature; then he chose to permit Hyde to exercise his energies in increasingly vicious courses while escaping the guilt and the punishment as Jekyll: 'Henry Jekyll stood at times aghast before the acts of Edward Hyde; but the situation was apart from ordinary laws, and insidiously relaxed the grasp of conscience. It was Hyde, after all, and Hyde alone, that was guilty . . . And thus his conscience slumbered' (pp. 65–6). The later status of Jekyll's repentance after Hyde's murder of Sir Danvers Carew is also rendered questionable: Hyde returns gloating over the crime to prepare the draught that will transform him back to Jekyll and safety:

> Hyde had a song upon his lips as he compounded the draught, and as he drank it, pledged the dead man. The pangs of transformation had not done tearing him, before Henry Jekyll, with streaming tears of gratitude and remorse, had fallen upon his knees and lifted his clasped hands to God.
>
> (p. 70)

The first reaction undercuts the second. The close juxtaposition of the two in such extreme form shows how illusory is Jekyll's belief that he and Hyde are quite separate. Yet even at the end Jekyll still makes a last desperate stand: 'this is my true hour of death, and what is to follow concerns another than myself' (p. 76); we recall how earlier Jekyll slipped into the first person when speaking as Hyde (pp. 69–70).

In Oscar Wilde's *The Picture of Dorian Gray* (1891) there is similar use of an apparatus to divide self morally from self, and there we know that the image of beauty in the picture is a lie, proven so finally by the picture's destruction. Both stories show that there is really no escape from the self, though the self may change. In *Dr Jekyll and Mr Hyde*, this comes over particularly in such passages as the following, written within one page of the end:

> I became, in my own person, a creature eaten up and emptied by fever, languidly weak both in body and mind, and solely occupied by one thought: the horror of my other self. But when I slept, or when the virtue of the medicine wore off, I would leap almost without transition (for the pangs of transformation grew daily less marked) into the possession

of a fancy brimming with images of terror, a soul boiling
with causeless hatreds, and a body that seemed not strong
enough to contain the raging energies of life. The powers
of Hyde seemed to have grown with the sickliness of Jekyll.
And certainly the hate that now divided them was equal
on each side. With Jekyll, it was a thing of vital instinct.
He had now seen the full deformity of that creature that
shared with him some of the phenomena of consciousness,
and was co-heir with him to death: and beyond these links
of community, which in themselves made the most poignant
part of his distress, he thought of Hyde, for all his energy
of life, as of something not only hellish but inorganic. This
was the shocking thing; that the slime of the pit seemed to
utter cries and voices; that the amorphous dust gesticulated
and sinned; that what was dead, and had no shape, should
usurp the offices of life. And this again, that the insurgent
horror was knit to him closer than a wife, closer than an eye;
lay caged in his flesh, where he heard it mutter and felt it
struggle to be born; and at every hour of weakness, and in the
confidence of slumber, prevailed against him, and deposed
him out of life.

(pp. 74–5)

How can he speak of 'I', here or elsewhere, as though 'I' were a pure,
respectable Jekyll, and not the double in one skin that it is?[8]—for when
he is Hyde, he is Hyde simple, but when he is Jekyll he is a mixture of
the two, and a mixture in which Jekyll has played a steadily decreasing
part. Thus it is that there is the shift here from speaking of himself as
'I' to speaking of himself as 'Jekyll', as though he could separate that
part from himself: he is no longer able to grasp what he is. So too the
passage seesaws between 'the sickliness of Jekyll' and a Jekyll who has
a 'vital instinct'. The passage then proceeds to a remarkable attempt of
Jekyll's to dissociate himself from Hyde even while his language admits
that he is implicated with him. First he says that Hyde is possessed of
'the raging energies of life' and the 'energy of life', but then he says that
Hyde 'usurp[s] the offices of life' and that he is not an expression of life
but of death, 'the slime of the pit . . . the amorphous dust . . . what
was dead, and had no shape'. Granted that Hyde is destructive: but is
it not Jekyll who is the more dead?—quiet, respectable Jekyll, who lets
himself loose to murder others while salving his conscience, Jekyll, who
translates all his energies into an external form and lets them out and
who has thereby given up half at least of what he is? Jekyll wishes to
separate himself from Hyde by calling him a horror, but even as he does
so he is forced unconsciously to acknowledge that this thing of darkness
is his own. Hyde is a horror, yet Hyde is knit to him closer than a wife

or an eye. He tries to suggest that it is Hyde who has forced this ghastly contiguity, but the imagery conveys a bonding with himself which the succeeding picture of the caging of a beast in his flesh would deny; and similarly he speaks of Hyde's 'struggle to be born', which suggests something begotten of Jekyll, and then counters with the notion of death and of Hyde having made a victim of Jekyll, 'prevailed against him, and deposed him out of life'.

The whole passage is shot through with these dualities. Hyde is 'co-heir with him [Jekyll] to death', he shares in that which separates; and 'these links of community' cause 'the most poignant part of his [Jekyll's] distress': that which is inorganic, formless slime of the pit speaks, takes form, and acts. Why is he so horrified by the last? We cannot write it off simply as moral horror at created evil. Looked at in one way, it is equally horror at having given birth. For what else, on this view, is the origin of a child, if it is not in slime, amorphous dust and shapelessness? What else does that voiceless slime eventually do but take form and speak and be a man? And is that not what Jekyll has become? Is he not the product of this process? And is it not he, with his respectability almost eaten away by Hyde, who is himself now more slimy and shapeless than Hyde's origins?—indeed, is it not the case that where Hyde has moved out of his slimy origins, Jekyll is moving back to them, moving back at least to that very nonentity, that absence of being, which he feigns to find abhorrent in Hyde alone?⁹ The pull of that syntax and phraseology—'that the slime of the pit seemed to utter cries and voices; that the amorphous dust gesticulated and sinned; that what was dead, and had no shape, should usurp the offices of life'—suggests that Jekyll himself feels he is being drawn back into that vortex of non-being: the cries and voices and gesticulations seem to refer not only to Hyde's growth but to Jekyll's decomposition.

Nothing else Stevenson wrote has quite the darkness of vision of this story. In 'Markheim' (1885) or 'The Bottle Imp' (1891) a degree of 'goodness' wins through in the end; even in 'Thrawn Janet' (1881), though the minister is driven mad by his experience of the devil's actions in his life, he is not himself the agent of these actions. As Stevenson wrote to J. A. Symonds, 'Jekyll is a dreadful thing, I own; but the only thing I feel dreadful about is that damned old business of the war in the members. This time it came out; I hope it will stay in, in future.'¹⁰ The 'war in the members' (see also p. 60) is painted here by Jekyll and others in moral terms, with Hyde as evil: yet Jekyll himself claims that the form he gave to this other side of himself need not have been the 'evil' one of Hyde at all, 'Had I approached my discovery in a more noble spirit . . . I had come forth an angel instead of a fiend' (p. 64). Such a duality would be put in potentially other terms by James in *The Turn of the Screw* or Conrad in *Heart of Darkness*, where we attend to the way the narrators may pervert or project the 'unacceptable' things they see.

Viewed in this light, Jekyll refuses the very sorts of connectiveness on which the entire story is founded: he divides things, making one black and the other white; he tries to cast off part of himself, only to find it devour him.

The idea behind the story is thus mirrored in its style: what appeared to be separated is shown to be more intimately joined than could ever have been supposed. Each isolated episode, event and figure, apparently so scattered, comes together in the final design. Hyde and Jekyll, who seemed independent of one another, come to fuse, mirroring the futility of Jekyll's own attempt to divorce his two selves. As the narrative proceeds, we get nearer and nearer to Jekyll, just as does Hyde. We move from the streets where Hyde was shut out to the interiors where he comes in. And all the divided details of the story move from the 'centrifugal' to the 'centripetal', closing in towards the final vortex of Jekyll's simultaneous self-revelation and loss of self. At the same time, placed at the end, Jekyll's 'full statement of the case' becomes an extreme analysis of the respectability of many of the separate characters of the story. Stevenson once referred to his story as a 'Gothic gnome':[11] he meant the term 'Gothic' in relation to its atmosphere, but it could equally be applied to its architecture, a mass of rambling and seemingly ill-assorted details ultimately resolving themselves into a unity beyond prior imagining. 'Style', Stevenson wrote elsewhere, meaning the expression of idea in form, 'is the invariable mark of any master':[12] the mark of such mastery is certainly present in *Dr Jekyll and Mr Hyde.*

Notes

1 Robert Louis Stevenson, *Dr Jekyll and Mr Hyde and Weir of Hermiston,* ed. Emma Letley (Oxford: Oxford University Press, 1987), p. ix. References to *Dr Jekyll and Mr Hyde* are to this edition.

2 Ibid., p. 207.

3 Stephen King makes a similar point in his *Danse Macabre* (London: MacDonald, 1981), p. 80, seeing the contrast in terms of that 'between superego and id'.

4 Much in the story is reminiscent of *Macbeth*—the murder of a good old man, the attempt to divide oneself from one's own evil ('To know my deed, 'twere best not know myself'), the idea of clothes hanging loose, as on 'a dwarfish thief', on the evil man. See also Julia Briggs, *Night Visitors: The Rise and Fall of the English Ghost Story* (London: Faber, 1977), pp. 67–8.

5 See also Barbara L. Berman, 'The Strange Case of Dr Jekyll and Mr Hyde', in Frank N. Magill, ed., *Survey of Modern Fantasy Literature,* 5 vols (Englewood Cliffs, N. J.: Salem Press, 1983), IV, pp. 1836–7; Peter K.

Garrett, 'Cries and Voices: Reading *Jekyll and Hyde*', in William Veeder and Gordon Hirsch, eds, *Dr Jekyll and Mr Hyde after One Hundred Years* (Chicago: University of Chicago Press, 1988), pp. 67–71; William Veeder, 'Children of the Night: Stevenson and Patriarchy', in Veeder and Hirsch, op. cit., pp. 116–22.

6 See also Katherine M. Morsberger, *'The Strange Case of Dr Jekyll and Mr Hyde'*, in Frank N. Magill, ed., *Survey of Science Fiction Literature*, 5 vols (Englewood Cliffs, N. J.: Salem Press, 1979), V, p. 2187.

7 Several critics have made this punning translation—see e.g. Rosemary Jackson, *Fantasy: The Literature of Subversion* (London: Methuen, 1981), p. 114; and Andrew Jefford, 'Dr Jekyll and Professor Nabokov: Reading a Reading', in Andrew Noble, ed., *Robert Louis Stevenson* (London: Vision Press, 1983), pp. 68–9. Jefford's essay, incidentally, portrays several hidden motifs within the story serving to bind its separate parts—particularly of wine versus the 'magic potion', warm sociable interiors versus cold lonely exteriors.

8 See also Morsberger, p. 2188; Garrett, pp. 62–7; Ronald R. Thomas, 'The Strange Voices in the Case: Dr Jekyll, Mr Hyde, and the Voice of Modern Fiction', in Veeder and Hirsch, op. cit, pp. 73–93 *passim*.

9 In Arthur Machen's *The Great God Pan* (1894), which imitates *Dr Jekyll and Mr Hyde*, is also found a devolutionary regress to the primal slime seen as the origin of life; on this see Briggs, p. 72, and Jackson, pp. 116–18.

10 Letter of Spring 1886, repr. in *The Letters of Robert Louis Stevenson*, ed. Sidney Colvin, 4 vols (London: Methuen, 1911), II, p. 274.

11 Letter of 2 Jan., 1886 to W. H. Low, repr. in *Letters*, II, p. 263.

12 Stevenson, 'A Note on Realism' (1884), repr. in *The Works of Robert Louis Stevenson* (London: Cassell, 1907), V, p. 262.

CHAPTER SEVEN

Women Writers: Margaret Oliphant and 'Fiona Macleod'

MRS OLIPHANT IS a woman writer; 'Fiona Macleod' is the pen-name of a writer called William Sharp who in the early 1890s decided that he was so drawn to the feminine psyche that he would take the name of a woman. So far as Scottish fantasy as a whole is concerned, they are not really exceptions, as it is part of the nature of this fantasy to be involved with the feminine: they serve in some ways only to make that tendency more explicit. What we shall find in them, for one thing, is an unflagging attention to the portrayal of emotion. In Mrs Oliphant's work this takes the form of compassion for lost spirits, where in Macleod the feelings evoked are the harsher ones of desperation, pain and loss; and where Mrs Oliphant locates her stories in an urban or domestic setting, Macleod chooses rather a more remote and often savage natural scene. The side of femininity that Macleod expresses is more that of the passionate lover or the fury than of the loving mother as with Mrs Oliphant. The two writers thus form a striking contrast, which encompasses the space from fireside warmth to moorland blast that is one range of the Scottish spirit.

MARGARET OLIPHANT (1828–1897)

For most writers of fantasy, the supernatural in their stories is there in some degree for the sake of the fiction, even while it is usually part of a vision of reality. An exception here would be George MacDonald, in whose work is felt the pressure of belief. Another is Margaret Oliphant, who herself knew MacDonald well and greatly admired his religious novels. In the tales of the supernatural that form a small but now best-known area of her prodigious literary output, Mrs Oliphant registers a particularly strong sense of the reality of the unseen. While her stories can be seen as part of the newly popular mode of the ghost story in the 1880s and 1890s,[1] they are highly individual and personally important to the writer. They emerge from a passionate but sorely-tried Christian faith, and from the frequent visits of death to Mrs Oliphant's family throughout her life—to three of her babies, to her husband Frank after nine years of marriage (1859), to her surviving daughter Margaret aged ten in 1864, and thereafter always threatening through the constant ill-health of her sons Cyril and Francis. Mrs Oliphant's desire to pierce beyond the veil of the unseen, both to anchor her faith and meet her loved ones, was very strong. But it was always tempered by an equally strong sense of realism, born of a hard practical life where she was forced to write copiously to make a living for her family, and to be an untiring mother to two sons who never left home—quite apart from many other duties she undertook to help others.[2]

The recurrent idea behind Mrs Oliphant's stories is how far the seen and the unseen worlds may meet—in short, with relative continuity and discontinuity. Those of her stories which deal with returning ghosts speak most immediately of the breach between the two worlds. The dead of the French town of Semur return in 'A Beleaguered City' (1879), but can make no more than oblique contact with the living citizens, who are forced to leave the town during the 'occupation'. In 'Earthbound' (1880), a beautiful lady met by the central character Edmund is a ghost, and can only register her pleasure at having been noticed by him, not enter into any further relation: when he seizes her there is in his head 'a roaring of echoes, a clanging of noises, a blast as of great trumpets and music; and he knew no more.' And if 'Earthbound' portrays a ghost which cannot leave the earth, 'The Open Door' (1882) gives us one who will not see the discontinuity of seen and unseen: the ghost is that of a youth who haunts the scene of his mother's long-past death, too foolish and weak-witted to realise that, as the minister who finally releases him tells him, her soul has long since gone to heaven. The door of the title, now a ruin opening on nothing, formerly fronted his mother's part of a house, and symbolises the discontinuity that the spirit refuses. 'Old Lady Mary' (1884) portrays the disjunction of seen and unseen in another way, through the vain efforts of the spirit of a once wayward and pampered woman to do some good: she returns to her house on earth and with her ghostly hands struggles to uncover from a secret cabinet drawer, where she irresponsibly hid it before her death, her will giving her property to her needy young relation and ward, also called Mary.[3]

While these stories highlight the severance of mortal from immortal, they also portray a poignant closeness of the two orders, as Edmund and the lady converse in the garden of the house like ordinary lovers, or as the voice of the crying youth in 'The Open Door' starts up from the ground directly next to the watchers, or as Lady Mary struggles with her immortal fingers to open the material cabinet. This mixture of 'so near and so far' gives an almost metaphoric power to these stories. The urge to overcome the barrier creates ripples in the mortal world: a baby and a child see Lady Mary, and in another story, 'The Portrait: A Story of the Seen and the Unseen' (1885),[4] a dead woman's anxiety over the evil ways of her husband enables her, through her portrait, to drive her son repeatedly to his father until the latter realises the source of these visitations, and yields.

Further, the very existence of these ghosts assures the reader that

James Hogg, by William Nicholson, about 1817, four years after the publication of *The Queen's Wake* and before the writing of his prose stories: here bright with his literary success in Edinburgh, but also full of native vitality and incipient mirth.

Thomas Carlyle, by Charles Linnell, in 1844. A surprisingly youthful, pre-'sage' Carlyle at almost fifty, ten years after the first serial publication of *Sartor Resartus* and at the height of his literary fame in London. Here the Romantic Carlyle still seems in the ascendant over the Victorian.

George MacDonald, by Cecilia Harrison, in 1897. Two years beyond the publication of *Lilith*, Mac-Donald is here burdened by exhaustion and illness. His favourite phrase of longing for heaven, 'I wis we were a' deid', seems here all too real.

The rather haggard and hunted-looking Robert Louis Stevenson painted at Vailima, Samoa by Count Girolamo Nerli in 1892, six years after the appearance of *Dr. Jekyll and Mr Hyde*, and two years before his death. This might be the Stevenson who could 'wonder why my stories are always so nasty'.

Margaret Oliphant, a pen-drawing by her niece Janet Mary Oliphant in 1895, with only 'The Library Window' still to come of her short stories. To any simple notion of her as a yearning mystic, this picture of alert and still amused intelligence is a corrective: J.M. Barrie 'wondered she ever fell asleep'.

'An unfinished sketch' of William Sharp ('Fiona Macleod') by Daniel Albert Wehrschmidt in 1898, two years from the appearance of Macleod's fantasy stories, and at the height of 'her' Celticism. The insistent maleness in the weight and impersonality of the heavy clothing and stiff pose here are offset by the full lips, bright eyes, and wild (golden) hair.

'Fairy Book' and essayist Andrew Lang by Sir William Blake Richmond in 1895, seven years after the publication of *The Gold of Fairnilee* and in the long summer of his literary powers and London fame. Lang has self-consciously draped his limbs about the chair: amid the studied nonchalance and ease the child still looks out.

Sir James Matthew Barrie by Sir William Nicholson, in 1904, the year of first production of *Peter Pan*. Barrie is here dwarfed within the frame, into which he appears to have strayed and been temporarily caught: suggestive of his own Peter Pan ('All children, except one, grow up').

David Lindsay, possibly around 1914, while gestating *A Voyage to Arcturus*. A carefully respectable, foursquare Lindsay here, reflecting the punctilious City clerk of some twenty years, while at the same time coolly indifferent to the world in the withdrawal of the eyes. 'Lindsay's imperturbable composure was but the surface-layer of a great deep', wrote his later friend E.H. Visiak.

Neil Gunn about 1947, three years after the publication of *The Green Isle of the Great Deep*, in the fullness of literary achievement. There seems a deep happiness here, a mixture of relaxed contemplation and bright-eyed insight: this is the Gunn who felt 'concerned with life in its vivid, living moments ... Incalculably living, aware that it should be beneath everything'.

George Mackay Brown in striking pose, in 1973, the year of
publication of *Magnus*. This seems to reflect more the strain of the
Norse raider than of the Christian in Brown: the sharp and
dynamic angles of the body and head seem directed by a force
quite other than that behind his self-effacement as an artist.
(Photo: Gordon Wright)

Alasdair Gray, photographed about the time of publication of *Lanark* in 1981.
This is a coolly interrogative Gray, whose narrow lips and strong nose, together
with the sheer hairiness of aspect, sufficiently suggest the academic manqué
who has outdone all academics. This is the Gray who refuses to be pinned
down: the Gray who wrote in 1988, 'So what are you for, Gray? … At present
I do not know.'

Margaret Elphinstone, photographed in 1988, when she had already written
some of the stories to appear in *An Apple from a Tree*. The mixture of warmth and
shyness in the features is countered in the exact and piercing eyes.

an unseen world exists, and is our eventual destination. All of them, however individually pitiable or absurd, are seen as part of a larger order. Lady Mary goes and returns to an audience of redeemed spirits; the lady in 'Earthbound' is 'appointed' 'for a time' to her lot; the spirit in 'The Open Door' is refusing the true open door, that of heaven. The 'reason' for the disjunctions between the unseen and the seen in these stories is that there can be at best only faint traffic between the two orders, when the supernatural is attempting to break back into the natural from which it is forever excluded. And yet it is a curious fact that while the best of Mrs Oliphant's stories describe this direction of travel, and thus are bound to register a division between the two worlds which in real life she longed to overcome, they are actually more effective in awakening a desire for reconciliation.

That longing did express itself in the opposite direction in another series of stories, *A Little Pilgrim in the Unseen* (1882) and *The Land of Darkness; Along with some further Chapters in the Experiences of the Little Pilgrim* (1888). The first of these, depicting the life and work of a dead woman's spirit in heaven, achieved considerable popularity both in Britain and America. The 'little Pilgrim' stories are Mrs Oliphant's attempt, in an age when orthodox Christianity was being weakened, particularly by scientific advance and ideas on evolution, to forge for herself a faith which would answer the human losses she had experienced in her life. While lower in literary worth than Tennyson's earlier *In Memoriam* (1850), which is also founded on a 'do-it-yourself' faith, her work tapped the same spring of need in the Victorian public for belief in a redeemed life beyond death—although hers shows the influence of the vogue for spiritualism in the 1880s.[5] Here, continuity between this world and the next is seen everywhere. Heaven is a rolling landscape like the Sussex Downs, with an Italianate city full of beautiful palaces. It is a place of continued earthly values—family life, work, education and charity.[6] The little Pilgrim is detailed to help newcomers adjust to heaven, then sent to the bedside of a dying sinner to assist repentance, and then travels with an angel to the pit of purgatory to help light halting souls on their way upward. What is always sought or portrayed is the seamlessness of the move from earthly to heavenly life, whereby what we best are here will go on there, and those who are there will be continually concerned to draw us to them. Moving though they are, these stories (apart from 'The Land of Darkness') are thin at the literary level, largely because they are lacking in complexity, and are driven by a wish for cosmic assurance rather than by the discontinuities of experience.

There are disjunctions of a more formal kind in the other, less assured stories, which also make them more effective in convincing us of the existence of the supernatural. For example, if they portray discontinuities between the seen and unseen worlds within the stories, they also exploit them in the relation of the stories to the reader. The reader expects a standard ghost story, but is given neither. The ghosts are many of them poor fumblers: there is little or no attempt to terrify the reader; and narrative excitement is kept to a minimum. There is often no culmination either: the ghostly visitors to Semur simply depart and the mortal inhabitants return to their old ways; the journeying figure in 'The Land of Darkness' (1887) turns back into hell, old Lady Mary fails in her aim, the lady in 'Earthbound' fades away. The tales are fictive but not quite fictions: they present imagined situations, but refuse the further illusion of self-contained narrative. And if their situations are imagined, they are at the same time depicted with almost banal realism, as Edmund in 'Earthbound' flies into a rage with a boy who rushes straight through the lady to whom he has just proposed, or old Lady Mary struggles to get a purchase on the cabinet containing her will. The supernatural here is not surrounded by a halo of mystery, but operates within sharply-portrayed domestic situations. Mrs Oliphant's long-acquired skills as a novelist of 'real life' here make themselves felt, whether in Edmund's predicament as a catch for Maud Beresford, when he finds himself falling in love with a strange lady he keeps meeting in the garden, or in Lady Mary's very different relations with her house and its inhabitants after she is dead. This is seen too in the way that we are sometimes allowed to speculate that what is seen is imagined: here again our assumptions are undermined, and we are left unable to settle. The most striking instance is Mrs Oliphant's last story, 'The Library Window' (1896), written two years before her death in 1897:[7] here the central young female figure, who is left strangely nameless amid a continually named circle of family and acquaintance, sees in a painted window on the wall of the library opposite her house the figure of a man writing, who gradually turns to face her. It is clearly implied that her vision of this figure could be a sexual projection, and yet at the same time it is also much more than that. Mrs Oliphant wrote this story at the height of the James/Conrad influence on English literature, and it certainly anticipates James's celebrated *The Turn of the Screw* (1898) in which a governess sent to look after children sees a male figure which is both a figure for her frustrated desires and a form of the devil.

These discontinuities and refusals of certainty have the effect of making us less able to be sure of anything, and this may in the context of these ghost stories be a way of removing our grasp on the seen and moving us towards the unseen and unknown. Here the celebrated 'A Beleaguered City' is an instructive example. The story is told through a range of variously biased narrators. Of these the main one is the respectable mayor of Semur, Martin Dupin, whose emotional range, of devotion to public service, vanity, outrage, piety, courage, and fear of the supernatural, finely embodied in a richly human portrait, makes him a fair witness to the facts, but not to the truth. For the 'truth', or something nearer to it, we have the account of the visionary Paul Lecamus, who alone of the citizens of Semur remains behind in the town when the supernatural host arrives, but whose nature may make him see and hear more than is present: to him, 'the thing which had happened to me was that which I had desired all my life' (p. 60). Then we have M. de Bois-Sombre, the mayor's representative while he re-enters Semur; the Mayor's wife; and her mother-in-law. Among all these what is going on is considerably obscured.

Indeed the whole story seems dominated by obscurity in the form of the darkness that falls on Semur. Hovering just at the edge of the narrative is the possibility that this is some 'great mystery of the unexplained', as modern parlance has it; or else that it is the result of some collective delusion or illness. Both Mme. Dupin and Lecamus ask themselves whether it was a dream (p. 85). And if, as we may suppose, it was a supernatural visitation, of what kind was it? Was it the dead of Semur returning, or was it redeemed spirits and angels (p. 55)? And why has this event taken place? M. Dupin's view is that the base materialism of many people in the town has provoked outraged heavenly response: but if so, nothing is done to cause the people to reform. The view of the pious is that the visitation is a response to the walling up of the access between the hospital and the convent in the town, so that the sick can no longer be helped by the devotions of the nuns. This is scoffed at by the mayor, but then on his own admission he has never 'professed religion' (p. 72).

Nor is Lecamus, for all his closeness to events in the city, an accurate authority. On his return he first says, '"They are not the dead. They are the immortal. They are those who dwell—elsewhere"' (p. 55); but when he recounts his experience he refers to them continually as the dead. He returns to say that he has been told, '"You are to send two—two whom you esteem the highest—to speak with them face to face"' (p. 56); but his account of what happened shows him receiving no such instruction, but rather becoming desperate to reverse what he sees as the spirits' failure; and when the mayor and the curé enter the city they are not met, and conclude that '"Lecamus must have deceived himself"' (p. 69). Lecamus' account of the spirits can be seen as reflecting his own aching need for contact with the other world, particularly since the loss of his wife (in this sense it is a comment by Mrs Oliphant herself on her own desire to reach beyond the grave): 'I have desired to investigate the mysterious and unseen. When I have walked abroad I have heard whispers in the air; I have felt the movement of wings, the gliding of unseen feet' (p. 57). He portrays the spirits as wanting desperately to speak with mankind, and as having failed to be heard, and then withdrawing once more. Yet as the mayor asks, if the spirits wanted contact so much, why did they drive the human inhabitants out of the town and close the gate against them (p. 48)? He asks this of his wife, who has advanced the view, which

she says has been 'given' to her, that the spirits ' "have come to convert
our people" ' (p. 48). Lecamus' view of spirits wanting contact is what
we might expect from a would-be mystic.

Equally, the mayor's view that they have come in judgment reflects
his own moralising position. Before their expulsion from the city the
people see a blazing sign on the cathedral door: the mayor reads it
as '*Sommation!*' which means 'summons' (to judgment), and assumes
without evidence that everyone else sees the same word and draws the
same conclusions:

> It was a summons to the people of Semur by name—myself
> at the head as Maire . . . to yield their places, which they
> had not filled aright, to those who knew the meaning of life,
> being dead. NOUS AUTRES MORTS—these were the words
> that blazed out oftenest of all, so that every one saw them.
> And 'Go!' this terrible placard said—'Go! leave this place to
> us who know the true signification of life.'
>
> (p. 25)

Yet we hear from the mayor how here everyone draws his or her
own picture on the darkness; as later too, when each person detects
a particular loved one in the supernatural upthrust. In this light the
mayor's priggish assertion, 'it has become my duty so to arrange and
edit the different accounts of the mystery, as to present one coherent
and trustworthy chronicle to the world' (p. 10), grows into its full ironic
lineaments.

In the face of all these ambiguities, we yet cannot dismiss what
occurred as mere delusion. The more the human agents confound the
nature of the visitation with their desires and prejudices, the more it
shines forth in a purity that does not register on the mayor's narrative.
The more each person fumbles for his or her deepest promptings in
the face of the unseen, the more power and reality that unseen draws
to itself. Whether it is a Christian power cannot clearly be said: the
setting in a French town means that all religious interpretations will
be in Christian and Catholic terms, but we are sufficiently aware of the
way the human mind imposes itself on the unseen throughout the story
to be able to draw back from this. It does not matter that we have Christ
in a chariot, or bejewelled angels, as seen by particular individuals: the
truth is merely provoked by such imagery.

Yet Mrs Oliphant's reticence here, her refusal, unlike her characters,
to write her own views upon the void, may be the strength of the story
at a Christian level. So far as the 'supernatural' itself is concerned, all we
can say is that we have a sojourn in Semur for an undetermined purpose,
followed by a disappearance—and we may even wish to dismiss these
events as a collective hallucination. But so far as the human world is
concerned, we have a group of people who all, variously, understand

in Christian terms what they think they have seen, and yet despite the strongest confirming evidence that they should reform, return at the end to their irreligion and materialism. If not at the level of revelation, then certainly at that of hortation, this story may work to Christian purpose. One of the most powerful moments in the story, shooting beyond the fabric of the narrative, is that of the Christ figure seen by Paul Lecamus, which rushes through the city, telling the saddened spirits, '"Neither will they believe—though one rose from the dead"' (p. 66). Then again, though not specifically Christian, the story may work to show the poverty of human response in the face of what all believe to be the supernatural. The very fact that the humans are driven out of Semur may depict the inherent antagonism between their natures and that of the pure beings who have come among them. Then, the desire to see the visitation as a judgment; or again the tendency to attend only to what is seen as one's own dead ones among the multitude: these also show human shortsightedness, or maybe the inability to understand or approach the free and unmotivated love that Lecamus sees all the spirits as offering and attempting to communicate.

> 'How was it, how was it that you did not hear? One time I was
> by the river *porte* in a boat; and this song came to me from the
> walls as sweet as Heaven. Never have I heard such a song.
> The music was beseeching, it moved the very heart. "We have
> come out of the unseen," they sang; "for love of you; believe
> us, believe us! Love brings us back to earth; believe us, believe
> us!" How was it that you did not hear?'
>
> (p.63)

Thus the very discontinuities of both content and form used in Mrs Oliphant's stories may serve to drive us closer to an apprehension of the unseen than might otherwise have been possible by more overt means clearly linking this world to the next—indeed *was* made impossible precisely by those means in the 'little Pilgrim' stories, where a too evident desire to create a consolatory heaven only leaves us with the image of our desires, not with the reality of a supernatural world beyond our own. It is a method of by indirections finding direction out—indeed, of being discontinuous with one's self and one's personal wishes, and by dramatising situations apart from one's own.

The preoccupation with continuity and discontinuity in Mrs Oliphant's work, or, to put it another way, with one order of being and another, means that her stories are centrally involved with relationship: there are always two terms in varying degrees of nearness to or distance from one another. Unlike the other fantasies we have considered, Mrs Oliphant's stories deal not with the solitary hero but with the interaction of two or more figures: Edmund and the lady in 'Earthbound', the townsfolk with one another and with their 'dead' in 'A Beleaguered City', the Colonel with others encountering the young man's spirit in 'The Open Door', the family of the living and the dead in 'The Portrait', old Lady Mary and her household and relations in 'Old Lady Mary', the girl with the figure in the window opposite who eventually looks at her in 'The Library Window'. The stories are full of door, window and house imagery, to suggest points of transition or of meeting—the door in 'The Open Door', the city gates in 'A Beleaguered City', the window in 'The Library Window', the elaborate gate of heaven in 'A Little Pilgrim in the Unseen', the locked door to the drawing room and the influence of Phil's mother in 'The Portrait', the hidden door to the wizard in 'The Secret Chamber' (1876),[8] the door opening into the byway through the park which is used by the ghost lady in 'Earthbound', the house and its rooms in 'Old Lady Mary'. All these are fulcra about which turn the various meetings and severances in the stories. And in a real sense all these stories are *about* relationship, from that of the little Pilgrim with the newly-arrived in heaven or those dying on earth or those struggling out of hell, to those of children with parents in 'The Secret Chamber', 'The Open Door' and 'The Portrait' or of a city with its dead in 'A Beleaguered City'.

This brings us to a story about which we have not said much, 'The Land of Darkness', a bleak work very reminiscent of James Thomson's *The City of Dreadful Night* (1874). This describes the arrival in hell of the soul of a dead man, and his subsequent journey. This hell is actually continuous with the worst forms of earthly life, just as heaven continued the best—it has a crowded and violent city and industrial wastelands, and is everywhere full of the whirr of machinery. But this place is founded on the reverse of relationship: it is each man for himself (one sees few women). In place of love, compassion and care, there are only indifference, cynicism or even hatred. Yet, for a time, the central character seems to suggest better than this. He cannot understand why people behave this way, or why sick or injured people spurn his attentions, or others mock him for trying to help them: '"it is a shame to let a fellow-creature suffer if we can prevent it."'[9] He can even (if inadvertently) use God's name, at which he causes all about him inexpressible pain (p. 242). He associates with a man who has a dim apprehension of the way out of this hell, and we begin to think that he himself has some intuitions of a better life. But he falls increasingly into the hellish idiom, and finally rejects this friend, who goes on towards the light he sees on his own, while our hero turns back into hell in a circular journey which images the self-enclosure of the damned. His last words to his erstwhile friend are '"There is no love!"'; and at the end, when in the darkness he sees 'a moving spot of milky whiteness', which is in fact the little Pilgrim trying to light the way up from hell for repentant sinners, he turns his back on it: 'On, on, across the waste! On to the cities of the night! On, far away from maddening thought, from hope that is torment, and from the awful Name!' (p. 285). He refuses the painful 'discontinuity' of God's love: rather the agonising hell that is ultimately congenial, than a wrenching change of the soul out of all recognition. And in a different way, the story mocks our own refusal of reality. For the tendency in reading is to assume that this hell is somewhere else, and only comes into existence after death. But suppose that this hell is our world, which we have seen it in many ways resembles? Suppose the hatreds, the selfishness, the glee in pain that we see in it are the idiom in which we ourselves move, in a materialistic world that has destroyed all the generosities of the spirit? To be encouraged to suppose that is to admit a greater continuity between this story and our lives than we would ever otherwise entertain.

All these stories deal with the breaking down of mortal certainties, the disestablishment of the conscious. In continually reiterating the existence of the unseen, Mrs Oliphant is as much showing the reality of that which lies beyond the conscious mind as of that which is transcendent: the seen and the unseen, mortals and ghosts, meet at the border of the mind as much as of life and death. In this her Christianity is akin to that of George MacDonald. In 'A Beleaguered City' we see the destabilising of minds in the face of the supernatural; in 'The Land of Darkness' we have a nightmare vision of the world that reason and complacency seek to deny. With Mrs Oliphant we find once again that interest of nineteenth-century Scottish fantasy with the hidden areas of being and of the mind.

FIONA MACLEOD (1855–1905)

If Mrs Oliphant deals with relationship and so far as possible the establishment of continuity, Fiona Macleod's work is much more shot through with broken relationships and abrupt discontinuities, springing often from a sense of the gulf between human aspiration and untamed fate.

'Fiona Macleod' is as said the pen-name of William Sharp, who took this name from about 1890 onwards, when he became aligned with the Celtic revival, and began to write numbers of novels, tales and essays springing from his interest in the 'Gael'. Sharp was sexually dimorphic, but for him that dimorphism related to areas of the mind rather than to compulsions of the body. A whole area of his being which had long been in revolt against the bleak bourgeois and mercantile values of his family crystallised into a separate individual, who could give free rein to feeling and to the unconscious.[10] It was not only that Sharp saw those qualities as peculiarly feminine, but that he felt that by 'becoming' a woman with a new name he had wholly severed himself from his oppressive past. But to try to live a new sexual identity, if only through writing, involves blurring what one is. It is just such refusal of identity, and indeed inability to give equal weight to opposites, that we find in Macleod's writing. It is ironic that the 'swimminess' he so felt to be a part of the feminine is not reflected in many women writers: and indeed that Mrs Oliphant's work, while it shows an interest in 'continuity', has a strong realism, sense of identity and awareness of the contradiction and complexities of life.

Macleod was one of the leading writers in the Scottish Celtic revival of the 1890s, heading with Patrick Geddes the *Evergreen* Circle in Edinburgh in 1895-6. For many years he had made long visits to the Highlands and Islands, absorbing the scenery and the cultural air, as well as listening to many Gaelic stories and songs; and he was well acquainted with collections of Celtic tales. He also brought out an edition of Macpherson's 'Ossian' in 1896. The introduction to this concludes, 'the ancient poetry, the antique spirit, breathes throughout this eighteenth-century restoration and gives it enduring life, charm, and all the spell of cosmic imagination.'[11] Indeed Macleod himself in his approach to Gaelic culture could be seen as a late nineteenth-century Macpherson, rewriting a tradition. Later writers we shall consider, Neil Gunn and George Mackay Brown, owe not a little to this side of his work.

And yet for Macleod it was not Celtic culture that mattered, it was what came through it, coloured doubtless by that particular source, but as available through different traditions and mythologies. Announcing with disdain, 'I, for one, care less to be identified with any literary movement avowedly partisan. That is not the deliberate view of literature, which carries with it the heat and confused passions of the many,' he declared:

> The 'Celtic Movement' . . . is not, as so often confusedly stated, an arbitrary effort to reconstruct the past; though it is, in part, an effort to discover the past. For myself (as one imputed to this 'movement') I would say that I do not seek merely to reproduce ancient Celtic presentments of tragic beauty and tragic fate, but do seek in nature and in life, and in the swimming thought of timeless imagination, for the kind of beauty that the old Celtic poets discovered and uttered. There were poets and mythmakers in those days; and to-day we may be sure that a new Mythus is being woven, though we may no longer regard with the old wonder, or in the old wonder imaginatively shape and colour the forces of Nature and her silent and secret processes; for the mythopoeic faculty is not only a primitive instinct but a spiritual need.[12]

This says that any mythology might provide 'the swimming thought of timeless imagination', even a modern mythology, since the urge behind them all is perennial. If Macleod really carried out his assertions concerning the possibilities of modern myth, he might have written like the later Yeats or J. M. Synge (to whom he has been likened[13]); and had he also been a modernist he might have written works akin to those different recreations of mythology in Eliot's *The Waste Land* or Joyce's *Ulysses*. But Macleod does also value the 'ancient Celtic presentments of tragic beauty and tragic fate' because they are old, and because what mythology is for him is very much tied up with wonder at remoteness, and with elegy and desire.

> I think that our people have most truly loved their land, and their country, and their songs, and their ancient traditions, and that the word of bitterest savour is that sad word exile. But it is also true that in that love we love vaguely another land, a rainbow-land, and that our most desired country is not the real Ireland, the real Scotland, the real Brittany, but the vague Land of Youth, the shadowy Land of Heart's Desire. And it is also true, that deep in the songs we love above all other songs is a lamentation for what is gone away from the world, rather than merely from us as a people, or a sighing or longing for what the heart desires but no mortal destiny requites.[14]

This is the language of Romantic *Sehnsucht*, or spiritual yearning: at best metaphysically-inspired as in Novalis or C. S. Lewis, it can equally slip into mere pleasure at the desire itself. The word 'vaguely' here is telling in Macleod's case: it would seem to align him with fantasy-writers of wish-fulfilment, such as William Morris and his contemporary romances of recreated Celticism (*The Wood Beyond the World* (1895), *The Well at the World's End* (1896), *The Water of the Wondrous Isles* (1897)), or with Lord Dunsany's later *The King of Elfland's Daughter* (1924). But Macleod is 'vague' here also in the sense of shifting position: for in the very next paragraph we learn that 'we dwell overmuch among desired illusions: beautiful, when, like the rainbow, they are the spiritual reflection of certainties; but worthless as the rainbow-gold with which the Shee deceive the unwary, when what is the phantom of a spiritual desire is taken to be the reality of material fact.'[15]

So far perhaps not promising: but when we look at the stories themselves, we find quite another mutation, for they are many of them far 'stronger' in character than this programme would suggest. Most of them first appeared in Macleod's collections of 1895 and 1896, *The Sin-Eater and Other Tales* and *The Washer of the Ford and Other Legendary Moralities*. They are as full of fate, death and darkness as of anything more happy. In 'The Washer of the Ford', the vengeful bard Torcall brings about the deaths of a boat-full of his enemies, and exults at the agony that awaits their souls at the hands of the terrible Washer at the Ford; there he sees each 'red soul' being taken and slashed to pieces by her sword before being trampled to annihilation, 'till under the feet of her was only a white sand, white as powder'.[16] This story ends in a Christian vision of the Washer as a purger of sins, which transforms this brutal and pagan view of life: but that view still retains its hideous force. 'Silk o' the Kine' and 'Ula and Urla' together make up a story of a pair of lovers who, in the first, manage to escape through murder the enforced betrothal of the woman, Eilidh (Urla), to the king's warrior-kinsman, and in the second, die through another king's lust.[17] In 'The Sin-Eater', a man 'eats' the sin of a dead man for money: but if he thus saves the other's soul, he loses his own. For the dead man is his enemy, and he is told that if a Sin-Eater bears a grudge against the dead man he helps, he will have gone against Christ (who 'ate' all man's sins out of love, and freely). The Sin-Eater here ends in spiritual torment, feeling that Christ has laid upon him '"all the nameless black sins of the world"' till Judgment Day; he is last seen trying to atone, self-lashed to a crossed spar, riding the waves out to the west from Iona to his death, calling, '"In ransom for my soul!"'

> 'And with that I saw the double-spar turn over and slide down the back-sweep of a drowning big wave. Ay, sure, it went out to the deep sea swift enough then. It was in the big eddy that rushes between Skerry-Mòr and Skerry-Beag. I did not see it again—no, not for the quarter of an hour, I am thinking. Then I saw just the whirling top of it rising out of the flying yeast of a great, black-blustering wave, that was rushing northward before the current that is called the Black-Eddy.
>
>   With that you have the end of Neil Ross: ay, sure, him that was called the Sin-Eater. And that is a true thing; and may God save us the sorrow of sorrows.'[18]

No easy sentiment or elegy here; no heart's desire or rainbow-land; no sunlit beauty nor wild unassuageable desire for an elusive glory. There are those who equate Macleod's work with Macleod's pronouncements as to its intentions, but this is mistaken: the sentimentality that supposedly informs them, and the 'Green Life' they are said to pursue, are not often in evidence at all.[19] A cursory glance at the further blacknesses of such stories as 'The Dan-nan-Ron', 'The Ninth Wave', 'The Song of the Sword', or 'The Dark Nameless One', will show the same thing.[20] There are stories with 'happier' or more spiritually uplifting endings, such as 'The Awakening of Angus Ogue', 'Cathal of the Woods' or 'The Last Supper'[21]—but even there the style, enthusiastic as it often may be (and it has more of the 'I' narrator than other tales), is only rarely as self-consciously indulgent as the ending of 'The Awakening of Angus Ogue': '"Go forth, eternal Hope!" she cried. And Angus Ogue passed away on the sunflood, weaving rainbows as he went, that were fair upon the hills of age and light within the valleys of sorrow, and were everywhere a wild, glad joy.'[22]

Then what is Macleod about? It seems that as in myth, he is able to strike levels of causality far beneath what is conscious or 'psychological', to suggest that people act out primal dramas with programmes that are set into the very nature of being. Indeed, it is here that his frequent mention of the basic Greek idiom is significant, and his sense of the 'Winged Destiny' that creates and laughingly manages all life from within the spirit. Constantly he reaches back to the primitive and the elemental, to the dark impulses of an Oedipus or a Medea:

> One does not need to know the Scandinavian story of Gunhild, or the Arthurian story of Tristan and Yseult, or the Gaelic story of Deirdrê and the sons of Usna, in order to know the mystery and the silent arrivals of destiny, or to know the emotion of sorrow at the passage of beauty. These emotions are not the properties of drama, which is but a fowler snaring them in a net. These deep elementals are the obscure chorus which plays upon the silent flutes, upon the nerves wherein the soul sits enmeshed.[23]

So too, 'The tradition of accursed families is not the fantasy of one dramatist or of one country or of one time. The *Oresteia* of Aischylos is no more than a tragic fugue wherein one hears the cries of uncountable threnodies.'[24] There is a distinctly Arnoldian note here.

Take 'The Sin-Eater' for example. The story decks itself in psychological causes. Neil Ross has returned to Mull from thirty miles to the east, ostensibly to see his family home, though he learns his relatives are all dead. He also, it appears, wishes to curse Adam Blair for causing his father to desert his mother for another woman. But these motives are no sooner uttered than dropped. We are left to wonder why Ross has come now, and in such poverty that he cannot find himself the next meal or bed, let alone take the ferry to Iona and his family place. When he is offered the chance to earn a few paltry shillings by eating the sin of the soul of the dead Adam Blair, he takes it, though he has no cause to wish to do any good for Blair, indeed the reverse. Nor are we given a character portrait of Ross as a weak and indecisive person, such as might explain his apparent shift of behaviour. Later he calls himself 'Judas', but that is only a name, an attempt to give an explanation for what he is doing. We could say he thinks he will be able to be rid of the sins himself, from the assurance of those about him: but he not only knows in himself that to hate the person whose sins you eat is to be doomed to be flayed by them, but is told this by the son of the dead man. What we have then at the surface level is psychologically a puzzle, a confusion: but that only drives us to a deeper level to see a web of compulsion that works through the souls of men. It is something to do with the fact that Ross comes from a blighted family, and that death, pain and guilt can earth themselves on just such a figure. It has nothing to do with personality, less to do with morality, but much to do with a primal choosing of which we are not aware. The sin-eater fits a pattern and plays a part, to be made the scapegoat: he thinks to escape the pattern after he has followed the rituals and 'eaten' the sins: but the pattern will not let him go. What happens seems almost independent of the agents, bound up in the bleak moorland marsh and the raging sea. In that sea Ross is one day seen to swim into the cave of a sea-monster, by which uniquely he is spared, to go on suffering. In this story, the normal categories we understand are broken down: chance seems to bring Ross to Mull, but destiny in fact makes a pattern; to eat a sin is literally to do so, as Ross partakes of salt bread and water laid on the dead man's flesh.

We know nothing of Ross, or of Blair, even of the old woman Sheen Macarthur, whom our cliché-making instinct is to see as a benign old lady who means for the best. Mere psychology is nothing here: we are below the old stable ego of the character, as Lawrence would have it, operating at levels dictated by primal gravity or the stars. It might scarcely occur to us that 'The Sin-Eater' is actually a story set in or near the present time, where others of Macleod's tales with a similar bent go further back to the period of the Vikings, or further still to the first men in these empty lands—'Ula and Urla', 'The Dan-nan-Ron', 'The Washer of the Ford'. The vision is Greek, or similar: these figures are here, they make marks in the boggy soil, but they are assemblages of spiritual electricity which will either blaze or be earthed. At the level of the individual, Macleod's stories are frequently elusive, just as is Macleod's own identity. Men turn into seals; and vice versa. 'Islâ' and 'Eilidh' (in 'Silk o' the Kine') already close in name, shift to 'Ula' and 'Urla' in the companion story, and each is joined in the third, their child, who speaks with an adult's knowledge. In 'The Washer of the Ford' we sense a shift from pagan to Christian as the vision of the washer changes from a flailer of souls to a woman who washes the sinful soul clean: yet such happy endings are no more true than sunny days to the weather. Macleod's stories entertain all different 'world-views'— 'pagan', Druidical, fatalistic, Christian—but settle for none. There is no justice, no fixed morality of good and evil. Indeed fixity is for mortals: no sooner are pledges uttered and promises made than the ground shifts.

So these stories, so close as they are to the tales and myths from which they spring, might seem to chill desire rather than awaken it, and scarcely ever speak of the land of the heart's desire, or the longing for a lost joy, that some of Macleod's criticism returns to. It is clear that his art was different from what he often made of it. Indeed he sometimes sees the creations of longing as an evasion of harsh reality: yet it is typical of his criticism that even as he does so he is half in love with the statement as he floridly puts it:

It is easy, then, by the illusions of the imagination, to avoid the dread shadow. Man has shaped and coloured many beautiful dreams, as much, perhaps, to elude this shadow as to create enchantment. Is it not for this, in so great a part, that he has taken the sigh of the sea and the cadence of the wind and the murmur of the leaf, and lamentations and delight and whispers, and made Music; that he has taken from the silent flower and wave-haunted shell, and wrought so the colour and sound of verse; that he has surprised the secret of light and shade, and the secret of the columnar suspense of the cypress in moonlight or the single image of life silhouetted against dawn or sunglow, and the secret of the sombre avenues of pine-forest at sunset or moonrise, and the secret of the swaying branch and the blue smoke of woods and the wave of the sea, and created painting and sculpture and architecture and the dance?[25]

Compare that, which is followed by, 'But below all art there is an austere whisper: How would it be with you, O Soul, in the wilderness; how would it be with you alone there, naked amid the great silence and before the eternal shadow, and with no least of your illusions to hide the one or inhabit the other?'—compare that with, say, the ending of 'The Laughter of Scathach the Queen', when the captured Vikings are hung by their hair in a tree:

> Soon all was dark in the rath. Flame after flame died out. Then there was but one red glare in the night, the watch-fire by the dûn. Deep peace was upon all. Not a heifer lowed, not a dog bayed against the moon. The wind fell into a breath, scarce enough to lift the fragrance from flower to flower. Upon the branches of a great oak swung motionless a strange fruit, limp and grey as the hemlock that hangs from ancient pines.[26]

The bleakness here is the truly moving thing: moving in no facile self-consciously sentimental way, but in the way of inspiring dread and a primitive sense of the numinous which exists beyond all taming creeds and wishes. So it is clear that Macleod's Celticism, while often an over-sweet thing in his thinking of it, is in practice, in the tales as we have them, the source of a far harsher and more elemental note. It is almost as though Macleod the commentator could ignore what Macleod the writer of tales had done: thus again we have two persons, and uncertain identity. Macleod writes about the Celts because of the elemental current of life they share with the deepest apprehensions of other mythologies; but also thinks to write such tales as a way of pleasing and warming through elegy and desire the spirit of a sad exile in flight from the hardness of modern urban and mechanical life. The one urge lives in identification with the experience, the other in distance. And the first lies in Macleod's best tales. Macleod writes fantasy not out of a belief in some definite or consoling supernatural being, but out of a sense that life is founded on, springs out of, some far current, constantly mutable, whose changes it forever reflects—the 'Winged Destiny', which while it exists eternally apart, can also 'descend upon your soul or mine as dew upon blades of grass, as wind among the multitudinous leaves, as the voice of sea and forest . . . that flitting shadow, more intangible than dew, yet whose breath shall see the wasting of hills and the drought of oceans.'[27]

Who else but Macleod, one now begins to wonder, could have told that dark tale, 'The Dan-nan-Ron', in which Mànus MacCodrum, whose forbears were of the seals, is driven out of his man-self by the mocking *feadan* or song of the seal of Gloom Achanna, his sworn enemy? Mànus took to wife the coveted cousin of the Achanna brothers; but his hold on humanity seems already forfeit when she and his child both die. At the end he is glad of the wild sea and the thought of the fish he will eat: he goes among the seals in the moon-flood off the reef, calling to them the lost rune of the MacCodrums:

> It is I, Mànus MacCodrum,
>
> . . . .
> Your brother, O Seals of the Sea!
> Give me blood of the red fish,
> And a bite of the flying sgadan:
> The green wave on my belly,
> And the foam in my eyes![28]

But when he strikes at the chief bull seal it turns on him, and with it all the rest:

> Mànus swayed this way and that. All he could hear now was the snarling and growling and choking cries of the maddened seals. As he fell, they closed in upon him. His screams wheeled through the night like mad birds. With desperate fury he struggled to free himself. The great bull pinned him to the rock; a dozen others tore at his white flesh, till his spouting blood made the rocks scarlet in the white shine of the moon.[29]

Again, a deep fate in the story beneath all will or morality; even Gloom Achanna is no more than an actor in this web, which locks souls in an indestructible filament of destiny that is woven out of their very essence. And here again no indulgence in description, no longing, only a deep and inevitable agony. It is not always easy to identify such stories with the feminine, with a Fiona Macleod. But for our purposes the main thing here is the reach for the unconscious, unknown, dark principle behind being. Macleod's characters are often driven not by reason or idealism, but by deep promptings of the spirit.[30] In this he is peculiarly a Scottish fantasist, his spirit aligned with those other fascinations with the unconscious we have seen in Scott, Hogg, Carlyle, MacDonald, Stevenson and Oliphant.

Notes

1 See Julia Briggs, *Night Visitors: The Rise and Fall of the English Ghost Story* (London: Faber, 1977).

2 For accounts of Mrs Oliphant's life and work, see Merryn Williams, *Margaret Oliphant: A Critical Biography* (London: Macmillan, 1978); and *The Autobiography of Margaret Oliphant*, ed. Elizabeth Jay (Oxford: Oxford University Press, 1990).

3 'A Beleaguered City', 'The Open Door' and 'Old Lady Mary' are reprinted in Margaret Oliphant, *A Beleaguered City and Other Stories*, ed. Merryn Williams (Oxford: Oxford University Press, 1988). 'Earthbound' and 'Old Lady Mary' are reprinted in Margaret Oliphant, *Selected Short Stories of the Supernatural*, ed. Margaret K. Gray (Edinburgh: Scottish Academic Press, 1985). References are to these texts. The quote from 'Earthbound' is from *Selected Short Stories of the Supernatural*, p. 61.

4 Repr. in Oliphant, *Selected Short Stories of the Supernatural*.

5 Colleen McDannell and Bernhard Lang, *Heaven: A History* (New Haven and London: Yale University Press, 1988), pp. 292–303.

6 This anthropocentric conception of heaven as continuous with earth was prevalent in the nineteenth century: see McDannell and Lang, chs 7–9 and p. 275.

7 Repr. in both Oliphant collections.

8 Repr. in Oliphant, *Selected Short Stories of the Supernatural*.

9 'The Land of Darkness', in *A Beleaguered City and Other Stories*, p. 241.

10 On Sharp's life and spiritual history, see Flavia Alaya, *William Sharp—"Fiona Macleod", 1855–1905* (Cambridge, Mass.: Harvard University Press, 1970).

11 *The Poems of Ossian*, translated by James Macpherson, ed. William Sharp (Edinburgh: Patrick Geddes, 1896), p. xxiv.

12 'Fiona Macleod' (William Sharp), *The Winged Destiny: Studies in the Spiritual History of the Gael* (London: Heinemann, 1910), pp. 183, 184. On Sharp's cosmopolitanism, his 'transcendent rationalism', see Alaya, pp. 168–74.

13 Roderick Watson, *The Literature of Scotland* (London: Macmillan, 1984), p. 312.

14 *The Winged Destiny*, p. 198.

15 Ibid., p. 199.

16 Fiona Macleod, *Reissue of the Shorter Stories of Fiona Macleod, Vol. II, Barbaric Tales* (Edinburgh: Patrick Geddes, 1897), p. 190. Vols I and III of this reissue, also 1897, are *Spiritual Tales* and *Tragic Romances*. 'The Washer of the Ford' is reprinted in Elizabeth Sutherland, ed., *The Gold Key and the Green Life: Some Fantasies and Celtic Tales by George MacDonald and Fiona Macleod* (London: Constable, 1986).

17 In *Barbaric Tales* and *Spiritual Tales* respectively; both are reprinted in Sutherland.

18 *Tragic Tales*, pp. 164–5.

19 Alaya calls her chapter on Macleod's Celticism 'The Celtic Never-Never Land', and sees the vision here as 'a fantasy overwhelmed with longing and nostalgia—a fantasy to which the "doomed" Celt has long lent his vocabulary, and which Sharp could only describe as a far-off land of beauty, "with the light of home upon it"' (p. 172). And Sutherland maintains that the tales are created in a dream of 'the green life' that takes no account of the harshness of reality (p. 139).

20 The first two appear in *Tragic Romances*, the third in *Barbaric Tales* and the fourth in *Spiritual Tales*.

21 The first and third are from *Spiritual Tales*; 'Cathal' is from *Barbaric Tales*. Sutherland reprints 'Cathal' and 'The Last Supper'.

22 *Spiritual Tales*, p. 208.

23 *The Winged Destiny*, p. 367.

24 Ibid., p. 368.

25 Ibid., pp. 383–4.

26 *Barbaric Tales*, pp. 59–60; repr. in Sutherland, p. 183.

27 *The Winged Destiny*, p. 389.

28 *Tragic Romances*, p. 110.

29 Ibid., pp. 111–12.

30 On the 'psychic dramas' of Macleod's stories, see Alaya, ch. 9, 'The Geography of Mind: Toward the Illimitable', pp. 182–90.

CHAPTER EIGHT

Scottish Fantasy and the Child: Andrew Lang and J. M. Barrie

L
ANG AND BARRIE both wrote within the vogue for children's literature in the decades around the turn of the century. This vogue was largely English, and both writers, as Scots living in London, thus gave to Scottish fantasy two classics it might not otherwise have had.

Whether Barrie's *Peter Pan* is properly to be seen as a children's book has been debated:[1] but both he and Lang are ostensibly addressing a child audience. The two form a remarkable contrast in their attitude to childhood, which for Lang is a long-past source of nostalgia, where for Barrie it is an ever-present and crucial issue. In Lang, as we shall see, we have an adult looking back at childhood, where in Barrie we often have a child who does not look forward to being an adult. But for both childhood is bound up with magic, with fantasy, and with features more recognisably Scottish—alienation, uncertainty of self, the unconscious.

LANG, *THE GOLD OF FAIRNILEE* (1888)

Stevenson's *Dr Jekyll and Mr Hyde* had as its epigraph this piece of verse:

> It's ill to loose the bands that God decreed to bind;
> Still will we be the children of the heather and the wind.
> Far away from home, O it's still for you and me
> That the broom is blowing bonnie in the north countrie.

It is an epigraph which might more obviously be applied to Lang's *The Gold of Fairnilee*. Lang was in fact a close friend of Stevenson's in London, and wrote on and edited his works, but there is small evidence that *Dr Jekyll and Mr Hyde* influenced him in any striking way. What the verse above registers, and the two writers must have shared, was a sense, sometimes guilty, of the pull of the land they had left. *The Gold of Fairnilee* is Lang's only memorable work of fantasy, and the only one to look back to Scotland, deriving much of its power from its setting in the Selkirk region of his own childhood, and from its foundation in Scottish legend and folk-tale. In this one story Lang realised the living power of myth which in others of his works (such as *Custom and Myth* (1884) and *Myth, Ritual and Religion* (1887)) he described much more theoretically.

The story describes the Borders home of the Kers of Fairnilee, where, after his father's death at Flodden, young Randal grows up with his widowed mother and an adopted girl, Jeanie, who was brought back accidentally from a reprisal cattle raid on an English holding. One day Randal explores a fairy wishing well over the hills and does not come back. Years of famine fall on the land, and much of the family wealth is sold by the Lady Ker to support her people. After seven years, Jeanie revisits the wishing well and through courage and Christian faith wins Randal back from the fairies. He has with him a bottle of magic liquid that can descry all truth through concealment. This accidentally proves the means of saving the family fortunes, for it uncovers the legendary treasure trove of Fairnilee. Randal and Jeanie marry.

The story is rooted in at least three Scottish traditional ballads, 'Lord Randal', 'Thomas the Rhymer' and 'Tam Lin'. Only the name of the protagonist comes from 'Lord Randal', which describes the poisoning of Randal by his 'true love'. 'Thomas the Rhymer' gives Lang the fairy queen who takes the hero, and the strange scenery through which she leads him to the garden of Faërie. There is also a sense of the hero's responsibility, even of a fall of man, in the way that Thomas gives himself into the fairy queen's power by kissing her and later by eating an apple she offers him in the garden; and Lang's story is to have similar overtones. 'Tam Lin' provides the theme of a girl who loves a man who has been captured by the fairies, and who must endure through three transformations of her beloved to win him back in his proper form; but the motive in this story is sexual, Janet being with child by Tam, whom she let seduce her. These traditional elements Lang weaves into a more realistic and historical setting, with a variety of themes.

One of the ideas of the story is what the true 'gold of Fairnilee' is. We do not get to the actual gold—coins, images and bars—until the very last. By that time we have had different losses and gains, all of them to do with people. The story starts with the loss of Randal's father through the larger loss for Scotland at Flodden. Randal one evening sees the ghost of his father ride by him wounded, and giving no sign of recognition: that night his dead body is brought back on a shield. The cattle raid brings back not only loot, but the far greater gift of Jeanie to both Randal and his mother: 'It came as if the fairies had sent it.'[2] But then the fairies take Randal away for seven years, and health and plenty are also taken from the land. The return of Randal is the greatest gift they could all have: 'This was the end of all their sorrow, and it was as if Randal had come back from the dead' (pp. 60–1). The discovery of material treasure later simply cements a joy already found. Nor should we forget that in himself Randal is the male heir of Fairnilee, the focus of the health of his family and his lands and the guarantee of its future: the story ends with still another human gold in the form of his children 'playing on the banks of Tweed, and rolling down the grassy slope to the river, to bathe on hot days' (p. 85).

Another related idea concerns how gain is achieved. In the realm of the fairies, all seems to Randal wondrously beautiful and happy: 'they came into the light, and into the beautiful garden that lies round the castle of the Fairy Queen. There they lived in a noble company of gallant knights and fair ladies. All seemed very mirthful, and they rode, and hunted, and danced; and it was never dark night, nor broad daylight, but like early summer dawn before the sun has risen' (p. 63). That 'seemed' gives it away; and Randal there finds a bottle of magic liquid which when rubbed on his eyes reveals this Fairyland for what it is, destroying the glamour, the patina of beauty and joy with which it is overlain. The happiness of this world is unearned, and therefore slight and easily dismissed.

Joy is to be gained, the story has us believe, only through loss and struggle. Out of the loss of the former Lord of Fairnilee grows Randal, who is to save the fortunes of his family. Out of his loss comes the true joy of his return. Out of famine comes renewed health and plenty. It is not for nothing that this story is set in the variable world of actual Scottish history in the early sixteenth century, with Flodden, border raids and famine through the economic isolation of Fairnilee; and the story ends where it begins, with a picture of the present-day ruin of Fairnilee.

The fairies, by contrast, live in a static world of pleasure, where there are no seasons, and time is stopped between night and morning. Because they are not part of mortality, their joys are thin. Nor is gain to be decreed or held: it is earned through courage and faith, as Jeanie restores Randal from Fairyland; or it comes by chance, as Jeanie happens to be caught up in a carpet looted in the raid on the English and is thus brought home, or as Randal and Jeanie happen to be by to see where the old nurse discovers the gold before the accidental breaking of the magic fairy bottle causes her to forget once more where she saw it. The treasure, held static in the earth since Roman times, and found, appropriately, in a large coffin-shaped container, is released to work in time and bring joy to people. The real gain is that which lives and moves with nature, not that which is frozen or hoarded.

There is much emphasis in the story on reality over false glamour. (This is interesting given Lang's usual preference for romance and adventure over realistic fiction.[3]) There is a place for wonder and beauty: the glory in which Randal's father sets out with his company to Flodden is not wholly banished by the death and loss that follow. But there is no easy romanticism either. When the company ride away, it is not on a clear road 'but along a green grassy track, the water splashing up to their stirrups where they crossed the marshes' (p. 5). Always the story is set amid the hard realities of sixteenth-century Borders life. Fairnilee may be secluded and far away enough to avoid the English reprisals after Flodden, but its very seclusion from commerce is its undoing in the years of famine. The old nurse with her country superstition concerning the fairies comes into conflict with Lady Ker, whose Christianity forbids her to entertain the existence of such beings (p. 44). Tam Hislop, a local man, disappeared just before Flodden and when he came back seven years later vowed he had been taken by the fairies, but some said they saw him in Perth, and he was thrashed for a runaway (pp. 27–9). But the main removal of false enchantment is that of the fairies themselves, when Randal sees them as they are:

> The gold vanished from the embroidered curtains, the light grew dim and wretched like a misty winter day. The Fairy Queen, that had seemed so happy and beautiful in her bright dress, was a weary, pale woman in black, with a melancholy face and melancholy eyes. She looked as if she had been there for thousands of years, always longing for the sunlight and the earth, and the wind and rain. There were sleepy poppies twisted in her hair, instead of a golden crown. And the knights and ladies were changed. They looked but half alive; and some, in place of their gay green robes, were dressed in rusty mail, pierced with spears and stained with blood. And some were in burial robes of white, and some in dresses torn or dripping with water, or marked with the burning of fire . . .
>
> And Randal wearied of Fairyland, which now that he saw it clearly looked like a great unending stretch of sand and barren grassy country, beside a grey sea where there was no tide. All the woods were of black cypress trees and poplar, and a wind from the sea drove a sea-mist through them, white and cold, and it blew through the open courts of the fairy castle.
>
> (pp. 64–5)

Fairyland and our world are not entirely separated. Quite when Randal has his sight of faërian disenchantment is not clear, but it seems quite 'late' in his seven-year term, for he begins to long for earth and its changes and 'Then the voice of Jeanie had come down to him' (p. 65). The famine that seizes Fairnilee occurs in the sixth and seventh years of Randal's absence. 'Fairnilee' and 'Fairyland' are similar names: indeed Lang tells us that 'Fairnilee' means 'the Fairies' Field' (p. 2). It may be that the disenchantment of Fairyland and the famine in Fairnilee are linked. As part of that disenchantment, Randal observes that the festivals of the fairies 'were not of dainty meats, but of cold, tasteless flesh, and of beans, and pulse, and such things as the old heathens, before the coming of the Gospel, used to offer to the dead' (p. 65). On his return the miseries of Fairyland and Fairnilee are likened (pp. 67–8). We may suppose that Randal undergoes a rite of passage, and as he does so, that larger community of which he is a part does so also—though Fairnilee has been through its own trial in the disaster of Flodden long before that.

But this omits the moral and Christian content of the story. Here, quite different links between the realms of Fairnilee and Fairyland are suggested, and Randal can be seen as more fallible. Before he is taken by the fairies, Randal ignores all warnings, drags Jeanie along with him and, when she is tired, deserts her at night and goes on alone: in the sense that he has not really cared for the feelings of other people, he has put himself outside his own race, and is thus ready prey for the fairies. In Fairyland he could be said to live a life of careless illusion, quite forgetting 'his mother and Jean, and the world where he was born, and Fairnilee' (p. 63). But while he is like this, those above him are distraught at his loss, seek him everywhere and never forget him. It is possible here to see Lang turning the traditional human forgetfulness while in Fairyland to moral purpose.

And the purpose may be more than moral. For the magic bottle that one day Randal 'happened to see' in Fairyland may not be there by chance but by grace. And it is through Christ that he is saved. For when Jeanie calls to him, and Randal is sent up by the Fairy Queen as a hideous dwarf to frighten her away, she is able to restore him to himself and his own world by making the sign of the cross over him three times: this transforms him because he is 'a christened knight, and not a man of the fairy world' (p. 66). The dwarf shape could be seen as that of his sinful nature, redeemed only through Christ's intercession. And one could go further: Randal's descent into the wishing well that is a forbidden place to Christians could even be seen as a fall of man. Then, the bitterness of his experience below and of men above could be the long consequence of that fall, which spreads to all men; and Jeanie (whose original name, Jane Musgrave, associates her with death, from which she was miraculously saved by being brought out of her burning home back to Fairnilee), becomes a Christ figure, or a form of the pure soul that can call man back and save him. All these possibilities are there: but it must be stressed that they remain possibilities, resting lightly on the story.

But here we should note Lang's attitude to the 'unconscious', in comparison to that of the other writers of Scots fantasy so far considered. (It is an attitude also mirrored in his other works.[4]) In one sense Randal's journey down to Fairyland also symbolises a journey into his inner self (from which, as Joseph Campbell would have it, he is to undergo a maturation process[5]), and along with this we can think of other archetypes such as the Anima and the Waste Land that must be healed. In that sense the journey to Fairyland is one that must be made. Like Mossy and Tangle in MacDonald's 'The Golden Key', the children must be divided and wander their ways through faërie until they meet again as mature man and woman: the difference here is only that the voyage into the darkness is one that the male child alone makes. The unconscious twines Randal in its coils: it is deceiving and dangerous here, no part of the divine as it is in MacDonald. But it is the place that must be traversed, the only way to a maturity which has seen through deceit and has learned also to accept its own mortality (for Randal's choice of this world in preference to faërie must be seen that way). And it is the dangerous realm from which is brought back the magic gift for the world above, the bottle that is to reveal the buried treasure.

In the end, though, that underworld is superseded, its gift used and broken, its very existence forgotten as Randal once forgot his own world: 'He remembered the long, grey sands, and the cold mist, and the white faces of the strange people, and the gloomy queen, no more than you remember the dream you dreamed a week ago' (pp. 67–8). The drive of the story is against the buried and the concealed. Everything is to be brought into the light, or it is to be forgotten. The emphasis falls on the rational. Randal is no longer the careless lad he was. He takes note of where the old nurse knelt with the magic bottle, and digs the treasure up by night, while Jeanie hovers near dressed in white clothes to look like a ghost and frighten off any passers-by. He and Jeanie hide the treasure in several secret locations. Subsequently, Randal sells parts of it in different countries and uses the proceeds to restore Fairnilee. And the story ends on a note of further rationality, as the narrator explains how it is that the treasure came to have among it not only Roman gold and images, but a 'kettle' full of coins from a period earlier than that of the Roman occupation. So we may say that if Lang sees the underworld or the unconscious as a place that 'must' be gone into, it is also one to be left utterly thereafter, for the levels of mind that exist away from the depths and in the light of the sun. Neither of his faërian sources in 'Tam Lin' or 'Thomas the Rhymer' actually blighted Fairy Land, turning it to wretchedness and poverty, as Lang did: he de-glamourises them, too. Certainly his story catches Fairy Land in a net of moral and Christian condemnation as his sources do not. But it is at least interesting for us that in making this one faërian journey back to his own roots, Lang should thereby feel drawn to go into the roots of the land and of the mind. His sources do not mention any descent into Fairy Land via a well.

In others of Lang's invented fantasies, *The Princess Nobody: A Tale of Fairy Land* (1884), *Prince Prigio* (1889) and *Prince Ricardo of Pantouflia, being the Adventures of Prince Prigio's Son* (1893), we are in the preposterous fairylands that have their origin in Thackeray's *The Rose and The Ring* (1855). The emphasis is light, comic and above all on wit: indeed it is Prince Prigio's problem that he is made too clever by half by one of his fairy godmothers, and must learn to tone it down. But then 'cleverness' was one of the motifs of Lang's own life, from his earliest university scholarships to his dominance of much London intellectual life. His attitude to fantasy was usually one of light amusement. Alone of all the writers we shall consider he directed his fairy-tales at children, if in a manner which just may escape being patronising[6]. In the introduction to the collection of tales in the first of his 'Colour' books, *The Blue Fairy Book* (1889), Lang wrote of the 'children to whom and for whom they are told', and declared, 'they represent the young age of man true to his early loves, and have his unblunted edge of belief, a fresh appetite for marvels.' This could come naturally to someone who believed that fairy-tales were created in the childhood of the race. By its light, one could almost see Randal's experience in Fairy Land as the story of someone learning to grow out of the illusion of fairy-tales. We will find quite a different story in J. M. Barrie's *Peter Pan*.

J.M. BARRIE, *PETER PAN* (1904)

Lang's *The Gold of Fairnilee* is fantasy for a child; but *Peter Pan* is also the fantasy of a child. In *Peter Pan* the desire is to stay a child, as does Peter himself. That fantasy of childhood is at once a yearning for an elusive truth and an escape from reality. Reality baldly announces itself in the first sentence of the prose version, *Peter and Wendy*: 'All children, except one, grow up.'[7] Peter Pan is both Pan, spirit of the woods, of nature and perhaps of something deeper than that, and also *Peter* Pan who ran away from his family to live with the fairies in Kensington Gardens and who declares, '"I want always to be a little boy and to have fun."'[8] That fantasy of never growing up was lived by the author J. M. Barrie: but in his story he shows the price of this, as well as the advantages, just as with growing up also. In *The Gold of Fairnilee* we follow a *rite de passage* in which the boy hero goes through magical experiences which mature him: the fairies there, caught in the eternal present of Fairyland, are seen by Randal to be blighted and in league with death; 'glamour' is there that which defrauds of life. *Peter Pan* is not so clearly a moral book in this way: the change from childhood to adulthood is seen as not so often the product of growth and maturation, as simply of time. Peter himself, who does not grow, is, as *Peter and Wendy* has it, at once 'gay and innocent and heartless' (p. 154). The tone on leaving Peter is one of elegy; something is lost, one's childhood and something else at the heart of childhood, as mysterious as the unattainable kiss on Mrs Darling's cheek. Yet even nostalgia itself is part-lost, for the picture of the ideal childhood fades to a vision of a creature who refuses growth, pain, love and commitment.

The essence of *Peter Pan* is elusiveness. Indeed the start of the adventure concerns the children eluding their parents' most strenuous efforts to keep them in reality. The centre of *Peter Pan* is the dream that is the Never Land, in which everything is dismantled and rendered fluid and uncertain before it is ostensibly rebuilt. The play is full of patterns and themes which seem to go somewhere and yet are also in the end subverted.

For instance, there is a pattern in *Peter Pan* which we see in some of Shakespeare's pastoral comedies such as *A Midsummer Night's Dream*, *As You Like It*, *The Winter's Tale* and *The Tempest*. We start in the city or the court, go out to the country, the fairies or the sea, and return. Childhood is here not left behind as in Lang, but is an agent in recovery. So here we start in London, in a normally regulated and 'policed' household, which would frustrate Peter's seizing the children, were it not for a lapse on the part of those in control—here parents, rather than rulers who go tyrannical and subvert civil behaviour. The parents go to a party, and Mr Darling ensures out of spite that Nana the guard dog will be chained up. Then the laws of nature are upended: the children can fly, time is suspended or reduced to the random ticking of a clock in a crocodile, direction is ' "Second to the right and then straight on till morning" ' (p. 15), and space is a land called Never. The Never Land itself is an island set in a dream sea, with pirates and redskins who live outside society and civility, and lost boys, and strange beasts. There are no buildings, no roads: the lost boys live with Peter in a natural cavern beneath the roots of the trees, and Wendy's house is made of branches with red sap and a roof and floor of moss. Wendy's house is in a sense an 'answer' to the Darlings' house, for here it is a matter of how many people can be got into it, not of how successfully it keeps things out. This 'destructuring' of the rules of ordinary life is part of a move not only from city to country, but as in Shakespearean comedy, from the rational area of mind to the imaginative and unconscious one, here identified with childhood. That we are dealing with mental realities in the Never Land is sufficiently evident from the frequent assertion that the Never Land and fairies are a product of make-believe, and from the way that while having their own reality, the redskins and the pirates under Hook are supremely literary creations, the products of clichés long domiciled in children's literature and games. The Never Land is journeyed to by the children when they are supposedly asleep: that is, in one sense they dream it.

And when they all come back? Everything—in this world—appears to be reconstituted. The children, who have forgotten them, meet their parents again as for the first time, as though reborn. Mr Darling, having learnt the error of his ways, emerges from his penitential kennel (literally 'in the dog-house') and is able to admit the six lost boys to his household before dancing round the house with all the children. The claims of the female are now before those of the male: now it is Wendy who chooses to do without Peter, and Mrs Darling's feeling for children which wins over Mr Darling. This is in many ways reminiscent of the return of the lost daughter Florizel in *The Winter's Tale*, with the former tyranny of the father-king Leontes now tamed and his wife Hermione dominant. And here Nana the dog is very like Paulina, the king's female counsellor in *The Winter's Tale*, thrown out for her warnings and then later (in *Peter and Wendy*) made his mentor by Mr Darling, 'Very touching was his deference to Nana. He would not let her come into the kennel, but on all other matters he followed her wishes implicitly' (p. 142). And we might here note, Nana is a *Newfoundland* dog. The statue of Hermione comes to life at the end of *The Winter's Tale*; here the static condition of the beds kept waiting for the children suddenly comes to life when they return, a return Mrs Darling herself has to come alive to, not at first believing that the three lumps now in the beds are her children come back. The motif of the lost being found is extended in the taking of the lost boys into the family. And of course the whole motif of children as agents of renewal to their parents is a central theme not only in *The Winter's Tale* but in all Shakespeare's late romances, *Pericles*, *Cymbeline* and *The Tempest*. In all of them as in *Peter Pan*, the older generation is at odds with the younger, and must lose it before eventually being brought to terms with it and renewed by it. And at the centre there is the theme of death, and of death overcome, as with Peter Pan himself.

Nevertheless, Peter Pan himself is a sign that not all can be brought together, that something vital remains lost and elusive. If children are to be reconciled with adults, they will in time become adults. This Wendy is shown doing at the end, until Peter visits her no more. And the Never Land is lost to all but believing children. Restored reality in London does not catch up the dream world, even though it benefits from it. Here *Peter Pan* is different from Shakespearean comedy, where the world of the wood, of fairies and of nature, is brought back into the city and court at the end; or, in other terms, the landscape of the unconscious mind, previously absent from the conscious and rational domain, is brought together with it to make a harmonious whole. But *Peter Pan*, 'jaggy' in nature, resists such benign conclusions, leaves us with still opposed sides and refuses to let us settle for either of them.

Peter Pan has particular affinities with Shakespeare's 'dream-comedies' *A Midsummer Night's Dream* and *The Tempest*: Peter is like Puck, there is frequent mistaken identity in the dark, there is a fairy squabble over a mortal child, vastly different groups of beings mingle in the one strange world; or, as with *The Tempest*, there is an island, an education process, and certain irredeemable figures. But *Peter Pan* owes as much to the far different world of children's fiction, in works such as R. M. Ballantyne's *Coral Island* (1858), R. L. Stevenson's *Treasure Island* (1883) or Kipling's *Puck of Pook's Hill* (1906). And at the same time the book is literary in quite the opposite way, in being a textual offshoot of an all too real and continuing adventure J. M. Barrie was acting out over years with the children of Arthur and Sylvia Llewelyn Davies, who are the originals for the Darling children in the book.[9] Continually the story is looking elsewhere, and in all directions elsewhere. And it is 'only a way of putting it', a momentary encapsulation of a situation continually in transit.

As a *text*, too, *Peter Pan* is elusive: it exists variously as a draft in *The Little White Bird* (1902), as a play first performed in 1904 and not given an authorised published form till 1928, as *Peter Pan in Kensington Gardens* (1906) which expands the chapters of *The Little White Bird* into a book for children, and as *Peter and Wendy* (1911), the prose version of the play.[10] It continually recreates and renews itself, just as it renews literary tradition: in a sense its literary existence is like Peter Pan himself. It has an author who not only frequently intrudes into the story, but also as frequently declares that the story can be altered. In the play we have, *'That is what we call the Darling house, but you may dump it down anywhere you like'* (p. 1), or *'THE NEVER LAND: When the blind goes up all is so dark that you scarcely know it has gone up. This is because if you were to see the island bang (as Peter would say) the wonders of it might hurt your eyes. If you all came in spectacles perhaps you could see it bang, but to make a rule of that kind would be a pity'* (p. 24). And in *Peter and Wendy*, which being a prose story is not so clearly 'managed' as a play, and thus calls for much more apparently arbitrary behaviour on the author's part, we have, 'Would it not serve them jolly well right if they came back and found that their parents were spending the weekend in the country?' (p. 140); 'Suppose, to make her [Mrs Darling] happy, we whisper to her in her sleep that the brats are coming back' (p. 143).[11] By such means, we are led to feel that the story is being invented from minute to minute, that all is arbitrary and could be quite other.

In short, everything is made to seem contingent. One of the key elements in this is make-believe. The whole of the Never Land is in a sense *make* believe: that is belief manufactured for the sake of something else. We are asked to believe in fairies so that Tinker Bell may be restored to life. We know that the adventures of the children are in part a wish-fulfilment fantasy. We know too that the character of the Never Land changes according to whether or not Peter is in it (for example, p. 24). The whole story seems continually to defy the rules it has set up. No sooner do we have the Darling family than we have a Newfoundland dog who is nursemaid, and a husband who behaves like a spoilt child before taking up residence in the dog's kennel. And no sooner do we have this bizarre family, than we are introduced to Peter Pan, and then through him to the still more fantastic Never Land with its disparate collection of pirates, redskins, animals and lost children, each society with its own peculiar psychology. In the midst of it, we, the audience, are asked to revive a character by an act of belief: reality is what we make it. And while we watch, Peter Pan is forgetting everything that is happening. 'Reality', to say the least, is never stable. There is no self-consistent world for our minds to enter. All these instabilities and changes could be said to make the whole story an image of the elusive character of Peter Pan himself: he is not just one character, but his essence is expressed through the very form and transitions of the story.

But the literariness of the story, the way it aligns itself with other texts, and the way it constantly calls attention to its 'made-up' character, relates to the theme of what is real. That question is a key one in *Peter Pan*. Behind the shape, the dreams, the model, there may be solid fact or there may not. Behind Peter's shadow there is Peter himself: and vice versa. The children dream the Never Land, but that is the only way to know how real it is. When in *Peter and Wendy* Mrs Darling dreams of Peter breaking 'the film that obscures the Neverland' that is 'really' what is happening while she sleeps, and she wakes to find Peter gnashing the 'little pearls' of his baby teeth at her (p. 15). Only by dreaming can one wake; only through fiction can one glimpse a truth.[12]

There might just be a vision of truth in the dream that is *Peter Pan*. For instance, there is a movement, again native to pastoral, whereby we start in winter, with snow on the ground, during the general frostiness of spirit that exposes the children to danger: and we notice that they return by the Azores 'about the 21st of June', that is, in mid-summer—or so *Peter and Wendy* has it (p. 140). Then there is something age-old, Christian but more than that, in the loss, departure and return. There seems something more than just comic, or more by being comic, in the way that Mr Darling's deceiving Nana by pouring his medicine into her milk is 'answered' in Tink's drinking the poisoned medicine intended by Hook for Peter. But more still than all this, there is Peter himself, who, as the quintessence of child, is a current of joy at the heart of life, relating to each individual Wendy, John or Michael, and to each adventure whether with Hook or some other fantastic villain, but 'heartlessly' beyond them all, forgetting and forgetting again as he re-appears for each new child and each new Never Land, 'so long as children are gay and innocent and heartless'. Each child, each adventure, is a passing act in Peter's never-ending play. And for a moment he alights in the play that is made by J. M. Barrie: yet as he does so the play twists and turns, will not be written, or if written turns continually into something else, or exists somehow independent of Barrie's authorship.

But all this has been very much to do with the play as essence. What of the particular story it tells, the individual children and characters it presents, the side of Peter himself that is not so much a spirit of nature as an irresponsible particular child (the side that is Peter rather than Pan)? Here again we see the play's elusiveness, in a seemingly clear pattern which is ultimately confounded. On the one hand we can find a movement from antagonism to harmony. At the outset the here ironically-named Darling family are squabbling over the children's bedtime, Nana the dog and getting ready to go to a party. Peter steals the children away to the Never Land. Tink has Wendy shot because she is jealous of her. On the island, the lost boys, the pirates, the redskins and the beasts are in continual pursuit of each other's blood. But when Wendy (in particular) arrives, some sort of civilising process begins: more than this, she becomes a mother to the lost boys and to Peter, making a family of them, one in which Peter is happy to believe he is a father, until he catches himself out. Hook himself wants to seize Wendy as a mother, but only for himself. Hook really knows only the law of eat or be eaten: he tries to poison the lost boys with a cake, and Peter through his medicine; and he spends his life in terror of being devoured by the crocodile, which has already consumed his arm. But if the pirates remain antagonistic, more acts of 'community' become evident everywhere else. Peter rescues Tiger Lily from Hook, and thus earns the undying friendship of the redskins; Peter is rescued from the Mermaid's Lagoon by the Never Bird on its floating nest after he himself has saved Wendy by tying her to a passing kite. Tinker Bell realises that Peter's medicine is poisoned, and drinks it in his place. The audience then has to help to bring Tink back to life. Peter rescues the children from their capture by Hook. He and Tink finally yield them back to their family. Mr Darling, now reformed and contrite, welcomes the six lost boys into the household. To this theme of increased community, we can perhaps add such symbols as Peter being at first disjoined from his shadow, Never Land being an island, and then Wendy sewing Peter's shadow back on to him, sewing together the clothes of the lost boys, telling stories (which bring people together as actors within the tales and as audience without). Then there is the wider literary community to which this story belongs: we have seen much of this already, but might consider also how the idea of Wendy keeping house for the six lost boys, and the jealousy of Tink and its consequences, owe much to the story of 'Snow-White and the Seven Dwarfs' in Grimm.

Yet beyond all this familial and loving drive of the story, we still have Hook, who remains antagonistic, and Peter, who forgets everyone, who is divorced from time and who in the end, while he knows much of honour and self-sacrifice, knows very little of family or of love—particularly sexual love. He says to Wendy, '"You are so puzzling . . . and Tiger Lily is just the same; there is something or other she wants to be to me, but she says it is not my mother"' (p. 53). Community is all very well, the story seems to say, and for most people a home and love are sources of joy and goodness; but there remain less comfortable things in life such as the antagonism of a Hook, the 'jaggy' nature of an irritable author, or the innocent heartlessness of a Peter Pan; and graver things too such as mortality and death, which Peter in his ignorance is only part-right to declare, '"will be an awfully big adventure"' (p. 48). The story will not, finally, be tied down.

The question of what is real is, as said, a key issue: and with it there goes a pervasive sense of insecurity. Both Peter and Hook are afraid of time. Peter does not want to go forward and age: '"I want always to be a little boy and to have fun"' (pp. 17, 58, 80); '"No-one is going to make me a man"' (p. 80). Hook, however, does not want to *degrade*, to go backwards: the devouring clock is at his back. He himself has already in part devolved: his arm has been lost to a reptile and in its place is a hook often referred to as a claw, after which he is now named; and in the end the reptile makes him wholly its own. Hook is radically unsure of his identity, which is one of the main reasons for his detestation of Peter's 'cockiness', his assurance of self. For Peter can stay as he is; but Hook cannot. Further, Hook is only one of Peter's adventures, and at the end he has forgotten him. Thus Hook's language is a series of melodramatic posturings and clichés, and he himself is a grotesque, dancing on the edge of his non-being. When Peter impersonates him on the Mermaid's lagoon, Hook begins to feel that *'his ego is slipping from him'* (p. 44). He is obsessed in *Peter and Wendy* about his identity as an ex-public-school boy, and keeps trying to live by the code of 'good form'; and in the play he slips on the eve of his death into a parody soliloquy from *Macbeth* and *A Midsummer Night's Dream*:

> 'How still the night is; nothing sounds alive. Now is the hour when children in their homes are a-bed; their lips light-browned with the good-night chocolate, and their tongues drowsily searching for belated crumbs housed insecurely on their shining cheeks. Compare with them the children on this boat about to walk the plank. Split my infinitives, but 'tis my hour of triumph!'
>
> (p. 64).

It would be fair to say that Hook is a linguistic construct, a series of absurd language gestures, and knows it and his own hollowness. We see something similar with Hook's *alter ego*, Mr Darling, early on, when he is a pompous and melodramatically self-pitying figure—*his* grip on 'reality' at this unreformed stage seems symbolised in his inability to tie his own tie. Indeed the males in this story come out rather worse than the females so far as their hold on reality goes, and continually have to be managed and protected.

Wendy is the one Darling child in the Never Land who keeps some hold on the world and the family they have left behind, and even she almost forgets. In the end, while she is telling the children a *story* of a family called Darling and how the children flew away to the Never Land, the fiction breaks, and the children realise who they are and how much they want to go back home. The whole story is threaded with different fictions. For instance, there are frequent deceptions, again raising the question of what is real. Mr Darling tries to pass off as her milk to Nana what he has contaminated with his medicine. The children pretend to be asleep. Peter allures Wendy with the Never Land. Tink tells the lost boys

Peter wants them to shoot Wendy. Peter tricks the pirates into believing that he is Hook; and later Hook into thinking he is the crocodile. Hook deceives the children into believing that their friends the redskins have defeated the pirates, and Peter with the poisoned medicine. Meanwhile the whole idea of telling stories that runs throughout adds to this; the first story-teller is Mrs Darling, and then there is Wendy, who in the Never Land 'plays' her mother. Then there are the trees that conceal the children. And there is Hook's obsession, in *Peter and Wendy*, with 'good form' and public-school 'show', and how far he lives up to them.

Peter Pan is a fantasy *about* fantasy and fantasists. At every stage the characters are defining or asserting themselves: they are supremely concerned with their being and whether or not they may lose it—Mr Darling asking whether he has authority any longer, Hook insisting on his while he doubts it, Peter telling us how fairies are brought to life or death by our behaviour, Peter insisting on his childhood. Many are makers, or re-make others. Hook is at once independent and the creation of characters from other books, as is Peter Pan. Peter sustains the Never Land, which wilts in his absence. The Never Land is also the image of the childhood desires for magic and adventure of the lost boys and of Wendy, John and Michael. Wendy re-makes the Darling household in the Never Land. Hook 'remakes', in the sense that he is another version of, Mr Darling. Peter Pan can make-believe things, such as food, into existence, as the lost boys cannot. And there is another fantasist, the author, who has himself made the magical journey back from adulthood to childhood, and has thus defeated time in a way that Peter cannot. This author has created the whole story; but then this author cannot remember either having made it.[13] And behind him, just as comes through Pan, may be some larger creative force. Everything is plastic: there are no rules: 'reality' is far more multiple than we think. *Peter Pan* teaches us about possible worlds, and how reality has as many shapes as there are seconds in a day or perceiving minds. There is no rest; we and the characters must be continually on the move, though there are way-stations such as the Bloomsbury home or the house underground. Reality continually falls away beneath us, and we are allowed no settled assumptions: elusiveness, symbolised in Peter Pan, is the essence. But that reality, it has to be allowed, is perceived only by a child: to the adults, the world seems as settled and clear as can be. It is only through dreams in the nursery, and in the plastic medium of a child's openly unconscious mind, that the wilderness of the world can be seen, and one can be a part of many other dreaming worlds, all of them perhaps the product of some far dreamer.

MARY ROSE (1920)

Peter Pan is, arguably, one of the most 'English' of the Scottish fantasies in this book: but Barrie wrote one other fantasy of the supernatural—a play, also on the topic of extended childhood, but one which has a much more Scottish derivation. This, his popular play *Mary Rose*, is from a similar folk tradition to that behind Lang's *The Gold of Fairnilee*—that of the enforced sojourn of mortals in Fairy Land, as seen in 'Thomas the Rhymer' and in the West Highland 'The Smith and the Fairies'. In the play, a young English wife is taken by the fairies during a visit while on holiday to a Hebridean island; after twenty-five years she comes back home, only to die when she finds that her infant child has long ago left home and disappeared. She then becomes a ghost and haunts her home for years in search of her child as she knew him; even when he returns as a grown man she cannot acknowledge him. Mary can be seen as losing her child (twice) by being the undeveloped adult that she is. Her faërian sojourn and her ghostly stasis can both be seen as symbolic of her paralysed emotional adolescence, her inability to grow or see others grow, and to be part of time. Thus the attitude to Mary as frozen adult is not so dual or shifting as it is towards the child-hero of *Peter Pan*: she is caught, just as she is immobile in time. And the fairies are here simply a danger, one opposed by the Christian supernatural, which comes forward at the end to give Mary a blessed relief she cannot find from her ghostly condition, in permanent sojourn in a far happier place than Fairy Land, as 'she walks out through the window into the empyrean.' But again the emphasis, as in most Scottish fantasy, and as in *Peter Pan*, is on the inner and unconscious world: the fairies, the island, the ghost-state, all symbolise a state of mind cut off from reality. The play, with its discourse between adult development and childhood stasis, and even between outer and inner rooms of the house in which it is largely set, suggests an inner drama, one portraying a radical breakdown of the unity of the mind and the spirit.

Notes

1 By Jacqueline Rose, *The Case of Peter Pan: or, The Impossibility of Children's Fiction* (London: Macmillan, 1984).

2 Andrew Lang, *The Gold of Fairnilee* (Bristol: J. W. Arrowsmith, 1888), p. 14.

3 Eleanor de Selms Langstaff, *Andrew Lang* (Boston: Twayne Publishers, G. K. Hall, 1978), pp. 93–4.

4 Lang was a founder member in the 1890s of the Society for Psychical Research, which investigated 'supernatural' occurrences, particularly sightings of ghosts: Lang was a rationalist, assigning all such experiences to the subconscious and to dreams. His fellow members of the Society were to include Freud and Jung (Langstaff, pp. 37, 130–1).

5 Joseph Campbell, *The Hero with a Thousand Faces* (Princeton: Princeton University Press, 1968).

6 Langstaff, pp. 137–40. J. R. R. Tolkien, however, has a sharply opposite view in his essay 'On Fairy-Stories' (1938–9), repr. in his *Tree and Leaf* (London: Allen and Unwin, 1964), pp. 36–43.

7 J. M. Barrie, *Peter Pan* [*Peter and Wendy*] (London: Collins, Armada 1988), p. 29. Since *Peter Pan*'s existence as a play first performed in 1904 is no more the 'authentic' text than the mode in which it is also widely known, that of the not substantially different prose version *Peter and Wendy* of 1911, textual references will be sometimes to the latter. The play had no fixed 'text' until 1928, when it first received authorised publication. The text is essentially elusive, as will be said later.

8 J. M. Barrie, *Peter Pan: A Fantasy in Five Acts* (London: Samuel French, 1988), p. 17.

9 For a full account, see Andrew Birkin, *J. M. Barrie and the Lost Boys* (London: Constable, 1979). Humphrey Carpenter argues that 'This drama was really his [Barrie's] greatest achievement, and in a sense *Peter Pan* was only an offshoot of it, an attempt to express it in other than realistic terms' ('J. M. Barrie and *Peter Pan*: "That terrible masterpiece"', *Secret Gardens: A Study of the Golden Age of Children's Literature* (London: Allen and Unwin, 1985), p. 176).

10 A full account of these and other versions can be found in R. D. S. Jack, *The Road to the Never Land: A Reassessment of J. M. Barrie's Dramatic Art* (Aberdeen: Aberdeen University Press, 1991), esp. pp. 164–5, 284–5. This book is the most ambitious and subtle of modern interpretations of Barrie's work, and justice cannot be done to it here, where the interpretation must seize on the immediate.

11 Compare also p. 74: 'Which of these adventures shall we choose? The best way will be to toss for it.' Barrie does so, and then suggests making the toss the best of three.

12 See also Jack, p. 162: 'For Barrie, the only possible glimpse of truth was that presented in art.'

13 'Some disquieting confessions must be made in printing at last the play of *Peter Pan*; among them this, that I have no recollection of having written it' (Dedication to *The Plays of J. M. Barrie* (London: Hodder and Stoughton, 1928), p. 1.

CHAPTER NINE

David Lindsay, *A Voyage to Arcturus* (1920)

L INDSAY'S *A Voyage to Arcturus* is one of the most extraordinary works of literature, let alone of fantasy, ever written. In form
and in some of its symbolic techniques it is highly indebted to the
work of George MacDonald: but for sheer inventiveness and intensity
of imagination it burns like some literary supernova. It is unique in
Lindsay's own work, everything written after it (for it is the first of his
books) being set not on a remote planet but on earth in a semi-realistic
English society: strange things may occasionally take place in *The Haunted
Woman* (1922), *Sphinx* (1923), *Devil's Tor* (1932) or the unpublished
'The Violet Apple' and 'The Witch', but nothing like the fountain of
extraordinary events that fills *A Voyage*. Yet the book had difficulty
finding a publisher, had few and uncomprehending reviews, and then
sold very poorly before being remaindered. The reviewer for the *Times
Literary Supplement* of 30 September 1920 called it 'a riot of morbid
fancy', 'a quagmire' and 'a noisome fog', and spoke of its 'uniform
unwholesomeness'. The book's sales of just 596 copies set the pattern
for all Lindsay's subsequent novels: Lindsay died convinced that he was
a failure.[1]

Since Lindsay's death the book has enjoyed some vogue. Indeed,
unknown to him, *A Voyage* was already in the 1920s having a profound
influence on the imagination of a not inconsiderable fantasy writer-to-be,
C. S. Lewis, who later wrote: 'The real father of my planet books [*Out
of the Silent Planet* (1938) and *Perelandra* (1943)] is David Lindsay's *A
Voyage to Arcturus*';[2] 'I'm one of the old guard who had a treasured
second hand copy before anyone had heard of it.'[3] In 1946, a year after
Lindsay's death, the book was reissued by Victor Gollancz, and again
in 1963 and 1968, helped by the growing vogue for fantasy through the
work of Tolkien and Lewis. It was published by Ballantine of New York
in 1968, by Gregg Press (a photographic reprint of the first edition) in
1977, by Sphere in 1980, Allison and Busby in 1985, and most recently,
in assertion of its Scottish identity, by Canongate Press in 1992. Now
that the fantasy vogue has largely passed, it may be that the book
will return to the shadows. It is not, while fascinating, an easy read;
and its philosophy is bleak to the point of being repulsive to ordinary
sensibilities. It has attracted some scholarly and critical interest—three
books and a number of articles, particularly in the period 1970–85.

But it is rightly to be seen as a Scottish book. Lindsay's father was

Scottish, his mother English; he traced his Scots ancestry back to Sir David Lyndsay. He was brought up in London, in Blackheath, though he spent some time at school at his father's home town of Jedburgh in the Scottish Borders, and later returned for several summers to Scotland, to Jedburgh or walking in the Highlands. At the Jedburgh school, he developed a hatred for the Scottish Celt, and also for the boys who, when one day he got into difficulty while swimming, appeared not to have heeded his cries for help. Little of this seems particularly favourable to Scotland, but there was that in the depths of Lindsay's character which responded to what he saw as its bleak and savage side: it is in a Scottish landscape peculiarly endowed with these qualities that he begins and ends the journey in *A Voyage to Arcturus*. And he clearly derived himself from Scottish, and Norse, roots: 'I trace my stock to the main stem of the Lindsays, whose history is in any book of Scottish families. Ivar, Jarl of the Norse Uplanders, is said to have been the original ancestor.'[4] It is in part to Norse mythology that *A Voyage to Arcturus* looks. But as fantasy the book is peculiarly Scottish in its destructured, non-rational, non-'respectable' form. Its primary literary indebtedness is to the fantasy of George MacDonald.

A Voyage to Arcturus is in striking contrast to the work of J. M. Barrie, which Lindsay would have scorned. Barrie's *Peter Pan* was in part a product of the new interest in children and in writing for them at the turn of the century, its nostalgia for childhood not least the expression of a sense of a golden age slipping away. Lindsay's book registers the new interest in science fiction and interplanetary travel, and reflects however indirectly the harshness of the war years (though Lindsay saw military service, it was in England). In *A Voyage to Arcturus* we see the portrayal of a fantastic and beautiful world which is shown to be inwardly corrupt. Here indeed we see a specific attack on fantasy-making itself. In place of childhood and retreat, Lindsay's spiritually Darwinist prescription is for self-denial, pain and willed growth forward out of the world.

Such an attack has to be viewed in a larger context also. Lindsay can be seen in part as a 'modernist': that is, some of his affinities are with the literary tradition of Yeats, Pound, Eliot and Joyce (Eliot's *The Waste Land* and Joyce's *Ulysses* were both published in 1922, two years after *A Voyage to Arcturus*). Modernism involved a rejection of nineteenth-century naturalism, nostalgia, traditional values and 'fine writing'. Lindsay's jagged fantasy world is the extreme antithesis of naturalism; he continually spurns the past and fixed views; and his style is the reverse of the conventionally literary. Like the modernists he is a subversive and sets out to disturb every fixed view and philosophy; though he is unique in the stress he puts on inventiveness, and in his orientation towards a wholly other world.

Briefly, *A Voyage* describes the meeting of a 'strong' man Maskull with two characters Krag and Nightspore, who persuade him to travel with them to Tormance, a planet of the double star Arcturus. Once Maskull is there, Krag and Nightspore disappear, and leave him to a series of adventures and encounters which end in the crossing of the planet's great ocean.[5] Each of these adventures is a different form of temptation offered by the planet, which is controlled by an evil deity Crystalman. At the end, Maskull meets again with Krag and Nightspore: through Krag Maskull is brought to die, and Nightspore now lives in him. Nightspore approaches a vision of the true god Muspel, who lives above and beyond the corrupting material world of Crystalman: but once there he finds that Muspel is closely besieged by Crystalman and fighting for his life. Together with Krag, who is a manifestation of Muspel, he returns to the world of the planet, and to the struggle against Crystalman.

Comparison with its prime source, George MacDonald's fantasy, provides a way into this extraordinary work. As with MacDonald's *Phantastes* and *Lilith*, the narrative is episodic: it could fairly be said of Maskull, as of Anodos, that he is '"wandering . . . without an aim."'[6] No constant urge directs Maskull: at first he is drawn by their wild grandeur to travel to the high mountains of the Ifdawn Marest far beyond the desert plain on which he first finds himself on the planet; then he thinks of his wanderings, however random-seeming, as those of a chosen 'man of destiny';[7] then he speaks of a 'moral aim', and says to one character, '"Can you grasp that it's possible to have an aim right in front of one, so big that one can't see it as a whole?"' (p. 89). And so on, through daily aim after aim, at one point even speaking of himself as '"travelling from curiosity"' and '"travelling at random"' (pp. 168, 169). None of this, however, is to suppose that Maskull's adventures do not have a pattern unknown to him, as in *Phantastes* or *Lilith*: indeed, that as in MacDonald's work, the less certain he is of an aim of his own, the more he may be driven by some further purpose within himself. In *Phantastes* we have the remarks, '"no one comes here but for some reason, either known to himself or to those who have charge of him,"' and '"for those who enter Fairy Land, there is no way of going back. They must go on, and go through it."'[8] And in *A Voyage to Arcturus*, Krag tells Maskull he is ripe to die because '"You have run through the gamut"' (p. 275), and that he was brought to Tormance to '"follow Surtur [the true God]"' (p. 276).

In MacDonald this lack of conscious purpose is part of an aim of taking us to the level below consciousness, the dreaming mind where God lives. But in Lindsay the object is rather to take us *above* consciousness, continually to transcend the perceptual awareness of the individual. In the sense that Maskull continually travels, and commits himself to no person and to no view, he may be taken as a symbol of this: and the process could be seen as finally accomplished in his own death, when he is transformed into Nightspore. Each of the figures met in MacDonald's

Phantastes or in *Lilith* has something to give or to take away from the protagonist: but in *A Voyage* the stress is on the limitations and frequent vanities of the figures met, which Maskull usually supersedes or even kills. In Tormance we deal with a wholly 'other' world, apart from the self, which the protagonist must pierce, understand and go beyond. The emphasis is on delusion and on true seeing. One of Maskull's temporary companions, a new prophet of duty and law called Spadevil, appears quite different when Catice, sage of the holy land of Sant, removes one of Maskull's previous 'probes' or sense organs: 'Spadevil's image-like clearness of form had departed for him; his frowning face he knew to be the deceptive portico of a weak and confused intellect' (p. 148). In death, the features of almost all the various and powerful figures met on Tormance relapse into the hideous grin that reveals the stamp on them of Crystalman's corruption. Muspel, the true god, is only finally 'seen' from the vantage point of the last landing of a tower whose stairway represents a painful ascent out of the earthbound spirit. In *A Voyage to Arcturus* we deal more with a gnostic search for the utterly and transcendentally 'other' than with a quest for union with the immanent force of deity within the world.

Assertiveness of the self, despite the final emphasis on its destruction, is however given a place in Lindsay as it is not in MacDonald, where the protagonists are much more passive. This may well, as frequently observed, owe much to Lindsay's readings in Nietzsche and in Schopenhauer (*The World as Will and Idea*),[9] but it also seems to emerge from some primal feeling that only the superman offers the best sacrifice. Or, to put it at a mundane level, one can only die when one has fully lived. In MacDonald the self is to be obliterated: Anodos has to learn to do without his 'white lady' and his possessiveness, Vane in *Lilith* to yield his own will and lie down with the sleepers. The consequence in both *Phantastes* and *Lilith* is that the boundaries of the individual melt away, and it becomes part of other people or of the world—'I lived in everything; everything entered and lived in me,' says Vane.[10] Maskull, by contrast, proceeds through *A Voyage* as a little fist of self, rejecting, destroying, overwhelming or even absorbing almost everything he meets. He slays the unpleasant Crimtyphon, husband of the beautiful Oceaxe, at her suggestion, and also kills the woman Tydomin and the ascetic Spadevil on the instruction of Catice: the females, Oceaxe, Tydomin and Sullenbode, submit to his violent charms; he is so powerful a player on the water-harp of Lake Irontick that his neural music dismembers the previous master, Earthrid (pp. 185–94); he engulfs the identity of Digrung, obstructive brother of the beautiful Joiwind (p. 121); he passes beyond even the insights of the mighty sage Corpang on his way. It is by pure will that Maskull accomplishes his unique journey over the inhospitable face of the planet.

And yet, at the same time, Lindsay also shows Maskull to be as much
a fool as a hero, or even a fool by being a hero. His whole journey is
in a sense futile, since his identity is lost to Nightspore. When he sets
out, spurred by restlessness, the kind and beautiful Joiwind, who has
helped him, asks him, '"Is this selfishness, Maskull? . . . or are you
drawn by something stronger than yourself?"' (p. 72): both are correct.
Immediately he leaves he is met by Shaping, or Crystalman, whom as
yet he does not know to be corrupt, and vows to serve him henceforth
(p. 76); and at the end of his journey he encounters him again as Gangnet
and still prefers his solicitations to the harsh correctives of Krag, also
present (pp. 276–90). Oceaxe sees him as inevitably Shaping's creature
(p. 121). Maskull is thus deluded as to the nature of the true god,
Muspel: it is only Nightspore who has a full vision of him. (This
strongly recalls the Arthurian Grail story in relation to Lancelot and
Galahad.) All of Maskull's adventures, from the standpoint of the world
heroic, are, from that of the divine, empty; Maskull's realisation at the
end, '"Why, Gangnet . . . I am *nothing*!"' (p. 289), is true at a level he
does not know. In one way, his journey is one of mythic daring, like
that of Prometheus, to whom Joiwind's husband Panawe compares him
(p. 58); in the transcendent view, it is futile, symbolised in its terminus
in the return to the stone tower from which he set out. The absence
of Krag during most of Maskull's sojourn on Tormance suggests the
loss of the larger view; while he is there he is to 'run the gamut' of
mortality; we may even see him as born into Tormance, mothered by
Joiwind and then following a course of folly till death, while his true
world, here represented by Earth and Starkness, lies elsewhere. In a
context such as this, Maskull's liaisons with women are to be seen as
at best dotage, his slayings of Crimtyphon, Spadevil and Tydomin as
nothing less than murder, and his whole journey as little else than
amoral tourism.

Here we have the central tension of the book. We are encouraged to
see Maskull as a hero on the planet, someone to identify with and to
admire, and yet we are also to see him as a corrupt dupe. And yet again,
Krag has *chosen him* for Tormance. The only way to reconciliation is to say
that Maskull is big enough to explore to the full and thus to represent
the potential of this strange new planet of *Torment* and *Romance*. His
journey over it could be said to capture all of it in him. And as previously
mentioned, the resultant process could be one whereby one can only die
when one has fully lived. There is also the point that, from whatever
possibly blighted motives, and mixed in whatever mortal corruption,
Maskull's journey is towards Alppain, the hidden blue star, and, on
the surface of Tormance, towards Surtur's Ocean, on the other side of
which lies Muspel: he is moving towards the transcendent, even while
to the last he himself is obstinately mortal in his vision. But this does
not remove the emotional tension of our attitude: indeed it is precisely

Lindsay's purpose to exploit that tension. He will both encourage and belittle our own mortality.

Doubleness it may be observed, is one of the motifs of the book. Tormance, planet of the dual name, has two suns—Branchspell, associated with Crystalman, and Alppain, associated with his opposite Muspel, and not visible till late in Maskull's journey. The females among the inhabitants espouse passion, while the males are many of them ascetics, denying it altogether: these two opposed ways of life are continually set before Maskull. The narrative is shot through with images of 'forking'—Slofork, Hator's Trifork, the forking will of Shaping's creativity, Maskull's other self Nightspore.

This doubleness is also seen in the very core of the book as a piece of creation. Creation itself is cast into question as we are told that the violently beautiful young world of Tormance was made by the evil Crystalman, and is completely corrupt. The true god Muspel emits from afar a spirit-stream that calls to mortality to transcend itself; but that spirit stream is intercepted by Crystalman, who captures and feeds on much of it, and then releases or excretes the product as matter and worlds (pp. 299–300). Some of the stream gets through, but 'shivered into a million fragments': these green corpuscles could, as Lindsay's follower C. S. Lewis later put it, be called 'gleams of celestial strength and beauty falling on a jungle of filth and imbecility.'[11] And yet at the same time the whole book seems to celebrate the very creation it thus condemns. *A Voyage to Arcturus* itself is the fruit of an amazingly fecund imagination, where not only do we have a thoroughly pictured planet, but each item in it is sheerly original in relation to the last. Panawe, husband of Joiwind, explains to Maskull that '"Life in a new planet . . . is necessarily energetic and lawless . . . The will forks and sports incessantly, and thus no two creatures are alike"' (p. 61). This provides explanation for Lindsay's own creativity as authorial Crystalman, but it does not explain it away. We have an extraordinary range of landscapes: there is the scarlet desert on which Maskull begins; then there is the amazingly active geology of the hills of the Ifdawn Marest, where suddenly whole tongues of land will collapse hundreds of feet, or others be sent surging as far into the air; there is the Sinking Sea, where the water is of such varying density that sometimes one sinks, sometimes one is practically choked in viscosity; there are the lake-harp Irontick, the Wombflash Forest with its giant trees, the huge and sullen mass of the mountain Disscourn, or the terrifying knife-edge across gulfs of Shaping's Causeway; there is even the attempt that nearly comes off to create in our minds an image of the new primary colours, jale and ulfire, found on the planet (p. 49). One could pursue the same stark differentiation through the objects, living things and the people of the book. Epitomising it is the valley of Matterplay on the far side of the Sinking Sea, where Maskull finds an extreme variety of living things being precipitated out of the apparently empty air, until 'every square foot of space was a tangle of struggling wills, both animal and vegetable':

> Other creatures sported so wildly, in front of his very eyes, that they became of different 'kingdoms' altogether. As an example—a fruit was lying on the ground, of the size and shape of a lemon, but with a tougher skin. He picked it up, intending to eat the contained pulp; but inside it was a fully-formed young tree, just on the point of bursting its shell. Maskull threw it away upstream. It floated back towards him . . . by the time that he was up with it, its downward motion had stopped and it was swimming against the current. He fished it out, and discovered that it had sprouted six rudimentary legs.
>
> (p. 200)

(It was this sort of invention that was later to fascinate C. S. Lewis, Robert Silverberg and P. J. Farmer.) The plenitude of Matterplay does not attract, rather it disgusts Maskull, and maybe that is because of its density and its continual flux. Yet the inescapable fact remains that *A Voyage to Arcturus*, as Lindsay's own world-creation, is (in this sense) a larger form of Matterplay itself. And the problem here is that Matterplay is the direct working of the evil Crystalman, or Shaping as he is also called. The act of making, even the process of harnessing spirit to matter (as the spirit stream of Muspel is dragged down to corporeality) is seen as disgusting. So we have a situation in which the very imaginative exuberance or riot—or fantasy—which constitutes the book is to be seen as a horror. Lindsay seems to have made a work of startling creativity and wonder only to tell us it is rotten to the core.[12] How are we to make sense of this duality?

One way might be by the principle of satiety: as at Matterplay, when we are crammed full of marvels we are nauseated by them. Something analogous to this is the way that Maskull is permitted to develop a fullness of heroic identity only to die. But we might also consider the way in which Lindsay has presented his wonders. We may be amazed, but there is rarely any leisure for contemplation, for we are continually travelling and moving from point to point. It is Crystalman who invites Maskull to enjoy the beauty of the planet, and whom Krag calls '"You eternal loller!"' (pp. 280–1); and Krag mocks Maskull for any luxuriating in the pleasures of Sullenbode or Gangnet's admired blue sun (pp. 284, 287–9). The contrast here, though it is not a fair one, is with C. S. Lewis's *Perelandra* (1943), directly based on Lindsay's work, in which an emotional and spiritual response to the landscape of a strange divinely-created planet is everywhere portrayed and enjoined: 'The very names of green and gold, which he used perforce in describing the scene [in the huge Perelandran ocean], are too harsh for the tenderness, the muted iridescence, of that warm, maternal, delicately gorgeous world. It was mild to look upon as evening, warm like summer noon, gentle and winning like early dawn. It was altogether pleasurable. He sighed.'[13] In Lindsay there is rarely such an emotional response, except perhaps in Maskull's early and slightly infatuated relationship with the pure-seeming Joiwind; nor as we find it in Lewis, is a single relationship, as that of the hero Ransom of Perelandra with the green Lady he finds there, made central and continuous. And we might add to the contrast George MacDonald here, in whose work desire, or *Sehnsucht*, is at the heart, as in *Phantastes*: all of MacDonald's fantasy has as one of its core themes the education of desire. Lindsay, however, would have us sick of our desires.

Much of the technique of *A Voyage to Arcturus* is in fact founded on making the reader experience this tension, this mixture of attraction and repugnance. The book has a style which refuses rest, continually jerking us out of any settled view. One of the methods by which it does this is that of violent undercutting. For example the book opens with the description of the preparations for a spiritualist performance, in which a celebrated medium, Backhouse, will produce from the air before an assembly of drawing room guests the material form of a person not previously there.[14] There is some account of the guests and of some of their interrelationships, before the abrupt arrival of two (actually invited guests), the giant Maskull, the sinewy Nightspore, and then finally the brutish Krag. The materialisation of a young man on the couch on the aesthetically-arranged stage having taken place, Krag unceremoniously approaches, and, with a wrench of his hairy hands,[15] twists the neck of the apparition round and breaks it;[16] upon which a vulgar Crystalman grin overspreads the countenance of the corpse, from which emerges 'a sickening stench of the graveyard' (p. 13).

After this disruption of illusion, coarser reality swiftly follows: for we travel with Maskull and Nightspore, sent by Krag to the lonely observatory of Starkness on the north-east coast of Scotland, to await a journey to the planet Tormance. The observatory is deserted, cold, scattered with broken glass, dust, dirt and old iron objects: the contrast with the civil urban surroundings of the previous chapter could not be more marked. Casual savagery seems the idiom: in order to be able to stand the gravity of Tormance, it is necessary to climb the tower of Starkness, but to do this is impossible without letting blood: Krag pulls out a pocket knife and with the big blade makes 'a careless and almost savage slash at Maskull's upper arm. The wound was deep, and blood flowed freely'; after which 'An awful agony, emanating from the wound, started to run through Maskull's body . . . [subsiding to] a gnawing ache in the injured arm, just strong enough to make life one long discomfort' (p. 34). And then, after the brief account of Maskull's journey to Tormance, his first experience is again a reverse, one of beauty and purity in the person of Joiwind, who has journeyed to help him from the scarlet desert: 'he seemed to see right into a soul which was the home of love, warmth, kindness, tenderness, and intimacy . . . She was tall and slight. All her movements were graceful as music . . . the love of her eyes . . . the angelic purity of her features' (pp. 41–2). After Joiwind, we shift to the sudden sexual violence of the woman Oceaxe; and so on. There are two symbols of this constant disruptiveness in the book: one of the land, in the Ifdawn Marest, where the ground collapses or thrusts up suddenly; and one of the ocean, the Sinking Sea, with its shifting viscosity whereby 'In some places he [Maskull] could swim, in others he could barely save himself from drowning, in others again he could not force himself beneath the surface at all. There were no outward signs to show what the water ahead held in store for him . . . The whole business was most dangerous' (p. 163). That word 'dangerous' sums up any commitment we try to make to any single one of Lindsay's fantastic images.

There is also a strange clashing of the casual and the organised. We start the book with the carefully arranged setting and audience for the medium Backhouse's promised materialisation: there is elaborate discussion of the need for props. Then there is the sudden irruption of Maskull and Nightspore, followed by the still less invited presence and quite un-aesthetic aspect of Krag. And at one point there is a sudden terrific crash from upstairs, sounding 'as if the entire upper part of the building had collapsed' (p. 8):[17] no sign of damage, however, is evident, and Nightspore bluntly remarks, ' "It was supernatural," ' with which Backhouse coolly agrees (pp. 8–9). These urban arrangements and disarrangements give way to the complete lack of them at Starkness. Maskull knows he is to go to Tormance, but can scarcely believe it, and is still less clear as to why he has been chosen, what the objective is, and whether Krag will indeed turn up there, especially since the whole place seems such a neglected ruin. When Krag arrives, no reason is given for their journey, which is made in a torpedo-shaped craft whose workings are given only the briefest and most contemptuous of explanations (pp. 38–9): it is powered by a dust-covered flask taken from a shelf, which apparently contains 'Arcturian Back-Rays' (p. 24), which Nightspore grudgingly implies is light from the star which will return there with any object to which it is attached. Once on the planet, Maskull is again with the apparently unplanned, for Krag and Nightspore have gone, and thereafter all his adventures seem random. At the same time, however, they are all to some extent linked by subtle patterns and gradations, recurrent motifs (such as that of drum-beats[18]) and organised on musical principles; and there is the hidden controlling agency of Krag behind Maskull's experiences. And so we may continue through plan and no-plan: Joiwind, whom Maskull suddenly finds standing by him in the scarlet desert, has come all the way from Poolingdred, forty miles away, seemingly at her own choice, to rescue him; and in order to do so she and Maskull must exchange blood, an operation which, in contrast to the recent coarse violence of Krag's slashing pocket-knife, she does with precise delicacy: 'she made a careful, deep incision on her upper arm' and then when Maskull has done so too, 'Joiwind delicately and skilfully placed the mouths of the two wounds together' (p. 44). Here again one episode is continually undermined by another.

And, as earlier suggested, we are invited to become attached to individual characters met by Maskull before we are then made aware of their limitations. (In this Joiwind is the only exception.) Oceaxe, whom Maskull meets after leaving Joiwind, represents the *femme fatale* to Joiwind's purity of soul, and she is also to encourage Maskull to murder her lover Crimtyphon: but for the time we see the encounter of the two in heroic and sexual terms. Symbolic of our shifts in view of Oceaxe is the nature of her death, wherein her rival Tydomin causes her to walk along a path which leads not to firm land but to an abyss, which she confidently does until realisation dawns too late. Tydomin herself, who then befriends Maskull, seeks to become male by taking his body and leaving him in torment, and is eventually slain by Maskull. Spadevil of the new law, whom Maskull follows to the holy land of Sant, is shown to be a fraud and killed. So too of course with Maskull himself, whom we follow with some enthusiasm, only to see him exposed and slain at the end. Every character seems to offer life, assurance or truth: and nearly everyone is shown to be '"false and deceitful, to the very core"' (p. 169).

This solicitation and refusal of security, this analogy with the eternal contest between Crystalman and Muspel, is seen even in the use of names in the book, which at once suggest and refuse clear meaning. 'Crystalman', for instance: how can that be appropriate to a deity who is the agent of continual change, metamorphosis and fecund growth on the planet, and who does not even have one name, but is known also as Shaping, as Faceny and as Gangnet? And yet there is truth there somewhere: for the object of Crystalman is to capture and fix the spirit-stream from Muspel; and every one of Crystalman's servants or creations assumes the same corrupt grin in death, as though behind all this variety there was one dead level of anonymity. 'Maskull', to take another, may be an Everyman figure, 'my skull'; or his name may refer to his being masked from himself; or again it may be 'Mass-kill', murderer of many. The house of Montague Faull in which the novel starts may by 'Faull' imply either 'foul' or 'fall'. Joiwind, Oceaxe, Catice, Dreamsinter, Polecrab, Haunte, Sullenbode, Leehallfee, these names are at least suggestive enough. But 'Krag'? Is that mere harsh onomatopoeia? And is his other name, 'Pain', meant to contrast in any way with the figure Corpang, whom Maskull meets towards the end? And what of the blue sun Alppain? Meanings cross and interweave, shimmer and lose form, much like the texture of the book. As for the names 'Surtur' and 'Muspel', those are importations from Lindsay's reading of the *Younger Edda*, with how much of their significance taken over from there indeterminate: in the *Edda*,

> 'The first world to exist . . . was Muspell in the southern hemisphere; it is light and hot and that region flames and burns so that those who do not belong to it and whose native land it is not, cannot endure it. The one who sits there at land's end to guard it is called Surt; he has a flaming sword, and at the end of the world he will come and harry and will vanquish all the gods and burn the whole world with fire.'[19]

From the *Edda* too we learn that Muspell is the source of sparks that give light to heaven and earth, and that the sun also was thus made.[20]

For all these underminings of certainty, the book also has a definite direction. It follows a process of analysis, of stripping away of the peripheral to reach the eternal. 'Analysis is well, as death is well,' George MacDonald once wrote in his opposition to the intellectual and the inquisitorial.[21] Yet inquisition is specifically what Maskull is inadvertently carrying out on the planet of Tormance. He is forever probing (indeed the limbs of several of the characters are called 'probes'). The entire process of the story can be seen as one of analysis, of pushing on and through to that which is irreducible, which here is Muspel. MacDonald's work might rather be called 'synthetic', in that it deals with an eventual coming together of all things and beings, an 'at-one-ment' as it is called in *Lilith*. The apparently random details of *Phantastes* come together to make a single truth concerning possessiveness in Fairy Land; the initially fragmentary episodes gradually become drawn together by such recurrent motifs as the white lady or the shadow; and Anodos ends presiding in love over all things in Fairy Land. We might even add that what start as isolated beings in *Phantastes* end as groups and even congregations. But in Lindsay the object is to dismiss the sympathetic imagination, which is seen as a source of corrupt delusion, and to perceive starkly and even clinically. (The name of the Scottish observatory, Starkness, is relevant here.) Characters live on their own or are divided from one another. The solitary Oceaxe has Maskull slay her lover; then is in turn slain by her rival Tydomin; and later Maskull, at the behest of Catice of Sant, kills both Tydomin and their companion Spadevil, also initially found alone. Polecrab the fisherman loses his wife Gleameil to the music of Earthrid. In the end Maskull dies and Nightspore becomes him. Then Muspel is found to be totally alone and surrounded. Isolation, reduction of being, death, these pervade Lindsay's book: and all these are functions of its analytic drive. At the end of that analysis is Muspel, whose spirit-stream is at once 'not the

One, or the Many, but something else far beyond either', and 'nothing
. . . Muspel consisted of himself [Nightspore] and the stone tower on
which he was sitting' (pp. 300–1).

All the time the hard questions are being asked. What is desire? What
is refusal of desire? Maskull meets with desire in a range of women; with
its refusal in a series of ascetic men. The women, from Joiwind to Oceaxe,
Tydomin and finally Sullenbode, increase in sexual force to the point
where Sullenbode can kill with a kiss (p. 254). Joiwind, most graceful,
most innocent and most maternal, awakens Maskull's purest feelings of
love; but Oceaxe is a vamp, and Tydomin seeks to take over his body. In
one sense Maskull leaves the best of desire behind in Joiwind: in another
he proceeds through deeper and deeper levels of it till he meets its
essence. The book of course has a strongly rejectionist attitude to desire,
which is another illusion and the strongest tie to darkened mortality.
And yet we are made aware of how some of Muspel's light gets through
to the world, and that from this point of view awakened desires for
women may be misinterpreted desires for Muspel. For Lindsay, music
in particular is the authentication of longing, if not longing as any kind of
luxuriant feeling. That is the nature of Earthrid's (symbolic name) music
on Irontick: '"my music is founded on painful tones; and thus its sym-
metry is wild, and difficult to discover; its emotion is bitter and terrible"'
(p. 187). If Maskull is not allowed to satisfy his lust on Tormance, if love
is continually associated with death, if in a real sense we go spiritually
downhill to Sullenbode, still, the existence of longing poses a role for
desire in the approach to Muspel. Love, as Sullenbode and Maskull see it,
is not happiness, but '"Restlessness . . . unshed tears . . . thoughts too
grand for our soul to think"' (p. 269), and although there is egoism and
vulgar pleasure in this (as seen in the 'phaen' Leehallfae's notion of love
earlier (pp. 208–9)), it is also a truth concerning Muspel and the effect of
his light. As Broodviol the sage puts it (to Polecrab, relayed to Maskull),
all attempts of creatures to escape the reductive nature of Crystalman
spring '"from the unconscious desire to find Surtur [Muspel], but . . .
in the opposite direction to the right one"':

> 'For Surtur's world does not lie on this side of the *one*, which
> was the beginning of life, but on the other side; and to get
> to it we must repass through the *one*. But this can only be by
> renouncing our self-life, and reuniting ourselves to the whole
> of Crystalman's world. And when this has been done, it is
> only the first stage of the journey; though many good men
> imagine it to be the whole journey.'

> (p. 171)

This is in reply to a (temporarily) rejectionist view of the world put
forward by Maskull (pp. 169–70): the journey it describes is one that
Maskull himself could be said to be making. Here, just as Muspel can

only reach us via Crystalman, so we can only work out to him by the same route. In this very limited sense the book could be said to follow the process of a kind of *via positiva*, whereby Maskull enters into an ever deeper knowledge of the world which is also an increasing awareness of Muspel.

But if we needed any corrective, we are certainly given it, in the sequence of ascetics and world-deniers on the other side, starting with Spadevil and moving on through Catice and Corpang to Krag, with certain legendary sages such as Slofork, Hator and Broodviol intermingled. Each of these male figures offers mental and spiritual values as opposed to the emotional and physical ones of the female figures; and most are engaged on a theological quest. Spadevil proposes adherence to law and duty: '"I destroy nature, and set up law"' (p. 146). Yet here too the urge to renounce the world is itself seen as often founded on self-pleasing and on pride. Underneath, Spadevil is shown by Catice to use his principles as a cloak for his own pride and pleasure (pp. 148, 150). The phaen Leehallfae, met by Maskull at the valley of Matterplay, is searching for 'Faceny' or 'Threal', the spiritual source of life: here again the apparent nobility masks the real Leehallfae, whose 'sensuality was solitary, but vulgar—it was like the heroism of a lonely nature, pursuing animal aims with untiring persistence' (p. 209). Corpang, a stronger figure, is in search of Thire, the afterworld, but his meeting with Maskull reveals to him that his Thire is really a disguise for the evil Crystalman, and he sets out with Maskull in quest of Muspel (pp. 222–33). Each of these world-renouncing figures portrays a deepening mode of the *via negativa*, the way to approach the divine by refusals of the world.

The analysis need not leave us only with so stark an opposition. If the one is a Hegelian 'thesis', and the other an 'antithesis', then there is the suggestion of a just tenable synthesis. For there is the idea that love's finest expression is in sacrifice, and that that is not *wholly* removed from the self-transcendence associated with Muspel: '"when the climax has been reached, love if it still wants to ascend must turn to sacrifice,"' says Sullenbode (p. 268). 'So long as men suffer, there is still room for sublimity,' writes Lindsay.[22] Sacrifice was seen in Tydomin, in Joiwind, even in Polecrab's wife Gleameil, who gave up her whole world to follow the desire awakened by Earthrid's music. The book may be full of world-renouncers and ascetics, but that is not quite what Sullenbode meant: she implies a full tasting of life before denial. This is analogous to the idea operative in Maskull's journey, that one can only properly die when one has fully lived: as if to say this, Maskull has two phantom rehearsals of his death during the narrative (pp. 123–5, 157–8). It is not for nothing that Sullenbode and Corpang, archetypes of desire and of desire's refusal, are brought together in the last stages of Maskull's journey.

But whatever direction there is to the analytic procedure of the book, whatever faint suggestions of a synthesis it may make, its general idiom is one of clashing opposites, and of the constant push and pull on emotion. Though life might make us wish to believe that truth rests in dialectic, the working out of oppositions within time, we are here forced to see it existing in paradox. There is both development and no development: Maskull comes to see more and Maskull also learns nothing. Muspel lives in the tower from which Maskull sets forth on his journey, ultimately in search of him; we are given final truth in Slofork's self-annihilation at the outset of the narrative (pp. 67–70). Tormance, creation of Crystalman, can exist only by oppositions, as in *tor*ment and ro*mance*; all truths formulated or 'crystallised' within it are both true and doomed to failure, just as all the matter forms Shaping uses to capture and solidify about the pieces of Muspel light are both wondrous and corrupt. The journey goes nowhere; the only true insight Maskull gains is that no insight is true; and yet at the same time the journey is heroic, and some insights are valid. Nightspore, the Muspel-self of what was once Maskull (p. 291), is at once the highest expression of Maskull and Maskull's utter cancellation, the release of the imprisoned spark of Muspel light from the cloying enclosure of the Maskull-self. With Nightspore the journey goes back on itself as he returns with Krag to the struggle on Tormance.

A Voyage to Arcturus is radically subversive: it appeals continually to our affections, imaginations and intellects only to deny them utterly: this world we find beautiful, these women we find noble, this man we see as a hero, all are also corrupt and corrupting creations of Shaping; and we, in having the ground so continually and brutally taken from beneath our feet, just as in literal terms the planet's geography frequently betrays Maskull, are forced to learn Muspel truths by literary experience of them. The 'fiction' is exploded in the way that we return to the tower to find Muspel: and all our strongest earthly impulses are invoked in order to be destroyed. But in that destruction lies, not nothingness (as Crystalman would have Maskull see himself at the end (p. 289)), but Muspel, the utterly transcendent other.[23] Even Nightspore's vision on the last level of the tower at the end is inaccurate, for he sees Muspel as reduced to the tower alone, fighting for his life against Crystalman: the truth is that Crystalman would die without Muspel, for he lives by devouring his light, while Muspel can live without Crystalman. Thus Krag tells the despondent Nightspore on his return, ' "I am the stronger and the mightier. Crystalman's Empire is but a shadow on the face of Muspel" ' (p. 302). No easy reassurance is offered, however, ' "But nothing will be done without the bloodiest blows" ' (ib.).

In relation to Scottish fantasy, *A Voyage to Arcturus* shows elements of the emphasis on the 'unconscious' that we have seen in other works. While Tormance is not an inner landscape but a vision, and while as we have said Lindsay's interest is in the super- rather than in the sub-conscious, his book has the destructured and image-filled quality of a dream, and we cannot but feel that its images and episodes flowed without prevision from Lindsay's mind. Certainly few of them have symbolic meaning, and most are portrayed as the products of a random and gluttonous creativity: ' "The will forks and sports incessantly, and thus no two creatures are alike" ' (p. 61). The mysterious images and disconnected episodes have their roots in George MacDonald's fantasies of the unconscious, even while Lindsay is doing quite different things with them. The book has a searching moral and intellectual analysis, but this analysis is rather draped about than made inherent in the images, which in themselves remain wildly diverse. Further, the analysis itself is, as we have said, continually undermining itself, denying order, pattern, and sequence, even while it also affirms them: in this way the book seeks to break down the certainties of the conscious mind, if to send it upwards out of itself rather than further within.

There is more of an aspect of a journey 'further within' in Lindsay's later fantasies, from *The Haunted Woman* (1922) to the unpublished 'The Violet Apple' and 'The Witch'.[24] The emphasis there is on stripping away the outward self of social convention and rationality and revealing the sublime world. The location of all these books is in buildings, in contrast to *A Voyage*, which starts by leaving one: in both *The Haunted Woman* and 'The Witch', for example, this is an ancient Saxon house, which is a gateway to another world; in *Devil's Tor* (1932) the centre is a huge exposed underground tomb.[25] But if the journey is now more introverted, and if the symbolism more directly suggests the unconscious mind than in *A Voyage*, the life of that unconscious is still not merely psychological, but is the sole portal to the super-conscious, the supernatural. Women are at the centre of these books, women as representatives of an age-old matriarchy linked to the world of the sublime; and marriage, founded in the sublime, is the objective in all of them. The focus is always inwards, to a point of conjunction: in *Devil's Tor* the eventual climax is the bringing together at once of the two halves of a long-split magic stone, and the powerful woman Ingrid with a man capable of matching her, Saltfleet. Here we deal not with an active outgoing hero such as Maskull, but with a more still and waiting power which is to be awakened, whether the long-dormant magic of a stone or an Edenic apple, or the latent supernatural power of ancient buildings. There is a sense here of often moving backwards, and the past, history, and memory play a part they do not have in *A Voyage*. In these books Lindsay finds a role for women, passion, union (rather than solitude) and creativity which he did not give them previously. (He himself remarked on the contradiction.[26])

The nature of these later books, however, is that of a search for something elusive or lost—a house that in certain circumstances opens on to a supernatural realm (*The Haunted Woman*), the missing fragments of a stone whose union will produce a new world, the recording of dreams in which glimpses of a wholly other world appear (*Sphinx*, 1923), the pursuit of the 'woman of heaven', Urda, in 'The Witch'. It would not be wholly inappropriate to trace the character of these books to a sense in Lindsay that the supernatural world that was so present to his inspiration in *A Voyage to Arcturus* has now largely receded from his view; certainly his own creativity struggles for expression with increasing difficulty over the rest of his life. Of course it is true that all these later books deal with finding the 'supernatural' in our obscuring world, where in *A Voyage* Lindsay was portraying its more immediate existence on another. Nevertheless it remains the case that these later books lack the creative tensions and the variety of *A Voyage*: their objectives become clear and narrow, and their worldviews are unambiguous and often laboured. They are fascinating and moving, but, with the exception of *The Haunted Woman*, they are not often art.

Notes

1 On Lindsay's life and writings, see Colin Wilson, E. H. Visiak and J. B. Pick, *The Strange Genius of David Lindsay* (London: John Baker, 1970); Bernard Sellin, *The Life and Works of David Lindsay*, trans. Kenneth Gunnell (Cambridge: Cambridge University Press, 1981).

2 Letter of 29 October, 1944, in *Letters of C. S. Lewis*, ed. W. H. Lewis (London: Bles, 1966), p. 205.

3 Letter of 1947 quoted in Donald E. Glover, *C. S. Lewis: The Art of Enchantment* (Athens, Ohio: Ohio University Press, 1981), p. 33.

4 Lindsay, quoted in J. B. Pick, 'A Sketch of Lindsay's Life as Man and and Writer', *The Strange Genius*, p. 6.

5 This, and the floating island on which it is done, find their way into C. S. Lewis's *Perelandra* (1943).

6 MacDonald, *Phantastes and Lilith* (London: Gollancz, 1962), p. 149. On Lindsay's debt to MacDonald, see also Gary K. Wolfe, *David Lindsay* (Mercer Island, Washington: Starmont House, 1982), pp. 11–13, 15.

7 David Lindsay, *A Voyage to Arcturus* (Edinburgh: Canongate, 1992), p. 77.

8 MacDonald, *Phantastes and Lilith*, pp. 24, 61.

9 See e.g. Wilson in *The Strange Genius*, pp. 8–9, 84–5; Sellin, pp. 53–5, 175–6, 179, 182, 189–90, 204, 208; Wolfe, pp. 15–17, 22–3, 24, 34–5, 36.

10 *Phantastes and Lilith*, p. 412.

11 Lewis, *Perelandra* (London: John Lane, 1943), p. 232.

12 Ian Watson feels the same discrepancy in 'From Pan in the Home Counties—to Pain on a Far Planet: E. M. Forster, David Lindsay and

how the Voyage to Arcturus Should End', *Foundation: The Review of Science Fiction*, no.43 (Summer, 1988), pp. 30, 32.

13 Lewis, *Perelandra*, p. 39.

14 Lindsay's mother and aunt used to hold séances in their house; Lindsay scorned these as a means of reaching the hereafter (Sellin, pp. 197–8).

15 It is typical of Lindsay to make the 'highest' form in the book, Krag, of a coarse and simian aspect.

16 Through Tydomin's agency, Maskull is later to find himself reliving this episode as the victim (pp. 123–5)—a piece of 'bilocalism' owing much to MacDonald's *Lilith*.

17 Lindsay once heard such an inexplicable crash in his own house, and also gave it supernatural explanation (Sellin, pp. 196–7).

18 References to drum-beats are at pp. 28–9, 62–3, 129, 154–60, 169, 170, 230–4, 271–2, 290, 292–3, 296. On their function, see Robert H. Waugh, 'The Drum of *A Voyage to Arcturus*', *Extrapolation*, 26, 2 (Summer, 1985), pp. 143–51.

19 *The Prose Edda of Snorri Sturluson: Tales from Norse Mythology*, sel. and trans. Jean I. Young (Berkeley and Los Angeles: University of California Press, 1966), p. 32.

20 Ibid., pp. 32, 33, 35–6, 38.

21 George MacDonald, *Unspoken Sermons: Third Series* (London: Longmans Green, 1889), p. 63.

22 Lindsay, 'Philosophical Notes', in a special David Lindsay issue of *Lines Review*, ed. Robin Fulton, no.40 (March, 1972), p. 23, no.133. On Lindsay's views on sacrifice, see Sellin, pp. 183–6. Lindsay saw women as the more self-sacrificing sex (Sellin, p. 185; see also *A Voyage*, p. 264).

23 In his unpublished 'Sketch Notes for a New System of Philosophy', Lindsay ended, 'Schopenhauer's "Nothing", which is the least understood part of his system, is identical with my Muspel; that is, the *real* world' (no.545, in National Library of Scotland MS accession no.5616). 'Philosophical Notes' (see note 22, above) is a selection from 'Sketch Notes'.

24 First published as David Lindsay, *The Violet Apple and The Witch*, ed. J. B. Pick (Chicago: Chicago Review Press, 1976).

25 On houses and buildings in Lindsay's work, see Sellin, pp. 72–98.

26 'Between the philosophies of *Arcturus* and *Devil's Tor* there seems to be a chasm of contradiction' (letter of 1932 to Putnam's, publishers of *Devil's Tor*, quoted by Pick in *The Strange Genius*, p. 30).

CHAPTER TEN

Neil Gunn, *The Green Isle of the Great Deep* (1944)

I F THE INTEREST of much of the fantasy we have looked at so far has been with loss of the self—the erosions of Jekyll, Wringhim or the 'sin-eater', the death of identity in MacDonald, Oliphant or Barrie, or the disappearance of the self into its own text in Carlyle's *Sartor*—in Scottish fantasy from about 1930 onwards we find much more emphasis on keeping one's self, on maintaining that 'atom of delight'[1] or displeasure that constitutes one's being. One prime reason for this is the increase of Scotland's own self-awareness, and together with that a sense of the threat to it. Practically all the fantasies we will be considering after this are works involving definition: they all constitute a struggle to arrive at a true self, sometimes even through death, which is subsumed in a larger growth in political and social awareness.

For Neil Gunn, who lived in Caithness for most of his life, the assurance of identity was a Highland one, of mingled identification with the land, a sense of being part of an age-old culture and a defiance of all who would destroy its values. Gunn was at first tempted by the fatalism of Fiona Macleod's work, but he turned away from the rhythms of defeat and elegy—themselves a very real strain in Scottish culture—to a more assertive idiom. That idiom is at first stentorian and harsh in some of his early novels, such as *The Grey Coast* (1926) and *The Lost Glen* (1932), but soon moves to a happier and more assured idiom as Gunn focuses on childhood as the root and guarantee of being and joy in such works as *Morning Tide* (1930), *Highland River* (1937), *The Silver Darlings* (1941) and *Young Art and Old Hector* (1942). In *Sun Circle* (1933), Gunn wrote a novel in the tradition of his friend Naomi Mitchison's *The Corn King and the Spring Queen* (1931), in which a young Celt has to contemplate the eclipse of much of his culture with the coming, equally, of the Vikings and Christianity: yet he sees that his spirit will outlast even these changes, because it is given a wholeness, like a ring, by the circled beauty of the land of which it is a part: 'As the Sun put a circle round the earth and all that it contained, so a man by his vision put a circle round himself. At the centre of this circle his spirit sat, and at the centre of his spirit was a serenity for ever watchful.'[2] In this novel the 'childhood' of the race is an extension of the childhood of the individual explored in others. Gunn's vision, regional, rocky, and child-oriented, is similar to Wordsworth's, though there is more sense of tradition (and sometimes of a remote and even geological past) in Gunn. Both are visionaries, sensing the metaphysical in the material world. But for Gunn the realisation is not only personal, it is cultural, collective and even political. Where Wordsworth found in the French Revolution an analogue for his own life, Gunn's Scottish Nationalism was a natural growth of his being; and Wordsworth could turn away from France and back to himself as Gunn never could from Scotland.

Gunn's main 'fantastic' work is *The Green Isle of the Great Deep* (1944); he himself called it a 'phantasy' in the dedication. He did however write two other novels which are metaphysical and at times even supernaturalist, *The Well at the World's End* (1950) and *The Other Landscape* (1954). *The Green Isle* was begun by 1941, and for all its lyrical-sounding title (true of many of Gunn's novels) is a highly political allegory, in the tradition of Yevgeny Zamiatin's *We* (trans. 1924) and Huxley's *Brave New World* (1932), on the consequences of the deification of the state at the expense of the individual. At the same time however, it is a sequel to *Young Art and Old Hector* (1942), which describes the childhood of a Highland boy and his developing relationship with a wise old man; at the end of the story Hector is about to take Art to the 'River' to poach salmon, and it is there that *The Green Isle* begins. *Young Art and Old Hector* gives us a sense of the richness of this world, centred on the village of Clachdrum, which is to sustain the characters as they move into another world in *The Green Isle*. It also 'grows' Art, in the sense that he develops through his childhood, to the point where he can take on the more complex spiritual role he is given in *The Green Isle*. And at the same time, the relation of Art and Hector, child and old man, the one being educated and the other drawing renewed life, joins the two ends of life into a circle like the sun's circle, tells us that the progress suggested by time and even by the narrative sequence of the two books has its counterpart in another and timeless level of being. Even the two books themselves suggest this, in the way that the first is centred mainly on Young Art and the second on Old Hector, and yet they are closely bound together.

The Green Isle was a popular book, selling 18,000 copies within four years, far beyond the publisher Faber's initial conservative run of 8,000. This we may attribute to its topicality, with such subjects as totalitarianism, concentration camps and mind-control; and perhaps to the interest in its treatment of an after-life, a subject made popular at the time, and in the context of war, by C. S. Lewis in particular, with his *The Screwtape Letters* (1942) and *The Great Divorce* (1945).[3] In it Gunn unites two strands, the 'individual' in Art and Hector, and the universal in the large, even ultimate, issues that are continually at the forefront of concern: indeed the joining of these two strands is in one way the 'meaning' of the book. Gunn could thus as readily claim (to his friend Naomi Mitchison) that he wrote the book simply to continue the story for the satisfaction of an old friend,[4] as he could write, 'I conceived the idea of letting these two characters drop through the bottom of a pool into their Gaelic Paradise . . . run on totalitarian lines, with the latest politico-metaphysical theories buzzing around, just to see what would happen to them.'[5] The first motive is one of friendship and continuity; the second of the detached, the experimental, even the scientific: both are shown to be needed, and both are here joined in the common impulse of *play*. The issue of play and seriousness is to be a central one in the book.

Gunn's book is a response to the Second World War, where Lindsay's may be to the First. Gunn saw the evil of the Second war as the destruction of mind more even than of body; the pains described in Lindsay's book are always very physical and brutal. The two differ in other ways. Gunn disliked Lindsay's 'nightmarish' vision and the 'inconceivability' of his Muspel world. Unlike Lindsay, he does not place supreme value on pain and loss as roads to the divine, but tries to overcome these, to annihilate them in a vision of an earthbound utopia. 'I think we could say that the actual experiencing of states of being that inhabit the other world momentarily are [sic] characterised by a profound sense of harmony, integration, unity, well-being—not "awful" etc.'[6] If Lindsay looks outside creation for his god, Gunn looks within, believing that though nature may be temporarily blighted by civilised man, it is inherently and divinely good. Gunn accepts Crystalman's world as Lindsay cannot.

The story of *The Green Isle* tells how Hector and Art fall into Hazel Pool while they are fishing for salmon in the River, and wake up in what seems a paradise. But nearly all the inhabitants prove to be human automata, their minds stripped and governed by a clique of thought police who have taken over this and other regions of paradise while God remains distant. These 'thought adjusters' do all they can to shape Hector and a recalcitrant woman of that land, Mary, to their wishes, in order to entrap the ever-elusive Art, whose name begins to take on allegorical dimensions. In the end Hector demands, as is his right, an audience with God, who comes to sit in judgment on His errant agents; after which Hector and Art come to themselves back near their Highland home, being rescued from drowning in the pool where their adventures began.

What happens in the other world seems international and even universal in scope, but we are not allowed to forget that it is all occurring within a very individual and Celtic world, that of the Gaelic paradise, or 'the green Isle that was about the heaps of the deep' ('Eilean uaine a bha 'n iomal torra domhain');[7] and the story not only begins and ends in Clachdrum, but is pervaded by it in the shape of Art and Hector or even of certain people and features of the landscape there. The Green Isle, if so it may be called, since we never hear of the sea, is arrived at by falling into an unfathomable deep in Hazel Pool. Quite what the place is is not clear, largely to allow it to be many things. It is a kind of utopia, where everyone seems happy in a beautiful pastoral landscape; and yet at the same time it is a dystopia, where all these happy people are brain-washed robots overseen by a city full of autocratic intellectuals. It seems at times to be a place where people go when they die;[8] and yet it also contains people very like some living in Clachdrum (such as Mavis/Morag, or Tom/Tom-the-shepherd (pp. 45, 81).[9] Old Hector does not know the place and yet ' "I seem to remember it, too" ' (p. 25; see also p. 38). It has God in it, somewhere: and He makes a very individual appearance at the end. It is also an image of the ills of Europe, or of man's compartmentalised mind. It is even, possibly, a picture of the divided parts of Scotland (pp. 38, 43, 48). If we speak of it as fantasy, it must be as partaking in all these aspects: it is as much, if not more, an image of the natural world as of a supernatural one.

Nevertheless, it has got God in it. It is not the God we 'know': there is no mention of Christ, of the Bible, the Church, apocalypse, heaven or hell; this, if we like, is a demythologised God. He is seen more as creator than as sustainer: He is called the 'Starter of the Race', which race is both the sports at Clachdrum and the human race. This God is rarely, if ever, invoked—certainly so rarely that not one of the governors of all the regions of the Green Isle knows of a time when He has come, not least because they have stifled such petitions as have been made. When He comes in this story, it is not just the case of his appellant Old Hector that is heard, but the whole organisation of that world is tried and found wanting. As judge, this God 'represents' certain ideas, such as heart over head, individual over state, freedom over control, but He is no mere abstraction, being also supremely personal: He appears as an old man, has adventures with Art, who at one point mistakes Him for Hector, and He departs from view in the midst of a jumping contest He is having with Art. This God, for all His absence and His transcendence, living alone on His far Peak, is as human, indeed as fully human, as can be; He is reminiscent of the God who comes to earth as a travelling wine-salesman in T. F. Powys' *Mr Weston's Good Wine* (1927). Perhaps we will understand best what this God is when we know a little more of the events that precede His arrival.

The place is called the Green Isle of the Great Deep: but depth is precisely what is not found in the ordinary people here. They seem at first like redeemed souls rejoicing in a pastoral heaven, but their laughter is 'bright and shallow' (p. 28). They are mere zombies, drained of personality and the capacity to think for themselves: happy as Wells's degenerate Eloi or Huxley's creatures of the test tube. They live in a utopia which in a sense mimics that of William Morris's *News from Nowhere* (1891); and yet this utopia is precisely not one, it is a hell. Their paradise is one in which they are bidden never to eat the fruit that they pluck and send to the City (p. 92): and yet eating the fruit is

the way not only to knowledge but to life itself (p. 98).[10] At the centre
of this are the intellectuals of the Seat on the Rock in the City, who are
stupid by virtue of their intelligence. They use the head only; they are the
rational mind; they impose ideas on the material world, the sterile rock
on living things and the city on the country. They are the simplifiers of
life, the 'Perfectionists', separating off the imagination, the personality,
the emotions, making a world founded on dualism between mind and
body. '"That's one thing about the mind," remarked the Questioner,
blowing an invisible speck from a lapel, "it is the ultimate, the final realm.
Nothing can transcend that to which we have been giving our attention"'
(pp. 214–15). He forgets God, who blasts mind with mind in out-arguing
them all. And the source of these simplifiers? They are '"Those who had
arrived from the earth with the new ideas"' (p. 96): doubtless some of
them idealists, but they are also the Stalinists, the Nazis, the eugenists,
the camp doctors, the ethnic cleansers, the religious bigots and purists,
all of them perpetuating schism and death in the name of their precisely
insane utopias. This of course is where the contemporary force of Gunn's
fable lies: it is a form of extended analysis of the ills of our time.

All these are shallow, living at the level only of the rational mind, or
as the mere passive tools of mind. Yet, until the arrival of Hector and
Art, this distorted world works: the people happily toil, the intellectuals
of the Seat on the Rock enjoy the refinements of their plans, and God
remains absent. Why then do Hector and Art arrive? They are about to
catch a salmon. And just before that, Art has plucked a branch of thirteen
beautiful hazel nuts from the topmost branch of a tree, which costs him a
fall. The nuts are knowledge; the salmon is wisdom; and beyond—'"You
see, first of all you get the knowledge. Then you get the wisdom . . .
Then," said Art, another tone down, "you get something else . . . The
magic"' (p. 226). And the magic, says Hector, was in the face of God
(ib.). Art and Hector, child and old man, in themselves unite opposites;
and in having the salmon of wisdom (for they find it lying beside the
pool on their return), they represent a far deeper level of understanding
than that possessed by anyone in the Green Isle. They are small in
themselves, but they constitute the seed (or the nut) of revolution;[11]
and on their hard shells the mighty intellects of the Seat break their
teeth. Here, then, depth is the issue. To the people of the 'single level'
who inhabit this strange land, a land whose very richness and wealth
have been tamed and flattened by the minds of its human inhabitants
(and we see few animals in that country), is opposed the increasing depth
that Art and Hector represent. The plunge that begins their adventure
goes on through it. The rulers of the city seek to brainwash Hector, and
in doing so go to deeper and further levels of his mind; detesting the
abyss, they plumb it, and themselves awaken what is there.[12] For the
Questioner, interrogating Hector when captured, 'Clearly, here was a
case of the primitive mind with its parallel in the lower forms of life.

Break it into bits, and each bit wriggles . . . For interest now lay in some new suggestion of an indefinable region where the old man might have achieved a primitive integration, a certain living wisdom':

> The Questioner decided to pursue the hunt into this primor-
> dial region. His lust grew on him. The cruel stroke on the
> mind could be used. Grunts and extraordinary cries became
> the speech of the jungle. Old Hector, like the wounded beast,
> floundered. Cried Yes and then cried No, meaninglessly.
> Relentlessly the Questioner pursued. Until at last the old
> man could bear no more, and crashing round, like some old
> stag of his native forest, raised his stricken head and stood
> at bay.
>   The Questioner felt a small shiver from that challenge. The
> whole primordial world stood still, this world, and all the
> universe of men and time.
>   And upon this silence, holding the Questioner by the eyes,
> Old Hector spoke deep out of his throat:
>   'I want to see God.'
>
> (pp. 154–5)

God, thus invoked, appears (p. 173): He is the 'direct consequence' of the analysis into Hector's deepest nature, his 'primordial world'. (This is reminiscent of George MacDonald, for whom God was to be found in the unconscious imagination.) This is the realm of magic, beyond wisdom, where all laws, including natural ones, may be suspended for deeper truths. Now we have an old man who can run or jump like a boy (pp. 173–5, 251–2), a magical escape from a prison and a room (pp. 208–10, 219), miraculous travels and invisibility (p. 227). Now Art, who should be exhausted from the constant hunt for him, appears to Hector full of vitality and 'a living grace' (p. 224); now, imbued with the presence of God, a more than mortal utopia is near (p. 250).

But this is not the whole of what happens. On the other 'side' of the narrative we have Art. Or rather, we do not have Art, since for much of the story he is in hiding. He contrasts with Hector as youth with age, and movement with stillness. He contrasts with the tamed utopians as a wild thing. And his elusiveness challenges the obsession with fixity and control that characterises the minds of the Seat on the Rock. It would be easy to allegorise him as Art itself (though it would have to be an unusual sort of art), or as the imagination, or individuality, or wild nature: but he defies such categorisation, whether by us or by the Seat.[13] Indeed his essence is his elusiveness: he is there to demonstrate the wild freedom of truth; he is only caught when he is in God's company. During the story his nature changes. When Hector sees him after one absence, 'He looked like a legendary boy, and to Old Hector it seemed he had grown two or three inches,' and he has 'that alien look which Old Hector had seen more than once before on Earth' (p. 87). Later, 'he was certainly growing. He was already more like a boy of ten or eleven than of eight past' (p. 119). Later still, this 'legendary boy', this 'vision of the immortal boy', has changed to a boy who is a legend, a creature of myth, whose physical prowess and ability continually to escape are magical (pp. 129–31). For the minds of the Seat it is inexplicable or impossible, and to preserve reason there must be '"a limit to credulity"' (p. 171). They identify the mythologising of Art as '"An interesting form of atavism . . . descent into the primeval abyss"' (p. 183). That makes Art identical with their view of Hector: and more than this, it reminds us that it was just such a descent into the primeval abyss of Hector's mind that unearthed God. Art's development is parallel to Hector's: he meets God when Hector has asked for Him. Hector is age, still and passive; Art youth, mobile, active and resistant. The relationship of Art and Old Hector is in itself a 'value' in the book, in that it embodies love of one person for another, as opposed to the atomising indifference of the rationalised society they find. But the old man/boy pairing (there is an ancient 'senex/puer' *topos* running through literature[14]) suggests that they are also a unity of opposites, two aspects of a single being. There are plenty of quite natural reasons for Art, as a boy, having run away in the strange land of the Green Isle, and even for his continued absence from Hector: but the story, thus divided between these characters, also suggests that Art's absence may in some way reflect Hector's 'dark night of the soul' in that land, or even, more broadly, the absence of spirit from the people.

If elusiveness, even absence, is at the centre, so is relationship. This is driven home by the very breaking of bonds: Hector is split from Art, and the still 'human' couple Robert and Mary are disjoined when Mary is taken to the Seat in the City to be brainwashed. The story itself becomes atomistic, as we move among Hector, Robert, Mary, the City officers Merk and Axle, or the Questioner at the Seat. The people do not even relate to the land, since they cannot eat its fruits. They are like the people of advertising, or the idealised workers of a communist state, who express a conformist happiness without depth: when Mary returns to Robert, apparently tamed by the Seat, and brightly invites them all in for a meal, 'It was the mood the harvesters and milkers understood. They laughed at her gay chattering. But the meal was over and they backed away, thanking her, still watching and laughing' (p. 166). This disjoining is reversed in the very existence of the bond between Hector and Art, and their arrival. They bring into that static land movement and time in their very natures as young and old (every person seems to be about the same age in the Green Isle, and while we hear of harvesting, we never hear of winter). And the love that leads both Mary and Hector to protect Art by hiding their true selves deeper and deeper like salmon from the probing gaze of the Questioner, eventually calls down God.

God arrives as judge, but unlike those he interviews, He is no disjoiner. The 'head', the rational part of man has gone outside its position and tried to make all that is man subservient to it, and to dismiss or erase all other human faculties. Reason has its place: God comes to teach it that place and to join it once more with the rest of mind and body. What God opposes is dualism, the splitting of one thing from another.

> 'There was a time when the Questioner had wisdom. He used his head and drew on his wisdom. But the more he used his head only, the paler his wisdom became, until at last the elements of wisdom were no longer so but only the ghostly bits he used for making a pattern with his head. He knew in his head that you suffered, but as the head itself does not suffer, he himself was not affected, for what is affected swims deep with the salmon. He has divorced knowledge from wisdom, the head from the heart, the intellect from the spirit—for man has many words for these two regions—and because of the divorce, the taste of life has gone bitter and its hope sterile.'
>
> (p. 242)

The God who says this is a reconciler, an 'atonemaker', though the reconciliation involved is no facile fusion, but a bond made out of wild and free individuals conjoined in love. The relation of Hector and Art is a central symbol of this, as is the larger Highland society from which they come. At the end, the poet Robert, his inspiration reawakened, begins to intuit 'round the corner' of the future, a vision of a world of harmony which resolves itself in paradox, 'in the ascending that goes deep and in the outward that penetrates, around the corner made visible, to-morrow and to-morrow and to-day' (p. 250). Whether that new Jerusalem founds itself on the magic that is in life, or sustains itself on some yet further supernatural power, is for us to determine in our own way.

The style of the book could be said to fit its subject. At first Hector and Art are travelling together, but then the narrative settles into a 'state', with Art absent and Hector oscillating between the Seat and the house of Robert and Mary. God is 'happened upon', while Hector's mind is being probed. There is no quest, no direction to the story, which suits with the lack of purpose in the ordinary people of the Green Isle and the fixities of the mind that emanate from the Seat. Indeed fixation seems to be a prominent feature of the Seat in the sense that the minds there become obsessed and fascinated by Hector and Art: they are '"interested, intensely interested, in any curious manifestation of the mind—for its own sake"' (p. 105). Expressing this could be said to be their continual recurrence to the same topic, gnawing it again and again.

The repetitiveness of the narrative (Art goes missing at least three times), the sense of going nowhere, the sterile reiteration of ideas, would thus become functional as an image of reason gone mad.

And yet, and yet . . . There is something necessarily contradictory in a book that can produce dissertations by God on dualism, intellectual analyses of where the intellect has gone wrong. In Art the book refuses us any ready identification of what he is: there is a section on the different interpretations of him by different regions of the Green Isle, whether as Art itself, or as Arthur, or as a part of a larger mathematical pattern (pp. 131–4). The patterning mind is mocked, and in particular because it sees only the meaning and not the individual that makes it. In this sense, it is the strength of Gunn's book to make Art supremely a young boy at the same time as a suggestive symbol and a legend. And yet there is still the patterning mind of the author. He is perhaps too often explicit where he might dramatise more. And for all the complexity of his proposed vision, he is often too simple or even sentimental in his response.[15] We learn throughout the narrative to hate the intellect; but then it is given a lasting role by God. We are shown how wrong all polarities are, and yet are asked on the one hand to respond with total love for Hector and Art, and on the other with complete revulsion at the evil of the Questioner at the Seat. We are reluctant to accept unreservedly such direct emotion as 'Old Hector looked as if he might talk now to Art of many things and of times long ago . . . A strange and silent smile, such as Art had never before seen, glimmered on his face, and in that moment Art entered into his heritage and he loved Old Hector and the presences of all those who had been here before, alive or dead' (pp. 23–4). The author's love of Highland values, and his loathing for the misapplications of the intellect, for all their worth betray themselves a little too nakedly. So far as the continual explication throughout the story is concerned, we could perhaps explain it as part of the nature of the utopian/dystopian genre: Bacon, Swift, Butler, Morris, Bellamy, Wells, Zamiatin, Huxley, Orwell, all of them take much time out to give us virtual pamphlets of discourse on their imagined societies. As to simplified responses, we might find these in the socialistic enthusiasms of Morris, the technological fervour of Bellamy or the unrelieved pessimism of Zamiatin: but more complex reactions are possible, as in the elusive position of Swift, the mockeries of Butler, the ironic interplay of the savage and the civilised in Huxley.

For all that *The Green Isle of the Great Deep* was popular in the immediate post-war years, it has not endured as has the work of Huxley or Orwell (*Nineteen Eighty-Four* (1949) possibly eclipsed it). Its appeal was to a particular sense of crisis and menace generated by the Russian purges and the discovery of the Nazis' calculated programme of genocide. It is, in the end, a little more propaganda than it is a novel. And while it is good in analysing the evils of the untamed intellect, not least in its clear grasp that *'in addition to the highest intention there can abide self-delusion and the last refinement of cruelty'* (p. 218),[16] it is less sure in its presentation of how Humpty-Dumpty is put together again—how, that is, outside the instinctual integration made freely available to a dweller of Clachdrum, a utopian unity of the mind is to be realised in the wider world beyond.[17] It is not quite enough to end with a mathematician smiling benignly at his new-found awareness of the difference between 'four' and 'four apples'. And the conclusion of the story, with Hector and Art back in Clachdrum, seems not wholly unlike a return to a cultural enclosure.

In Gunn's work we once again find the peculiar and specific concern with the mind that is often seen in Scottish fantasy—in Hogg, Carlyle, MacDonald, Stevenson, Barrie and others. And once again the emphasis is on the value of the unconscious and the imagination. God is found far within Hector's mind and sets about dismantling the tyrannies of the intellect. Art, the elusive Art, whose name must go for something, is the inspiration itself, never to be trapped.[18] A creature in part of mythology—as Arthur and as Cuchulain with his hounds—he belongs to the collective unconscious of the folk. During the story he dilates in size, runs at increasingly amazing speeds, and even flies: in a sense the imagination is expanding in its own seclusion and freedom, until it can meet naturally with its God. And throughout, the unconscious imagination is suggested through the imagery of depth.

There is a similar stress on the imagination in Gunn's less specifically fantastic, but still metaphysical, novels, *The Well at the World's End* (1950) and *The Other Landscape* (1954). *The Well* starts with a touring professor and his wife being directed by an old highland woman to a well where the water is so clear it is invisible, giving the professor the feeling that they are '"setting out to find the—the something in life that we think isn't there"'.[19] The narrative is full of images of wells, suggesting descents into a dark and refreshing region of the mind:[20] but it is a descent that is never fully completed, owing to the central figure Peter's flippancy and intellectual habits of mind. Peter knows the 'trick' of pushing beyond the ego: but because he sees it only in terms of advantage to himself, he cannot perform it (p. 263). He pursues a 'wild man', an ex-ghillie called Peter Mackay, who looks remarkably like him, and who can be seen as the primitive side of himself he cannot meet; this Peter Mackay is killed. In *The Other Landscape*, the central figure Menzies is trying to come to terms with his wife's death by the composition and playing of music, and through metaphysical speculation: he has an acute sense of an other and supernatural world of which he can give no more than hints through symbols and musical modes. (The novel seems indebted to David Lindsay's *A Voyage to Arcturus* for its setting, its sense of the sublime and its use of musical imagery, particularly of drum beats). Like Peter Mackay in *The Well*, Menzies falls down a cliff and is killed. In this novel the innermost self, and the vision of the world that it reveals, give rise to a world not of the imagination only, but of the imagination made fact. It is that world which we are to suppose Menzies has at last entered at his death.

In *The Other Landscape* Gunn in a sense faces harder and deeper issues than in *The Green Isle of the Great Deep*: for in the former it is the doings of man that are at fault and God is benign, but in the later novel the very fabric of the universe is under question, and God is for long seen as a 'Wrecker'. The values of Clachdrum will not sustain us if the earth on which they stand is the creation of a malevolent being. One cannot blame man, or seek for remedy, for the 'natural' death of a beloved wife. It is here that Gunn puts his vision to a further and deeper test. If *The Other Landscape* is not a fantasy, that to some extent is the measure now of fantasy in Gunn's mind: there are no longer any clear answers, or certain and supportive Gods, only 'the sheer wonder of man's being on its quest'.[21]

Notes

1 Title of Gunn's autobiography.

2 Gunn, *Sun Circle* (Edinburgh: Porpoise Press, 1933), pp. 365–6.

3 A remarkable parallel to Gunn's book is C. S. Lewis's *That Hideous Strength* (1945), which also has control by a rational/scientific elite dominated by a Head, and brainwashing procedures.

4 Letter of 9 June 1944 in Neil M. Gunn, *Selected Letters*, ed. J. B. Pick (Edinburgh: Polygon, 1987), p. 79. On the inception of the book, see also Francis Russell Hart and J. B. Pick, *Neil M. Gunn: A Highland Life* (London: John Murray, 1981), pp. 194–8.

5 *Selected Letters*, p. 140 (letter of 17 April 1958 to Alexander Reid); see also p. 209 (letter of 26 June 1965 to Professor Tokusaburo Nakamura).

6 *Selected Letters*, pp. 192–3.

7 As featured in e.g. J. F. Campbell, ed., *Popular Tales of the West Highlands*, 4 vols (Edinburgh: Edmonston and Douglas, 1860–2), I, pp. 164–70 ('The Brown Bear of the Green Glen').

8 As with the woman Mary of that land, who seems to have lived on earth near Clachdrum many years before Hector (Gunn, *The Green Isle of the Great Deep* (London: Faber and Faber, 1944), pp. 69–70, 84).

9 Even God is identified as the Starter of Clachdrum (the starter of the races at the annual Games), p. 224. On the other side, Art reminds Robert and Mary in the Green Isle of their son who died on earth (pp. 91, 151).

10 Andrew Noble, 'Fable of Freedom: *The Green Isle of the Great Deep*', in *Neil M. Gunn: The Man and the Writer*, eds Alexander Scott and Douglas Gifford (Edinburgh: Blackwood, 1973), p. 209, remarks: 'for

Gunn the tree of knowledge is also the tree of life, because without knowledge of good and evil man is not free.'

11 Noble, p. 201, refers to Gunn's presentation in *The Atom of Delight* of a child's innate ability to sense evil, and how throughout *The Green Isle of the Great Deep* Art is 'the only person who understands the pragmatism of what is happening for what it actually is, evil. He therefore, is the exception that breaks the rule. "In the end," says Gunn, "the diversion becomes the deviation that wrecks the system"' (The last quote is from Gunn, *The Atom of Delight* (London: Faber and Faber, 1956), p. 10.)

12 Noble remarks on 'Gunn's belief that analysis finally comes to that which its paranoid self-awareness has perhaps always feared' (p. 206).

13 Such attempts at explanation of Art are made by the various intellects of the Green Isle (pp. 131–4). Gunn probably took Art from the wondrous Little Art, Highland child and confidant of Christ, in Fiona Macleod's 'The Last Supper', in *The Washer of the Ford* (1896).

14 See Ernst Robert Curtius, *European Literature and the Latin Middle Ages* (New York: Pantheon, 1953), pp. 98–101. Curtius sees this as 'an archetype, an image of the collective unconscious in the sense of C. G. Jung' (p. 101).

15 And yet Gunn had intended this book as a corrective to the sentimentality readers had found in *Young Art and Old Hector* (*Selected Letters*, pp. 140, 208–9).

16 A notion previously explored by Gunn in 'On Belief', *Scots Magazine*, XXIV, no.1 (Oct. 1940), p. 55.

17 An issue also raised by Hart and Pick in *A Highland Life*, pp. 197–8. However, Richard Price, in *The Fabulous Matter of Fact: The Poetics of Neil M. Gunn* (Edinburgh: Edinburgh University Press, 1991), writes, 'The Council of the wise men . . . is politically naive, but we should not expect a full-blown Constitution in an ostensible fable' (p. 128).

18 As pointed out by Noble, p. 202. Noble also identifies Art with 'the capacity for vision and imagination' (p. 203).

19 Gunn, *The Well at the World's End* (London: Faber and Faber, 1950), p. 10.

20 A point made by Price, *The Fabulous Matter of Fact*, pp. 173–4.

21 Gunn, *The Other Landscape* (London: Faber and Faber, 1954), p. 318.

CHAPTER ELEVEN

George Mackay Brown, *Magnus* (1973) and Others

NEIL GUNN AND GEORGE MACKAY BROWN lived all their lives in places close together—the one in Caithness, the other in Orkney, and shared a sense of the value of human community moored in nature and tradition, and a particular love of the elements of rock, water, air and light. Brown registers his own sense of the modern threat to these things in his novel *Greenvoe* (1972). However, the two writers never met, though Brown dedicated one of his stories to Gunn.[1] Gunn was ending his literary career as Brown was beginning his; and for all their proximity in space and social outlook, there are marked differences between them. Gunn was not directly a Christian, more a visionary of glory made manifest in this world; but Brown, a Roman Catholic, believes that the tangled web of this world is caught up in a larger supernatural reality which sanctifies it. Brown, too, is a poet, and uses imagery and language under more pressure than Gunn. He has, also, a more continuous preoccupation with the past of his land than does Gunn: he will look back in his stories as far as the remote prehistory of Orkney, or, as he frequently chooses, to the period when Orkney was an earldom of Norway. This concern with tradition and the past is also a characteristic of the Catholic Church—and in each case it is born of a belief that no time is lost in eternity, but that in God and through Christ and His body all times are co-present. One further feature that influences Brown's outlook is the peculiar geography of his realm—a cluster of islands huddled in a cold sea, at once suggesting human community and yet, in their history of violence, continually denying it; a place of bare earth over rock surrounded by water; a scene of continual arrivals and departures, a land for all its permanence always in a state of transition. There is no settled assurance of community in Brown's stories: assurances, such as they are, are either violated or wrested with pain from shifting circumstance. Where Gunn's Hector or Art speak with the voice of a whole people, Brown's characters are much more often isolated, or alone.

Born in 1921 the son of an Orkney postman and tailor, and schooled at Stromness Academy from 1926 to 1940, Brown was held back by tuberculosis until in 1951 he was encouraged to study at the adult education centre of Newbattle Abbey, near Edinburgh, under the benign tutelage of its then director, the fellow Orcadian poet Edwin

Muir. Later he went on to read English at Edinburgh University from 1956 to 1960, and thereafter to do postgraduate work on the poet Gerard Manley Hopkins (1962 to 1964). All the time he was developing poetic skills he had first discovered in himself at school, his first poetic publications (*The Storm* and *Loaves and Fishes*) appearing in 1954 and 1959, and a more substantial work, *The Year of the Whale*, in 1965. His first collection of short stories, *A Calendar of Love*, came out in 1962. After Edinburgh, he returned to Stromness, where he has lived ever since, writing about Orkney life. In 1972 came out his first novel, *Greenvoe*, portraying an Orkney island community and its (temporary) expulsion by a military-technological project.

Brown's *Magnus* (1973) is one expression of a central interest of his life in Earl Magnus, patron saint of Orkney, immortalised in the early thirteenth-century *Orkneyinga Saga*. As early as 1948 Brown interrupts the information in a tourist guide, *Let's See the Orkney Islands*, with the declaration that 'Near Rousay lies a little island, Egilsay, on which, in 1116 AD, occurred the most vital event in all Orkney's rich history—the martyrdom of Earl Magnus.'[2] Brown returns to Magnus in two poems in his collection *The Storm* (1954), in two stories in his *A Calendar of Love* (1967), and in his celebration of Orkney, *An Orkney Tapestry* (1969).[3] When in 1972 the Cathedral of St Magnus in Kirkwall appealed for funds for restoration, Brown wrote a play, *The Loom of Light*, on Magnus' life; and this provided the framework for the novel *Magnus. Magnus*, transformed to an opera by Peter Maxwell Davies as *The Martyrdom of St Magnus*, was later performed in churches all over Europe. For all Brown's reservations about novel-writing ('I don't particularly like the novel form'[4]), *Magnus* is of unique power, catching up the poet and the fabulist as well as every other aspect of his being, in a beautiful synthesis.

Apart from his Orcadian sources, Brown's literary debts are not much to Scotland, though as a poet he may owe something to his mentor Edwin Muir. In *Magnus* particularly he looks to the sacramental vision of the Catholic poet Gerard Manley Hopkins; there too he seems evidently indebted to T. S. Eliot's *Murder in the Cathedral* (1935), which dramatises the martyrdom of another medieval saint, Thomas à Becket. Brown's Christian view of history, his sense of all acts as eternally co-present, is close (though not indebted) to the vision of the Anglo-Catholic writer Charles Williams, whose supernaturalist novels and plays of divine action appeared during the 1930s. If there is any Scots work to which Brown may owe something in *Magnus*, it is to Carlyle's *Sartor Resartus* for the imagery of clothing that runs through the novel—but he could as readily have derived it from Jonathan Swift's *A Tale of a Tub* (1704). We have in Brown someone who speaks for and with the voice of Orkney, and yet whose voice finds support beyond nationality and place. This is in keeping with the mixture of intense localism and universality in his work.

The core of the story is the division of the earldom of Orkney between two cousins, one of whom, Hakon, eventually seeks sole power and the death of the other, Magnus. In the original story from the *Orkneyinga Saga*, Magnus and Hakon had contended for power until Magnus was trapped in a situation where his death was demanded: upon this he courageously accepted his end.[5] Magnus had previously been a devout and unworldly figure, who preferred to hold a psalter rather than a sword in battle, and the Church was willing to see his death as martyrdom and to make him a saint. Brown modifies this story somewhat, making Magnus more continuously pure of heart, and portraying his entrapment and death as acts of deliberate sacrifice on his part; this makes Magnus a more acceptable saint. But Brown not only modifies, but transforms his material. He does not focus only on the rivalries of the earls, but sets everything in an Orcadian tapestry. We start with two peasants, Mans and Hild, struggling to till their patch of coarse ground; we meet tinkers, attend a noble wedding, go on a military expedition (with Mans as our witness), visit school and church, watch rival factions ravage the land and people at whim, or attend a conference of landowners; and all the time we are aware of the changing seasons and the land and the sea and the people who are part of it. This is not only through a desire to celebrate Orkney, but through the wish to make Magnus' death not just his alone, not just that of a single and singular devout earl, but one that somehow incorporates all Orkney. If Magnus is Orkney's patron saint, then it is right and indeed supernaturally true that not only he but Orkney is present in his sacrifice. The larger sacramental vision on which the novel is based is that through Christ we are all members of one another, that corporately we could be said to form a single body sustained in His.

A stream of imagery in the story relates to weaving, looms, and garments. Some of this is applied to the notion of an interwoven society; some to the garment of state.[6] The two should be the same, the earl seeking only the binding together in love of the different individuals and activities within his rule, and they finding themselves perfectly knit together in the coat of state that he wears: but of course this is not the case. Brown quotes an imaginary homily of Bishop William of Orkney, *Concerning the Two Coats, of Caesar and of God, that cover Adam's Shame*: this describes the splendid coat of state that can only be worn by 'A man approved of God and by the people', and which 'In a mystical way . . . gives warmth and dignity not to the chosen wearer alone, [but] . . . enwraps the whole community':

'all the people from the highest to the lowest help in the creation of this marvellous coat. Every lawful transaction in the market-place, every courteous greeting on the road, every civil and charitable act—yes, every time a young man kisses a maid in the harvest field because of the plenitude of the season—whenever these things are done a creative stitch is put upon the mystical garment. Pictures of tranquility are woven thereon. A crofter with a plough. A fisherman with a net. A monk kneeling. A shepherd with sheep. A merchant despatching a ship. A woman at a hearth-stone. A tinker on the road. Many simple acceptable things sing together in harmony on that garment.'[7]

'But conversely'—the bishop then gives a list of the same people *not* behaving as they should, not creating a harmony—

'conversely, when men of the same community act with malice and pride one towards another, then it may be said that the fabric is endangered. Here and there threads must always be working loose. The fishermen come with cut mouths from the ale-house on a Saturday night. The bread at the croft table never breaks in five equal pieces. Even in the monastery the choir-master howls at a chorister that sings a note wrong. But these are expected attritions, random incursions of the moth, and there are not wanting instant patches and needles to remedy the matter.

(p. 112)

However, there is a question concerning the bishop's attitude here. He considers people as misbehaving through individual choice, but he does not allow that the social hierarchy itself may be at fault. Such a claim is made right at the start of the story by Mans the peasant, who demands a more egalitarian society where the landowners and the powerful no longer feed on the miseries of the poor (p. 20). That message of man's equality was one that Christ brought (though Mans does not practise it himself in his harsh attitude to two travelling tinkers). But the Church, as part of the social fabric thus described, as a beneficiary of hierarchy, has no wish to question the system, or make a more fully loving garment of the social order; it is happy to picture, as expression of the beauty of the coat-of-state, the 'symbol of the unity and peace of the people', the great farmers feasting in their lord's house at harvest home while 'The poor wait at the gate outside.' For the bishop, any fault in the social order is not inherent, but the product of particular circumstance—here, of the division of the kingdom and the subsequent feud: 'Two men lay claim to the earldom. The mystical coat-of-state is riven, it comes apart in their hands. The fissure runs through field and croft and family' (p. 112); of this Mans' scarecrow, which is also the title of Chapter 5, seems an apt symbol.[8] Here then, with the cries, albeit coarse, of Mans and others in mind, we are invited to criticise the good bishop as he pursues his eloquent intellectual embroidery; and in this way the book forces us to weave our own garment of truth as we read. For we, as readers, are weavers too.

Brown has refused to focus on Magnus and Hakon alone because he is writing about all Orkney, a whole community involved in and causing the acts of these two. He has written in the way he has, with abrupt shifts of context, time and place—with Mans the peasant in his field, then Thora the bride at the Hall, then boys going to school in an island monastery, the court of the King of Norway at Trondheim, the sea battle of Norsemen and Welshmen off Anglesey, and so on, without links and transitions—so that we will be forced to make the links ourselves into a larger garment, and at the same time, before we do, each stitch and thread will have its own exclusive and stark identity.

> When Mans came to his corn rig carrying the scarecrow he saw Hild on the slope above. She was searching here and there among the heather [for a missing black hen]. She probed and poked among the tough springy meshes. It was a beautiful morning in early summer. The sun glittered out of loch and the wind went in fluent undulations among the tall grass. The first faint flush of green had gone over the ploughlands of Birsay. Mans' scarecrow stood in the centre of his rig. It creaked in the wind and fluttered its rags. The monks uttered plainchant under a distant arch.
>
> (p. 93)

Brown feels into every detail, plays small views against large (the heather, the sudden vista of the morning) or near against far (the scarecrow, the ploughlands). He lets the scene dilate, pauses, refuses us narrative, just as in the novel as a whole, contemplation, delays, excursions, thread themselves among the 'great' events going forward and impending. Each word is carefully placed, and each bare sentence sits vividly on its own before it becomes part of a paragraph, and so on into larger and larger units of the book. The whole procedure is that of a poet—though a poet who is also a sacramentalist; but then because the poetry and the vision are one it is also a natural expression of that marriage of community with free individuality which was, at the secular level, Brown's (and Gunn's) social ideal. 'The sacrament deals with the actual sensuous world—it uses earth, air, water, fire for its celebrations, and it invests the creatures who move about among these elements with an incalculable worth and dignity. Sacramentally seen, the poorest beggar is a prince, every peasant is a lord, and the croft wife at her turning wheels of stone and wood is "a ladye gaye"' (p. 140). In this vision Brown is closest to his admired Hopkins.

But this novel is 'mainly'—insofar as Magnus may be seen to embody all that rightly is Orkney—about another kind of community and another kind of garment from those we have been discussing. That community is fellowship in Christ and beatitude among the saints, and that garment is the white one of innocence lost in man's sin and offered once more through Christ to the pure in heart (p. 137).[9] The attainment of this coat precisely demands that Magnus should not have a 'position' in society, whether as earl or even as monk. He does not enter the monastery school with the other boys, preferring to help a wounded seal, and when asked his name, says, '"Names are wrong. Men are imprisoned in their names. Angels and animals don't need names. I do not like my name. It means 'great, powerful'. I don't want to be great and powerful"' (p. 46). He takes no part in the sea fight, reading his psalter in the bows of the ship *Sea Eagle* while arrows strike the wood about him (pp. 53, 56). He cannot give himself physically to his wife Ingerth, and is told in a dream that while physical love is a good, '"there are souls which cannot eat at that feast, for they serve another and a greater love, which is to these flames and meltings (wherein you suffer) the hard immortal diamond"'; after this, 'Magnus enrolled himself in the company of the virgins' (p. 71). He is only half an earl; seems absent even from the feuding carried on on his behalf against the followers of Hakon. When offered a place in a monastery, he refuses it. In the end he wants his own death, a death which will be a communal act in that all Orkney is caught up in it, but also an act of final renunciation of the world. His whole life has been a struggle against sin and temptation towards that purity which will enable him to don a garment quite other than the jewelled coat-of-state, and to sit down at a table and in a company which would never be found in the Hall. Yet for all this, there is no lack of love in Magnus for the world: his very renunciations make him see its beauty more fully. The fire of his physical passion, turned from one woman, embraces all: '"this regard—it extends beyond human beings to the animals, it longs to embrace even water and stone. This summer I began to handle sea, shells, larks' eggs, a piece of cloth from the loom, with a delight I have never known before, not even as a child"' (p. 72).

The life in Christ, even of a spiritual apprentice, is a life within a garment or a web of being that can transcend space, time, or causality as we know them. 'We operate, mostly, in sequence, but sequence is not all,' says Charles Williams.[10] Magnus is the chosen one: a special significance invests the moment of fertilisation that begets him out of a myriad of possibles: 'Before dawn Arnor Earlsskald composed Three Sacred Bridal Songs for the high-born pair who, even as he gave the strings a first delicate fingering, were laid together in love; and while a great sacrificial host surged between the loins of bridegroom and bride, and among them a particular chosen seed, a summoned one, the sole ultimate destined survivor of all that joyous holocaust' (p. 26). Magnus is approached—whether or not in 'reality' does not matter—by a stranger before his marriage, who tells him, ' "The loom is set for thee now," ' and that he must weave well upon it; he also says that he is there to protect Magnus from another who will come, a tempter (p. 67) But Magnus also hears of a coat that is being woven *for* him, for the marriage feast of Christ with his Church (p. 70; see also pp. 126–7, 142–6). That marriage feast is not only a 'future' event of the soul's meeting with its Maker, or of the beatitude of the Saints, but is 'past' and continuous, in that Christ has married the Church through His life on earth, and the Church and its members continually marry Him through worship—here in the form of the Mass. Magnus sees that the Mass is not so much an event that takes place in ordinary time as one that contains all time: 'The end and the beginning. All time was gathered up into that ritual half-hour, the entire history of mankind, as well the events that have not yet happened as the things recorded in chronicles and sagas' (p. 139). If that is so, the acts of any communicant in the Mass 'have an immense importance; what he does and says and thinks reverberates through the whole web of time' (p. 141). It is this that is behind the 'extraordinary' event that follows, concerning the death of a German Lutheran pastor during the Second World War.

For as Magnus endures his dark night of the soul in the cold church on the night before his death, he has a vision of sacrifice that moves both backward and forward in time. Now he is simply 'the man', because now he is Everyman:

> The man whispered, and the whole web of history trembled. He breathed out pain on the gray air. Two images came unbidden into his mind. He saw himself in the mask of a beast being dragged to a primitive stone. A more desolate image followed, from some far reach of time: he saw a man walking the length of a bare white ringing corridor to a small cube-shaped interior full of hard light; in that hideous clarity the man would die. The recurrence of pattern-within-flux touched him, momentarily, with wonder.
>
> (p. 141)

That second scene is the execution of the Lutheran pastor (suggestive of Dietrich Bonhoeffer) by Nazi officers in a concentration camp in April 1943, possibly close to the saint's day (April 16) of Magnus himself. This is later described in the novel, as though part of the narrative. We have had Magnus' meditations in the church; we then move outside to the cynical negotiations going on between his chief followers and those of Hakon (pp. 147–64); have a disquisition on the nature of sacrifice (pp. 164–70); momentarily watch Magnus come towards the place of his death (p. 170). And then, abruptly:

> I lived at that time in an old forester's hut just outside the compound.

We are with Lifolf, cook of the Nazi concentration camp: shortly to be invited to the office of the commandant, where he will be asked to exercise his skills as a butcher on a particular human subject. This Lifolf is identical in name and trade to the Lifolf who is asked by Hakon to execute Magnus—as also are a Lieutenant-Colonel Sigurd and a Captain Sighvat (both names of Hakon's chief officers). We thus follow the death of Magnus through the description of that of the twentieth-century pastor (though it is more the circumstances leading up to the death than the death itself that is described in each case). It is not only the martyrdom that is shared: the act of murder is itself recurrent. There is a similar group of savage officers, for some reason unable to do the act itself but passing it to the camp cook as expert, though in fact since it is a hanging that takes place, his skills are not needed at all. It is as though the pattern will have its way against 'normal' courses of behaviour; even while there are differences in the particular stories of each of the 'central' characters (pp. 139–40). Through the Church, which is Christ's body, the novel shows us that we are all members of one another, and participate across time and space in one another's lives, and deaths. More specifically, within Christ we are able to reach out across time and help others: 'A man can . . . direct his purified will into the future for the alleviation of the pain of the future' (p. 141).

And the same is true looking backwards, for Christ catches all history into Himself. Before the account of the Lutheran pastor, there is a discourse on pre-Christian sacrifice and its changes over time. First we learn how, for a tribe living in Orkney four thousand years before Magnus, sacrifice was a means of communal purification, in which 'the god and the tribe and the slain beast share in each other's life', and whereby through this renewed relationship the god working through man may continue to make the ground and the race fruitful (pp. 164–6). Sometimes even, in places other than Orkney, human sacrifice was preferred, as more worthy (pp. 166–8). We are given an account of such a sacrifice: a beautiful young man of physical purity, who is prepared over months for the event. This young man is a type of Magnus too, but his virginity is more accident than abstinence, and his purity is more physical than spiritual: he comes to the sacrifice as a pampered and sleek Adonis, to have his heart ripped out. The people of this latter race are more rational, and therefore feel that they can *earn* the god's acceptance through a better sacrifice, where the others only renewed a continuing bond, as is in a sense done in Christian communion and confession. An agricultural people followed these, now offering bread and wine instead

of beasts and blood, but even so still slaying rams on occasion. But for
all these 'the god himself remained an enigma' (p. 169). The last part
of the threefold relation of god, man and animal altered all this: for the
god himself came down and was sacrificed, 'himself the deity and the
priest and the victim'. This sealed the relation more fully than had ever
been known before.

> That was the one only central sacrifice of history. *I am the bread
> of life*. All previous rituals had been a foreshadowing of this;
> all subsequent rituals a re-enactment. The fires at the centre
> of the earth, the sun above, all divine essences and ecstasies,
> come to this silence at last—a circle of bread and a cup of wine
> on an altar.
>
> （p. 169)

In this sense Magnus' death also incorporates long past pagan sacrifice.
He is killed, we learn, because at certain times of particular misery in the
world, 'men still crave spectacular sacrifice. . . . [W]hen . . . the deep
sources are seemingly hopelessly polluted—then bread and wine seem
to certain men to be too mild a sacrifice. They root about everywhere
for a victim and a scapegoat to stand between the tribe and the anger
of inexorable Fate' (p. 170). We may suppose that this primal motive
operates beneath the search for 'peace' and undivided rule by the chief
men of the islands. Magnus' death thus also travels backwards in time.
His sacrifice at the stone is at once part of a 'pagan' ritual of renewal
and a sealing of his own nature in Christ. The bishop catches both
aspects: '"What is needed in Orkney is something more in the nature of
a sacrifice, the true immaculate death of the dove"' (p. 119). In Magnus'
death the web and cloth of all history comes together; and his garment
of innocence and immortality is made finally complete.

Counter to the imagery of garments, webs and weaving that runs
through the story is that of rags, of tearing, of division. Man is
self-divided by his sin, the fabric of his spirit stained and torn (p. 126).
The earldom is divided between two leaders. The world is riven with
dualities: 'The body-spirit dichotomy, or the body-intellect dichotomy,
is a bitter prideful cleaving of the wholeness of a man's nature' (p. 140).
In Christ alone is man made whole and division overcome. Yet few in
this story save Magnus give any attention to Christ. The children who
met together at school become divided as men: 'in the complex web of
their relationship many strands had been severed, sometimes savagely'
(p. 107). Yet still there is another kind of cleaving that is allowed,
glorified: the cleaving of the soil or of woman to implant seed. The
book starts with the parting of the earth by Mans and Hild as they
force their plough through it—a more fertile union for them than that
of the childless bed from which they have just risen. These wounds,
though painful, are natural, and common to earth and woman: 'I am

wounded. I have taken a wound in my flesh. The lips of it will never come together' (p. 28).

Not so the wounds of a land at war. War, violence, antagonism: these are the real destroyers in the book. There is, it must be said, a side in Brown that continually returns to scenes of acute savagery, blood-letting and pain in the Orcadian past: these seem to create a kind of touchstone for him. In his novel Brown continually measures violence against the template of language. Words, sentences, a book: these all unite to communicate. Isolated acts, and people become symbols, full of meaning, through poetry, art, and music (p. 140). The ceremonies of the Church and of the Mass are a grammar of spiritual order (p. 145). But suppose the words pervert? Suppose, say, a poetic ritual is made out of slaying? At the fight in the Menai Strait, the bards in each ship call to one another in a traditional language which makes the whole event a decorous and ordered exchange. *'The channel is narrow, Welshman. There's not room for two ships to pass.* The answer came at once, *Turn round then. Back with you to the whales and mermaids'* (p. 51); *'Well hunted, hawks,* cried the Welsh herald. / *The falconry has only begun, little birds,* sang the Norse herald' (pp. 53–4). At the end, with the Welsh massacred, the two bards, who are sacrosanct, meet and exchange 'formal well-turned phrases' in which they glorify the battle, the fame it has begotten and the poetry it will enrich (pp. 58–9). This is to be the gloss on the butchery of the Welsh or the death of their leader Hugh of Shrewsbury, fraudulently attributed by the Norse King to his own arrow. The actual death of Earl Hugh is thus described:

> Then a second arrow struck the Earl of Shrewsbury on the face: it shattered nose-plate and nose and passed on into his skull. The body was borne backwards by the impact. It passed out of the hands of his guardsmen. It fell among the Welsh oarsmen. They flung the blood and brains and bone splinters from them, and screamed. The Earl clattered on the deck and lay awry there. At once the whole Welsh host understood that their leader was dead. A terrible cry arose. (p. 57)

The words of the bards serve only to heighten the brutality, not to transform it. The only transformations possible here are those contained in the counterpoint of words uttered throughout by Magnus as he sits reading from his psalter, *'They have eaten sour grapes . . . and now the teeth of the children are set on edge'* (p. 53); *'Thou preparest a table before me in the presence of my enemies. Thou anointest my head with oil. My cup runneth over'* (p. 56).[11]

Then there are the words that feebly dignify the rotting allegiance of Magnus' followers when they meet those of Hakon on Egilsay to make an agreement and find themselves outnumbered. First, they dress up Hakon's trickery, in coming with eight shiploads of men instead of the agreed two, as a perfectly common mistake; but, as Sighvat denies this and expresses his boredom with words, Magnus' men are led to accept the eight ships for what they are, and to begin smoothly to speak of how one earl is best for Orkney, how for various reasons Hakon would probably be the most practical choice, how Magnus would be content to live his life out in Scotland, or if that did not suit in some monastery, perhaps one so far away and so strict that it would be as though he had died (pp. 147–60). Not for one moment is there any mention of the enmity that brought eight ships there and the desire for Magnus' death. All the time the language is formalised as though it is entirely dispassionate, the minutes of a committee meeting debating a particularly knotty administrative problem: 'Sighvat Sokk said that in his opinion . . .'; 'Finn Thorkelson said that he would like to offer a solution that would, he felt sure, be acceptable to Earl Hakon Paulson'; 'Earl Hakon Paulson said that he was considering Finn Thorkelson's proposal closely' (pp. 156–61). Here the counterpoint to this spray of words is Sigurd Kalison's hatred of all talk (pp. 150–2), or a sense we gain of the fabric of language breaking down: when first he speaks, the phrases of Earl Hakon Paulson are 'interspersed with broken uncertain silences' (p. 153). In the end, all the talk is a waste of time, eroding back to the simple prior arrangement that Magnus is to die. Here, as at the sea-fight, false civilised language serves to heighten the true brutality of what is going on. And the same might be found, for example, at the Norse court in Trondheim, where Magnus is politically solicited by Aristius the King's chancellor (pp. 74–6); or in the fraudulent periods of Magnus' other tempters (pp. 68, 77–9).

'Style is the garment of thought.' The aphorism loses its banality with Brown here. To the corruptions of words he answers with his own poetic sense of their integrity. To the disjoining of words from the deeds they cover, he replies with a sense of their sacramental value. His are magic words. 'The symbol becomes a jewel enduring and flaming throughout history' (p. 140); 'The man whispered, and the whole web of history trembled' (p. 141). These words can move across time, can use the diction of the sagas to make us meet the past (p. 123), or the language of a twentieth-century newspaper report to make us see how our present partakes in the story (pp. 130–6). And all the time, as garment, the style is weaving diverse episodes and characters, from Mans to Aristius, Sighvat or the bishop into the seamless community of the book. Here the way that the novel is largely a series of reflections around a few actions finds its place. For language here is a means of weaving about each person and events the universal pattern from which it springs. Only through continual analyses—which are also in their own way sacred actions—can each stitch of being and doing find its position in a whole tapestry that unites and transcends all times and places. And this involves the kind of dismantling of certainty that we have seen throughout Scottish fantasy—here of localism, the narrow conviction that only one's own time or place is real.

At the end of the book, two old tinkers we have met previously come by night to the kirk where Magnus is buried. The man, Jock, prays to Magnus to give his wife Mary her sight back. Magnus, thus summoned, grants the prayer. No raptures follow: Mary's response is ' "I'm supposed to be grateful, am I? Well, I'm not. Can I get the dark years back again? There's one place I do want to see though, more than any other place, and that's the Birsay ale-house"' (pp. 205–6). As with Christ, grace is given to the meanest and most deprived of mortals: here again is that marriage over distance that has characterised the book. And yet we are left with an enigma. The act of grace seems useless, seems to have fallen on sterile ground. But who, the words go on, is to say?

> Not the frailest thing in creation can ever be lost. A word, a smell, a flower, may be the hard rich symbol, recurring again and again in a man's life, by which we instantly recognise him. Spume on the psalter in a Welsh battle; the quenching in a rockpool of the fires of lust; a cascade of spray over a hand steering a ship to an island—a single sea-drop has wandered through a certain man's life, signing the supreme moments, a symbol and a leitmotif. (p. 204)

The least thing may be the greatest; what seems useless may have huge unseen influence; what seems enclosed in the self may only by virtue of that be social on some further shore of time. And this, curiously, has also been the way with Brown's style and his sense of community: one can only be part of a larger whole when one is fully oneself. Even while he weaves everything and word into a larger garment, Brown devotes himself to sensing to the full the being of each piece of creation:

> There was a crude stair of undressed stones from the beach up the shallow cliff-face to the grass. Jock mounted the steps easily by the nakedness of the bride-moon. His bare feet made no noise over the grass. The island was utterly quiet. He stood in front of the black hulk of the kirk. He paused, listened. The brothers were breathing in this cell and that. He heard whispers of Latin and the low clack of beads. The kirk was deserted. He depressed the latch and opened the door into an immense sweet-smelling cave. It was dark but for one small hard light at the side of the altar—a wound in the darkness, a rose petal carved out of ruby-stone—and, under a stone cross at the side of the kirk, a guttering candle weeping last gray tears.
>
> (p. 196)

In an island world such as Orkney, such a picture of a society made

out of supremely individual selves may come naturally. And peculiarly
Orcadian, too, is its saint, who dies to seal his own virginity of spirit,
and yet contains all Orkney in his going.

Magnus is Brown's main work of fantasy, a sort of summary vision
of his Christian outlook. His one other longer work that could just be
called a fantasy is his *Time in a Red Coat* (1984), but there the fantasy
is only a framework: his subject is the savagery of warfare, in all times
and places, and this is presented through the time- and space-travelling
gaze of a young princess with a flute and a bag of coins who heals the
suffering as she goes. Her object is to pursue and tame the dragon of
war, and this we are to presume she accomplishes, at least figuratively,
at the 'end' (which also turns out to be the beginning). But the nature
of war and its effects is the primary concern. The large number of
Brown's short stories, which are almost all of them about Orcadian
life, present and past, do have occasional stories which could be called
fantasies—particularly in his *Hawkfall* (1974), *The Sun's Net* (1976) and
Andrina (1983). Brown's vision is not an exclusively fantastic one: he is
as much concerned with Orkney's 'secular' history and identity as with
its more evidently sacred one, and invokes his own faith only where
the subject needs it, as with Magnus, or for example when he comes to
write of Christmas (though even here we can have the brutal 'The Fires
of Christmas' in *Hawkfall*). This said, certain of his stories stand out,
such as 'Sealskin', 'The Drowned Rose', 'The Interrogator' (*Hawkfall*),
'A Winter Tale', 'The Book of Black Arts', 'Brig-o-Dread', 'The Pirate's
Ghost' and 'Soldier from the Wars Returning' (*The Sun's Net*).

Most of these tales deal with the persistence of life after death, and
the return of ghosts. 'The Interrogator' involves evidence being given by
ghosts of the dead to a supernatural circuit judge, concerning the death
of a young woman on the island of Norday. 'Brig-o-Dread' describes the
post-mortem existence of the murdered worthy Arkol Andersvik, and
how he has to accept the revealed truth of his life before he can join
the blessed. John Gow the pirate returns to his love Thora Gordon as
a ghost after his execution in London, and asks her to go to Wapping
to touch his dead body and release him from love to his torment ('The
Pirate's Ghost'). A soldier who fought on the royalist side against the
Covenanters in Caithness returns home, as he thinks, victorious from
the battle: but he gradually realises that he is dead and a ghost, that the
battle was lost, that there is no place for him in his lady's heart any more,
and that he must return to the battlefield to forgive his slayer so that
he may find his proper destination. Female ghosts come back in 'The
Drowned Rose' and 'Andrina'. Christ returns in the Christmas stories 'A
Winter's Tale', 'An Epiphany Tale' (*Andrina*) and 'The Christmas Dove'
(*The Masked Fisherman*, 1989). As in *Magnus*, these stories emphasise life
as lived in this world, but that makes all the more potent their message
of another and supernatural realm. They are however more moral than

sacramental in emphasis: humanity is being assessed, the dead have to come to terms with their lot, or set right their moral accounts or receive their quietus. They could be said often to be concerned with 'tying up loose ends': to that extent their involvement with the fabric of existence is less complex than with the weaving in *Magnus*. In themselves they show the poetic, compressive character of Brown's writing, his habit of making the single person, action or moment incandescent: but in *Magnus* he makes a whole shining web of such individual filaments.

Much of Brown's work is concerned with loss—not loss in the elegiac sense of regret, but loss as a condition of being and dying. The supernatural tales often deal with the topic of how the dead reconcile themselves to parting from their past lives. In Orkney history as Brown records it, every attempt to make a secure life is continually being washed away. This is the way he portrays international history in *Time in a Red Coat*, as a series of civilisations like islands, destroyed by the seas of war. Loss enters Brown's work in every shape. In 'Sealskin' he describes the unhappy marriage of a seal-woman to a fisherman, and how she finally leaves him and escapes back to her kind in the sea; in 'The Book of Black Arts', a story in the same family as Stevenson's 'The Bottle Imp', he portrays the efforts of a series of people to get rid of a devilish book they have ignorantly acquired. Separation is here the form loss takes: and it is also seen in the way few relationships last in Brown's work, people often ending stripped of lovers, friends, marriage partners, families or home. There is lost opportunity in 'A Winter's Tale', where Christ is born again, and none heed or recognise Him; brief remission in 'An Epiphany Tale', where a blind, deaf and dumb boy is for a short time given back his senses by Christ; or abrupt loss of beauty in 'The Pirate's Ghost', as the handsome pirate Gow's body is transformed at his execution to a blackened lump. Loss is everywhere seen as a condition of our mortality, and in a Christian context the measure of our distance from God. Brown has little to say directly of any afterlife: his one essay in that kind, at the end of 'Brig-o-Dread', reads as a rather limp picture of beatitude in a heavenly village. Brown's vision is rather the one that closes 'Sealskin', where the exiled son of the marriage of man and seal-woman, now become a world-famous violinist, broods on the role of his art in late nineteenth-century life:

> He thought of the men who had thrown off all restraint and were beginning now to raven in the most secret and delicate and precious places of nature. They were the new priesthood; the world went down on its knees before every tawdry miracle—the phonograph, the motor-car, the machine-gun, the wireless—that they held up in triumph. And the spoliation had hardly begun.
> Was this then the task of the artist: to keep in repair the

sacred web of creation—that cosmic harmony of god and beast and man and star and plant—in the name of humanity, against those who in the name of humanity are mindlessly and systematically destroying it?

If so, what had been taken from him was a necessary sacrifice.

Notes

1 'The Burning Harp' (1973), for Gunn's eightieth birthday; repr. in *Hawkfall and Other Stories* (1974).
2 Brown, *Let's See the Orkney Islands* (Fort William: W. S. Thomson, 1948), p. 56.
3 Alan Bold, *George Mackay Brown* (Edinburgh: Oliver and Boyd, 1978), p. 100, supplied this and the previous information.
4 Quoted in Bold, p. 110.
5 Bold, pp. 100–1. For the original story, Brown used both the *Orkneyinga Saga* and the scholarly account of Magnus' life, the Kirkwall businessman John Mooney's *St Magnus—Earl of Orkney* (1935).
6 Brown may have taken his weaving and garment imagery from ordinary life in Orkney (and also from his own father's occupation of tailor), but there is also striking anticipation in Fiona Macleod's 'The Last Supper' and 'The Washer of the Ford' (repr. in Macleod's *Spiritual Tales* and *Barbaric Tales* respectively).
7 George Mackay Brown, *Magnus* (Glasgow: Richard Drew, 1987), pp. 110–12.
8 Bold, p. 105, makes this point.
9 See Zechariah 3.3–5; Matthew 22.11–13; 2 Corinthians 5.2–5; Ephesians 4.18–24; Revelation 3.4–5 and 19.8.
10 Charles Williams, *He Came Down From Heaven and The Forgiveness of Sins* (London: Faber and Faber, 1950), p. 92.
11 Ezekiel 18.2; Psalm 23.5

CHAPTER TWELVE

Alasdair Gray, *Lanark* (1981)

G RAY'S *Lanark* WAS BEGUN around 1952 but was only published in 1981, through Canongate Press of Edinburgh: it is not only the longest of Scottish fantasies, but the longest in the making. It started as a semi-autobiographical account of the upbringing in Glasgow of an artist (later named Duncan Thaw), which forms Books 1 and 2. Gray actually submitted Book 1 as a novel in itself to the literary agents Curtis Brown in 1963, but it was rejected. At an early stage however Gray intended to make the book more epic by mixing it with another and quite contrastive work he was writing, 'a Kafkaesque adventure book of politics in an underworld': this became Books 3 and 4, the story of Lanark, whose life follows on Thaw's, and who lives in a bizarre other world of deprivation and mind-control, ruled by a bureaucratic council.[1] The patchwork quality of the book that results is part of its problematic nature, being both accidental and intentional.[2] Few other Scottish fantasies give us two or more worlds as *Lanark* does.

The story is a complex one. It opens with Book 3, with the character Lanark living in a strange lightless city, and eventually being transported, via a giant pair of lips in a graveyard, to another and subterranean world run as a hospital. The 'patients', including Lanark, are all suffering in some degree from their skins having turned to tough 'dragon-hide': if that hide covers them completely, they explode. All those who are cured, such as Lanark, are made doctors; but the hospital, which also turns out to be something of a power station, harvests the energy that is generated by the detonations of the dying. The hospital (known as the institute) is thus a place that both feeds off death and tries to prevent it. Lanark tries to help a supposedly hopeless case, a woman called Rima, and succeeds, after which the two become lovers. Rima says she dreamt of knowing Lanark as Thaw in a previous life: he then calls up an 'oracle' to try to find out about his past. We now shift to Books 1 and 2 of the novel, in which we are presented with the past life of Lanark as Duncan Thaw, struggling artist, in Glasgow, and his eventual suicide. Book 4 returns us to Lanark, who quits the hospital institute; he travels with Rima back to the darkened city, now named as Unthank, and thence, to save the city from being finally drained of life by the giant corporation now running the earth, to a world assembly in another city called Provan. In Provan his mission fails, but the world council is overthrown in an apocalyptic earthquake and deluge, and

Lanark, now an old man, is granted final death by a new 'ministry of earth'.

If we call *Lanark* a fantasy—and there is reason to do so, even if parts of it have all the lineaments of a realistic novel—it is certainly unlike most others considered in this book. For one thing, it very definitely locates itself in the modern city, and even names itself as a town. In doing so it involves itself in a world of the man-made: there is not much of 'nature' here, nor of nature's answers—only human nature, and what may be wrung from that. Its concerns are metropolitan: politics, society, art, bureaucracy. Its setting is in the collective, too: the central characters are always moving within a larger social fabric. Secondly, it is not a single literary mode, but a mélange, a fictional city, of allegory, novel and fantasy: we are not allowed to settle to any one world or genre, but find that what starts as apparent realism (with Lanark in a café in a city) slips away as we see Lanark growing 'dragonhide', and then switches back as we move in the next book to the very 'realistic' history of Thaw, living in Glasgow; and so on. Unlike most other fantasies, it refuses us clear direction and sequence in the narrative: here again it denies assurance, while at the same time it multiplies possibilities. Its nearest likeness in this is perhaps Carlyle's *Sartor Resartus*, but its more obvious affinities are with the dislocations and manifold realities of the postmodern novel, as in Pynchon or Calvino.[3]

However, *Lanark* has one feature in common with many other Scottish fantasies: the hero is in some sense a freak, a social misfit. Most English fantasies deal with 'perfectly normal' individuals, from Kingsley's knockabout Tom to Tolkien's down-to-earth hobbits, who have or find a place in society (C. S. Lewis's Ransom is a Cambridge philologist, T. H. White's Wart becomes King Arthur, Mervyn Peake's Titus cannot escape from being Earl of Gormenghast). But in the Scottish variety we move from Wringhim or the absurd Teufelsdröckh to Peter Pan, Young Art or Magnus, all in some sense grotesques or wonders, and all refusing or refused a place in the world. Scottish fantasy is often generated out of the eccentricities of its protagonists, as in *Phantastes* or *Peter Pan*, where the structures of the works could be said to reflect the natures of the central figures. In this *Lanark* is no exception.

Both Thaw and Lanark are 'displaced persons'—Thaw most evidently. This is seen at the level of sex and love: neither, despite longing to do so, can form a lasting relation with a woman. Sex is actually one of the strongest currents in *Lanark*. It would be fair to say that Thaw's whole existence revolves around the question of his acceptability to women: and since he is not accepted, he lacks a hold on life which finally manifests itself in his suicide. And Lanark, in his sections of the novel, is unable to keep his beloved Rima: he saves her from death in the institution, protects her on their daring journey to Unthank and fathers a child with her, but she leaves him for a stronger acquaintance of his, Sludden. At one point on their journey she says, '"I like you, Lanark, and of course I depend on you, but you aren't very inspiring, are you?"' (p. 387); later, she blames him for dragging her on the journey, for being nervous, pathetic, heavy, dismal, humourless, and unloveable (pp. 429–30); and in her departing note tells him she loves Sludden because he '"needs me more than you do . . . You're the most selfish man I know"' (p. 456). The whole book is full of agonised heart-searchings and embarrassments for both Thaw and Lanark. All Thaw has near the end of his life is the practice of his art in a neglected Glasgow church, and even that activity collapses under him after a fleeting visit from the girl he once loved, in the company of her fiancé.

But sex is not all there is to it. It is the feeling of being a misfit, of not being able to bond with others or with the world. Arguably, Thaw reappears in another world as Lanark because he cannot live fully in any world. *Lanark* is about the emotionally crippled, the socially disabled: it is about the embarrassment of being, or rather, the embarrassment of not being able to be properly. Thaw is afflicted by asthma, which he is told is partly psychosomatic (p. 186), and which mirrors the frailty of his hold on the world, for all his determination to keep trying. 'The only imaginable future was a repetition of a present which had shrunk to a tiny painful act, a painful breath drawn again and again from an ocean of breath' (p. 184). His every effort collapses: 'he was tired of being thought a bookish hermit and meant to forge a new, confident, sardonic, mysterious character for himself' (p. 224). The God he sees about him is one who has created an abortive world, a hell, in which his soul can find no place: '"it's a big continual loving man I want who shares the pain of his people. It's an impossibility I want"' (p. 296). And Lanark? '"I was faithful to her [Rima] not because I loved her but because I *wanted* love, it is *right* that she left me *right* that I'm locked up here, I deserve much worse"' (p. 527). Both Thaw and Lanark are made to feel shameful, disgusting or unwanted (on a walk Thaw can simply become dislocated from himself, can see himself as 'a small figure starting across the moor like a louse up a quilt' (p. 140)); but they are themselves also unable to conform. They are out of joint with the world not only because it finds no place for them but because they find no place in it. Thaw will not follow the pressure of society and train for a regular job as a librarian. He cannot fit into art school, and has to have special leave to paint murals in Cowlairs Parish Church. The elders of that church ask him for completion dates he cannot manage; his whole activity in the church—dirty, materials scattered all over the place—is an affront to the congregation, not least when a newspaper gives a lurid account of him headed, 'Atheist Paints Face of God' (p. 326); and only the kindness of the minister keeps him there. Frequently he sees the world as hell, and acknowledges, '"I have no choice but to cooperate with my damnation"' (p. 211). To his father's insistence on the progress of human society, he responds with images of Belsen, Nagasaki, imperialism, malnutrition, human power, lust, hatred and indifference. Often he comes close to a misanthropic wish to be done with the human world altogether:

> 'I wish I was a duck on Alexandra Park pond. I could swim, and fly, and walk, and have three wives, and everything I wanted. But I'm a man. I have a mind, and three library tickets, and everything I want is impossible.'
>
> (p. 294)

On the other side, Lanark mirrors this non-conformity in seemingly more heroic mode. He defies Ozenfant, chief doctor of the underground institute, he ignores all warnings and manages to save the terminally ill Rima through love, he is revolutionary in his demand to be allowed to leave the institute, he refuses, as the emissary of the disaster-stricken Unthank to the world council in Provan, to withdraw his complaint.

These personal issues, the fact that this is a novel about acute personal discomfort, deserve as much attention as the cultural and political analyses which *Lanark* has so far received. It is not *only* a book about entrapment, class-division, social deprivation or the condition of Scotland—though it certainly is also about these things.[4] From the personal point of view, Thaw is frequently in a position to 'do as well as the next man' by following society's patterns: it is he, idiosyncratic he, who refuses or is unable to do so. What 'social analyses' there are in the Thaw narrative come late, though they are more present in the Lanark one: the two narratives themselves are divided as more and less personal. And the same, arguably, goes with the novel's 'postmodernism': this too is both 'real' and subjective. In the latter view, because they are not in tune with the worlds about them, Thaw and Lanark are, precisely, dislocated: they have no 'location'. The lack of sequence in the story, the very procedure of shuttling between Glasgow and Unthank, Thaw and Lanark, the disruptions of time in the 'intercalendrical zone' between the institute and Unthank, the very breaks in comprehension we as readers frequently experience as the story or even individual sentences shift assumption or mode—these need not emerge only from a 'postmodernist' impulse to depict the chaotic and inconsequential character of modern life, but can also stem from something quite specific, which here is simply the fact that dislocated stories may express dislocated individuals. Thus, because neither Thaw nor Lanark is at home in the self, they shift worlds, and we as readers are allowed no home or secure point of vantage in the novel: the object is to make us as formally embarrassed as the characters are psychologically.

However, while this more personal view of *Lanark* is first as important as the socio-political one, both still make up the overall picture. It is still the case that part of the thrust of the novel, particularly in the Lanark books, is to show the individual as at the mercy of the collective. In *Lanark* as a whole we are thus given opposed views of human nature: one, that it is trapped and driven by society; the other, that it defeats itself. And we will find that in fact the novel is pervaded by such incompatible views and realities—indeed that it is part of its nature as fantasy to offer not only alternative words but alternative philosophies.

We have looked at the nature of Gray's characters, and the effect on his fantasy. What then of the fantastic medium, the worlds in which they move? Is the world of the institute, for instance, a purgatory, or simply a different version of Thaw's secular world? Is it natural, or supernatural? Typically of Gray it will be found that the answers to these questions are again divergent.

At one point in the book (pp. 485–99) we are given a set of acknowledgments of books to which *Lanark* is indebted. One such acknowledgment is to Charles Kingsley's *The Water-Babies* (1863), and while we cannot take this simply at face value, since it is put in the mouth of a 'prepostmodern academic'[5] called Workman, it cannot be dismissed either, especially when we consider that *The Water-Babies* had considerable early influence on Gray and that for him it is one of the 'masterpieces of European literature'.[6] *The Water-Babies* is set largely in a divine purgatory. Tom the chimney-sweep falls into a stream and becomes a water-baby; as he develops morally he moves downstream to the sea, where he meets other water-babies and the great 'fairies' who run the world for God; finally he advances far enough to be admitted to heaven. When we are told that 'Most of *Lanark* is an extended Difplag [Diffused Plagiarism] of *The Water-Babies*' (p. 491) we may follow this in the two narratives.

Thus we have the realistic Glasgow world of Thaw, his final journey to the Highlands, eventually to drown himself in the sea; then there is his new incarnation as Lanark and his descent into the earth into the hospital-institute, followed by his rediscovery of his beloved Rima there; from there we have his journey with her across an 'intercalendrical zone' back to Unthank (where he loses her), and on to Provan and finally death. This parallels the journey of Kingsley's Tom, first from the world of industrial Yorkshire to a valley stream where he is transformed to a water-baby; thence to the sea, and beneath the sea to the fairy isle of St Brandan, where he re-encounters the little girl Ellie who bewitched him in his old world; and so on via the strange upside-down land of the Other-end-of-Nowhere to the world's end, and then heaven. To this we could add parallels between the great figures of Professor Ozenfant and Lord Monboddo we find in the institute and the Fairies Doasyouwouldbedoneby and Bedonebyasyoudid of St Brandan's Isle; between the 'author' of *Lanark* itself whom Lanark meets near the end, and Kingsley's creative Mother Carey, who (more freely) 'make[s] things make themselves'; and between an uncertain view Lanark has of 'God' at the end and the indefinite vision Tom has at the end of *The Water-Babies*.

The details of the two books are close enough to make it possible to see *Lanark* as a re-creation of *The Water-Babies*.

Whether however *Lanark* in any way shows the same outlook as Kingsley's story is another matter—or rather, whether it *can* share it: '"Where we had Christ's vicar upon earth we have now . . . Lord Monboddo, president of the council!"' (p. 80). What immediately attracted Gray to *The Water-Babies* was 'the business of mixing genres' and its use of two worlds:7 characteristically he is interested in it because it is multiple and will not settle to one view of reality, or truth. He can just as readily refer us to the more secular afterworlds of Wyndham Lewis's *The Human Age* (1955) or Flann O'Brien's *The Third Policeman* (1967) as possible sources for *Lanark* (p. 489, note 6).

Most directly the world of Lanark seems a secular one: but it is so not just in one but in several different ways. On one view, life in Unthank is only a way of describing Thaw's life in Glasgow in different terms. For instance, the social system whereby life in 'this' world is governed by examinations and follows pre-set paths, then becomes the hospital institute in another life; and what in Glasgow was life from the viewpoint of the dispossessed and poor, is in the other world existence as seen by those in power. In this light, for example, the hospital becomes a sort of metaphor for life in Glasgow: a vast system in which the state seeks to manage human misery. (Compare T. S. Eliot's more religious 'The whole earth is our hospital' in *East Coker*, 1940.) A hospital is the location because that is where most caring should be present: but the fact that the place is so systematised, and indeed also the fact that patients' ills are treated exclusively as physical rather than spiritual, means that real caring is absent. What should happen is the kind of love that Lanark, who after his cure is automatically made a doctor in the place, gives to his apparently hopeless female patient. All this would serve as commentary on the draining of humanity from our own world, the increase in bureaucratic impersonality, the indifference to the individual, the death of emotion. In these and other ways one world may act as a metaphor for the other. Yet any reader of *Lanark* knows that such translations, while suggested, are never quite certain: as Lanark is told by a military man, ' "Metaphor is one of thought's most essential tools. It illuminates what would otherwise be totally obscure. But the illumination is sometimes so bright that it dazzles instead of revealing"' (p. 30).

But there are other ways of seeing the two worlds in such secular terms. For instance, just as there may be an infinity of possible universes, so one universe has Lanark, and another Thaw. Or, conceivably, the world of the institute or Unthank may be a dream in the mind of Thaw, who certainly does not have a sunlit subconscious: indeed the quest for sunlight drives Lanark in Unthank from the beginning. Again, the maker of these worlds may be simply and insistently the artist, who frequently draws attention to his constructs, portrays himself as a 'conjuror' and refers to the true physics of the world as founded not on atomic particles but on printed words (pp. 484–5). This author can speak of Lanark as a more advanced saloon model built on Thaw:

> 'My first hero was based on myself. I'd have preferred someone less specialised but mine were the only entrails I could lay hands upon. I worked poor Thaw to death, quite cold-bloodedly, because though based on me he was tougher and more honest, so I hated him. Also, his death gave me a chance to shift him into a wider social context. You are Thaw with the neurotic imagination trimmed off and built into the furniture of the world you occupy. This makes you much more capable of action and slightly more capable of love.'
>
> (p. 493)

All these possibilities are present, and each excludes the others. But Gray is enough of a Scot, and sufficiently reared amidst Calvinism, to add God to the mixture, and further complicate matters. Thaw's mother tells him, ' "You know, Duncan, you would make a good minister . . . You have a minister's way of talking about things" ' (p. 194); and a girl tells him he sounds ' "like an old highland minister" ' (p. 258). Though he is the unchristened son of a 'pious atheist' father (p. 258), his mother is a believer and he is knocked off balance by an old lady in a pub who is living witness of the love of Christ (pp. 329–32). His only true artistic productions are on religious themes from the Book of Genesis, and are painted on the walls and ceiling of a church (Gray himself once did this.[8]) Throughout his life he is in continual active dispute with God for having created a world so full of pain. He writes, '*I want to make a series of paintings called Acts of God showing the deluge, the confusion of Babel, the walls of Jericho falling flat, the destruction of Sodom. Yes, yes, yes, a hymn to the Old Testament Catastropher who makes things well but hurts and smashes them just as well*' (p. 236). But that very vision allows existence to God while it attacks Him. And it is a view of the world which is precisely circumscribed by Calvinism, which holds that the world is a hideous place because man has sinned and God has withdrawn from it. A highland minister tells Thaw,

> 'You talk, Duncan, as if I believed that the world as it is is the work of God. That is not true. The world was made by God, and made beautiful. God gave it to man to look after and keep beautiful, and man gave it to the Devil. Since then the world has been the Devil's province, and an annexe of Hell, and everyone born into it is damned . . . Mibby you've been searching the world for a sign of God's existence. If so, you have found nothing but evidence of his absence, or

less, for the spirit ruling the material world is callous and malignant. The only proof that our Creator is good lies in our dissatisfaction with the world . . . and in the works and words of Jesus Christ.'

(p. 183).

This Calvinist view of the world as blighted fits with Thaw's; but he tries to depict a different sort of God as its author. In other words, he is a theist, whose belief in God is measured by his hostility to Him. He, Thaw, tries to recreate the world as it should be, as it was before man's loss of Eden, in his church murals, but his sense of God, the destroyer and the butcher as much as the creator, keeps creeping in. He is outraged by the discrepancy between the biblical picture of God as '"the one perfect man of whom we are imperfect copies"' and the absurd reality of a god who wrecks what he creates and then creates again (p. 321): '"I want to like the world, life, God, nature, et cetera, but I can't because of pain"' (p. 264). But he is trapped like Job in relationship with God:

'Very few men are as nasty to their children as you are to yours. Why didn't you give me a railway station to decorate? It would have been easy painting to the glory of Stevenson, Telford, Brunel and a quarter million Irish navvies. But here I am, illustrating your discredited first chapter through an obsolete art form on a threatened building in a poor province of a collapsing empire. Only the miracle of my genius stops me feeling depressed about this, and even so my brushes are clogged by theology, that bastard of the sciences . . .'

(p. 321)

This ruined faith was certainly not espoused by Thaw's literary prototype in painting Genesis in a church, Gully Jimson in Joyce Cary's *The Horse's Mouth* (1944).

Lanark's journey in his narrative can be seen as one through a series of false gods—the sexually powerful Sludden, Ozenfant at the institute, Monboddo at the institute and the world council, and the 'author' himself. But beyond all those, glimpsed once as Lanark flies from Unthank to Provan, on his mission to save the former, is God Himself, seen as a gigantic eye from a mile up in his aircraft, and heard as a voice saying, '"Is . . . if . . . is . . ."' (p. 468). This God is enigmatic and faintly absurd; but the tiered sequence of the narrative, whereby Lanark proceeds through greater and greater people of power, suggests some reality for His existence, an existence which has been banished to obscurity by those who have usurped His power and taken over the earth. The author, who at one point admits that he is no longer a part of God, having been 'excreted' by Him for going bad (p. 481), later claims, ' "I'm like God the Father . . . and you [Lanark] are my sacrificial son . . .' (p. 495). Lanark finds himself in a world not wholly unlike that of David Lindsay, where the true God Muspel exists in absence, and the pleasure-loving Crystalman usurps his place[9]—although in Gray's case it might be better to speak of a world of pain and sensuous deprivation rather than pleasure. But in both cases the world is seen as given over to the corrupt, and this squares precisely with the view of Calvinism. In this limited sense then we may say that Gray's outlook demands God, even while He may be reviled, denied or expelled. *Lanark* could, just, be called a fantasy founded on the supernatural. This is further supported by the way the book parallels Christian history, in moving from Genesis, which Thaw paints and abortively lives, to the ending of the world, which Lanark beholds.

But such an identification is of course conditional. In this post-modernist fantasy, the afterword is equally dream, metaphor and purgatory. Once again we have a situation in which one truth or reality is countered by another. And we find a similar series of incompatible views if we consider Lanark's moral development.

Suppose we look at Lanark's experience in Unthank and the institute in the light of its being a kind of purgatory. It is possible to trace a moral pattern in which he develops to the point where he may die completely, as happens to Tom in *The Water-Babies*. In Unthank he develops dragonhide, which covers one of his arms and is only cured when he enters the institute. Dragonhide expresses an ill, but not as in Kingsley simply a moral one: rather, as one would expect of Gray, it is also a personal one, the deformity depicting a neurosis. And that neurosis is basically an inability to go out of the self to others or to the world: it is the disease of isolation, one which Gray finds peculiarly a modern one. The consequences are bizarre, just as were Tom's prickles in *The Water-Babies*:

> Some [dragons] had glossy hides, some were plated like tortoises, some were scaled like fish and crocodiles. Most had quills, spines or spikes and some were hugely horned and antlered, but all were made monstrous by a detail, a human foot or ear or breast sticking through the dinosaur armour.
>
> (p. 66)

This is devolution from human to Jurassic reptile, and is explained by Dr Ozenfant to Lanark in physico-spiritual terms as a progressive refusal of the human being to let out its heat ' "in acts of generosity and self-preservation" ' (p. 68). Self-preservation comes into it because, as the heat is retained by the individual, the armour is formed, and when that armour is complete the individual explodes, that is, becomes both nothing and at the same time the involuntary donor of a vast amount of stored heat, which is used as fuel for the benefit of the wider humanity so long refused. Lanark, however, is capable of love and care: he starts his narrative by coming in to the Elite Café in Unthank from the isolation of the balcony outside it. And he is unique, in the sense that he is continually in search of sunlight (which he finds at the end (p. 558)). In the rather hard group of the habitués of this café (led by Sludden), he is the only one who struggles with love for someone (Rima, who for her refusals is in the institute all but engulfed by dragonhide); he makes friends with the children of his landlady, Mrs Fleck. Friendship and generosity of heart are his special gifts; and certainly he has to use them to the full as he is deserted by Rima and manipulated by Sludden. One other gift he has, and that is the willingness to fight inhumanity, whether in refusing the cruelties of the hospital, or in acting as ambassador to the council to save Unthank from destruction. The very fact that, uniquely, he is continually journeying in the narrative, suggests his development: and for this in the end he is granted the '"extraordinary privilege"' of knowing that he is to die the next day, this time a death after which '"nothing personal will remain of you"' (p. 559). This latter promise could mean several things, and certainly does not point readily to immortality of the sort that is granted to Tom in *The Water-Babies*, but it does mean that Lanark will have done with being and with darkened worlds, purgatorial or not, as he has known them.

But this idea of evolution is, like everything else in *Lanark*, contradicted by other aspects of the book. For one thing, it involves a linear movement, which the book, with its jumbled narrative sections, also denies. Here *Lanark* diverges from the Victorian *The Water-Babies*, which is wholly informed by the idea of progress. While it is true that Lanark is in many ways an older version of Thaw, and that the whole novel traverses a biography from Thaw the child to Lanark the dying old man; and while we are told that Lanark is an advance on Thaw, who after his suicide was flung back into the world by '"the infinite bright blankness . . . which only selfishness fears"' (p. 219)—still we are left with an assemblage of displaced pieces of story, and have to try to work out where each goes. There is the suggestion that we could read in *any* direction: most plainly that the story may go backwards as readily as forwards. If Lanark is an 'improved' Thaw, then Thaw is the devolved version of Lanark; in *The Water-Babies* too Tom is told that if he had not gone forward he would have gone back, and dwindled to an 'eft', or newt, in a pond. In other words it would be possible, just possible, to read Gray's novel as Lanark's 'decline' into Thaw rather than the other way round. This could be symbolised in the *Alice*-like road that Lanark and Rima find after they leave the institute to journey to Unthank, a road which goes downhill on one side of its centre line and uphill on the other (p. 377); and equally, by the way they repeatedly return to the door of the institute, which has the same name on the outside as it did from within, 'EMERGENCY EXIT 3124' (pp. 376, 378, 381).[10] Beyond the issue of moral advance or decline, the dislocated narrative asks us which is 'first', Thaw's world or Lanark's; and which is more fantastic, the world of Glasgow or of Unthank.[11] These are the same questions of reality Kingsley asked in *The Water-Babies*, but he supposed an ultimate Reality in God. Our notions of what is real, what fantastic, what first, what last, are thus displaced, at the same time as being confused. It is in these terms no less a fantastic world in which Thaw struggles with his asthma than it is a real one in which Lanark flies in a mechanised eagle which accepts as the fare a credit card which draws on units of his own future. At the same time as inviting a linear reading, the story calls for a circular one: Thaw's narrative is 'enclosed' by that of Lanark (p. 484)—'"The snake eats its tail"' (p. 438)—and Lanark is in another way enclosed in Thaw's story, for at the end as he passes over Provan he returns to long-forgotten childhood memories:

> 'Did I have a sister once? And did we play together on the grassy top of that cliff among the yellow gorse-bushes? Yes, on that cliff behind the marine observatory, on a day like this in the summer holidays. Did we bury a tin box under a gorse root in a rabbit hole? There was a half-crown piece in it and a silver sixpence dated from that year, and a piece of our mother's jewellery, and a cheap little notebook with a message to ourselves when we grew up. Did we promise to dig it up in twenty-five years? And dug it up two days later to make sure it hadn't been stolen? And were we not children then? And was I not happy?'
>
> (p. 470).

Just as the children themselves telescoped time, so here does Lanark. He wonders at the familiarity of the place, to which he can put no names and which it seems he has wanted all his life: '"And if I really lived here once, and was happy, how did I lose it? Why am I only returning now?"'[12]

Here we approach the darker vision of the book. This also works against its linear and evolutionary side. If the world of *The Water-Babies* was water, that of *Lanark* is earth—which suggests resistance not only to progress, but to all movement. For all that the worlds of *Lanark* are continually shifting, names and identities changing, there is also a remarkable impression of the solid and the unalterable. Fantasy often deals with the elusive or the mysterious, but there is little of that here. From the start the atmosphere is oppressive, whether it is the circumscribed world of Thaw's Glasgow, a heavy, organised city slumped under the soot of its own creating or the 'thin smirr' that nature deposits on it, or whether it is the frequently enclosed, darkened world of Lanark in shrivelling Unthank or the subterranean world of the institute. Both Thaw and Lanark stay seriously and solidly themselves:

their strength is measured in their resistance, their refusal to submit to other identities or collectives. Thaw's first question of his father concerns the law of gravity: '"Grrrrrravity is what keeps us on the earth"' (p. 121); gravity varies in Lanark's world, but still his most constant impression is of falling—falling into Unthank, falling down the mouth in the Unthank necropolis, falling on ice in a subway, falling as Monboddo turns him away at the end. Thaw, with his asthma, constantly struggles with air; at the end he has his final revenge on air by filling his lungs with water: his death by choking fits his experience and his element. Lanark is frequently rebuked by Rima as being 'too solid'; she, on the other hand, is named after the flittering insubstantial creature with whom W. H. Hudson's hero falls in love in *Green Mansions* (1904). Lanark's son is called after earth, Sandy. When Lanark is given his death, he is given it by 'the ministry of earth' (p. 559). 'Thaw' suggests Hamlet's wish of the 'too, too solid flesh'. And overall there is little or no wild nature, only city, human beings, and organisation, and the extent to which one can resist that organisation before it drives one to death, whether in the north west Highlands or in Provan.

This world, as seen by Thaw and Lanark, continually refuses escape, that impulse of much fantasy. Even when Thaw commits suicide, it is only to be driven further into the earth as Lanark in another world and another life. No prescription for a happier life is available within the worlds of these characters: if a suggestion of social amelioration is made, as by Thaw, it is withdrawn; Lanark, in his darkened world of powerful bureaucracies, can make individual protests, but his reasoned assault on Monboddo's corrupt treatment of human nature is swept aside, and he can only end, '"I am useless. I should never have come here"' (p. 552). There are consolations to be wrung from within these bleak existences, such as Lanark's joy in his son, or Thaw's sense that a painting well done will be eternal even if it is destroyed (p. 337), but the vision generally is of a stoical Calvinist trudge through the gloom, with such triumph as there is in the making of the stern journey itself rather than in any far outcome. On this view there may be a God beyond the borders of the narrative, but of Lanark's prospects with Him the book can have nothing to say.

Where in Kingsley's fantasy world there is a sense throughout of expansion from stream to river, sea and ocean, in *Lanark* there is continual narrowing and confinement. This is particularly seen in the imagery of ingestion that runs through Gray's novel. The perspective is one in which the material world is dominant, and intellectual and spiritual life either marginalised or engulfed. The system of examinations, job, marriage, family, mortgage, pension and grave is a conveyor belt that Thaw resists: to him it processes people into things who feel, eat, think and act only as they ought and according to social patterns. Like his asthma, society seeks to choke his free breath. Thaw's opposition to this is futile, and leaves him only the resource of his own suicide: he is driven into a corner. (In the Victorian progressivist medium of *The Water-Babies*, by contrast, Tom dominates the world and wins.) A more nightmarish version of this digestion of the individual is seen in the Lanark narrative. In the institute the food is the processed meat of dead patients. Lanark's entry to the institute is via a mouth in a graveyard, and he falls, as down a digestive tract, into the stomach that is the institute-hospital. The institute is powered by the energy releases from exploding dragons, fed by the flesh of compressed 'softs', and staffed by cured patients made doctors. The analogy with bodily digestion needs little underlining. Lanark, who opposes and disrupts the system, or in other words cannot be used by it, is excreted by it—though here through an exit rarely used, since the institute only devours, it does not defecate. Later we learn that the world council, which is a 'creature', is about to swallow Unthank (p. 369): it is to prevent this that Lanark is sent as ambassador to the assembly at Provan. There he finally encounters a plain picture of feeding made an international and even an interplanetary imperative, from the mouth of the Lord Monboddo, whose name also transcribes as 'my body'. Monboddo sees the world as '"enclosed in a single living city"' (p. 543); and that city grows because '"it is a living body, its arteries are the rivers and canals, its limbs are the trade routes grappling goods and men into its stomach, the market"' (p. 540). However,

> 'The fuel supply of the present planet is almost exhausted. The food supply is already insufficient. Our deserts have grown too vast, our seas are overfished. We need a new supply of energy, for energy is food as well as fuel. At present, dead matter is turned into nourishment by farming, and by the consumption of uneducated people by clever ones. This arrangement is a failure because it is inefficient; it also puts clever people into a dependent position. Luckily our experts will soon be able to turn dead matter directly into food in our industrial laboratories—*if we give them access to sufficient energy.*'
>
> (p. 546)

That energy is to come ultimately from 'harpooning other planets' (p. 539). No morals here, not a rag of human feeling—and no place in this world for them either, as Lanark's objections are overwhelmed and he is given his final exit from life. That this 'civilisation' of happy eaters should do any more than consume and survive is not said: no value, no creation, nothing of art or artefact matters, only a continuation of the 'creature' and its creatures. This is devolution as Kingsley would see it, from human to devouring worm on a world scale. This world does not give out, it only draws in.

Where in Kingsley the fantasy element is a picture of the divine

coherence behind the world, in *Lanark* it is often a vision of a world
gone mad. Within Thaw's narrative it is the very normality of the mania
which is so striking to him:

> The ten-to-eight factory horns mourned over the city roofs
> and he curled more tightly into the nest of warmth his
> body made in the mattress, for like all bad sleepers he
> enjoyed bed most in the minutes before leaving it. Faint
> sounds came from the kitchen where his father prepared
> breakfast. Hundreds of thousands of men in dirty coats and
> heavy boots were tramping along grey streets to the gates
> of forges and machine shops. He thought with awe of the
> energy needed to keep up a civilization, of the implacable
> routines which started drawing it from the factory worker
> daily at eight, from the clerk and the shopkeeper at nine.
> Why didn't everyone decide to stay in bed one morning? It
> would mean the end of civilization, but in spite of two world
> wars the end of civilization was still an idea, while bed was
> a warm immediate fact.
>
> (p. 223)

This idea of the world as creatures feeding themselves on one another's
energy to no purpose extends itself to nature: 'He felt the natural world
stretching out . . . in great tracts of lumpy earth and rock coated thickly
with *life*, a stuff whose parts renewed themselves by eating each other'
(pp. 184–5); and beyond that he has hallucinatory visions of people
as assemblages of pulsating sacs, or of the world as full of maggots
devouring living people and eventually one another till only a giant
one is left curled about the earth, 'content' (pp. 232, 233). In Lanark's
world the madness makes overt fantasy. The sun's light has been choked
off; people, systematised, are covered with mouths or isolated from one
another in dragonish or crystalline forms.

But what we feel in this narrative is a breakdown of coherence.
(Kingsley uses incoherence within his narrative, but only to reveal the
deeper divine pattern within nature.[13]) The institute is indiscriminately
hospital and death-factory. Roads go both up and down. Time disintegrates, in the 'intercalendrical zone' (perhaps derived from Angela
Carter[14]), which itself is spreading over and devouring the world. On
the way to Unthank, huge wrecked chariots loom out of the mist: the
past is jumbled with the present in distorted size, and later we learn that
the present can feed on the future (pp. 437, 466). The eighteenth-century
savant Monboddo runs the institute. By the end of Lanark's story,
names and identities have changed to the point where '"Time changes
all the labels"' (p. 473). The love of Rima for Lanark becomes uncertain
and disintegrates. Even a drink is such that Lanark says, '"The taste
of this makes no sense"' (p. 503). And that is true: no *sense* unites the

world, only eating. The fiction itself loses coherence. Its very existence as little broken worms of time expresses this. At the end it loses its boundaries, and lets its author in to talk with his own characters; and it provides lists of its own sources to show how it has itself fed on others. In its portrayal of the Thaw story as 'enclosed' within the Lanark one, it suggests a form of narrative ingestion (p. 484). The fantasy, the disintegration, increase throughout the Lanark sections as the madness of society is revealed to him and as it advances; the process is not unlike that in Pope's *The Dunciad*. The suggestion through all this increase of chaos, is of approaching entropy. Thaw's vision of the stasis of the gigantic maggot curled about the devoured earth approaches realisation.

On this reading, Gray uses fantasy because the world offers no meaning to his characters, only absurdity. Both the Thaw and Lanark narratives are analyses, probings of the world we accept, always interrogative, never accepting, going further in and down. In a sense they are like journeys from the complacent rational-seeming exterior to the riot of unconscious drives beneath—journeys into dream. But the dreams, the madnesses, these are the reality for Thaw and Lanark. In the Thaw narrative we may sometimes question whether Thaw himself does not ask too hard questions of the world, and whether his father, who selflessly and cheerfully works to give his wife and family a good life, has not a better idea. But Thaw thinks he does see through to a view of the ultimate nonsense of life, and he cannot conduct his affairs sensibly in the face of that knowledge; and his view is extended in that of Lanark. At times the book does also suggest that everything we see is *his* view, that the Lanark afterworld is the one that suits Thaw's nature and vision, that Thaw's friend McAlpin, say, might have had quite another and happier afterlife; and Rima tells Lanark that the oracle told her story, not his (p. 357). But that way—true madness lies.

Such madness (we may close by remarking) is in fact explored in Gray's recent novel *Poor Things* (1992), in which for a long time we are absorbed in a semi-fantastic narrative in which a doctor revives a drowned woman with the transplanted brain of her unborn child, only to be greeted near the end with a letter from this same woman in which she says that the previous story has been a fabrication. Here again Gray explores multiple views, fictions, worlds. Which account we are to believe we do not know: the first appeals because we have been with it for far longer, and it does not immediately seem founded on any personal bias of its narrator; but the second persuades both because it is the last word and because it provides all too human reasons for the construction of the fantasy. While we are left suspended, the book has in a sense followed another fantasy, inasmuch as the series of anatomical drawings with which it is punctuated suggests a journey, not unlike that of *Lanark*, through the various regions of the body. The world of blood, muscle and bone on which our civilised gestures are founded seems here as elsewhere to Gray to provide an interesting counterpoint itself to the fictive worlds we construct.

'Modern afterworlds are always infernos, never paradisos, presumably because the modern secular imagination is more capable of debasement than exaltation,' remarks the commentator Sidney Workman in _Lanark_.[15] This suggests an element of the facile in dark views of the world which can make them questionable. In _Lanark_ no one view goes finally without its opposite. It is true that the bleak view has the loudest voice: but we have seen how while neither Thaw nor Lanark can better the worlds in which they live, and are indeed killed by them, they are still seen as effecting change and hope in their individual struggles, however ultimately futile in this life. There is also the stress Gray puts on the personal and the idiosyncratic, particularly in Thaw, a stress which negates generalisation and defies 'world views'. He sees a value for love and for creativity which has nothing to do with their endurance; and he finds a limited place for God, and Christianity, and faint, sneaking hope. At the moment that he gives us the bleak view of the world, Gray offers us a way out of it; only to undermine that way in turn with a 'Death is the only dependable exit' (p. 116). Gray's feeling for life's complexity, and his creativity, win out over any one philosophy.

Notes

1 For the account of the novel's inception here, see Bruce Charlton, 'The Story So Far', in Robert Crawford and Thom Nairn, eds, _The Arts of Alasdair Gray_ (Edinburgh: Edinburgh University Press, 1991), pp. 10–21.

2 The 'author' who at one point introduces himself to Lanark in the novel says, '"[Thaw's] death gave me a chance to shift him into a wider social context. You [Lanark] are Thaw with the neurotic imagination trimmed off and built into the furniture of the world you occupy."' But another 'author', in a footnote to this, comments, 'But the fact remains that the plots of the Thaw and Lanark sections are independent of each other and cemented by typographical contrivances rather than formal necessity. A possible explanation is that the author thinks a heavy book will make a bigger splash than two light ones' (Alasdair Gray, _Lanark: A Life in Four Books_ (Edinburgh: Canongate, 1981), p. 493.

3 See Randall Stevenson, 'Alasdair Gray and the Postmodern', in _The Arts of Alasdair Gray_, pp. 48–63.

4 For such a reading (a good one), see Cairns Craig, 'Going Down to Hell is Easy: _Lanark_, Realism and the Limits of the Imagination', in _The Arts of Alasdair Gray_, pp. 90–107. This interpretation effectively

adopts the vision of the Lanark narrative, and reads it back on to the Thaw one. Alison Lumsden takes issue with it in her 'Innovation and Reaction in the Fiction of Alasdair Gray', in Gavin Wallace and Randall Stevenson, eds, *The Scottish Novel Since the Seventies* (Edinburgh: Edinburgh University Press, 1993), pp. 115–26.

5 Letter from Gray to me of 19 November, 1993.

6 Ibid. and Alasdair Gray, 'Alasdair Gray Interviewed by Jenny Renton', *Scottish Book Collector*, no.7 (Aug./Sept. 1988), p. 3.

7 Ibid. and *Lanark*, pp. 491–2.

8 For an account, with plates, see Cordelia Oliver, 'Alasdair Gray, Visual Artist', in *The Arts of Alasdair Gray*, pp. 25–9.

9 Monboddo's council chamber is a perversion of a divine throne-room (p. 366).

10 3124 is also the sequence of the four books of *Lanark*.

11 There is a village of Unthank near Penrith in north England. 'Unthank' however is also the surname of the main character in James Bridie's play, *The Girl Who Did Not Want to Go to Kuala Lumpur* (1930).

12 Another and more terrible circularity is seen in the Prologue of the oracle, pp. 108–17.

13 On this see the chapter on Kingsley and *The Water-Babies* in my *Modern Fantasy: Five Studies* (Cambridge: Cambridge University Press, 1975), pp. 20–32.

14 That is, from the 'Nebulous Time' of her 'postmodern' fantasy *The Infernal Desire Machines of Dr Hoffman* (1972).

15 *Lanark*, p. 489, footnote 6.

CHAPTER THIRTEEN

Margaret Elphinstone, *An Apple from a Tree* (1991)

ITH MARGARET ELPHINSTONE we return to pastoral fantasy. But, in contrast to Gunn or even Brown, this pastoral has less of a community to give it assured life. There is no Highland village life as we find it in Gunn, no Orkney history as we see it in Brown. Here we have occasional and fugitive figures within landscapes equally fragile. Indeed in the paired novels *The Incomer* (1987) and *A Sparrow's Flight* (1989) the landscape is a blighted, post-holocaust one, and the community is maimed, in need of a healing that can only come from an outsider, not from within itself. In the short stories contained in Elphinstone's *An Apple from a Tree*—stories which will be our main concern here—nature is under threat or betrayed. We have now moved on to a Scotland of tourism, urban sophistication, college degrees, and state exploitation: and the way back is much harder, indeed the conditions for writing fantasy itself are much less assured.

But then the author herself is an enigmatic figure in this context. Brought up in Somerset, and living from 1983–9 in the Galloway countryside, she is urbane and highly educated herself, now living in Edinburgh and teaching English at the University of Strathclyde. She appears literally to have worked herself away from her roots: her occupation was first a gardener, but then she wrote two books on organic gardening, *The Green Gardener's Handbook* (co-authored, 1987) and *Organic Gardening* (1990), and turned to novel writing. While pastoral values are at the centre of her work, they are filtered through intellectual causes such as feminism, ecology and anti-nuclear views. She negotiates with these, aiming to pierce to an elusive reality both in and beyond them, but as her starting points they give her writing an intellectual and urban air.

In all Elphinstone's books we find the steady pressure of a feminist view:

> 'I did find my way into the forest, after all.'
> 'I thought you would, the first time I saw you. It was only a question of recognising what you knew already. Like the music. If I hear it played enough times, I begin to know it. Even the music you gave to Davey.'
> 'I wish I could have taught it to you. But I've left it with

you, and it's yours, as far as it ever can be.'

'You couldn't wish for more. After all, we're not the same. All we do is create worlds for ourselves, I suppose, and when one touches another, there's a tension between one image and another. But the images we use reflect the same thing.'[1]

Music, creation, giving, sharing, even 'I suppose', catch that simple, tentative, delicate quality of woman that Margaret Elphinstone puts over rather less as plain description than as a programme for living. Her male characters do best when they surrender to these qualities, as with Thomas and his relation with Naomi in *A Sparrow's Flight*. Men are seen as imposing their minds on the natural world and on women alike, whether as gardeners ('Islands of Sheep' in *An Apple from a Tree*), or rapists (Patrick in *The Incomer*), or nuclear scientists (*A Sparrow's Flight*). Nearly all the novels and stories put women and women's values at the centre of their concern. The result is a certain one-sidedness, and one which over long distances, as in the novels, can be stifling. Together, too, the novels explore the history of the same character Naomi, travelling with the music of her fiddle through a post-holocaust world, trying to rebuild a civilisation in contact with nature—though they are contrastive to the extent that Naomi is an 'incomer' in the first, staying throughout in the village of Clachanpluck, where in the latter she is an 'outgoer', a traveller with a destination.

Despite their still programmatic character, Elphinstone's short stories are less evidently one-sided; and their constant shifts of world from one story to another suggest the sense of alternative views as much as of realities. Also, there is in them often a more muted quality to the message—whether through the use of irony or the indirection of symbol—which gives them an urbanity that at once hides and strengthens their designs on us. At the same time, they are very inventive. One could place *The Incomer* in the genre of Tolkien, or *A Sparrow's Flight* with that of post-holocaust fiction, but the short stories are much more original and imaginative—and powerful through their compassion. Curiously too, for all their diversity, they collectively give the author a far more personal voice than is present in the novels.

We shall be concerned here primarily with these shorter stories. There is one further and seemingly more formal reason: they are most of them concerned with the 'supernatural', or what may so be identified. No such magical being or event is present in the novels, which are nearer to science fiction than to fantasy. There is superstitious dread, whether of the shadow in the forest in *The Incomer*, or of the empty lands in *A Sparrow's Flight*, but the shadow is a projection of mind, and the empty lands a product of man; and the only magic that is worked is the human magic of changing relationships or of the harmonising influence of music. By contrast, in the short story 'Conditions of Employment', a girl acts as guardian of a magical mountain well while its protector, a spirit of water called Oddny, is on holiday; and in a companion-piece to this, 'The Cold Well', we find Oddny putting a binding-spell on a nuclear power station that is polluting the land and water about it. 'Green Man' describes an art teacher who meets a man from another dimension, camping in the wilds of Galloway. In 'Islands of Sheep', an academic living in the Fens takes a young woman lodger who gains peculiar influence over his mind: she is associated with the power of the sea. In 'An Apple from a Tree', a bite from an apple in Edinburgh's Botanic Gardens enables the heroine to shuttle between worlds. The sixth and last story, 'A Life of Glory', contains a spirit from some far realm unwilling to enter and be bound to flesh as two people conceive a child on earth. All these supernatural elements are seen as associated with nature, whether defending it, living it or restoring it: in a sense they fit with Tolkien's view of the supernatural in fantasy as super-*natural*.[2] If any metaphysic is implied in this use of magic, it is one whereby the earth itself is seen as inherently divine, as Gaia, '"Before any god was thought of . . . there was the image of a woman, and she was the whole world."'[3] When the world was pure, woman rather than man, not governed by rules and penetrated by questions, not polluted by effluent or nuclear power, then it was most magical. Ecology, feminism, the unconscious, creativity, these are here given a religious base.

But the most constant use of the supernatural in these stories is to deconstruct modern rational awareness through its 'otherness'. Most of the central figures of the stories are intellectuals who have lost touch with their primal, instinctual selves, and those lost selves are for them precisely 'supernatural' and 'other'. So it is the object of several of these stories to show those sophisticated people being variously confronted by the primitive, the mysterious and the suppressed; just as, in their different way, the longer novels show people struggling with their fear of woods or of unknown lands after a catastrophic war. The difference between the science fiction and the fantasy is that in the one it is ignorance that is to be overcome, and in the other, too much knowledge; in the one superstition is banished, and in the other it is invoked.

The blurb on the back of *An Apple from a Tree* declares, 'The author's ironic, stylish blend of magic and realism subverts conventional views of normality.' While that could be said of any fantasy, it does have a special relevance here. Subversion, if we like, is there from the start of the first story, 'Green Man':

The most human feature of the valley was the railway. It emerged from a cutting between the hills and swept out above the bogland on a narrow embankment, the loch lying to the north of it. All that was left of the halt was a rusted shed, ramshackle and crazily tilted, by the solid little bridge that spanned the burn. A smaller burn flowed out of the loch, and the two, conjoined, wound their way through heather-tufted marshland, round the long green curve of Airie Hill. Drifts of trees fell across the northern slopes like blown leaves, winnowed away from the bare bones of the hills. There seemed no reason why anyone should have stopped here. Forgotten passengers on the ghost of a departed railway, shooting-parties in tweeds and brogues, solitary salmon fishers in season, shepherds who dropped off here to cover the grazings on these hills which no farm or cottage overlooked. There was nothing else here, nor ever had been. Lochskerrow Halt. A name on a map which lent it meaning only by the dotted line where there was once a railway. The cuttings remained, the long embankments, the grey shingle that crunched under feet that followed the tracks of the departed trains.

At first sight the opening sentence makes the railway the valley's only redeeming constituent, but then we have to think again and ask ourselves whether it might not rather be the valley's sole repulsive aspect, and whether our conventional idea of human as 'warm, personal' is relevant here. Conventional ideas about humanity are to be questioned throughout the story. Then, the first paragraph of the novel gives us a scene of a desolate spot called Lochskerrow Halt (actually a real place in Galloway); while the second seems to continue there but in fact does not, for it and the next describe the progress of a woman hiker along the track from a place called Mossdale some miles to the east. Moreover, what was described as a 'railway' in the first sentence, a railway which had determination and purpose, is shown to be a disused line, with only the track bed left. We are thus disoriented. And the woman hiker, who, analogously with the railway, is 'An efficient and determined person, a person with a destination in view, who had not strayed into this territory idly' (p. 4) is soon to lose all sense of direction, all contact with the world of normal motivation, in an unexpected meeting. She is to find a strange tent, with an even stranger being on the far side of it, by the loch near Lochskerrow Halt. No such tent or being were described in the first paragraph, which said only that 'The most human feature of the valley was the railway': that could have meant there was a creature other than human there, but it did not describe it. Alternatively

the tent and its owner are not there till the hiker is: in which case the one
begets or calls down the other, which is to be suggested in the story.
But we do not know. And not knowing is to be one of the journeys of
this story. To this opening description we might add one last aspect: the
woman is to turn out to be an art teacher and a painter. What happens
to her today is going to transform her art from 'small landscapes drawn
from the surrounding woods and hills, portraits of people she knew'
(p. 54), to a terrifying vision from 'dim regions beyond the compass of
the waking mind', 'strange pictures, as from another world, or the same
world seen through other eyes' (pp. 53, 54). The opening paragraphs are
themselves a painting, and one which changes in character as we read
also, from the level of a straightforward landscape to something much
less definable, much more strange and full of haunting possibility.

The dislocations here show how 'other' the world is capable of being
at any moment to our rational minds. What simpler thing than a loch
and a fire with a man by it? 'But the tent was an odd shape, an attractive
shape, like a breast . . . It was something about the tent, the shape of it,
or the colour. It was not quite like anything that she had seen before. It
certainly didn't come out of any camping catalogue' (p. 5). And the man?
'The person sitting by the fire had its back to her.' Already something
has gone in that 'its'. And then, when he turns,

> He was green.
> Completely, uncompromisingly green. The vivid, vibrant
> green of fresh spinach plants, or bogland grass, or young
> hawthorn. His hair was thick and green, and hung over his
> forehead in a green fringe. His skin was green, his eyes were
> green, even his lips were green. Under the russet cloak he
> wore strange loose garments of dark green, but his feet were
> bare—and green. He watched her with gentle interest, and
> stretched out a green hand to her.[4]
>
> (p. 6)

The abruptness of this, the vegetable insistence of it, inclines us to laugh,
until we remember that this is precisely the mood of recollected shock
and struggling irony with which Sarah's educated mind is trying to deal
with it. Immediately, too, our minds try to place the man, whether as
fertility god, fairy, extraterrestrial or import from the pages of C. S.
Lewis.[5] Our instincts are again mediated by Sarah, to whom 'He
appeared to have come from another planet' (p. 13; see also p. 66).
Whatever assumptions we try to make are undercut. He has not come
by any space-ship; and if he were some kind of god, he is solid enough to
have a tent, need a fire and food and, when asked, to be good at making
love. He tells Sarah that, like her, '"I . . . started from my home"'; and,
when asked how near that is, answers, '"Only a thought"' (p. 8). But if
we want to assume 'thought travel', he replies that we all live a thought

away from home; and in reply to Sarah's '"Have you come from another world?"' he replies, '"Just as you have"' (pp. 8, 9). He is telling Sarah that he is just as much or little 'supernatural', 'other' or 'mysterious' as she is. Then he says that he has seen Airie Hill since the earliest times of man, and that he is some kind of watcher (pp. 35, 40–1). Sarah herself has a vision that connects him with beings some might call fairies, 'Beings grown insubstantial for want of food and offerings, small deities denied their due, guests bringing gifts from beyond the stars drifting upon the hills because there was no one left to receive them' (p. 31). Later she associates him with the rejected gods of earth and sea, Pan and Poseidon (p. 40). We may say that he is strongly linked with nature and the land: yet he is left without certain identification, while still strongly inviting it; our minds are teased out of thought. Even language itself, and its grammatical forms and parameters, are disrupted.

> 'Who are you?' she asked at last, and was annoyed to hear her voice sounded frail and squeaky.
> 'Not yet,' he said. 'I hope so, by the end of my journey.'
> 'Hope to what?'
> 'Who I am,' he said. 'But perhaps in this country you are already who you are.'
>
> (p. 7)

But Sarah is precisely not who she is, her real self, yet. And she is continually asking questions. He, however, feels no surprise, knows his destination, speaks almost always in the indicative, already knows her name. He says to her, '"I think you could ask questions for a thousand years. It must be very important, this knowing of yourself"' (p. 42).

The green man (whose name is Lin) matters for himself, of course. He brings all the freight of mystery, of the possibly supernatural, of an astonishing new relationship, of the agonising grief and guilt when he is lost. But he is also a person seen in a landscape, the landscape of Lochskerrow Halt. He is only met there: he cannot be abstracted from the place. When Sarah paints the landscape and it is recognised at an exhibition of her work, the green man is also exposed, even though he was not in the painting;[6] and when she returns it is to find units of the army there, searching for him. In all Margaret Elphinstone's stories we find the importance of the land, of nature, of the earth, which through civilisation, progress, mind itself has become 'A land laid waste, bound by words, spells, questions, concepts in the minds of men' (p. 31). The 'otherness' of the green man here stands as proxy for that of the land. In all of Sarah's paintings of her experience of him after the first, his figure has gone and she is painting landscapes made alien, 'They were strange pictures, as from another world, or the same world seen through other eyes' (p. 54).

To make similar strange pictures of the land, to give it back its wild nature, is the object in the other stories too. In 'Islands of Sheep', we are in the Fens, a land forced out of the sea by man, drained and walled and farmed. Amid this scene sits the Cambridge geography lecturer Peter, academic of landscape, his name meaning 'stone', in a neat modern bungalow; and to that bungalow comes as tenant Anna, doing postgraduate work on psychology, an academic of the unconscious, to make up a dualism. The interaction of the pair is in a sense that of land and sea, of the drained Fens and the prowling ocean; Anna is the daughter of an Orkney lighthouse keeper. Metaphorically like the flat Fens, Peter has no unconscious, but Anna has; and Peter's secret investigation of her diary puts the record of her dreams into his mind. That record is one in which the Fens are once more returned to their ancient form by a storm-led incursion of the sea; and just such an incursion subsequently happens within the dry Fen-like mind of Peter one night, and gives him a nervous breakdown. 'There was a roaring in his ears, crashing of the sea against rock, sea sucked down into the caves under the island'; 'The light from the falling tower [Anna's lighthouse] blew apart, fiery bolts tore into the sea. Then the tower broke, and crashed, washing him down with it into the hungry sea' (pp. 111, 112). At the level of the unconscious the land has been transformed, has become 'other'. At the end of the story, as Anna, now in control of the house, negotiates with a second tenant to take Peter's place, we know that at another level we are in the calm of a placid sea dotted with islands, as Anna once dreamt it:

> Islands of sheep. Islands of sheep. The sea so calm and still, flat as a field on a summer's day. The islands were bright green like toys, like the scenery on our model railway at home, and the sheep were white as plastic snow. Islands of sheep like lily pads, floating towards the sun.
>
> (pp. 103–4)

In the story 'An Apple from a Tree', Elphinstone uses a technique of 'bilocalism' she may have got from George MacDonald to juxtapose Edinburgh as it is with Edinburgh as it might have been. Another intellectual alienated from all but the most tamed forms of nature, an urban cynic called Alison, is found mentally pecking about in Edinburgh's Botanic Gardens. 'I have always enjoyed walking there, not only to commune with nature, such as it is, but also to watch people in the throes of conversations and encounters that are obviously about to change their lives' (p. 179). However, despite herself, she has certain yearnings, which the blue sky above the trees calls up. Then she does something instinctual, like a child, and jumps up to catch falling leaves: 'Seven years' good luck, we used to say. I don't know who taught me that. You don't catch luck falling off a tree . . .' (p. 180). At that point an apple, from no visible apple tree, falls on her. She deliberates a while, but the apple smells so pleasant (reminding her of 'the apple-scented bottles in the Body Shop'), that despite not knowing where it has come from, she eats it. At once her world changes; she is whirled into another dimension. If the apple in Eden gave knowledge, this one restores a kind of innocence. She finds herself on ground scattered with windfall apples, watched by a naked woman. Her responses, however, are fallen.

> That [her nakedness] was the first thing that I noticed about her. If that makes you think that I pay too much attention to trivia, you should read the regulations governing the conduct of visitors to the Botanics, and you will see at once why this should seem so startling.
>
> (pp. 181–2)

The woman introduces herself as Nosi¹a—Alison's reverse. In one sense she is 'supernatural', but in another she is Alison's other self, her primal and unconscious being, with which she has lost touch. The rest of the narrative in one way consists in a dialogue between the two Alisons, the one rational, urbane and common-sense, the other instinctual, uninhibited, chaotic, and sexy. And it also comes down to a matter of preferred landscapes. 'The forest badly needed clearing. No one had thinned out the young saplings, or cleared away the masses of fallen trunks and dead wood . . . Even the sky shocked me' (p. 186):

> We were at the top of the hill and the slope below us stretched down to open ground. When I looked again I saw it was not ground but water. It was black in the half-light, uncannily calm, and on the far side it was lost in shadow where a great precipice towered over it. I found it weird, as though the place were full of hidden things I did not wish to think about.
>
> (p. 187)

Here the land has become alien: Alison cannot recognise Edinburgh Castle Rock, and has no reason to identify the water she sees as the loch that was once below it (supposing it is that). And she—that is, the rational she—is afraid of the hidden things, the deeper parts of the self. So the story continues, with Alison being introduced to Nosila's world and she in turn to Alison's, with equal repugnance on both sides, until the point of decision is reached, and Alison refuses to stay in the other world she has seen. She reaches this decision after Nosila has met a naked man in her world and made love to him. But she would not be Alison if she did not want power. She will go back with an apple 'so all the worlds I wanted were now open to me' (p. 200): that will put her in control of strangeness, of the 'other'. When she finally leaves Nosila, she feels a 'splitting away from my side like my heart being torn out'; but she ends with the apple, 'secure in my own knowledge' (p. 201). Here the rational self has 'won', to its impoverishment: here the victory gained is nothing to the primal and unending delight that might have been.

In the last story in the collection, 'A Life of Glory', Elphinstone tests her own vision of the spirit of the land. For the story is set in the empty lands of Arizona and Colorado, and these prove to have nothing human about them, to answer to nothing in the depths of the human psyche, but rather to reflect, like E. M. Forster's Marabar Caves in *A Passage to India*, an indifferent abyss of time devoid of life. In this place, Helen, on holiday from Scotland and visiting James, an American friend she once met in Edinburgh, unintentionally conceives a child. The spirit of the embryo is described as drawn in, reluctantly, from the interstellar spaces to this one spot. The story is full of shallow commitments. Helen and James will not make a lasting relationship, even though each loves the other; neither of them wanted a baby; the baby's spirit does not want to be enclosed in matter; and Helen rejects the baby when she knows of its presence, so that it spontaneously aborts. Similarly Helen cannot connect with the American desert and mountain landscape, which baffles her with its violent contrasts, its freakishness and its vacancy; and James, while he lives there for the time, is a traveller who can live anywhere. Back in Edinburgh, however, Helen feels a quite different landscape, one full of geological process, history and life, and one far more real to her. In a sense her rejection of the child becomes the defeat of one landscape by another. The spirit of the child sees its approaching release from the earth in this way:

> Around me in the darkness was red rock, sand beaten into rock, rock worn down by water, strange petrified shapes, canyons going thousands of years down into the red earth. In the heart of the desert I saw a sea, grey and icy, with black clouds blowing over it. The clouds parted. The stars were cold and far away, and beneath them was a city, clinging to the stubborn rock that ice could never wear away, a road winding down the dragon's tail towards a palace, the whole hill drenched in blood and history. The sky was cold and clear as death. I saw the earth turning, one side and then the other coming face to face with me.
>
> (p. 260)

Edinburgh has 'obliterated' Arizona. Now, set free, the spirit once more feels 'the desert stars'.

This story differs from others by Elphinstone, where she shows the 'otherness' of the land: here she shows someone learning rather where she is at home. Here, instead of juxtaposing an 'everyday' with a fantastic Edinburgh to show the poor surface we prefer to live with, as in 'An Apple from a Tree', she is showing someone coming to value the known place against the alien. By going away from her landscape to its opposite, Helen learns where she truly lives:

> Here, Helen was no longer a visitor: she belonged. She was
> made here, and eventually born here. The idea of belonging
> became real to her, in a manner it had never done before,
> when she walked across the town on a September Sunday,
> shortly after her return. Absence makes familiarity all the
> stranger, for never having been noticed before.
>
> (p. 247)

Helen begins to think *within* this landscape: her decision not to have the child is made during a walk to Cramond Island. In disconnecting the 'foreign' child from herself she is recreating an almost umbilical connection between herself and her home. In this story Elphinstone is not concerned with rural values against urban ones, but rather with home against abroad; and thus this is the only one of her stories in which a city landscape is celebrated. But then, for her purposes, Edinburgh is just right: for in it landscape and man have entered into a unique marriage. There seems something autobiographical about this final story, the sense of someone coming to terms with herself and her place: it may be that it records Elphinstone's own growing acceptance of the city, her perception that town and country are not always to be seen as opposed. But what we also have here is a strong sense of landscape itself as an active agent in the shaping of human lives, whether as individuals or within a city, deciding things for them more than they do themselves, operating both in and outside their minds at levels far beyond perception. Of this the unseen spirit of the child, which takes so large a part of the story, seems an apt symbol: and so too the for long invisible and unknown embryo itself.

The remaining stories of *An Apple from a Tree*, 'Conditions of Employment' and 'The Cold Well', portray the need to maintain the health of the land under present-day threats from man. In the first, the girl Miranda's short job as guardian of a mountain well involves her also in using the living powers of the well to answer the questions and problems of the various individuals, both human and supernatural, who come to it. In 'The Cold Well', we have a picture of the blighting of the land by a nuclear power station and the departure of the mountain-guardian of the deer: the water-spirit Oddny only just succeeds in binding the destructive influence of the nearby power station, where 'the very stuff from which the earth was made was being torn apart' (p. 168). These are less subtle stories than the others in the collection, the one rather too flippant and the other too strident and hectoring in its ecological aims. Both however celebrate the living, spiritual power of water. This emphasis on water is seen in others of the stories: the green man Lin is met by Sarah in the watery context of a loch and rain, and his tent has liquid designs on it; Peter's dry little certainties, like the artificial land, are overwhelmed by water in 'Islands of Sheep'; the wildness of primitive 'Edinburgh' in 'An Apple from a Tree' is associated with water; and Helen in 'A Life of Glory' finds Arizona repellent in its dryness, 'Perhaps those endless cliffs should have been damp with spray, facing a living sea, but at their feet the rock was the same, merely empty' (p. 224).

There is one other recurrent feature in all these stories apart from the concern with the otherness of the land, a topic which follows on from that interest. This is the motif of duality. '"I should have remembered . . . that there are two sides to everything,"' Oddny tells Miranda (p. 142). If the land is other, then that supposes a separation. All the stories involve division between two orders of being, whether natural and supernatural, earth and water, town and country, male and female—Sarah and the green man, Peter and Anna, the Fens and the sea, the wild spirit Oddny and the tamed water in the terrible artefact, Alison and Nosila, Helen and James, Edinburgh and Arizona. Together with this goes an interest in the struggles of the two orders to get into relationship, whether that be a relation of harmony as with Sarah and Lin, or one founded in oppugnancy, as between Peter and Anna. There are frequent conversations and negotiations where one 'side' tries to accommodate to or find out about the other, as between Sarah and Lin, or Alison and Nosila, or Peter trying to find out about Anna, or even Miranda in 'Conditions of Employment' entering a business contract with the water-spirit Oddny. Always there is a sense of dialectic, a dance of differents, or opposites.

Together with that there is a tremendous sense of fragility. The seemingly least thing can turn everything wrong. In 'Green Man', Sarah's mention, to one person who knows the place, that her paintings are of Lochskerrow Halt, causes the place to be invaded; and she thereby loses the green man and the other reality he had come to represent to her. By 'earthing' or identifying the green man at one point, his whole world is discharged: 'I have stripped you of shadows' (p. 66). In 'Islands of Sheep', Peter's curiosity, and his breakage of Anna's treasured possession, her sand dollar, in some way precipitates or lets through the whole disaster. In 'The Cold Well', the actions of the nuclear power station involve an invisible destruction of atomic matter which in turn causes far wider destruction. The hold of the foetus on life in 'A Life of Glory' is as frail as its mother Helen's commitment to its distant father James: as flesh it falls out into the world long before its time, as spirit it feels 'the desert stars'; the story ends in dualism. These stories, then, are often tense, poised on the 'edge of the world' (p. 206), full of a sense of their own frailty: one wrong touch, and the whole delicate balance is overthrown. Not surprisingly, they are frequently imbued with a sense of loss, of elegy. So much was possible, and so much was lost. 'I have nothing left of you now, only stale images hanging in a gallery that I shall never see again' (p. 69); 'It was possible that she was the only one of her kind upon whom the sun still rose . . . She would miss him, even if she stayed here until the end of time, and nothing that the earth brought forth would take his place for her' (p. 176); 'She was crying, for loss and relief all at once' (p. 260). In the end every one of the protagonists is alone.

To a large extent these stories deal with aliens because the humans in them are alienated. (We may notice too that any relationship is lost.) Part of Elphinstone's concern is with the hardness of the self, the degree to which it will not flow or be 'deconstructed' into harmony with its surroundings. Sarah in 'Green Man' approaches very nearly to that desired loss of self; others retreat within the city, or the ordered and regulated world or mind, or to islands, lighthouses, dry lands. Here again, water is of symbolic value. '"Water is much more powerful than you think,"' says Oddny (p. 142); and later we are told, 'No power on earth prevails against water' (p. 172). So too the world will not stay still, but is continually shifting and fluid; and each of these stories creates a quite different imaginative world, while at the same time they all lie together in shimmering relationship, like the inside of Lin's tent where 'everything was infinite and complicated, lines softened into nothing, endless patterns with no solid shape as if it were all shifting, changing in the uncertain light' (p. 24). Even the alienating definiteness of words and sequences is one which Margaret Elphinstone as a writer must herself seek to undermine and dissolve to recreate, just as happens in 'Green Man'.[7] Her very name, Elfin-stone, seems somehow peculiarly appropriate to this task.

Yet what is also being recorded in these stories is the threatened loss of the supernatural itself. The Green Man has departed, the guardian of the hills has been driven out by a power station, the wild abundance of Nosila's world is disdained, the spirit from beyond the stars is cast out of its tenuous hold upon flesh. As Oddny, spirit of the water, sees it,

> It was a curious thing, there were worlds upon worlds which had once been open to one another but the people now believed that there was only one, and that was dying fast enough. That frightened her. People had one power that other kinds did not, which was the power to dream things and make them happen, or the power to destroy, merely by the act of forgetting.
>
> (p. 156)

The existence of magic is made possible so long as the land is healthy, so long as feminine values, freedom, individuality, the unconscious, continue to play a central part in the life of man. What Elphinstone records is her fear that this may now be in danger. It has always been the province of elusive faërie to awaken feelings of loss—witness for example Bishop Richard Corbett's 'Farewell, rewards and fairies' of 1647—but here we come to a sense of a radical impoverishment of the human spirit which is a more final quietus. Here, in a world stripped of mystery, severed from its past and consumed by man's wish to control the environment and others, the magic is going away, 'dismissed into a world of shadows' (p. 31). Now, to quote it again, we have 'A land laid waste, bound by words, spells, questions, concepts in the minds of men'; and now the 'supernatural' is 'Beings grown insubstantial for want of food and offerings, small deities denied their due, guests bringing gifts from beyond the stars drifting upon the hills because there was no one left to receive them' (ib.). In one way what we see in Elphinstone's work is a sense that fantasy, 'the power to dream things and make them happen', may itself be coming to an end.

Notes

1 Margaret Elphinstone, *The Incomer* (London: Women's Press, 1987) p. 229.
2 J. R. R. Tolkien, *Tree and Leaf* (London: Allen and Unwin, 1964), p. 12.
3 Margaret Elphinstone, *An Apple from a Tree and Other Visions* (London: Women's Press, 1991), p. 40.
4 On fairy green men in Scottish folk tradition, see Hannah Aitken, *A Forgotten Heritage: Original Folk Tales of Lowland Scotland* (Edinburgh: Scottish Academic Press, 1973), pp. 19, 20, 23.
5 With Lewis, there are similarities between the green man and the green Lady and Lord of his *Perelandra* (1943), and with the Marshwiggles of his *The Silver Chair* (1953).
6 But Sarah does feel that the landscapes grew out of her one direct painting of the green man (p. 47).
7 In that story the green man says that Sarah's language is difficult for him because it '"travels only in straight lines"', and that words are dangerous because '"They change everything"' (pp. 12, 14). There, too, Sarah's paintings also dissolve and recreate what she saw: 'The picture kept on shifting inside her head. The hill would not be all black, not really. Now the red moon had come, there would be a reflection, like another possibility. One planet turning into another. No, it wasn't a Mars landscape after all. That was just an image, an analogy. It had merely been a step on the way' (p. 47).

CHAPTER FOURTEEN

Other Writers

T HIS CHAPTER WILL deal with works which approach, but are not quite, fantasy, and with less central fantasies. Among these are historical fantasies, 'discussion' fantasies, moral, comic, and children's fantasies, and 'fantastic' or 'magical' realism. Most of these are fine works on their own terms, and some of them form the contemporary mutation of the genre. They several of them serve to put fantasy in a broader literary context, and show it tapering away into other literary modes.

1. HISTORICAL FANTASY

John Buchan, Witch Wood (1927)

This novel is a brilliant recreation of the Covenanting period in mid-seventeenth-century Scotland, and portrays the shift in sympathy from stern theology to royalism in the heart of a newly-appointed minister of the Covenanting Kirk. Young David Sempill comes to the Borders village of Woodilee in 1644 to find his Calvinist certainties being undermined both by acquaintance with the views of their opponents (including a meeting with the Duke of Montrose) and by the increasing repulsiveness of his fellow-votaries.

The opposition of royalist and Covenanting worlds is put in supernatural terms. David is to fall in love with Katrine Yester of the Border keep of Calidon, whose family support the King and harbour Montrose. David first sees her in the reputedly haunted woods about Woodilee, and thinks she is a fairy. Certainly she is elusive enough: when one day he is in a beautiful glade, which his imagination depicts as having been used by the fairy folk, he hears a rustle; and then

> at the far end of the glade behind the red bracken he saw a figure. In two steps he was certain. A green gown fluttered and at his third step broke cover. He saw the form of a girl—nymph, fairy, or mortal, he knew not which. He was no more the minister of Woodilee, but eternal wandering youth, and he gave chase.[1]

Later, he finds her favourite resort in the wood, where 'the whole place was Paradise. Never before had he felt so strong a natural magic. This

woodland, which he had once shunned, had become a holy place' (p. 81).
Katrine retains her elusive quality till the last, for as she mutates from
fairy to loved woman, she is finally an unacknowledged saint, as she
helps David tend the sick of the parish in a visitation of the plague and
is herself struck down and lost. At the end David senses that 'Katrine
was his forever among the eternal fields' (p. 275).

Buchan gives us another side to the wood however, and that is the
association of its darkest parts with the sinister and the demonic. The
Black Wood of Melanudrigill has roots going far back into the pagan
and Pictish past and beyond: its very name is secret, being 'given' by
the 'Guid Folk' to the village natural, Daft Gibbie. In that wood, David
finds, dark things are still being enacted at certain times of the year:
more, he finds that it is his own upright parishioners who partake in
hellish sabbats and dances there.

Both in the faërian and satanic directions the book awakens our
wonder or dread, only to give us 'perfectly natural' explanations:
the fairy is Katrine, Satan's followers are hypocrite Covenanters. But
for the time the opposition between royalist Calidon and 'unco' guid'
Woodilee is put in terms of supernatural imagery: at its purest, the
one is fairy and natural, the other satanic and unnatural. And in
a way the sense of the supernatural remains, through Katrine and
through the ancient wood, both brooding and sunlit, capacious home
to every superstition. Buchan may use the different magics as symbolic
touchstones, but having invoked them, having invited them into his
story, they will not finally be dispelled (any more than the wood can
be fully penetrated). Katrine may turn from apparent fairy to human,
but her humanity still calls for the faërian to express it; and the sabbat
of the people of Woodilee calls down the very Satan that they and their
church execrate. Indeed it is possible that the devil is in fact present at
their furtive festivals (pp. 128–9) and in the final pursuit of the coven's
high priest (pp. 273–4).

The supernatural—if we may call it that, since it is so much a part
of the wood—is present in another sense in the story as a whole. One
legend has it that David Sempill, who mysteriously disappeared from
Woodilee at the end of the story, was taken by the fairies; another that the
devil secured his own (pp. 2, 286–8). We have good reason to disbelieve
both accounts, but their mere existence gives enduring reality in some
sense to these supernatural beings. And 'Buchan' enters to tell how in
his own childhood, he believed that the fairies took him (p. 2). But more
than this: the story assumes a more than natural force as he considers
writing it. He has gone back to Woodilee with the tale strongly in mind,
but has found that the modernity of the place makes it impossible to bring
the legend back to life: 'I could not re-create the picture out of glistening
asphalted highway, singing telegraph wires, spruce dwellings, model
pastures, and manicured woodlands' (p. 3). But then, one evening, he

sees 'with other eyes': sees the place as 'a thing antique and wolfish, tricked out for the moment with a sheep's coat'; and passes further into a vision—

> It was the Woodilee of three hundred years ago. And my mind, once given the cue, set out things not presented by the illuded eye . . . There were no highways—only tracks, miry in the bogs and stony on the braes, which led to Edinburgh on one hand and Carlisle on the other. I saw few houses, and these were brown as peat, but on the knowe of the old kirkton I saw the four grey walls of the kirk, and the manse beside it among elders and young ashes. Woodilee was not now a parish lying open to the eye of sun and wind. It was no more than a tiny jumble of crofts, bounded and pressed in upon by something vast and dark, which clothed the tops of all but the highest hills, muffled the ridges, choked the glens and overflowed almost to the edge of the waters—which lay on the landscape like a shaggy fur coat cast loosely down. My mouth shaped the word 'Melanudrigill', and I knew that I saw Woodilee as no eye had seen it for three centuries, when, as its name tells, it still lay in the shadow of a remnant of the Wood of Caledon, that most ancient forest where once Merlin harped and Arthur mustered his men . . .

(p. 4)

The past and legendary thus break through into the present. This magical sense of history, by which the past is not so much animated as itself becomes active, is something that will also be felt in the historical novels of Naomi Mitchison. Here just as we are challenged concerning the supernatural as it is given an apparently 'natural' explanation, so our notion of history as past and inert is also questioned. No *conclusion* is possible, only the knowledge that life is more than it seems, that reality is greater than the fences our minds put round it. So here, the huge symbol of the forest of Melanudrigill that broods over the story, breaks through the neat little lines of modern civilisation; so too, in the story the grid of Covenanting theology is transgressed by the passions of its own adherents.

Naomi Mitchison, The Corn King and the Spring Queen (1931)

In Naomi Mitchison's major work *The Corn King and the Spring Queen* (begun in 1925) we have a more 'epic' history than Buchan's, involving a recreation of several pre-Christian societies, in Scythia, Sparta and Egypt. The 'supernatural' appears most directly in it in the person of Erif Der (Red Fire reversed), a Scythian woman of the third century BC who can do magic. In a sense the book is a piece of cultural anthropology, setting the values of an agrarian, magic-based society (Marob) against others more urbane (Sparta, Egypt). Mitchison also wants to create a society in which there is a place for the free expression of feminine energies: she gives us a heroine who is sexually uninhibited and who learns to make her own independent choices.[2] The contrast with Buchan's male-centred and Edwardian view of women as delicate sprites and self-sacrificing nurses is marked. Beyond these issues, the book is also about art, politics, religion, philosophy—indeed it is amazing that this compendium of interests and a whole gallery of sharply observed characters cohere within this history of several worlds.

The history here is much more imagined than in Buchan, being about a remote time and (in Scythian Marob) a place for which records are sparse—and they certainly were for Mitchison, who often had to rely on the likes of Plutarch. So we get both a sense of the romantically distant and of the invented. What heightens the 'fantasy' is the thoroughness with which Mitchison has imagined her lost worlds, so that she makes them as real as they are remote. This is the house of the Corn King Tarrik's sister in the main town of Marob by the Black Sea (she calls herself by the Greek name of Eurydice, because she wishes to emulate the culture of Greece, but she is also called Yersha by the Scythians):

> Her room looked partly over the sea and partly over the gardens, where there were lawns of scythed grass between great rose hedges, carved marble seats under apple trees, and narrow borders of bee-flowers and herbs round fountains and statues that came once from Hellas. But Yersha who was Eurydice sat at the other window, watching the sea. She had been copying manuscript; there was pen and ink beside her, and half a page of her slow, careful writing, and now she was quite still, beside her window. Along her walls there were chests of book rolls; above them their stories were repeated in fresco, black lines filled in softly with tints of flesh or dress—Achilles in Skyros, Iphigenia sacrificed, Phaedra and Hippolytos, Alkestis come back from the dead, horsemen with the thick, veiled beauty of a too much copied Parthenon, women with heavy eyelids and drooping hands and lapfuls of elaborate drapery, all framed in borders of crowded acanthus pattern that repeated itself again and again on the mouldings of doors and windows. The floor was of marble from Skyros, white streaked with brown and a curious green, the couches and table of citron wood and ivory, with worked silver feet. There were a few vases, light colours on a creamy ground, with palely florid borders and handles, and one or two marble groups, a swan or so, and the little winged, powerless Erotes, like mortal babies.[3]

This is no mere historical pedantry—it reflects the particular character of Yersha. She is trying to better herself by emulation of the best model of civilisation. Feeling that she is trapped in the vulgar little world of Marob, she is looking over the sea where she may sail away to her beloved Greece. She can, however, only copy, and the copies reveal her nature—the slow, careful writing, the overdone and crowded decoration, the lavish expense to make a room into a museum, a room which, in refusing existence to Marob, itself lives in a sub-cultured limbo. Again, having no babies—that other tie to nature—she has collected a leash of stone ones. But if she has made her room a dead thing, she and her world come vividly alive for us in this description. It brings into reality for us a world we had never imagined as having this kind of local and recognisable existence; it gives its life back to the past, or even peoples vacancy, like a kind of resurrection. That sympathetic, animating magic of Mitchison's is highly appropriate in this book, which in Marob at least expresses itself in the annual dance of the Corn King and the Spring Queen to restore life to the dead soil of winter.

As for the magic itself, as it works in Marob through Erif Der and through the fertility dances of the Corn King and Spring Queen, that is 'real' enough—or rather it is allowed as much reality as the more suave rationalism of the court of Kleomenes of Sparta (which Tarrik and then Erif Der visit). Hyperides the Spartan, writing from shared captivity with Tarrik King of Marob in the hands of the predatory Red Riders, is forced to admit the reality of the magic, though he still tries to bend it to his own worldview, 'I am beginning to accept all this about plowing and the Harvest. I am beginning to see the way in which it is compatible with science' (p. 417). But the 'facts' are that if the dance is good, the corn does come in abundance (pp. 149–50); and if the dance or the dancers fail, as once when there is no Corn King present, then the year will be blighted (pp. 195–6, 202). And the Corn King can heal the sick, as he does with the mortally wounded Kotka (pp. 427–9). As for Erif Der, she has her magic from her forbears, and power to harm or even to slay: at the instigation of her family she damages the ritual performance of her husband Tarrik as Corn King at the Midsummer and Harvest festivals, and is only just diverted from having him killed at the bullfighting (pp. 45–7, 50, 54, 56, 70–6, 247); with her magic she can make Yersha sick (pp. 84–5), control the movements of crabs, or even in Sparta, join broken thread (pp. 186–7). But Marob magic has less power in Sparta. Tarrik, when he arrives there, finds the hot magic of Erif Der's wooden star go cold (pp. 127, 128); and in Marob itself Erif's power will not work on the 'Greek' side of Tarrik's nature (p. 54).

The book gives us two main societies, one founded on magic, the other on reason; one passionate and joined to the earth and nature; the other controlled, virtuous, and citified. Each fades into two extremes, the barbarity of the Red Riders who make raids on Marob, and the effete civil degeneracy of Ptolemy of Egypt, where Kleomenes of Sparta and his exiled followers eventually meet their end. Thus Mitchison portrays two currents in human nature. She makes no prescriptions, nor presses hopes concerning their union: there they are, and perhaps it is something in human nature that it can only express itself richly where it pursues one side of the duality. To the civil and spiritual beauty of Kleomenes' court in Sparta is contrasted the ecstasy and magic of the dance on Plowing Eve in Marob:

> She raised her head a little to give another answer and saw that the plow-oxen were quite near, that the fallow field was almost plowed. Suddenly Erif Der was unreasonably and beautifully glad. Her voice, as the crowd was hoping it would, grew louder. She was the spring and she would come with flowers and small leaves and lambs and a growing child. The plow came again across her field of vision and then turned inward towards her. She did not know at all how violently she was shivering. The painted horns of the oxen swung together and apart. She saw the Corn King's eyes over the backs of the beasts. The plow came at her. The singing stopped. At the last moment she leapt to her feet, ran under the horns of the oxen, between their panting flanks, and leapt the plowshare itself as it made the last furrow right through the centre of the fallow field, tearing apart the warmed, flattened grass where she had been sitting. (p. 212)

It is not that Mitchison 'believes' in magic in this novel in the sense of having any religious or metaphysical vision: it is rather that she sees magic power itself as a part of human conviction and a certain kind of society; in such a world it comes naturally to make the corn grow, or to heal the incurable, or even to stop one's hair falling out (p. 30).

Mary Stewart, the 'Merlin' trilogy (1970–9)

This series, *The Crystal Cave* (1970), *The Hollow Hills* (1973) and *The Last Enchantment* (1979), is of a similar historico-fantastic genre to *The Corn King and the Spring Queen*, though now we are dealing with history seen through a considerably embroidered myth—here the legendary story of Merlin and Arthur, set in fifth-century Britain. This 'history' is one reflective of the vogue for fantasy in the 1970s, though its sources go back to Nennius and Geoffrey of Monmouth. The skill which Mary Stewart puts into recreating what it could have been like to live in the Britain of the period just after the departure of the Romans is considerable, even if it does not often reach the kind of literary sophistication that we find in Mitchison's work. The type of magic present is as modest as that in Mitchison's story, though here it involves the ability to see through time and space, and is believed to come from a god: we follow the story through the eyes of the recipient of this magic sight, Merlin.

Part of the force of the story is watching a perfectly 'normal' boy develop imperceptibly into a man who is also a wizard. Stewart is perhaps at her best in the first book, when she is setting the scene, and when the growth of Merlin's power goes together with his unknown father Ambrosius' military skill in founding a new British order which Arthur will inherit. In the second book, we have a long account of the concealment of the young Arthur by Merlin until he is ready to claim the throne; and in the third we are with Merlin's struggles to direct Arthur until he himself is caught by Nimuë and his power ended. The emphasis of the trilogy is rather less on Merlin's magical powers than on his courage, humanity and sense of mission: although the last book effectively portrays the ending of Merlin's magic and the departure of supernatural help from Arthur, the focus is much more on the inevitable letting go of young life that the old have in the end to accept or endure.

Sian Hayton, Cells of Knowledge (1989), *Hidden Daughters* (1992) and
The Last Flight (1993)

Sian Hayton's three novels (the first of which won the Scotsman Saltire First Book of the Year Award in 1989) make up a trilogy set in tenth-century Scotland near to the millennium. Here history has become a backcloth, and the legendary and the fantastic are at the centre. We are presented with the daughters of a giant, and shown their various interactions with mortal men—particularly men of the Church, through whose agency the story is told. The fantastic element is mainly to be found in the first book, where we have shape-shifting, magic castles, prodigious powers—and even, adding a dash of science fiction, wondrous machines. In addition, to win one of the giant's daughters, Marighal, the suitor Kynan must accomplish three fairy-tale feats, with supernatural help, including cutting his bride-to-be to pieces and using her bones to climb a huge tree to a bird's nest. There is also an amazing vision at the end of *Hidden Daughters*. Hayton's inventive and fantastic powers are considerable, and they are joined with what comes over as a powerfully felt vision of the world. But 'magic' for magic's sake is not her interest: the trilogy also shows a steady decrease in the presence of the supernatural.

The books are 'history' to the extent that we have recreations of the life of that period, with an embattled Christianity struggling with paganism and awaiting the end of time, and with a world full of invasion and struggle and yet at the same time witness to a spread of humanity across previously unoccupied lands. In the form of the giant and his daughters, we have an embodiment of an older and magical Celtic culture with which the Church is in conflict. In the first book the giant is slain, and his daughters, previously immortal, then become subject to death. The trilogy is often concerned with how much the Church rejects, or how much it can assimilate, of this dying culture without which it is both arrogant and effete. The picture of continual ecclesiastical refusal is not on the whole a happy one. The title of the first novel, *Cells of Knowledge*, says it all.

The opposition recounted is also between man and woman. For the monks, a woman is almost inherently evil, the serpent's prey, redeemed only by God's grace towards Mary. The giant oppresses his daughters. Husbands are tyrannical to wives. Women are treated as cattle by raiders. In turn, the giant is overthrown by a woman he cast out from his protection, and his a daughters are themselves brought low. But the issue is not only a sexual one. It is one of freedom—and energy. The giants in the story suggest the enormous forces of the human spirit. Unfettered, that spirit can become violent and renegade, as with the giant himself. Too much contained, and it dries into the little terrified certainties of some of the monks. Bound down by mortality, and sustained by self-control and common humanity, it is better seen in the giant's daughters and their acceptance of their fate. Within the world of humanity, which they embrace and the monks refuse, hope is renewed through time and generation, as we move through the three books from a father and his daughters, to bereft sisters, and to mothers and sons and then lovers.

In this trilogy the nature of history itself has become problematic. With another intelligent people beside the human, who take their ancestry from Vulcan and chaos, and who themselves are immortal, being continually reborn in new bodies, time has a different shape from the one we know. Nor is human history any more secure a concept, since for the Church, whose voice we largely hear, spiritual history has only occasional connection with time, and the approaching millennium is seen as the ending of the world. Then again, given the predominance of daughters on the giant side, there is the gender issue: are we to see it as his-story or her-story? Thus it could be said that history itself has here become a series of alternative readings or texts, each fantastic in relation to the others. In short it has become what is called postmodernist.

2. DISCURSIVE, COMIC AND MORAL FANTASY

In these fantasies we do not find a spiritual vision so much as the discussion of ideas: and this gives a measure of detachment, and with it the potential for comedy. Here commitment, zeal and intensity are often set against a worldly-wise and Olympian view, which sees both sides of an issue. Here too the supernatural provides rather more a platform for moral education, philosophical insight and even plain thrill at the absolute, than any transforming metaphysical view of life.

'James Bridie' [O. H. Mavor], 1888–1951

James Bridie is, with J. M. Barrie (much of whose *Peter Pan* he knew by heart), one of the founders of modern Scottish theatre, writing over forty plays from 1928 onwards and encouraging Scottish drama at the Glasgow Citizens' theatre. Bridie's plays, full of a sense both of life's variety and of theatrical effects, are shaped by moral issues and an acceptance of life which were eclipsed in the new 1950s theatre of Osborne, Beckett and Pinter. In addition they are many of them fantasies—of a kind.

Not the least of the features which 'dated' Bridie's plays was their frequent use of the supernatural, particularly of the Christian supernatural, if often in disguised forms such as dreams. Thus in his first play, *The Sunlight Sonata* (1928), we have the devil, the seven deadly sins and the three virtues of faith, hope and charity, all very much alive among a group of modern people; *The Amazed Evangelist* (1931) has the devil and, perhaps less unusually, a seaside landlady who is a black witch; *Tobias and the Angel* (1930), *Jonah and the Whale* (1932) and *Susannah and the Elders* (1937) rework Old Testament and Apocryphal stories involving the supernatural; *Babes in the Wood* (1938) is a vision of contemporary loose morals in terms of hell; *Mr Bolfry* (1943) involves the invocation and questioning of a devil in the manse of a Highland Calvinist ('Wee Free') minister; in *The Queen's Comedy* (1950) we have the Trojan war, surrounded by the discourses and interferences of deities of Olympus and of the sea; and in *The Baikie Charivari* (1952), Bridie returns full circle to the theme of the seven deadly sins under the devil, to show the ignorant evil of seven prophets of modern views.

Bridie's use of the supernatural, and its relation to any system of belief, is however as various as the plays themselves. Bridie rings all the changes: his nature is essentially that of a spiritual jack of all trades. In some of his plays his interest is more in the moral than in the supernatural. Thus in *Tobias and the Angel* the angel is concerned with 'developing' the naive Tobias both morally and personally: here, when Bridie comes to describing the angel Raphael's conflict with the demon Asmoday, he puts it in a little separate 'Pantomime' which he says may be omitted. In *Mr Bolfry*, even the moral is abandoned for the speculative, as the devil engages in a fireside discussion of the nature of the true world conflict rather than in any suggestion that the characters he addresses are his potential prey.

In other plays we have the apologetic Bridie. He is trying to find a role for the supernatural apparatus of Christianity in the modern world. Charles Williams had done it, with more conviction, in his novels, and C. S. Lewis in *The Screwtape Letters* (1942; possibly a source for *Mr Bolfry*); and T. S. Eliot was to do it in *The Cocktail Party* (1949). Here Bridie's devils are urbane, personable figures, modestly dismissive of the medieval horrors attached to them. In *Mr Bolfry*, the devil has to spend much of his time proving his existence to his more sceptical human hearers, and his nature to a more conventionally outraged minister. He tells the disillusioned squaddy Cohen that his view of the world and the war with Hitler is irrelevant and trivial: '"Look up! The real war is beyond and about it [the world]. The War between Good and Evil. The Holy War. It is a War not to destroy but to create."'[4] This devil is an advanced version of the old one, remodelled via Blake: the Reverend McCrimmon can find nothing exceptionable in his existence, but is outraged at his 'heresies'—he preaches dialectic, he fights for 'the New Disorder' which may '"prevail against the armies of the Cherubim"', he depicts God as the oppressor of man through His commandments, and 'Hell' as a mere rude label affixed by repressed individuals such as God and McCrimmon to all that is delightful in life. If Hell wins the war, '"Man's genius will burst its bonds and leap to meet the sun. The living, glorious animal in you will riot in the fields, and the soul will laugh for joy naked but not ashamed"' (pp. 205–6). The devil may be a liar, but his existence here at least is meant to be a truth: and the purpose of showing us that existence is to remind us of the existence of the Good and Evil that underfund it: '"neither you nor I nor anyone else can tell anything about Heaven or Hell, or this very imperfect makeshift of an Earth on which we stand, without our blacks and our whites and our greys, which are whites mixed with black"' (p. 192).

But the moral vision in Bridie, though omnipresent, is rarely so intense, and not always the sole one. The comic element of the plays, their easy acceptance of mundane reality, can mute it. A mere whim has Mr Bolfry called up from the infernal regions, in the midst of a play which for half its time has been concerned with the mating drives of two billeted soldiers. *Tobias and the Angel* is a fine merging of the archangelic with the domestic, so that we are always aware of Raphael's true nature even while he acts as Tobias's paid servant Azarias: but the price is that Raphael's contest with the demon Asmoday, or his refusal to bathe because his wings may be revealed, can only appear comic.[5] Just how much Bridie fully means what he says, and is not compromised by the very world he would anatomise, is difficult to determine. His frequent reliance on past narratives, particularly from the Bible, suggests a need for a literary authority he himself cannot generate. Even in *Mr Bolfry* the use of Blake's 'theology' is a convenient screen. Nor can we be quite sure always of his message. On the one hand the world as we see it is a mere surface, beyond which a cosmic war of Good and Evil is being waged; on the other the everyday reality and vivid individual characters of the plays are the life and soul. On the one hand Blake's view that energy and self are eternal delight seems to be espoused; on the other every human desire can be analysed in terms of the seven deadly sins or the three cardinal virtues.

Bridie is to *some* extent a dabbler—but only because he is a lover of the individual. He tries out a whole series of different stories in his plays—of Burke and Hare, of John Knox, of Malory's Sir Lancelot, Chaucer's *Pardoner's Tale*, several biblical tales, Homer's *Iliad*, fairy-tales. Each of his plays so absorbs itself in the world of its source as to make it appear almost that a different set of beliefs could be behind each. We should not underestimate either the extent to which Bridie could have seen the 'supernatural' as an exciting theatrical device. Impulses far other than the moral and polemical also go into his plays. His theatrical sense is more for the individual scene and character than for the larger design and narrative. In *Mr Bolfry* we do not have a clear overall vision; and the devil himself is, from one point of view, brought in to provide a little spice for the characters, the author and the audience when the other dramatis personae have shown us all there is to know about them. (The other narratives on which Bridie so often relies may also be a way of providing him with a sequential story and design.) His plays are bursting with life, amusement and insight, but his inspiration is more local than architectonic, and more occasionally discursive than consistently visionary. Yet of that he still makes a virtue:

> *'Listen to this. "She came downstairs. She went to an office and sat there all day. She went back to her divan room at six-thirty and stayed there reading library novels. She had no friends and no money to spend . . ." If I make her alive then I have told a story, a story out of which you can take your own meaning, a story you can round off with your own moral. If I put in a murder in the next flat, a love affair with her employer or any such miserable incident I put it in because otherwise no one would buy this story. But they are not the story. The story is the girl herself, coming to life, reaching to you over the footlights and telling you that you are not alone in the world; that other human beings live, suffer, rejoice and play the fool within the same limitations that bind you.'[6]*

That, if we like, is for Bridie the true fantasy, when a made-up person comes 'to life' and can make 'real' people think about their lives. The theatre here almost performs the office of the supernatural in his plays.

Bridie's light touch can be seen in fantasies by other writers of his generation, such as Eric Linklater and Bruce Marshall. Marshall's *Father Malachy's Miracle* (1931), for instance, portrays the vain attempts of a Catholic priest to restore human faith in God, by persuading Him to transport an Edinburgh dance hall called the Garden of Eden to the Bass Rock in the Forth estuary. Though the miracle occurs, it is disbelieved and ignored by humanity at large, to the frustration of Father Malachy, who now asks God to restore things to their proper place. The novel's moral is that 'proof' will not persuade us of the existence of God (who is beyond proof), and that each person must come to faith within him- or herself, and through the Church and the sacraments. Meanwhile, the novel has been a delighted and comic picture of 'fallen' Edinburgh human nature in 1930, which accepts that it is on that fallen nature that salvation must be built. Nevertheless, as comic fantasy, as a correction of religious assumptions, it does mark a stage on the way towards the removal of a basis for the supernatural in fantasy itself. The existence of three able writers producing fantasy of this sort at this one time cannot be other than significant.

3. SCOTTISH FANTASY FOR CHILDREN: A NOTE

Given the hospitality of Scotland to fairy-tales, it is surprising that it has not proved a fertile ground for the re-creation of such tales for children. In England, from the time of the publication of Edgar Taylor's translation of Grimms' tales, 1823–6, there has been a long tradition of fairy-tales for children, from Ruskin's *The King of the Golden River* (first written 1841), Thackeray's comic *The Rose and the Ring* (1855), Kingsley's *The Water-Babies* (1863), the *Alice* books (1865, 1872), and so on down through such writers as Edith Nesbit, Walter de la Mare, J. R. R. Tolkien, C. S. Lewis, Diana Wynne-Jones and hosts more. From Scotland in the nineteenth century we have only George MacDonald's fairy-tales and Lang's *The Gold of Fairnilee*:[7] both were writing in London, and MacDonald placed a unique 'Romantic' value on the child, while Lang's story is a single gleam in his work, which so far as invented fantasy is concerned is otherwise in the Thackeray vein. In the early twentieth century we have of course Barrie's *Peter Pan*: but there again we know that Barrie had a unique obsession with childhood. There does not seem to be that in Scottish culture which particularly values the child as child. Perhaps it is the influence of Calvinism, with its emphasis on serious adult matters; perhaps it is the frequent absence of a sense of relaxed playfulness.

At any rate, what we usually have, apart from the figures mentioned, and works such as Mollie Hunter's stories, or George Mackay Brown's retellings of Orkney folk-tales in his *The Two Fiddlers* (1974), are magic adventures befalling Anglo-Scottish or even English middle-class children on holiday in remote (often Hebridean) parts of Scotland. Of these an early example is W. W. Tarn's *The Treasure of the Isle of Mist* (1919; reissued 1938, 1950, 1959); others are William Croft Dickinson's *Borrobil* (1944) and *The Eildon Tree* (1944; based on 'Thomas the Rhymer'), Katharine Briggs's *Kate Crackernuts* (1965), Winifred Finlay's *The Singing Stones* (1970) and *Beadbonny Ash* (1973), Rosemary Harris's *The Seal Singing* (1971), Joan Aiken's *Winterthing* (1973), or Catherine Storr's *Thursday* (1974; based on 'Tam Lin').[8] Dickinson's *Borrobil* takes off from Tolkien's *The Hobbit* (1937), having a similar quest with dwarves and a dragon; the other works represent a high flowering of Scottish children's fantasy in the surge of interest in the genre from the mid-1960s, and owe a considerable debt to Scottish folklore and fairy-tales, on which their stories are often based. Briggs and

Storr are English writers quarrying Scottish material. All of these books are well and observantly written, and Tarn's book in particular has a vein of mysticism running through it, whereby the fairies reward the courage and good behaviour of the girl-heroine Fiona by giving her not the lost Spanish treasure she thought she was seeking, but the spirit of the island of Skye that she loves. In all of them moral values abound, and with them the implicit purpose of educating children spiritually. The ethic is frequently a caring and sometimes a Christian one: those who are unselfish, those who sympathise with others and look after them, are the blest. Several of these children's fantasies are written by women, and in nearly all of them it is the girl-child who is the heroine. A recent exception so far as the feminine element is concerned, is the late William Raeper, whose *A Witch in Time* (1991) and especially *Warrior of Light* (1993) are fantasies portraying a Christian worldview, if in the latter with rather too much enthusiasm for supernatural machinery to allow the human characters to be very credible. It has to be said, though, that there is little that is identifiably Scottish in Raeper's stories.

4. THE FANTASTIC

Under the head of 'the fantastic' are included those works which essentially have the 'real' world as their subject and use fantasy and the supernatural not for themselves but as a means of expressing or portraying the self or this world. A fantasy is a story involving the supernatural, but the 'fantastic' is a descriptive technique.

James Thomson's *The City of Dreadful Night* (1874) uses fantastic techniques and allusions to Dante's *Inferno* to describe the poet's despair amid the cityscape of Victorian London:

> The street-lamps burn amidst the baleful glooms,
>   Amidst the soundless solitudes immense
> Of ranged mansions dark and still as tombs.
>   The silence which benumbs or strains the sense
> Fulfils with awe the soul's despair unweeping:
> Myriads of habitants are ever sleeping,
>   Or dead, or fled from nameless pestilence!
>
> (I, 43–9)[9]

Thomson, an atheist, had little time for the supernatural save as a poetic device, and for metaphysical systems not at all.[10] The pressure of his vision is downwards to extinction: in his Swiftian satire, 'Proposals for the Speedy Extinction of Evil and Misery' (1868), the best way forward he finds for mankind is universal suicide.[11] *The City of Dreadful Night* is of the same genre as T. S. Eliot's later *The Waste Land* (1922), another dark picture of London using fantastic techniques, if with rather more juxtaposition of times, places and planes of reality than in Thomson. Apart from the often phantasmagoric savagery of John Hay's *Gillespie* (1914), or the mutating visions of Hugh MacDiarmid's *A Drunk Man Looks at the Thistle* (1926), which follows on from T. S. Eliot, this fantastic technique is not found strikingly in Scottish literature again until after about 1970, with such poets as D. M. Black and Liz Lochhead, and novelists such as Emma Tennant, Ian Banks or James Meek.

Both D. M. Black and Liz Lochhead recreate Grimms' fairy-tales—Black in 'The House of Felicity' (1976–7), and Lochhead in her sequence *The Grimm Sisters* (1981). Black's poem is, as he says of his poetry generally, 'an attempt to understand some area of feeling which has arisen, and will be resolved, elsewhere.'[12] The poem is a lattice of different human relationships, father-daughter, mother-son, husband-wife, set in a fairy-tale idiom designed to heighten their typicality and continual recurrence: it explores a psychological sequence, against a literary template that suggests something patterned, determined, archetypal, behind all the apparently free negotiations of the human will. As for Lochhead's *The Grimm Sisters*, this is not dissimilar, though it is more concerned with specifically feminine experience.

> yes, Rosebud, I
> suppose you were right.
> Better than hanging around
> a hundred years for Someone
> to hack his way through the thorns
> for the shoe that fits
> for chance to have you cough up
> the poisoned apple
> wodged in your gullet.
> So you (anything for a quiet
> life) embrace the beast, endure.
>   ('II: Beauty & The')[13]

As for the novelists, it is particularly recent women novelists, such as Jessie Kesson, Emma Tennant and Sharman MacDonald, who use fantastic techniques in their work, such as doubles, abrupt shifts of time or place, intertextuality and dream sequences, as part of their explorations of feminine identity.[14] Fantasy has for long been a neglected literary genre, just as women have been repressed and their voices unheard: we have seen how Scottish fantasy from the beginning has explored and often celebrated the feminine side of human nature; and it is not surprising that the recent popularity of the fantastic and the new confidence of women should bring the two together in literary creation. But the interest is not in fantasy and the supernatural for themselves, but only as a means of expressing and exploring the human problems of identity, repression and relating in this world. There is a similar character to the work of Angela Carter (whose father was a Scot), particularly in her *The Infernal Desire Machines of Dr Hoffman* (1972) a novel whose very title is a series of subversions: identity, sexuality and the unconscious are its recurrent concerns.[15]

Ian Banks portrays a unique form of female repression in *The Wasp Factory* (1984). Here, a father whose wife treated him badly and deserted him, comes so to hate the female sex that he brings up his daughter to believe that she is a boy whose genitals were bitten off by the family dog, when 'he' was three. The child murders a series of its infant relations, in rage, it later surmises, that they will grow to full adulthood where it (so it believes) will not. The child also has elaborate rituals for propitiating the rent in its existence, in the form of sacrificial poles for the heads of animals it slays, and an elaborate 'factory' in which wasps select the doom of their choice. Fantasy here is a function of a psychic inferno: and the sense of that inferno is increased by our not being given any explanations for the grotesque behaviour of the child until the end of the novel. Here fantasy is being portrayed as a function of the unnatural. It is interesting that this is a novel of anxiety by a man. The modern use of the fantastic by male writers is rather more to create a sense of something wrong than to explore the possibilities of life, as often with women. Still more recently we have a work such as James Meek's *Last Orders* (1992), a collection of stories written mainly as a satire on Scottish mental self-enclosures, mediated by a series of often sinister images and fantastic inversions.

The 'fantastic' does constitute the present direction of fantasy, which might broadly be called magical realism, whereby visions of this world are heightened by the grotesque or subverted by postmodernist disjunctions. This strain in fantasy is actually a long one, going back to E. T. A. Hoffmann, Poe, Lautréamont, Rimbaud or Kafka.[16] It has taken over from the fantasy which looks beyond the world to a supernatural order or realm, partly because the contexts of belief that sustained a supernaturalist view of life have been worn away. Whether it will retain this pre-eminence, whether indeed the fantastic itself will continue to be a significant medium through which to view the world, is for time to tell.

Notes

1 John Buchan, *Witch Wood* (Edinburgh: Canongate, 1988), p. 67.
2 Jill Benton makes the feminine issue the central one in her *Naomi Mitchison: A Biography* (London: Pandora Press, 1992), pp. 64–9. While clearly the novel gives a powerful new role for women, other issues are just as crucial.

3 Naomi Mitchison, *The Corn King and the Spring Queen* (Edinburgh: Canongate, 1990), p. 23.

4 James Bridie, *Mr Bolfry*, in *Plays for Plain People* (London: Constable, 1944), p. 205.

5 Bridie, *Tobias and the Angel*, in *A Sleeping Clergyman and Other Plays* (London: Constable, 1934), pp. 25, 49, 55–6.

6 Passage from the close of Bridie's autobiography, *One Way of Living* (1939), cited in Terence Tobin, *James Bridie (Osborne Henry Mavor)* (Boston: Twayne, 1980), p. 75.

7 There are also Catherine Sinclair's comical short tale 'Uncle David's Nonsensical Story of Giants and Fairies', in her *Holiday House* (1839), which is one of the first of British invented fairy-tales, and the Rev. Norman Macleod's story 'The Gold Thread' (1861), a more solemn allegorical tale enjoining faith in God throughout life.

8 See Marion Lochhead, *The Renaissance of Wonder in Children's Literature* (Edinburgh: Canongate, 1977), pp. 141–8, 155–62.

9 A not dissimilar vision, expanded to interplanetary proportions, is found in Thomson's prose piece, 'A Walk Abroad' (1866), in his *Essays and Phantasies* (London: Reeves and Turner, 1881), pp. 257–68.

10 Thomson, 'On the Worth of Metaphysical Systems' (1876), in *Essays and Phantasies*, pp. 296–302.

11 *Essays and Phantasies*, pp. 51–103.

12 D. M. Black, *Collected Poems, 1964–87* (Edinburgh: Polygon, 1991), p. xi.

13 Liz Lochhead, *Dreaming Frankenstein and Collected Poems* (Edinburgh: Polygon, 1984), p. 80.

14 On these see Carol Anderson, 'Listening to the Women Talk', in Gavin Wallace and Randall Stevenson, eds, *The Scottish Novel Since the Seventies* (Edinburgh: Edinburgh University Press, 1993), pp. 170–86.

15 See my '"In the Demythologising Business": Angela Carter's *The Infernal Desire Machines of Dr Hoffman*', in Kath Filmer, ed., *Twentieth-Century Fantasists: Essays on Culture, Society and Belief in Twentieth-Century Mythopoeic Literature* (London: Macmillan, 1992), pp. 148–60.

16 See Rosemary Jackson, *Fantasy: The Literature of Subversion* (London: Methuen, 1981).

CHAPTER FIFTEEN

Conclusion

W E CAN NOW see that in its fantasy literature Scotland has a vital and so far largely unacknowledged tradition of writing, which represents the other side of Scottish fiction from the realist mode. It should also be clear that most of these fantasy works are both powerful and subtle as imaginative literature, easily able to bear comparison with more established books. Scots can therefore be aware that they have a richer and more various literature than they may have thought, and one of which they can be justifiably proud.

If we are now to make some wider generalisations concerning Scottish fantasy, the preliminary point to reiterate is the great variety of the works we have grouped together under this heading. The worlds of the Never Land, Tormance, Fairnilee or Unthank, for instance, would appear to be so different as to admit no feature in common. Such diversity is not, as already observed, unique to Scottish fantasy: it can be found also in England, in the contrasts between, say Kingsley's *The Water-Babies*, T. F. Powys' *Mr Weston's Good Wine* or J. R. R. Tolkien's *The Lord of the Rings*. It emerges, first, from the individualism of British culture, and second, from the fact that no such genre as 'fantasy' is really thought of till about the time of Tolkien. Scott writes what he sees as 'the supernatural in fictitious composition', Hogg recreates folklore or imitates German Romantic models, MacDonald writes 'fairy-tales' or 'romances', Stevenson an urban Gothic novel, Lindsay a vision, Gunn a dystopia, Brown a sacramentalist novel, Gray a life in two worlds. While some of them are part-indebted to one or more of each other, such as MacDonald to Carlyle, or Stevenson to Hogg, or Lindsay to MacDonald, many are not evidently so, such as Carlyle, Macleod, Barrie, Gunn or Brown. Nevertheless, as already seen in the Introduction, there is a remarkable number of features shared by these works, features which can be largely predicated on their use of the supernatural and their explorations of the imagination. If they all involve looking at that which lies 'beyond' nature as we understand it, and if they are all in some distinct way Scottish, then they begin to give out similar signals. One of the interests of writing this book has been the way these works are at once so diverse and yet have so much in common, held together apparently by threads but actually by strong ligaments. To talk of Scottish fantasy is not to speak of that which immediately presents itself with any single or obviously recognisable face: we are dealing with what looks like an assembly of individuals all appearing to gaze in different directions, and yet all united by hidden relationships below the level of sight.

Now to the generalisations. We saw in the introductory chapter that Scottish fantasy could be said to be inward-looking: and during the book we developed an idea of it as continually interested in, or even imitative of the form of, the unconscious. Practically all nineteenth-century Scottish fantasies explore this area of mind: the unanimity here, even given the then international cultural interest in promptings of the mind below the respectable and rational, is striking. Scott can show the rational mind overthrown; Hogg and Stevenson depict the growth of the mind's dark forces; Lang and Barrie variously enter the unconscious world in its association with childhood; MacDonald goes into the depths of his fantastic imagination to find God; Macleod reveals some of the primal patterns underlying life; Oliphant looks at the super-conscious, that intuition of a transcendent world which manifests itself only to certain states of mind; Carlyle tries to break down our rigid ways of seeing to display the supernatural wonder in life. These works often mirror the unconscious in their form, being unstructured, mysterious or even fragmentary. Many of them work to dislocate the certainties of the conscious mind through paradox, discontinuity, uncertainty and clashes of idiom. This interest is continued in the twentieth century, even when the stimulus born out of Victorian suppression of the unconscious is removed. Lindsay is drawn to the 'sublime', which, while it is not part of the perceiving mind, is associated with the dislocation of fixed mental categories, in a narrative which has the lineaments of a dream while also being a vision. Gunn looks to the 'great deep', to the promptings of a world which in its true form overthrows rational control for magic. Brown gives us a world whose true spiritual patterns are beyond common sight, and make a supernatural garment both of civilisation and of sainthood. Gray's Thaw breaks through all the structures of life into death, and so too his reincarnated self Lanark in the life beyond that, until he has so discovered himself at a primal and instinctual level that he can die indeed. Every one of Margaret Elphinstone's stories is written in support of unconscious and intuitive ways of seeing. This is all in marked contrast to much modern English fantasy, which places value on order, control and structure—witness the patterned Christian worlds of Charles Williams or C. S. Lewis, the minutely organised universe of J. R. R. Tolkien, the Arthurian civilisation of T. H. White, the separation of individual consciousness from the unconscious world of Gormenghast in Mervyn Peake's 'Titus' books. One exception here is Angela Carter's *The Infernal Desire Machines of Dr Hoffman* (1972)—and as previously observed, Carter's father and a small part of her childhood were Scottish. In America it is the ordered Lewis-Tolkien type of fantasy that has most taken hold.

Scotland's fantasy, then, is unusual in this interest in the unconscious. And this interest, moreover, is one we cannot simply leave with fantasy, but seems rather something of a national characteristic whose presence is heightened by the action of fantasy. The same can be said of the recurrent interest of Scottish fantasy in questioning of the self—a theme also seen throughout Scottish literature. There is an interrogative character to Scottish fantasy, which is involved continually with the potential of identity to disintegrate. The use of the doppelgänger, the alternative self, is frequent, more so even than in European literature—Wringhim/Gil-Martin (Hogg), Lilith/Mara in MacDonald's *Lilith*, Jekyll and Hyde, Mr Darling and Captain Hook, Hakon and Magnus, Thaw and Lanark. (English fantasy tends to deal much more with the 'other'—the Red Queen in no way reflects Alice, nor the evil Sauron Tolkien's Frodo, nor Peake's Steerpike his Titus.) In several of the visionary poems of the medieval and Renaissance Scottish 'makars', the individual is marked out and excluded by the collective. Thus there is the imprisoned James I of *The Kingis Quair*, whose whole struggle is to become acceptable to his lady and to life in general, and win release from the prison of his isolated self; Cresseid in Henryson's *Testament*, cast out and made a repulsive leper by the gods who are in a sense projections of her inability to live with herself; Dunbar's lover in 'The Goldyn Targe', overwhelmed by the forces of love when he reveals his presence to them, and then abandoned by them; Gavin Douglas's similar unfortunate in 'The Palice of Honour'. All of these visionary poems are in a sense journeys into the self and its deepest windings; and this is seen also in Montgomerie's *The Cherrie and the Slae*. In Macpherson's 'Ossian' poems, the boundaries of the self are blurred. In Burns's, Scott's and Hogg's tales the self and its securities are continually under attack. In Carlyle's *Sartor Resartus* the identity of the elusive Teufelsdröckh is in question; and his story is itself a picture of how his old identity and place in the community are lost for a new and freer being—rather the process that is followed in Gray's *Lanark* (and Gray's *Poor Things* is precisely about the identity of the supposedly resurrected lady). MacDonald's *Phantastes* portrays a journey in part into the unconscious self of Anodos; and his *Lilith* is full of questions of Vane's being. In Lang's *The Gold of Fairnilee* the self is subject to illusion and is forfeit to the fairies; in Mrs Oliphant's stories there is questioning of ghostly continuations of the self; the characters in Fiona Macleod have their being dissolved or destroyed in larger patterns of action; *Peter Pan* explores the struggle to keep the self from change. Maskull in *A Voyage to Arcturus* is 'my skull', and has his identity at once explored and destroyed: the whole book is written against the self and its desires. In *The Green Isle of the Great Deep* Neil Gunn describes attempts by thought police to turn all the people of their country to automata by brain-washing. George Mackay Brown shows in the plot and the framented structure of *Magnus* the attempt to destroy the being of Magnus and the loss of integrity of his followers, till Magnus finds another identity for himself founded in that of Christ. In almost every one of Margaret Elphinstone's stories the civilised self is under threat, or its premises challenged. In sum, in every Scottish fantasy we have looked at, the self is either outside society, open to question, subject to doubt or shame, undermined, divided, defiantly asserted, or transformed.

What are we to make of this? At the level of individual works, this assault on the self is sometimes seen as a good (MacDonald, Lindsay, Elphinstone), sometimes as a destructive evil (Stevenson, Gunn). But at the deeper level of the recurrence of this motif, it seems to express a continual desire to reach bedrock, to plumb a depth of certainty or a completeness of experience beyond what life can normally offer (hence the very reach to the fantastic). Even Gunn's *The Green Isle of the Great Deep*, which 'asserts' the self, follows an analytic process towards a ground of all being in God. Whether the repeated portrayal of the self under attack can be construed as a version of Scotland itself under threat—either through its own cultural self-divisions or in relation to the perceived rapacity of England—can only be aired, not answered here. But what Scottish fantasy seems to register is a fundamental lack of confidence in the conscious or civil self. And this distrust is often peculiarly expressed in a journey away from that self, into the innermost or unconscious areas of the mind. While the theme of the uncertain self is found elsewhere in Scottish literature, it appears in unique form in Scottish fantasy—and with particular force, for the medium of the supernatural throws divisions into sharper relief.

To these characteristics we may add one more which distinguishes Scottish fantasy, and that is its emphasis on the power of women and the worth of feminine values. Such a stress on the feminine might be said to fit naturally with the themes of the unconscious and of identity. Women dominate to a marked degree in the poems of the 'makars'. James I is virtually treated as a child by Venus, Minerva and Fortune in *The Kingis Quair*. Cresseid, punished though she is, is Henryson's central interest in the *Testament*. Dunbar in 'The Goldyn Targe' and Gavin Douglas in 'The Palice of Honour' are overpowered or directed by women. Only Montgomerie's *The Cherrie and the Slae*, where a man has to try to make up his mind, is different here. Burns's Tam o' Shanter escapes one group of women (the witches) only to fall into the hands of another, his wife. Scott's General Browne is unmanned by a female spectre, as is the son by his mother in 'The Highland Widow'. Those of Hogg's fantasies that we looked at all put women at the centre, even *The Confessions of a Justified Sinner*, where the 'masculine' brother is killed and the effeminate one dominates the story. In Carlyle's *Sartor Resartus* it is the destructive influence of a woman that provokes the formation of Herr Teufelsdröckh's philosophy. Female figures control and direct in many of MacDonald's fantasies, whether for good or ill. The deluded

Randal in Lang's *The Gold of Fairnilee* has to be rescued by the girl Jeanie. Women are great survivors, in contrast to men, in Macleod's tales, all of which are the productions of a man who decided to write as a woman (contrast his English near-contemporary E. Nesbit in her fantasies, who chose to pretend to be a man). Peter Pan and the lost boys get the mother they have longed for in Wendy. David Lindsay increasingly stresses the power of individual females and of ancient matriarchy in his fantasies. It is Mary's protective love that saves Art in Gunn's *The Green Isle of the Great Deep*. Brown's Magnus gives us a gentle, 'womanly' man as hero. In Gray's *Lanark* the masculinity of the protagonists is continually being challenged or defeated. Margaret Elphinstone is overtly feminist, to the point where her women take on some 'male' heroic characteristics.

These three features—the stress on the unconscious, on uncertain identity and on femininity—draw together some of the characteristics of Scottish fantasy we explored in the introduction. They seem to be not only defining features of Scottish as opposed to other fantasy, but literary expressions of one side of the Scottish character itself—the inwardness and love of mystery and dream that are often ignored, the uncertainty and passion that are so often denied. These features of Scottish fantasy come together in a current of longing. Most striking, more perhaps than any other national fantasy, this is a fantasy of desire. Think of Teufelsdröckh's painful sense of the wonder in life, the longings of MacDonald's heroes, the desire of Stevenson's Jekyll for forbidden pleasures, of Lang's Randal for treasure and glamour, of Macleod's heroes for a savage joy, of Barrie's Peter Pan for everlasting childhood, Lindsay's Maskull for Muspel, Mitchison and Buchan for a lost past, Gunn for a fading Highland utopia, Brown's Magnus for a heavenly garment, Elphinstone for a sweet, elusive freedom and Gray for the mere sense of being able to breathe freely beneath a sky not mortgaged to the social system. In their fantasy the Scots seem continually to express a lost wholeness, a sense of a threatened or dispossessed self, an acute sense of a distant paradise that beckons, and mocks, and frustrates, and which sometimes, when not looked at, is momentarily there. And so for them their own country, Scotland, is always not fully there, a presence beneath a distant hill, a desire that runs like blood through every frail imagination of the place.

Bibliography

Aiken, Joan, *Winterthing* (London: Cape, 1973)

Aitken, Adam J., Matthew P. MacDiarmid and Derick S. Thomson, eds, *Bards and Makars* (Glasgow: Glasgow University Press, 1977)

Aitken, Hannah, *A Forgotten Heritage: Original Folk Tales of Lowland Scotland* (Edinburgh: Scottish Academic Press, 1973)

Alaya, Flavia, *William Sharp—'Fiona Macleod', 1855–1905* (Cambridge, Mass.: Harvard University Press, 1970)

Anderson, Carol, 'Listening to the Women Talk', in Wallace and Stevenson, eds, *The Scottish Novel Since the Seventies*, pp. 170–86

Avery, Gillian, with Angela Bull, *Nineteenth-Century Children: Heroes and Heroines in English Children's Stories, 1780–1900* (London: Hodder and Stoughton, 1965)

Banks, Ian, *The Wasp Factory* (London: Macmillan, 1984)

Bannatyne Manuscript, 1568, The, 4 vols (Glasgow: Hunterian Club, 1896)

Barrie, J. M., *Mary Rose: A Play in Three Acts* (London: Hodder and Stoughton, 1925)

——, *Peter Pan: A Fantasy in Five Acts* (London: Samuel French, 1988)

——, *Peter Pan [Peter and Wendy]* (London: Collins, Armada, 1988)

——, *The Plays of J. M. Barrie* (London: Hodder and Stoughton, 1928)

Bawcutt, Priscilla, *Dunbar the Makar* (Oxford: Clarendon Press, 1992)

Benton, Jill, *Naomi Mitchison: A Biography* (London: Pandora Press, 1992)

Berman, Barbara L., 'The Strange Case of Dr Jekyll and Mr Hyde', in Frank N. Magill, ed., *Survey of Modern Fantasy Literature*, 5 vols (Englewood Cliffs, N. J.: Salem Press, 1983), IV, 1834–9

Birkin, Andrew, *J. M. Barrie and the Lost Boys* (London: Constable, 1979)

Black, D. M., *Collected Poems, 1964–87* (Edinburgh: Polygon, 1991)

Bold, Alan, *George Mackay Brown* (Edinburgh: Oliver and Boyd, 1978)

Bridie, James [pseud. of Osborne Henry Mavor], *Plays for Plain People* (London: Constable, 1944)

——, *A Sleeping Clergyman and Other Plays* (London: Constable, 1934)

Briggs, Julia, *Night Visitors: The Rise and Fall of the English Ghost Story* (London: Faber, 1977)

Briggs, K. M., *The Fairies in Tradition and Literature* (London: Routledge and Kegan Paul, 1967)

——, *Kate Crackernuts* (Edinburgh: Canongate, Kelpies, 1987)

——, and Ruth L. Tongue, eds, *Folktales of England* (London: Routledge and Kegan Paul, 1965)

Brookes, G. H., *The Rhetorical Form of Carlyle's Sartor Resartus* (Berkeley: University of California Press, 1972)

Brown, George Mackay, *Andrina and Other Stories* (London: Triad Grafton, 1990)

——, *A Calendar of Love and Other Stories* (London: Hogarth Press, 1967)

——, *Hawkfall and Other Stories* (London: Triad Grafton, 1990)

——, *Let's See the Orkney Islands* (Fort William: W. S. Thomson, 1948)

——, *Magnus* (Glasgow: Richard Drew, 1987)

——, *The Masked Fisherman and Other Stories* (London: Triad Grafton, 1991)

——, *Pictures in the Cave* (Edinburgh: Canongate, Kelpies, 1990)

——, *The Sun's Net* (Edinburgh: W. and R. Chambers, 1992)

——, *Time in a Red Coat* (London: Grafton, 1991)

——, *Three Plays: The Loom of Light, The Well and The Voyage of Saint Brendan* (London: Chatto and Windus and the Hogarth Press, 1984)

——, *The Two Fiddlers* (London: Chatto and Windus, 1974)

Buchan, David, ed., *Scottish Tradition: A Collection of Scottish Folk Literature* (London: Routledge, 1974)

Buchan, John, *Witch Wood* (Edinburgh: Canongate, 1988)

Burns, John, 'Myths and Marvels', in Wallace and Stevenson, eds, *The Scottish Novel Since the Seventies*, pp. 71–81

Burns, Robert, *The Poems and Songs of Robert Burns*, ed. J. Kinsley (Oxford: Clarendon Press, 1968)

Byron, George Gordon Noel, 6th Baron, *The Poetical Works of Lord Byron* (London: Oxford University Press, 1959)

Campbell, J. F., ed., *Popular Tales of the West Highlands*, 4 vols (Edinburgh: Edmonston and Douglas, 1860–2)

Campbell, Joseph, *The Hero with a Thousand Faces* (Princeton: Princeton University Press, 1968)

Carlyle, Thomas, *Critical and Miscellaneous Essays*, 5 vols (London: Chapman and Hall, 1899)

——, 'Extracts from a Note Book', in J. A. Froude, *Thomas Carlyle: A History of the First Forty Years of his Life*

——, *Sartor Resartus*, eds Kerry McSweeney and Peter Sabor (Oxford: Oxford University Press, 1987)

Carpenter, Humphrey, 'J. M. Barrie and *Peter Pan*: "That terrible masterpiece"', *Secret Gardens: A Study of the Golden Age of Children's Literature* (London: Allen and Unwin, 1985), pp. 170–87

Charlton, Bruce, 'The Story So Far', in Crawford and Nairn, eds, *The Arts of Alasdair Gray*, pp. 10–21

Child, F. J., ed., *The English and Scottish Ballads*, 5 vols (New York: Folklore Press, 1957)

Craig, Cairns, 'Going Down to Hell is Easy: *Lanark*, Realism and the Limits of the Imagination', in Crawford and Nairn, eds, *The Arts of Alasdair Gray*, pp. 90–107

Craik, Thomas W., 'The Substance and Structure of *The Testament of Cresseid*', in Aitken, Adam J., *et al*, eds, *Bards and Makars*, pp. 22–6

Crawford, Robert and Thom Nairn, eds, *The Arts of Alasdair Gray* (Edinburgh: Edinburgh University Press, 1991)

Crawford, Thomas, 'James Hogg: The Play of Region and Nation', in Gifford, ed., *The History of Scottish Literature, Volume 3*, pp. 89–106

Curtius, Ernst Robert, *European Literature and the Latin Middle Ages* (New York: Pantheon, 1953)

Daiches, David, *Carlyle: The Paradox Reconsidered*, Thomas Green Lectures no.6 (Edinburgh: The Carlyle Society, 1981)

Dickinson, William Croft, *Borrobil* (Harmondsworth: Puffin, 1964)

——, *The Eildon Tree* (London: Cape, 1944)

Douglas, Gavin, *The Poetical Works of Gavin Douglas*, ed. John Small, 4 vols (Edinburgh: William Patterson, 1874)

Dunbar, William, *Poems*, ed. James Kinsley (Oxford: Clarendon Press, 1958)

Elphinstone, Margaret, *An Apple from a Tree and Other Visions* (London: The Women's Press, 1991)

——, *The Incomer* (London: Women's Press, 1987)

——, *A Sparrow's Flight* (Edinburgh: Polygon, 1990)

Finlay, Winifred, *The Singing Stones* (London: Harrap, 1970)

——, *Beadbonny Ash* (London: Harrap, 1973)

Froude, J. A., *Thomas Carlyle: A History of the First Forty Years of his Life, 1795–1835*, 2 vols (London: Longmans, 1882)

——, *Thomas Carlyle: A History of his Life in London, 1834–1881*, 2 vols (London: Longmans, 1884)

Garden, Mrs [Mary Gray Hogg], *Memorials of James Hogg, the Ettrick Shepherd*, 3rd edn, (Paisley: Alexander Gardner, 1903)

Garrett, Peter K., 'Cries and Voices: Reading *Jekyll and Hyde*', in Veeder and Hirsch, eds, *Dr Jekyll and Mr Hyde after One Hundred Years*, pp. 59–72

Gifford, Douglas, *James Hogg* (Edinburgh: Ramsay Head Press, 1976)

——, ed. *The History of Scottish Literature, Volume 3, The Nineteenth Century* (Aberdeen: Aberdeen University Press, 1988)

Glover, Donald E., *C. S. Lewis: The Art of Enchantment* (Athens, Ohio: Ohio University Press, 1981)

Gordon, Patrick, *The First booke of the famous Historye of Penardo and Laissa other wayes callid the warres of Love and Ambitione* . . . (Dort: George Waters, 1615)

Gray, Alasdair, 'Alasdair Gray Interviewed by Jenny Renton', *Scottish Book Collector*, no. 7 (Aug./Sept. 1988), pp 2–5.

——, *Lanark: A Life in Four Books* (Edinburgh: Canongate, 1981)

——, *Poor Things: Episodes from the Early Life of Archibald McCandless M. D., Scottish Public Health Officer* (London: Bloomsbury, 1992)

Gunn, Neil, *The Atom of Delight* (London: Faber and Faber, 1956)

——, *The Green Isle of the Great Deep* (London: Faber and Faber, 1944)

——, 'On Belief', *Scots Magazine*, XXIV, no. 1 (Oct., 1940), pp. 51–5

——, *The Other Landscape* (London: Faber and Faber, 1954)

——, *Selected Letters*, ed. J. B. Pick (Edinburgh: Polygon, 1987)

——, *Sun Circle* (Edinburgh: The Porpoise Press, 1933)

——, *The Well at the World's End* (London: Faber and Faber, 1950)

——, *Young Art and Old Hector* (London: Faber and Faber, 1942)

Harris, Rosemary, *The Seal Singing* (London: Faber, 1971)

Hart, Francis Russell, and J. B. Pick, eds, *Neil M. Gunn: A Highland Life* (London: John Murray, 1981)

Hartland, Edwin Sidney, ed., *English Fairy and Other Folk Tales*, (London: Walter Scott, 1890)

Hayton, Sian, *Cells of Knowledge* (Edinburgh: Polygon, 1989)

——, *Hidden Daughters* (Edinburgh: Polygon, 1992)

——, *The Last Flight* (Edinburgh: Polygon, 1993)

Henryson, Robert, *The Poems and Fables of Robert Henryson*, ed. H. Harvey Wood (Edinburgh: Oliver and Boyd, 1958)

History of Scottish Literature, The, gen. ed. Cairns Craig, 4 vols (Aberdeen: Aberdeen University Press, 1987–8)

Hogg, James, *Memoir of the Author's Life and Familiar Anecdotes of Sir Walter Scott*, ed. Douglas S. Mack (Edinburgh: Scottish Academic Press, 1972)

——, 'Nature's Magic Lantern', in *Works*, II, pp. 459–62

——, *The Private Memoirs and Confessions of a Justified Sinner*, ed. John Carey (London: Oxford University Press, 1969)

——, *Selected Poems*, ed. Douglas S. Mack (Oxford: Clarendon Press, 1970)

——, *Selected Poems and Songs*, ed. David Groves (Edinburgh: Scottish Academic Press, 1986)

——, *Selected Stories and Sketches*, ed. Douglas S. Mack (Edinburgh: Scottish Academic Press, 1982)

——, *The Three Perils of Man*, ed. Douglas Gifford (Edinburgh: Scottish Academic Press, 1989)

——, *The Works of the Ettrick Shepherd*, ed. the Rev. Thomas Thomson, 2 vols (London: Blackie, 1876)

Holbrook, David, Introduction to George MacDonald, *Phantastes* (London: Dent, 1983)

Hook, Andrew, 'Scotland and Romanticism: the International Scene', in Hook, ed., *The History of Scottish Literature, Volume 2*
——, ed., *The History of Scottish Literature, Volume 2, 1660–1800* (Aberdeen: Aberdeen University Press, 1987)

Jack, R. D. S., *Alexander Montgomerie* (Edinburgh: Scottish Academic Press, 1985)
——, *The Road to the Never Land: A Reassessment of J. M. Barrie's Dramatic Art* (Aberdeen: Aberdeen University Press, 1991)
——, ed., *The History of Scottish Literature, Volume 1, Origins to 1660* (Aberdeen: Aberdeen University Press, 1988)
Jackson, Rosemary, *Fantasy: The Literature of Subversion* (London: Methuen, 1981)
James I of Scotland, *The Kingis Quair*, ed. John Norton-Smith (Oxford: Clarendon Press, 1971)
Jefford, Andrew, 'Dr Jekyll and Professor Nabokov: Reading a Reading', in Andrew Noble, ed., *Robert Louis Stevenson* (London: Vision Press, 1983), pp. 47–72

King, Stephen, *Danse Macabre* (London: MacDonald, 1981)
Kingsley, Charles, *The Water-Babies, A Fairy Tale for a Land-Baby* (London: Macmillan, 1863)

Lang, Andrew, *The Gold of Fairnilee* (Bristol: J. W. Arrowsmith, 1888)
——, *The Princess Nobody: A Tale of Fairy Land* (Bristol: J. W. Arrowsmith, 1884)
——, *Prince Prigio* (Bristol: J. W. Arrowsmith, 1889)
——, *Prince Ricardo of Pantouflia, being the Adventures of Prince Prigio's Son* (Bristol: J. W. Arrowsmith, 1893)
——, ed. and introd., *The Blue Fairy Book* (London: Longmans, 1889)
Langstaff, Eleanor de Selms, *Andrew Lang* (Boston, Mass.: Twayne Publishers, 1978)
LaValley, Albert, *Carlyle and the Idea of the Modern* (New Haven: Yale University Press, 1968)
Lawler, Donald, 'Reframing *Jekyll and Hyde*: Robert Louis Stevenson and the Strange Case of Gothic Science Fiction', in Veeder and Hirsch, eds, *Dr Jekyll and Mr Hyde after One Hundred Years*, pp. 247–61
Le Quesne, A. L., *Carlyle* (Oxford: Oxford University Press, 1982)
Lewis, C. S., *The Allegory of Love: A Study in Medieval Tradition* (London: Oxford University Press, 1958)
——, *Letters of C. S. Lewis*, ed. W. H. Lewis (London: Bles, 1966)
——, *Surprised by Joy: The Shape of my Early Life* (London: Bles, 1955)
——, ed. and introd., *George MacDonald: An Anthology* (London: Bles, 1946)
Lindsay, David, *Devil's Tor* (London: Putnam's, 1932)

——, *The Haunted Woman* (Edinburgh: Canongate 1987)

——, 'Philosophical Notes', in David Lindsay issue of *Lines Review*, ed. Robin Fulton, no.40 (March, 1972), pp. 22–7

——, 'Sketch Notes for a New System of Philosophy', National Library of Scotland MS accession no.5616

——, *The Violet Apple and The Witch*, ed. J. B. Pick (Chicago: Chicago Review Press, 1976)

——, *A Voyage to Arcturus* (Edinburgh: Canongate, 1992)

Lindsay, Maurice, *History of Scottish Literature* (London: Robert Hale, 1977)

Lyndsay, Sir David, *The Works of Sir David Lyndsay of the Mount*, ed. David Laing, 3 vols (Edinburgh: William Patterson, 1879)

Lochhead, Liz, 'The Grimm Sisters', *Dreaming Frankenstein and Collected Poems* (Edinburgh: Polygon, 1984)

Lochhead, Marion, *The Renaissance of Wonder in Children's Literature* (Edinburgh: Canongate, 1977)

Lumsden, Alison, 'Innovation and Reaction in the Fiction of Alasdair Gray', in Wallace and Stevenson, eds, *The Scottish Novel Since the Seventies*, pp. 115–26

McDannell, Colleen, and Bernhard Lang, *Heaven: A History* (New Haven: Yale University Press, 1988)

McDiarmid, Matthew P., 'Robert Henryson in his Poems', in Aitken, Adam J., *et al*, eds, *Bards and Makars*, pp. 27–40

MacDonald, George, *At the Back of the North Wind* (London: Dent, 1956)

——, 'The Fantastic Imagination', *A Dish of Orts; Chiefly Papers on the Imagination, and on Shakspere* (London: Sampson Low, 1893) pp. 313–22

——, 'The Imagination', *A Dish of Orts*, pp. 1–42

——, *The Light Princess and Other Tales* (London: Gollancz, 1967)

——, *Phantastes and Lilith* (London: Gollancz, 1962)

——, *The Princess and the Goblin and The Princess and Curdie*, ed. Roderick McGillis (Oxford: Oxford University Press, 1990)

MacDonald, Greville, *George MacDonald and His Wife* (London: Allen and Unwin, 1924)

Macleod, Fiona [pseud. of William Sharp], *Reissue of the Shorter Stories of Fiona Macleod, vol.I, Spiritual Tales; vol.II, Barbaric Tales; vol.III, Tragic Romances* (Edinburgh: Patrick Geddes, 1897)

——, *The Winged Destiny: Studies in the Spiritual History of the Gael* (London: Heinemann, 1910)

Macpherson, James, trans., *The Poems of Ossian*, ed. William Sharp (Edinburgh: Patrick Geddes, 1896)

MacQueen, John, *Robert Henryson: A Study of the Major Narrative Poems* (Oxford: Clarendon Press, 1967)

Mack, Douglas, ' "The Rage of Fanaticism in Former Days": James Hogg's

Confessions of a Justified Sinner and the Controversy over *Old Mortality'*, in Ian Campbell, ed., *Nineteenth-Century Scottish Fiction: Critical Essays* (Manchester: Carcanet, 1979), pp. 38–50

Manlove, Colin, *Christian Fantasy: from 1200 to the Present* (London: Macmillan, 1992)

——, 'Circularity in Fantasy: George MacDonald', in *The Impulse of Fantasy Literature* (London: Macmillan, 1983), pp. 70–92

——, ' "In the Demythologising Business": Angela Carter's *The Infernal Desire Machines of Dr Hoffman* (1972)', in Kath Filmer, ed., *Twentieth-Century Fantasists: Essays on Culture, Society and Belief in Twentieth-Century Mythopoeic Literature* (London: Macmillan, 1992), pp. 148–60

——, *Modern Fantasy: Five Studies* (Cambridge: Cambridge University Press, 1975)

——, ' "Perpetual Metamorphoses": The Refusal of Certainty in Carlyle's *Sartor Resartus'*, *Swansea Review*, 2 (Nov., 1986), pp. 19–36

Marshall, Bruce, *Father Malachy's Miracle* (London: Heinemann, 1931)

Meek, James, *Last Orders* (Edinburgh: Polygon, 1992)

Mitchison, Naomi, *The Corn King and the Spring Queen* (Edinburgh: Canongate, 1990)

Montgomerie, Alexander, *Poems of Alexander Montgomerie, and other pieces from Laing MS No 447*, Supplementary Volume, Scottish Text Society 59, ed. George Stevenson (Edinburgh: Blackwood, 1910)

Mooney, John, *St Magnus—Earl of Orkney* (Kirkwall: W. R. Mackintosh, 1935)

Morgan, Edwin, 'Scottish Poetry in the Nineteenth Century', in Gifford, ed., *The History of Scottish Literature, Volume 3*, pp. 337–51

Morsberger, Katherine M., 'The Strange Case of Dr Jekyll and Mr Hyde', in Frank N. Magill, ed., *Survey of Science Fiction Literature*, 5 vols (Englewood Cliffs, N. J.: Salem Press, 1979), V, 2184–9

Nairn, Thom, 'Ian Banks and the Fiction Factory', in Wallace and Stevenson, eds, *The Scottish Novel Since the Seventies*, pp. 127–35

Noble, Andrew, 'Fable of Freedom: *The Green Isle of the Great Deep'*, in *Neil M. Gunn: The Man and the Writer*, eds Alexander Scott and Douglas Gifford (Edinburgh: Blackwood, 1973), pp. 175–216

Novalis [pseud. of Friedrich von Hardenberg], *Fragmente* (1798–9) in *Schriften*, eds Paul Kluckhohn and Richard Samuel, 3 vols (Stuttgart: Kohlhammer, 1960–8), III

Oliphant, Margaret, *The Autobiography of Margaret Oliphant*, ed. Elizabeth Jay (Oxford: Oxford University Press, 1990)

——, *A Beleaguered City and Other Stories*, ed. Merryn Williams (Oxford: Oxford University Press, 1988)

——, *The Land of Darkness; Along with some further Chapters in the Experiences of the Little Pilgrim* (London: Macmillan, 1888)

——, *A Little Pilgrim in the Unseen* (London: Macmillan, 1882)

——, *Selected Short Stories of the Supernatural*, ed. Margaret K. Gray (Edinburgh: Scottish Academic Press, 1985)

Oliver, Cordelia, 'Alasdair Gray: Visual Artist', in Crawford and Nairn, eds, *The Arts of Alasdair Gray*, pp. 22–36

Orkneyinga Saga, eds Hermann Palsson and Paul Edwards (Harmondsworth: Penguin, 1978)

Pick, J. B., *The Great Shadow House: Essays on the Metaphysical Tradition in Scottish Literature* (Edinburgh: Polygon, 1993)

Price, Richard, *The Fabulous Matter of Fact: The Poetics of Neil M. Gunn* (Edinburgh: Edinburgh University Press, 1991)

Raeper, William, *George MacDonald* (Tring, Herts: Lion Publishing, 1987)

——, *Warrior of Light* (Tring, Herts: Lion Publishing, 1993)

——, *A Witch in Time* (Tring, Herts: Lion Publishing, 1992)

Ratcliff, Ruth (reteller), *Scottish Folk Tales* (London: Frederick Muller, 1976)

Reid, David, 'Prose after Knox', in R. D. S. Jack, ed., *The History of Scottish Literature, Volume 1*, pp. 183–97

Richardson, Thomas C., 'Carlyle and the Scottish Tradition of the Double', in Horst W. Drescher, ed., *Thomas Carlyle 1981*: Papers Given at the International Thomas Carlyle Centenary Symposium (Frankfurt am Main: Peter Lang, 1983), pp. 351–64

Roberts, Ruth ap, *The Ancient Dialect: Thomas Carlyle and Comparative Religion* (Berkeley: University of California Press, 1988)

Röhrich, Lutz, 'Elementargeister', in *Enzyklopädie des Märchens*, gen. ed. Kurt Ranke (Berlin and New York: Walter Gruyter, 1977–), Vol.3 (1981), pp. 1316–26

Rose, Jacqueline, *The Case of Peter Pan: or, the Impossibility of Children's Fiction* (London: Macmillan, 1984)

Rosenberg, John D., *Carlyle and the Burden of History* (Oxford: Clarendon Press, 1985)

Royle, Trevor, *The Macmillan Companion to Scottish Literature* (London: Macmillan, 1983)

Scott, Sir Walter, 'On the Supernatural in Fictitious Composition', in Scott, *On Novelists and Fiction*, ed. Ioan Williams (London: Routledge, 1968), pp. 312–53

——, *The Supernatural Stories of Sir Walter Scott*, ed. Michael Hayes (London: John Calder, 1977)

Sellin, Bernard, *The Life and Works of David Lindsay*, trans. Kenneth Gunnell (Cambridge: Cambridge University Press, 1981)

Smith, Lesley (née Willis), 'George MacDonald's Fantasy for Children:

"Light out of Darkness" in *At the Back of the North Wind*, *The Princess and the Goblin* and *The Princess and Curdie'* [unpublished MS]

Smith, Nelson C., *James Hogg* (Boston, Mass: Twayne Publishers, 1980)

Spark, Muriel, 'What Images Return' (1962), repr. in Karl Miller, ed., *Memoirs of a Modern Scotland* (London: Faber and Faber, 1970), pp. 151–3

Spiller, Michael, 'Poetry after the Union, 1603–1660' in Jack, ed., *The History of Scottish Literature, Volume 1*, pp. 141–62

Stevenson, Randall, 'Alasdair Gray and the Postmodern', in Crawford and Nairn, eds, *The Arts of Alasdair Gray*, pp. 48–63

Stevenson, Robert Louis, 'A Chapter on Dreams' (1888), repr. in Stevenson, *Dr Jekyll and Mr Hyde and Weir of Hermiston*, pp. 198–209

——, *Dr Jekyll and Mr Hyde and Weir of Hermiston*, ed. Emma Letley (Oxford: Oxford University Press, 1987)

——, *The Letters of Robert Louis Stevenson*, ed. Sidney Colvin, 4 vols (London: Methuen, 1911)

——, 'A Note on Realism' (1883), in Stevenson, *Essays in the Art of Writing* (London: Cassell, 1905), pp. 93–107

Stewart, Mary, *The Crystal Cave* (London: Hodder and Stoughton, 1970)

——, *The Hollow Hills* (London: Hodder and Stoughton, 1973)

——, *The Last Enchantment* (London: Hodder and Stoughton, 1979)

Storr, Catherine, *Thursday* (Harmondsworth: Puffin, 1974)

Strout, Allen Lang, *The Life and Letters of James Hogg, the Ettrick Shepherd, Vol.I, 1770–1825* (Lubbock, Texas: Texas Tech Press, 1946). Vol.II, 1825–35, is in typescript in the National Library of Scotland

Sturluson, Snorri, *The Prose Edda of Snorri Sturluson: Tales from Norse Mythology*, sel. and trans. Jean I. Young (Berkeley: University of California Press, 1966)

Summers, Montague, *A Gothic Bibliography* (London: Fortune Press, 1941; repr. 1964)

Sutherland, Elizabeth, ed., *The Gold Key and the Green Life: Some Fantasies and Celtic Tales by George MacDonald and Fiona Macleod* (London: Constable, 1986)

Tanner, Tony, 'Mountains and Depths—An Approach to Nineteenth-Century Dualism', *Review of English Literature*, 3, 4 (Oct., 1962), pp. 51–61

Tarn, W. W., *The Treasure of the Isle of Mist* (London: Oxford University Press, 1938)

Temperley, Alan, ed., *Tales of Galloway* (London: Skilton and Shaw, 1979)

Tennyson, G. B., *Sartor Called Resartus: The Genesis, Structure, and Style of Thomas Carlyle's First Major Work* (Princeton: Princeton University Press, 1965)

Thomas, Ronald R., 'The Strange Voices in the Case: Dr Jekyll, Mr Hyde, and the Voices of Modern Fiction', in Veeder and Hirsch, eds, *Dr Jekyll and Mr Hyde after One Hundred Years*, pp. 73–93

Thompson, Stith, *The Folktale* (New York: Holt, Rinehart and Winston, 1946)

Thomson, James, *The City of Dreadful Night and Other Poems* (London: Reeves and Turner, 1880)

——, *Essays and Phantasies* (London: Reeves and Turner, 1881)

——, 'On the Worth of Metaphysical Systems' (1876), *Essays and Phantasies*, pp. 296–302

——, 'Proposals for the Speedy Extinction of Evil and Misery' (1868), *Essays and Phantasies*, pp. 51–103

——, 'A Walk Abroad' (1866), *Essays and Phantasies*, pp. 257–68

Tolkien, J. R. R. 'On Fairy-Stories' (1938–9), *Tree and Leaf* (London: Allen and Unwin, 1964), pp. 11–70

Urquhart, Sir Thomas, and Peter Le Motteux, trans., Rabelais, *Gargantua and Pantagruel*, 2 vols (London: David Nutt, 1900)

Veeder, William, 'Children of the Night: Stevenson and Patriarchy', in Veeder and Hirsch, eds, *Dr Jekyll and Mr Hyde after One Hundred Years*, pp. 107–60

——, and Gordon Hirsch, eds, *Dr Jekyll and Mr Hyde after One Hundred Years* (Chicago: University of Chicago Press, 1988)

Watson, Ian, 'From Pan in the Home Counties—to Pain on a Far Planet: E. M. Forster, David Lindsay and How the Voyage to Arcturus Should End', *Foundation: The Review of Science Fiction*, no.43 (Summer, 1988), pp. 25–36

Watson, Roderick, *The Literature of Scotland* (London: Macmillan, 1984)

Waugh, Robert H., 'The Drum of *A Voyage to Arcturus*', *Extrapolation*, 26, 2 (Summer, 1985), pp. 143–51

Whittaker, Ruth, *The Faith and Fiction of Muriel Spark* (London: Macmillan, 1982)

Williams, Merryn, *Margaret Oliphant: A Critical Biography* (London: Macmillan, 1978)

Wilson, Colin, E. H. Visiak and J. B. Pick, *The Strange Genius of David Lindsay* (London: John Baker, 1970)

Wittig, Kurt, *The Scottish Tradition in Literature* (Edinburgh: Oliver and Boyd, 1958)

Wolfe, Gary, *David Lindsay* (Mercer Island, Washington: Starmont House, 1982)

Wolff, Robert Lee, *The Golden Key: A Study of the Fiction of George MacDonald* (New Haven: Yale University Press, 1961)

Index